FURTHER UNIVERSITY OF WISCONSIN MATERIALS: FURTHER DOCUMENTS OF F. TAYLOR OSTRANDER

RESEARCH IN THE HISTORY OF ECONOMIC THOUGHT AND METHODOLOGY

Series Editors: Warren J. Samuels, Jeff E. Biddle and Ross B. Emmett

RESEARCH IN THE HISTORY OF ECONOMIC THOUGHT AND
METHODOLOGY   VOLUME 23-C

FURTHER UNIVERSITY OF WISCONSIN MATERIALS: FURTHER DOCUMENTS OF F. TAYLOR OSTRANDER

EDITED BY

WARREN J. SAMUELS

*Department of Economics, Michigan State University,
East Lansing, MI 48824, USA*

2005

ELSEVIER
JAI

Amsterdam – Boston – Heidelberg – London – New York – Oxford
Paris – San Diego – San Francisco – Singapore – Sydney – Tokyo

ELSEVIER B.V.	ELSEVIER Inc.	**ELSEVIER Ltd**	ELSEVIER Ltd
Radarweg 29	525 B Street, Suite 1900	**The Boulevard, Langford**	84 Theobalds Road
P.O. Box 211	San Diego	**Lane, Kidlington**	London
1000 AE Amsterdam	CA 92101-4495	**Oxford OX5 1GB**	WC1X 8RR
The Netherlands	USA	**UK**	UK

First edition 2005

Library of Congress Cataloging in Publication Data
A catalog record is available from the Library of Congress.

British Library Cataloguing in Publication Data
A catalogue record is available from the British Library.

ISBN: 0-7623-1166-5
ISSN: 0743-4154 (Series)

∞ The paper used in this publication meets the requirements of ANSI/NISO Z39.48-1992 (Permanence of Paper). Printed in The Netherlands.

Working together to grow libraries in developing countries

www.elsevier.com | www.bookaid.org | www.sabre.org

ELSEVIER   BOOK AID
International   Sabre Foundation

CONTENTS

MATERIALS FROM CHESTER WHITNEY WRIGHT'S COURSE,
ECONOMIC HISTORY OF THE UNITED STATES, ECONOMICS
220, UNIVERSITY OF CHICAGO, 1933–1934

MATERIALS FROM CHESTER WHITNEY WRIGHT'S COURSE,
ECONOMIC HISTORY OF THE UNITED STATES, ECONOMICS
320, UNIVERSITY OF CHICAGO, SPRING 1934

LIST OF CONTRIBUTORS

Kirk D. Johnson	Dover, DE 19901, USA
F. Taylor Ostrander	Williamstown, MA 02167, USA
Warren J. Samuels	Department of Economics, Michigan State University, USA

FURTHER UNIVERSITY OF WISCONSIN MATERIALS

NOTES FROM HANS H. GERTH'S SEMINAR, MASS MOVEMENTS, SOCIOLOGY 250, UNIVERSITY OF WISCONSIN, 1955–1956

Taken and Edited by Warren J. Samuels

INTRODUCTION

This is the second set of notes from a course given by Hans H. Gerth published in this annual. This set, like the first, was taken by the editor while an Economics graduate student at the University of Wisconsin with an outside minor in Sociology. Notes from his course on Democratic and Totalitarian Societies were published in Volume 6 (1989).

The notes published here do not indicate the year, only that the class met on Thursdays at 7:30pm in 312 Sterling Hall. Most likely the course was taken during the 1955–1956 academic year.

Hans Gerth was a well-known and respected political sociologist, a German emigre. A Max Weber expert, he was well versed in economics. He co-authored with C. Wright Mills, *Character and Social Structure: The Psychology of Social Institutions* (1953). He translated and edited *From Max Weber: Essays in Sociology* (1946) and Weber's *The Religion of China* (1951). A collection of Gerth's work, *Politics, Character, and Culture* (1982) was edited by Joseph Bensman, Arthur J. Vidich, and Nobuko Gerth.

Further University of Wisconsin Materials: Further Documents of F. Taylor Ostrander
Research in the History of Economic Thought and Methodology, Volume 23-C, 3–14
Copyright © 2005 by Elsevier Ltd.
All rights of reproduction in any form reserved
ISSN: 0743-4154/doi:10.1016/S0743-4154(05)23201-7

The notes run to some ten pages. The text has been only slightly edited. Full accurate author name, title and year of publication have been substituted for incomplete originals. My comments are within { }.

Published with the notes, as a second document, is a summary of the notes (not including the readings) written in preparation for the final examination. I do not recall preparing such a summary in any other course; usually, sufficient materials were presented in lectures to call for an outline (and in one or two courses an outline of the outline). Found with these documents are notes from the Earl of Cromer's *Ancient and Modern Imperialism* (1910), and Thomas Brockway's chapter on economic imperialism in Glenn Hoover's *Twentieth Century Economic Thought* (1950). Other notes were disbursed, my having later put them to various uses, and unfound. They included numerous notes on Weber's writings.

Gerth's lectures were a combination of organized presentation and flow-of-consciousness exposition. Accordingly, it was difficult to take well-structured notes; hence the organized summary. But Gerth frequently had something deep, important and/or interesting to say. His German background and training and his wide reading resulted in the powerful mind of a first-rate social theorist and commentator. Moreover, his interests had already become part of mine.

One idiosyncratic aspect of the course was that Gerth taught the theory and practice of imperialism as fulfillment of the course title, Mass Movements. Assuming the mass-movement aspect of imperialism, another defect of the course, in retrospect, was Gerth's concentration on the events of the then-prior two decades rather than a broader base encompassing a variety of mass movements per se, revolutions, and so on. Of course, such a base was acquired through reading the textbook in the course, Rudolf Heberle's <u>Social Movements</u> (1951).

The very first line in the notes indicates his interest and focus: "Orientation to power orders and problems of power." The second line helped to reinforce a point that I had learned as an undergraduate and has remained important to me: the idea of "different definitions of situation, i.e. of reality." Not only did Gerth have a European orientation, his level of analysis transcended the typical American one, which was guided by positions on immediate issues themselves guided by the manufacturers of public opinion. (The only economist at Wisconsin of whom something like this could be said was Selig Perlman – European with a Russian education.) This did not necessarily signify the correctness of his views, but it did indicate the depth of his analysis and the topics that formed it at that level. For the U.S. to be labeled a competitive imperialist nation, and still be on the right side of world conflicts, was an unusual experience. Gerth had an ability to identify and concentrate – alas, not a great length – at arm's length on topics that had an elevation and ubiquity unusual in my experience before or since. These topics, for example (from the first lecture), include imperialism as a mass movement, the psychology of deception in politics, the psychology of treason, ideologies of imperialism, and so on.

It was difficult to discern – for example, when he spoke of the "acceptance of greater responsibilities" – whether and when he was being ironic or merely echoing the language of the manipulation of political psychology.

NOTES FROM HANS H. GERTH'S SEMINAR, MASS MOVEMENTS, SOCIOLOGY 250, UNIVERSITY OF WISCONSIN [1955–1956]

Lecture

Orientation to power orders and problems of power.

German rearmament, c. 1936 – different definitions of situation, i.e. of reality.

Britain: poise against weight of USSR; hence concessions.

America: funny toy soldiers of Nazis.

Neglected play by U.S.S.R. balancing Germany in West.

Germany: after Molotov-Ribbentrop accord, USSR neutralized; later double cross.

West unprepared for and disillusioned by start of war – rapid change in image of reality.

[In margin: American recognition of USSR aided by steel and other interests seeking markets and foreign investment outlets; not oil: had been expropriated]

[In margin, added later: e.g. of position jockeying]

Politically inspired mass movements: extension and expansion of great power (de facto) jurisdiction, i.e. imperialism (territorial); competitive imperialisms – U.S. vs. USSR – the new internationalism (assumption of new responsibilities per press).

[In margin, added later: Imperialism as mass movement]

West German labor movement disillusioned re future of classical (Marxiaan) socialism; American prototype didn't recover from World War One. Italy – still Marxist.

Comparative study of anti-capitalist mass movements; and psychology behind nationalism and imperialism; source points and supporters of imperialism. Sources in business and law; neo-mercantilist approach. [Research topic, in margin: History of American thought on imperialism.]

Theories of Imperialism (must also have theory of war)

(1) Earl of Cromer: (*Modern Egypt*, 1908; *Ancient and Modern Imperialism*, 1910)
  1. "moral task of British people"
(2) John A. Hobson: *The Evolution of Modern Capitalism*, 1926; *Imperialism*, 1938
(3) V. I. Lenin: *Imperialism*, 1933
  2. Rosa Luxemburg: *The Accumulation of Capital*, 1951
  3. Fritz Sternberg: *Capitalism and Socialism on Trial*, 1951
(4) Hannah Arendt: *The Origins of Totalitarianism*, 1951
(5) Joseph A. Schumpeter: *Imperialism and Social Classes*, 1951

Political Sociology
(1) Robert Michels, *Political Parties*, 1949
      Problems of vigor, leadership, tactics.
      Thesis: larger the organization, less the democ[racy] due to apathy, necessity. "Natural law" of democratic political parties. [In margin: professional leadership]
(2) Max Weber: *Max Weber on Law in Economy and Society*, edited by Edward Shils and Max Rheinstein, 1954; Chapter, Domination in Political Communities, pp. 323–348
      Max Weber, *From Max Weber: Essays in Sociology*, edited by Hans H. Gerth and C. Wright Mills, 1946; Chapters, Politics as a Vocation, Structures of Power, including The Nation (pp. 159–179), Psychology of Charisma (pp. 245–252)
      Max Weber, *The Theory of Social and Economic Organization*, edited by A. M. Henderson and Talcott Parsons, 1947. Types of Authority and Imperative Co-ordination (pp. 324–386)
(3) Harold D. Lasswell and Abraham Kaplan, *Power and Society*, 1950.
(4) Rudolf Heberle, *Social Movements*, 1951.
(5) Hans Speier, *Social Order and the Risks of War*, 1952.

Sources of imperialism: (1) demise of isolation and (2) sense of mission.

Materialistic tenor of American politics: mass hedonism; implies definition off happiness. Growth of bureaucracy, security feelings, growth of pressure groups.

[In margin at top of page: John Wheeler Wheeler-Bennett, *Wooden Titan: Hindenberg in Twenty Years of German History*, 1936.]

Psychology of deception in politics. [In margin, added later: Deception]

Technique of secrecy:

[name illegible] – The Secret and Secret Society. [Possibly John Heron Lepper, *Famous Secret Societies*, London: S. Low, Marston, 1932; Una Birch Pope-Hennessy, *Secret Societies and the French Revolution*, London: John Lane, 1911; Hutton Webster, *Primitive Secret Societies: A Study in Early Politics and Religion*, New York: Macmillan, 1932; Nesta Helen Webster, *Secret Societies and Subversive Movements*, 7th ed., London: Britons Pub. Society, 1955.]

Edward A. Shils, *The Torment of Secrecy*, 1956.

Underground movements in totalitarian states. Is mass rebelliousness and even revolt possible under such conditions? General consensus of sociologists: impossible.

Psychology of treason, of treachery. ("Concentration camps the democratic way.") Speir – Treachery and War essay in book noted above. [In margin: "Treason and the 20th Century"] [In margin, added later: Treason]

Arthur Rosenberg, *Democracy and Socialism*, 1939.

V. I. Lenin, theory of the labor aristocracy [added below line: labor elite] and vanguard of labor.

Dictatorship and democracy (Jacobins, Lenin).

Ideologies of imperialism.

"Natural law"

(a) geopolitical
(b) racism
(c) Italian
(d) German
(e) American
(f) British

[In margin:

Ratzel – geopolitics [Friedrich Ratzel, author, e.g. of *Politische Geographie*, 1903]

Also New World Review.

Kennan – Lectures [George F. Kennan, *American Diplomacy, 1900–1950*, 1951 (Charles R. Walgreen Foundation Lectures), *Realities of American Foreign Policy*, 1954 (Stafford Little Lectures)]

Morgenthau – [Hans J. Morgenthau, *Politics Among Nations*, 1948; *In Defense of the National Interest*, 1951.]

Modern terror techniques – technical and psychological management of wholesale fear.

Monroe Doctrine.

Political intelligentsia.

Lecture

[To be] Isolationist is to be non-expansionist, i.e. re acceptance of greater responsibilities.
[In margin: Re American foreign [word indecipherable] – U.S. in early 19th century was self-conscious re British investment in U.S. Bank etc.]

[In margin:
Cromer.
John R. Commons on bargaining.
Robert K. Merton, *Science and Technology in 17th Century England*, Harvard PhD thesis.]

Lecture

Weber on Dominancy (Law in Economy and Society)
Pervasive in all relations (power; super- and sub-ordination)

[In margin, added later: Power]

Power to command by virtue of authority or constellation of interests plus interest in obeying by obeyer.

Europe: emphasis on power structures

America: Emphasis on leadership and power without background of structure.

[Power] ubiquitous.

Bargaining vis-à-vis <u>command</u>.

Thesis: nature (substance) of power structure.

Freedom as antithesis to power: talk former; study latter.

Great sociologists – concern with power – differentia specifica.

Edward Hallett Carr, *The Twenty Years Crisis, 1919–1939*, 1940 – phase between World Wars I and II.

Lecture

Methods of Soviet imperialism in East Europe after World War II
(1) Provisional governments formed – communists in top offices, acceptable to West. [In margin: Interior ministry (police); communications; transportation. Working-class militia in factories (action committees)]
(2) Establishment of coalition government after elections; undermine and exclude bourgeois parties.

LECTURE

[In margin at top of page: Beck and Godwin, "Russian Purges" [unable to identify]; cf. Character and Social Structure. Cairnes – *The Slave Power*, 1862. Read Encyclopedia of the Social Sciences – Imperialism, Tribute, etc.]

Conservatism emphasizes constants of human nature and ways of man, unchanging characteristics. Wiese, Burke, Parsons [Presumably Leopold von Wiese, Edmund Burke and Talcott Parsons]. Change a function of different construction of eternal verities {why not reconstruct}. Lord Bryce: man by nature is indolent. If recognize change, cyclical; more the change, more it is the same. [In margin: Kaufman, Philosophy of Nietzsche [Walter Kaufmann, *Nietzsche: Philosopher, Psychologist, Antichrist*, 1950] – return of the ever same]

Change must seek to support and preserve the heirlooms of the past.

See as whole; no emphasis on preconceived ideas. Contemplation, description.

Thought after fact[,] not as midwife thereto. No emphasis on rational delineation of well-defined principles {? ws}. [In margin: E.g., gestalt psychology]

Lecture

[In margin at top of page: Cf. Raymond Aron, <u>Partisan Review</u>, November–December 1951, "Leninist Myth of Imperialism"]

Hobson:

Imperialism stems from political protection given to economic middlemen (primary source is in middlemen).

Foreign nation unable to exert de facto control over foreign investment (China vs. Japan) – establish[ment] or not of a foreign sphere of influence (political sovereignty over own markets) – function military strength.

Lenin:

Investment bankers plus industrialists (not middlemen).
Differential development and re division of world power through war.

Gerth:

Imperialism source point not merely capital expansion; also military and political pressure.

Lecture

Schumpeter: Imperialism and Social Classes

Groups and origins etc. of imperialists. Part of theory of economic growth. The carriers – warriors.

Defined as objectless proclivity to expansion – power for power's sake.

Rosa Luxemburg:

Pure capitalism doesn't exist due to imperialism (capital export to realize surplus value). Capitalist structural properties require imperialism (not classes); page 6 of paperback edition.

Psychology of power – same just desire power and power begets more power.

All people have interest in expansion.

Conquest Theory

Ibn Khaldun [*An Arab Philosophy of History*, 1950]

Ludwig Gumplowicz [*Geschichte der Staatstheorien*, 1905; *Grundriss der Soziologie*, 1905; The Outlines of Sociology, 1899; *Sociologie und Politik*, 1892]

Gustav Ratzenhofer [*Wesen und Zweck der Politik*, 1893]

Franz Oppenheimer [*The State: Its History and Development Viewed Sociologically*, 1914; *Histoire des doctrines économiques*, 1913]

Alexander Rustow [*Ortsbestimmung der Gegenwart*, 1950, abbreviated translation as *Freedom and Domination*, 1980]

Joseph A. Schumpeter

Lecture

Elite thinking in Lenin

Marxian theory of social change

Per contradictions.

Creation of class conscious proletariat.

Proletariat not as class conscious as it should be.

Karx and Engels: lead and educate proletariat.

Intellectual bodies from another class (Marx himself).

Lenin: went further

(a) Vanguard to bring revolutionary consciousness
(b) Vanguard must be stable organ of professionals.

Upper-class men go to aid of rising class.

Rationalize and "prove" humanism, universalize their demands – assure general [word indecipherable: approval?] value; attract others to progressive force.

"Actual" not illusory proletariat – the last class struggle.

(1. class: 2. trade union: 3. party) consciousness; fusion of militant worker and intellectual ideologist.

[In margin, alongside *supra*:

Imperialism: old vs. new liberalism; old now has affinity to anarchism, e.g. Cola Parker.

Imperialism: differences re automaticity as function scarcity- vs. abundance-psychology (cf. Selig Perlman) [Most likely my comments]

Lecture

[In margin at top of page: Simon-Hexy – Tory MPs [unable to identify]]

Mass movement – the creation of loyalty to an organized power-seeking group.

Lecture [likely by student]

Rise of Landless in Indian Villages: Kudaravalli, Kistna, Andra

498 families of which 439 are agricultural; total population of 2079.

Non-cultivating owners	3
Cultivating owners	127
Partly cultivating owners	3
Cultivating tenants	22
Agricultural with land	111
Agricultural without land	173
	439

Below 2 acres	128
2–5 acres	53
5–10 acres[a]	35
10–15 acres[a]	17
15- acres	36
	249

[a] Middle class.

Cultivated area (water): 1700 acres

Minimum of subsistence acres per family: under 5

Employment for all – planting and harvesting – i.e. seasonal.

Traditionally, free agricultural labor; now plus artisans out of work.

Over-production of intellectuals in India and [other] undeveloped countries.

Landless not good ground for Reds [Communists]; middle class – land owning – looks to future for children – listens to plebian intellectual who has all [the] answers. Appeals to plebian intelligentsia who can't get educated; activist.

Communism gives psychological appeal value: conception of world history.

(1) a firm orientation – has all answers; visionary; never surprised
(2) intellectual and therefore systematizer

(3) gives birthright re future
(4) activist plus a cause

Walter M. Kotschnig, *Unemployment in the Learned Professions*, 1937, under League of Nations; [found unemployed supported revolutionary movements]

Communism as failure of capitalism to industrialize the world (as its world-historical mission); on the contrary, reduces them [word indecipherable] factory industries – a void.

SUMMARY WRITTEN IN PREPARATION
FOR FINAL EXAMINATION

Mass Movements

The subject of mass movements requires an orientation to power orders and problems of power. Problems of power, whether intra-national or international, involve differing definitions of the situation, some "official," others non-official. The definitions are functions of domestic and international strains, ambitions and interests both private and public. A most important type of influence is the economic, which involves markets, investment outlets and supply sources. Swift changes in objective phenomena leave some disillusioned; for most it involves rapid changes in the image of reality.

Alongside economically inspired mass movements are the politically inspired mass movements – the extension and expansion, de facto or de jure, of great-power jurisdiction, i.e. territorial imperialism. This often involves competitive imperialisms: the new internationalism and the press's "assumption of new responsibilities."

Interesting would be a comparative study of anti-capitalist mass movements and the psychology and source points behind the supporters of nationalism and imperialism.

Noting such aspects as the psychology of deception in politics and the technique of secrecy, the psychology of treason, of treachery, and the techniques and psychology of terror, the question may be posed, "Is mass rebelliousness and even revolutions of underground movements in totalitarian states possible under such conditions?" The general consensus of sociologists is that such is impossible.

Weber, on Domination, notes that dominancy is pervasive and in all relationships: re power, and super- and sub-ordination; power to command by virtue of authority or the constellation of interests plus the interest in obeying by the obeyers. Power and domination, command, is ubiquitous.

Europeans emphasize the power structure; Americans emphasize leadership and power without the background of the structure.

Methods of Soviet imperialism in Eastern Europe after World War Two include: (1) formation of provisional governments with communists in top offices, acceptable to Western powers; (2) undermining and exclusion of bourgeois parties, establishment of coalition governments after elections; (3) construction of working-class militia in factories, with action committees; (4) securing top ministerial positions: interior (police), communications, transportation.

FURTHER CORRESPONDENCE
OF SELIG PERLMAN

Edited by Warren J. Samuels

Correspondence and other materials pertaining to Selig Perlman may be found especially in Archival Volume 8 but also in Volumes 4 and 18B. Perlman was the author of a major history and a psychologically rich interpretation of labor and trade unionism in the United States (*A History of Trade Unionism in the United States*, New York: Macmillan, 1922 and *Theory of the Labor Movement*, New York: Macmillan, 1928). Published below, thanks again to the generous cooperation and permission of his son, Mark Perlman, is further correspondence, principally from Selig Perlman to his former student, Ben Solomon Stephansky.

Perlman (1888–1959) was born in Bialystok, Poland, and emigrated to the U.S. in 1918. Stephansky (1913–1999) was born in Bogoslav, Russia (that part which is now the Ukraine) and was brought to the U.S. in 1915. He received the bachelor's degree in 1939 and doctorate in economics in 1952, both from the University of Wisconsin. He taught at Wisconsin during 1938–1942 and 1948–1949, at Sarah Lawrence College between 1945–1947, and at the University of Chicago during 1947–1956 (social science).

Stephansky became a professional diplomat in the service of his adopted country. A Foreign Service Officer since 1956, he served as Labor Attaché in the United States Embassy in Mexico City, 1956–1957; Labor Advisor in the Bureau of Inter-American Affairs, Department of State, 1957–1960; Ambassador to Bolivia (1961–1963); and Deputy Assistant Secretary of State for Latin America (Bureau of Inter-American Affairs), 1963–1964. He was executive secretary of the United

Further University of Wisconsin Materials: Further Documents of F. Taylor Ostrander
Research in the History of Economic Thought and Methodology, Volume 23-C, 15–33
Copyright © 2005 by Elsevier Ltd.
All rights of reproduction in any form reserved
ISSN: 0743-4154/doi:10.1016/S0743-4154(05)23202-9

States-Puerto Rico Commission on the Status of Puerto Rico, 1964–1966, and Deputy U.S. Representative to the Organization of American States, 1967–1968.

He was associated with the Carnegie Endowment for International Peace, the Cooperative Housing Foundation, and International Voluntary Services, Inc. IVS was established in 1953 by a group of Peace Churches – Quakers, Mennonites and the Church of the Brethren. It was commissioned by later Secretary of State John Foster Dulles to promote self-development through local institutions in third-world countries to combat hunger, poverty and human suffering – a precursor if not model for the Peace Corps.

Stephansky published *Latin America – Toward a New Nationalism* (New York: Foreign Policy Association, 1972).

Almost all the letters published below are from Perlman to Stephansky, sent from Madison. Two of them are short notes to Perlman from Charles Beard and John Dewey, the eminent historian and philosopher, respectively. Perlman had apparently sent them copies of his *Labor in the New Deal Decade* (New York: Educational Department, International Ladies Garment Workers' Union, 1945), comprised of three lectures he gave to the I.L.G.W.U. Officers' Institute, 1943–1945.

Only those parts of Perlman's letters of substantive interest are reproduced below; personal matters have been deleted (without indication), with a few exceptions. Perlman's letter to Daniel J. Boorstin (the only one of Perlman's that is typed) is addressed to him at the History Department of the University of Chicago. The letter concerns a planned new edition of the *History of Trade Unionism in the United States*, which never came to fruition, though the additional chapters prepared by Perlman for that edition are published in Volume 8 of this annual. Boorstin was the editor of the series in which the book was to appear; a copy of the letter was included with Perlman's letter to Stephansky of April 8, 1955.

Minor corrections have been made; abbreviations, completed. Editorial addenda are in brackets. I have taken the liberty of excising some names, where identification is unnecessary and potentially grief-causing.

Perlman's letters manifest the view of the world and issues of organized labor resulting from/embodied in his theory of the labor movement. They also show something of Perlman's position on Israel.

Also evident is the precarious disciplinary position of Perlman's theory of the labor movement. Perlman, like most other scholars, self-identified with his theory, such that it became a normative prescription for him, not solely a hypothesis as to why U.S. trade unions were different from those of Europe (a matter of a different psychology bred by different, classless institutions and history). In one letter he speaks of the test of time. Fifty years later – double the period he specified – it is not entirely clear how his theory has fared. A strong case can be made, however, that organized labor has not done well, for several reasons. U.S. unions are more conservative than European ones and labor has become/remains more conservative still. The reason can be articulated in Perlman's own terminology: U.S. labor, notwithstanding relative stagnation of its position during the last thirty years, retains the opportunity consciousness of the middle class with regard to their children if not for themselves; this is the ethic of property, and it applies as well, for example, to the ideas of Henry George (Samuels, "Why the Georgist Movement Has Not Succeeded: A Speculative Memorandum," *American Journal of Economics and Sociology*, Vol. 62, July 2003, pp. 583–592). The Cold War mentality, the managerialist and individualist points of view (ironically) further spread among the population, legal restrictions on unionization, the eclipse of some labor issues and the failure of other ones (health care), massive ideological assault, and so on, in a process of cumulative causation also contributed. In other words, job consciousness has been weakened, first, by other elements of consciousness two of which were status emulation and achievement motivation as substitutes for class consciousness and, second, by effective social control. Without class consciousness, job consciousness was fragile.

All that notwithstanding, Perlman was able to hold in abeyance, and in that sense transcend and escape from, the common – loaded and ideological and hence inconclusive but nonetheless selectively instrumental – categories of the day. "Capitalism," "socialism" and the like paled in comparison before a mind that opened up to students some of the institutional and psychological fundamentals of his form of labor economics and institutional economics. *What* he had to say was, in a way, not as important as his identification of the *topics* about which he said what he thought needed to be said.

One is tempted to wish that Perlman had become a general social theorist; but he was, as a historian and theorist of the labor movement, already a social theorist. Looked at differently, as an economist Perlman was on the left what Joseph Schumpeter of *Capitalism, Socialism and Democracy* was on the right, only less ambitious and less flamboyant but equally confident. One emphasis that they had in common they shared with Frank W. Taussig and Vilfredo Pareto – and the early 20th century American psychological school – was on the nature and significance of psychology; economic psychology to be sure but psychology across the social sciences. This emphasis was arguably more important than that centering on instinct theory vs. behaviorism. One wonders how Perlman's theory of modes of consciousness would have fared in the hands of a synthesizer who tried to make sense of and integrate all these different systems of psychology. For example, what is the relation of job- and opportunity-consciousness to what Taussig called the instinct of domination?

In any event, we see in this correspondence something of the opportunity-conscious intellectual who elevated job consciousness over opportunity consciousness and the matter-of-fact, down-to-earth, bread-and-butter issues of working people over the esoteric formulations of intellectuals. We also see something of a dichotomy of moods: elation over his theory, despair over criticism. Those who have studied under Perlman typically were in awe of the man, his intellect and his theory; here we see the human being, his joys and his travails, as well as his intellect at work. And we learn something of his private reactions to his critics.

Charles Beard to Perlman, September 11, 1946

Dear Mr. Perlman:

Not in many a day have I read such a thoughtful and informative statement on labor relations in our time as you have made in your little collection of lectures. I am grateful to you for sending me a copy. Too many of our leaders in high places seem to live on current news and noise and have no sense of time or institutional history. I am sure that were dear John Commons with us, he would say of your lectures: "Well done, my young friend." Since he is not here, I shall venture to say it myself in his name!

Yours cordially

Charles Beard

John Dewey to Perlman, October 1, 1946

Dear Mr. Perlman:

I didn't get around to reading your pamphlet when I first received it, now some weeks ago. I've read it now and want to thank you for sending it to me. I found it more enlightening about our confused American political-economic scene than anything I've ever come across. It is "realistic" in the real sense of that word in getting one in closer contact with the facts of the situation.

Sincerely yours

John Dewey

Perlman to Stephansky, November 11, 1946

Dear Ben:

I enjoyed your post-mortem on last Tuesday and you were too generous about my "theory." I took the occasion to lecture to my class on the Roosevelt Phenomenon now that the New Deal was <u>formally</u> closed (its substantive closing was 1} years ago). I found in Frances Perkins' statement that FDR never read any books in economics a clue to his mentality: it was a pre-economics mentality. That accounts for his freedom from the bugaboos which have stemmed from the dismal science;

fear of an unbalanced budget, of "waste," of going-off the gold standard, of "juggling the dollar," etc. Hence he could spend 40 billion in lend-lease, 2 billion for atomic research at the suggestion of Einstein who had never "met a payroll," etc. This takes him back to the glorious Virginia period in American statesmanship (Jefferson, Madison, Monroe) in which, likewise, there was no "economics consciousness" but the leaders were experimenters in the "grand manner." I also told them that the new "progressive innings" – in about 8 or 12 years – would have to be another New Deal, with the same intellectual fuzziness, and, let us hope, with a leader equally blasé as far as the economics-begotten phobias are concerned.

I am enclosing the Beard and Dewey comments on my ILGWU lectures. They will have to console us all for the very low opinion some thousand economists have of our Wisconsin labor economics, labor history, etc. . . . wrote to Mark, in reply to his inquiry about fellowship prospects at Harvard, a very frank and courageous letter spelling it all out. I replied thanking her for her honesty, and added that since it was not Periclean Athens but Justinian's "Rome" that was sitting in judgment, it was not too serious.

As I go over in my own mind my emotion-stirring "interests," I find that nothing touches the Palestine matter, not the statehood aspect (who cares for another puppet state?) but the immigration aspect. I wrote to . . . in reply to a note from him about a British labor leader's visit to Madison (I did that at the end of a long letter in a friendly, personal vein) that on that issue (throwing tear bombs and directing fire hose at girls on board a refugee ship who have "nur für Offiziere" tattooed across their breasts) I have nothing but my curse for those who talk about parochial-mindedness when the Jews' side is presented. If he wants to take it as addressed to himself . . ., it is up to him.

Selig P.

Perlman to Stephansky, December 4, 1946

Dear Ben:

I am delighted with your letter. It proves that civilization is possible – that the most scratchy matters can be handled without leaving a scratch.

Your paragraph about the effect of the split in the present labor union drama is going to be read in my seminar this afternoon. The Macmillan people have forwarded to me an "opinion" by a labor economist of my revised Theory. He is dead opposed to my interpretation. He thinks my America chapter as of 1928 was full of bad guesses. He is especially outraged at my "dark forebodings" about the effects of the split, which, according to him, has infused organizing energy into both movements and has tended to allay the apprehensions of the American people on the score of a labor monopoly. My reply reached them on the day when the miners' strike began and I did not neglect my opportunity. Petty bourgeois notions die hard and also the propensity to think in silly analogies. If two grocers in a block means a better servings of the consumers, so two labor movements means more attention to the membership – whereas the analogy is with Yugo-Slavia (after U.S.S.R.) and Holy (or Anglo-American) "competition" for Trieste. Although I have promised the Macmillans not to speculate about the authorship of that "opinion," I feel pretty certain who it was.

Yours,

Selig

Perlman to Stephansky, September 29, 1949

Dear Ben

Your letters always enhance my <u>joie de vivre</u>. About my theory of "job-consciousness" I have a good one by way of illustration and confirmation, but unfortunately I can relate it at most to graduate groups. A young woman active in the Madison Federation of Labor was arrested a short while ago in a hotel in a room with a man other than her husband. She immediately resigned all her labor offices (including a state-wide one) and, forfeiting her bond, left town. Fleming in discussing it with a labor man was interested to find that labor people thought as much of her as ever – they knew that it was a semi-permanent liaison and that both were suing for divorce – but what griped them was that she patronized or acquiesced in patronizing a non-union hotel! What better illustration could you get of the "job-territory" concept and what better proof of the ideological stratification as between the businessman (and his fellow-respectables or hypocrites) and labor – "job-conscious labor."

You always give me a lift by your appreciation of my intellectual work. I am referring to your discussion of the multiplicity of economic attitudes in society. I do not think that I have ever shown you this sketch of an array of ideologies among four social groups – farmers, small business men, big business men, and labor. The "theory" tieing them up is that in each array the needle lodges in accord with the "opportunity appraisal" in the concrete situation.

Speaking of a cordial appreciation of my theories, this time you have been joined by a more widely known person but to me not above your class – Harold J. Laski. In his book just off the press, *Trade Unionism in the New Society*, he speaks with great respect of my dissent from the views he holds.

[Postscript] The exam is two weeks early.

Best wishes,

SP

Perlman to Stephansky, October 23, 1949

Dear Ben:

It so happened that your examination paper on my question came in most opportune in a discussion Mark and I had on the subject of the Wisconsin approach. We both agreed that it is shaped above all by the basic assumptions and by a wide cultural frontage.

Yours,

S. P.

Perlman to Stephansky, November 12, 1949

Dear Ben:

I fully accept your addenda to my Lewis statement in Alinsky. [Saul Alinsky, *John L. Lewis, An Unauthorized Biography*, New York: Putnam, 1949] I have never fallen for John L, even in 1936–1937 and always been aware of his cannibalistic propensities when balked in his drive for power. I made it, however, stand out as a loss of an historical opportunity rather than as a positive detriment to labor. To a Lewis it is the former that hurts.

We are both glad that the prelims are over. To have you get one of the three A's in theory (the other two were theory majors) was an "experience."

I had a short talk with Frances Perkins about the Alinsky book. She said she had not put into her book all she had about JLL. Alinsky advocacy is pretty "Ich wach" is not it?

Yours,

S. Perlman

Perlman to Stephansky, December 14, 1949

Dear Ben:

Am very interested in your plan. The leadership of the American labor movement in the Western world requires a clear formulation of its "mentality" today. Am enclosing an "array of labor programs" which I shall distribute to the group before which I'll lecture on January 3. I am also having mimeographed my 1942 New Leader article where I used the term "nuclearity" borrowed from you. The account of the new Trade Union International as presented in the Manchester Guardian Weekly for December 10 stresses the defeat of socialism and the victory of what I have called "dynamic job consciousness." This latter with its transfer of the emphasis from who owns the means of production and names (?) management to the control of the job on the ground is worth pursuing.

I received an offer from Clark Kerr to teach the second summer school (August 1–September 10) at Berkeley. I thankfully declined. I do not think that the chance to see the Pacific Coast for the first time is worth the extra drain. Also, I feel committed to the School for Workers here.

Are we to have the respective branches of the State and Labor departments fight it out as to who is the more effective champion of the Wisconsin School in labor thought? It makes me smile.

I am deriving a powerful kick from Ben-Gurion's defiance. Elizabeth Brandeis who when troubled about a Jewish matter, comes to my "confessional" was in on the Jerusalem matter. My reasoning goes as follows. The Assembly of the UN is not a government but a moral entity. As such it should behave morally and democratically. Two hundred thousand humans (Jews and Arabs) are not thrown about like so many pieces of rubble to please a dogma-worshipping church hierarchy. The voting was like a game by a Notre Dame team under a Knute Rockney – coached and controlled. The human factor did not have a chance to assert itself. Hence, the decision carries no moral weight. Ben-Gurion is splendid under such crises – his decisiveness is just the thing.

Yours,

S. P.

[Postscript] Mark has written interesting letters about the election. He had written earlier about the strong Catholic influence in Labor. Hence I was not surprised at Australia's lead on Jerusalem.

Stephansky to Perlman, December 14, 1949, from the University of Chicago

Dear Mr. Perlman:

Remembering your comment, when you were here, that the American Labor Movement was infusing its ideology into the international labor scene, I thought this enclosed piece would interest you. The writer appears to be very astute, and knows some history of the international labor world well.

The wrangle over representation seems very interesting. I account for it as follows: The socialist-oriented predecessor organizations, apparently conceived a rather basic disharmony between nationalism and trade unions, the latter being the embryonic purveyors of the eventual socialist internationalism. Basic trade unionism of the American-Gompers variety has no such inherent conflict. In fact, the new organization puts nationalism (democratic) and trade unionism side by side as allies in the scrap against dictatorship. If the orientation were merely socialist-internationalist, the problem of representation would be a minor one; the newly articulate orientation, the nationalist-trade union one, creates a problem of representation.

The proposed regional form of representation is obviously a crude compromise, and it seems to me will not last. I think the trade union organizations, by national origin, is the logical form. The solution, it seems to me, is a kind of two-chamber affair, like that of the UN. Along the lines of the articulated philosophy, an "upper" chamber or council, and a "lower" assembly, allowing room for complete representation of all labor movements, by nation, would seem to be in order. This seems to be especially important from the viewpoint of, for example, the Italian labor movement, as expressed in the article.

Yours,

Ben

Perlman to Stephansky, January 2, 1953

Dear Ben:

[Perlman tells Stephansky that the translation of his "Theory" has gone to press in Germany (see the Introduction, or Nachwort, published in Archival Supplement 8, 1999) and that he awaits the French and Italian translations. Kelley has just brought out a new printing of the 1949 reprint.]

I really do not know of a good short labor history – certainly not the Dulles one. There's "The Labor Movement in America" by Marjorie R. Clark and S. Fanny Simon, W. W. Norton, 1938, which is so-so.

There is quite a "run" on my Jewish trade union booklet. David Riesman has been talking it up (as, for instance, to Joel Seidman who asked for a copy). But I have been reduced to about 4–5 copies. Your Mexicans, unless they fancy themselves a part of Ten Lost Tribes, would not be interested.

Yours,

Selig

Perlman to Stephansky, March 3, 1953

Dear Ben and Anna:

My health subject to ups and downs, has settled to a gratifying "uppiness." I am busy, very busy, preparing detailed suggestion-outlines under 24 or so big heads, dealing with the combined research project with the Illinois group – American Labor History, 1928–1938. In Volume IV we've slurred over the 1928–1932 stretch. My wife fetches me back in a cab on teaching days, as I am not too good at walking in the cold, even a couple of blocks. However, indoors I feel my old self.

Our University is going through a budget crisis. It is really serious this time, as it may deprive us of our graduate assistants and shrink the enrollment in general (a general raise in incidental fees in contemplated). We, we shall see.

I am most interested in your Mexican stuff. With Guatemala in the other camp, Mexico is more than ever the battlefield. I have not too much confidence in the realization at the highest level of this most important point. Well, we'll see.

Our best wishes,

Selig and Fannie Perlman

Perlman to Stephansky, July 27, 1953

Dear Ben and Ann:
. . . From him I got an accurate description of what's going on over in Washington. In "labor," the union boys have a home to return to, the unattached technicians are walking the plank or are anticipating to.

Professor Charles Gulick of Berkeley has come out with a full dress attack on my Theory in the (Cornell) Industrial and Labor Relations Review – about 17,500 words. It is nearly all logic-chopping and unimpressive at that. I'll let the next quarter century add its time-test to the one just past. It's a most passionate piece and accuses me, among other things, of having crucified the intellectuals. The expression brings back my boyhood activities of the Easter-season. I do not know how the editor let that word stand.

Yours,

S. P.

Perlman to Stephansky, September 5, 1953

Dear Ben and Anna:
This is something of a topsy-turvy world. At a time when the New York Times dispatches from Britain, and other sources as well, are using the categories of trade unionists vs the intellectuals in regard to nationalization, as though these were as accepted as man and women (or better man and mother-in-law – Ann forgive this stale joke). The Berkeley group has chosen to make a grand attack on my Theory. If the people of our ilk perhaps . . . is most in the news, as the chief economist and brain truster of Dave Beck – in connection with longshoreman's situation and also the pulling up of internal discipline in the teamsters. . . . spent a few days here and he had plenty to tell about the ILA situation and Meany's acceptance of "union sanction" with the aid of government (New York plus New Jersey in concerted action). These days it's perhaps most comfortable to be a Dewey Republican – you then know the score and you are kosher!

What's ahead is hard to say, except that Ike's popularity is, if anything, on the increase. Somehow he seems the "last refuge." Stevenson is very good, but one has a feeling that he may be too much to the taste of the liberals to appeal to the generality, at a showdown. I notice he has disappointed the British leftists (the milder ones, to say nothing of the leftist <u>dons</u>) because he has been cautious in his references to McCarthy, "loyalty," Korea, etc., while in London recently. These British "know it alls" forget that they do <u>not</u> vote in American elections, and a terse reminder would not hurt. However, we've just had another kind of a don, Hugh-Jones of Oxford, who was a joy to have around. He stayed 3 months. The other "foreigners" come for a few days at the most. The State department that used to send us a man "on training leave" for a year, has been too busy with other matters and too short of funds. Our man for 1952–1953 had to shift for himself for the last month of the year.

I have not yet found it necessary to depart from my firm view on what the USSR is after. Nothing to look forward to, there. Yet when for a short while she ceases to scowl, the non-Communist Left falls as men used to fall for Peggy Hopkins in the twenties and thirties. La femme fatale in the international field!

I see it's close to three A. M. Time for another nocturnal nap! My sleeping and waking schedules have for years been twisted.

Yours,

Selig

Perlman to Stephansky, September 27, 1953

Dear Ben:

In regard to the American scene, is it not remarkable that the only force on the progressive side that is tackling new and risky jobs is the A F of L, in regard to the water-front situation. The other progressives are just reciting Jeremiads.

I am trying to function on my job, but it's a day to day proposition.

I think there is a new "vogue" – against the general labor history approach. The word is to go after specific problems and use the new techniques. I wonder whether the bankruptcy of ideas on the "left" is not in a measure responsible for this turn. I deplore it as it's bound to limit the horizon and to end in another bankruptcy.

Yours,

S. P.

Perlman to Stephansky, October 20, 1953

Dear Ben:

I got your article this morning and by this time, the early afternoon, I've read it twice. Needless to say that I am immensely grateful for your eminently successful "aggressive defense." No defense attains the purpose of turning the enemy away unless it has also turned him to flight. And we no longer dispose of the aid of the force which "did in" Saaheril and his Assyrian host when Jerusalem's fate appeared sealed.

Because my personal reaction is what it is (and what else could it be?) I consider it imperative to refrain from suggestions except where I felt myself misunderstood. I have not yet found any such passage; on the contrary, in a number of spots you have done what seems to have become a standard practice in public life: "So and so's attitude has been further elucidated by the X Department 'Official Spokesmen.' " The second shot is usually closer to the target than the original one and in this instance, invariably so. So it's better to have those inside the besieged fortress to refrain from offering advice (although not quite identical in circumstance, do you remember the Lincoln anecdote about Blondin?) to the [word indecipherable] army, but be content, as the Russian General in Simanou's Stalingrad, to feast his ear on the growing noise of the army marching in from the East.

A Perlman analysis of Perlman's reception over the years: In 1928, such men as . . . were happy to hear a fresh note. . . . Then came the New Deal, with all the fine intellects drawn into it, and no time to bother about theorizing. Now the New Dealers are "free" again for the first time, and the fodder that is available is dry and unappetizing (the "inter-disciplinary" business is merely re-discovering what the "ancients" – Barnett, Commons, Hoxie, Perlman – had talked about and "wage theory" is just "wage theory") that a miraculously preserved juicy morsel is a godsend. I expect more Gulick campaigns, since everyone must try to prove to himself and others that he is alive. Hence, your taking up arms may mean a commitment not just to a battle but to a campaign. But then you are an old warrior. I have more than a suspicion that you have prepared one of the big shells which was shot off by my side in the IRRA conference in December 1950.

Very cordially yours,

Selig

Perlman to Stephansky, October 21, 1953

Dear Ben:

In re-reading your letter I saw that I have failed to answer one of your key questions, namely whether I was getting up a personal reply to Gulick. The answer is no. The student in question is "on his own," except that I have served as a "resource."

Hastily,

Selig

[Postscript] And is it ever brilliant!

Perlman to Stephansky and wife, November 23, 1953

Dear Ben and Ann:

Ben's calm acceptance that the anti-Perlman campaign it [sic] just a private vamp, has done wonders in giving me the requisite self-confidence in facing my class and seminar: I could not do a thing at fairs or horse races, "harness" or by jockey!

The television set was a wise move. I'll have to stand a lot of "guying" from colleagues and neighbours: See, how the highbrows have struck their colors at last!

Affectionately,

Selig and Fannie

Perlman to Stephansky, March 1, 1954

Dear Ben and Ann:

My health has taken a turn for the better. I have a large class of 160+ in Capitalism and Socialism, a graduate section of 13 meeting at the house, participate in the Wednesday seminar and have a longish list of dissertation writers who likewise come to the house for weekly conferences. Yesterday (Saturday) it was a "continuous show." Fannie accompanies me to my large class and in the eyes of the multitude has the rating of an "associate lecturer," a rank she richly deserves. I do feel more re-assured with her in the front row. In my graduate section a smart young lady opened up the reports by one on Dostoyevsky's "The Possessed" (based on the Nechaw [?] incident) and surprised me with her insight into Dostoyevsky psychology. . . . Long live the youth of America! They keep me young.

Speaking of America, the current events scarcely contribute to one's "joy of living." America's non-friends (a Russianism more accurate than the sharper term "enemies") are rubbing their hands in glee at our self-flagellation! It is astounding how far people in responsible places will go in "playing with matches." Our conservatives are too emotional to "conserve" anything, and are that way even though the "menace" is not an anti-capitalist revolution but a Professor Douglas or a Senator Humphrey, whom they hanker to defeat.

The German trade union federation is discovering for itself why such a movement needs a Gompersian wage and job consciousness. It has lost its grip on the situation. Since the younger workers do not see why they should part with one hour's wages each week in union dues (our workers pay one week's wages each <u>month</u>) to any organization headed by leaders too shy to demand real wage increases but forever repeating the old gospel taught them about 1890. Perhaps it would have added something to their effectiveness had they gone through with their contract to publish my <u>Theory</u> (they sent me the small honorarium, which I took, but I have not received nor do I expect to see the nine <u>printed</u> copies as per contract). I still wish them well, of course, ass they are real idealists, but why must they forever be looking to the past?

Yours,

Selig

Perlman to Stephansky, January 11, 1955

Dear Ben and Ann:

I have been under a "house arrest" decreed by Dr. Kay after I have had a relapse of the flu (I had gone out to Sterling [Hall] a bit too soon). Now my temperature is normal again but the doctor says to stick around at home until Thursday and so it shall be.

I am whiling away my confinement by letter writing and by a "line by line" reading of the German translation of my "Theory," which arrived a week ago. It was brought out by the Verlag für Gewerkschaftspolitik und Sozialwissenschaft (Gulick et Cie, take notice!), rather than by the Federation of Trade Unions' publishing house, as first planned. It is all to the good as the translation has been improved beyond recognition, the translator has added a number of footnotes (marked Der übersetzen [translator]) for the benefit of the German reader, and the volume itself is just a "thing of beauty." It has paid to wait, even if that included the frustration of the feeling of having been neglected in "the house of one's friends," fortunately but a temporary "rejection."

Yours,

Selig

Perlman to Stephansky, January 22, 1955

Dear Ben:

Thank you for the long letter and for the copy of the anti-Gulick piece. I have reread it with great pleasure indeed. However, I will not avail myself of the chance to bring it out by finding you a collaborator or even of having it mimeographed for intra-mural consumption: I think it is better not to polemicize but let time decide. There was an article in the January 1955 issue of the Cornell <u>Review</u> by Kerr and Siegal which advances a new theory against all the so-called traditionalists: Webb, Commons, Hoxie, Perlman and Marx. The new theory charges that we have all followed the British model with its juxtaposition industrial capitalism-labor movement, whereas the better way is to array it all on the juxtaposition industrialization-the "structuring of the labor force." This would presumably make it possible to have the theory of the labor movement cover the Fascist, Peronist and Japanese varieties. To my mind, it is a more realistic and better methodology not to hanker for a formula that squeezes out all the cultural-historical juices but to deal with the several varieties undehydrated so as not to build a theory on mere "pulp." Again, I'll pass it over in silence.

Jack Barbash has sent me the text of Walter Reuther's speech on political action at the CIO convention. He has come along a good way.

Yours,

Selig

Perlman to Daniel J. Boorstin, April 4, 1955

Dear Boorstin:

I think that I shall very soon be in a position to send you the manuscript of my History of Trade Unionism in the United States. I wish to bring out the following points.

(1) The coming generation needs to be shown that the American labor movement and the shape of American industrial relations are not at all a case of a "cultural lag" (as compared with Britain and Germany), but an American phenomenon of first importance, certainly for America but also fraught with importance for other countries.

(2) American labor history is an organic part of American history and has been a strand in the latter on a par with Puritanism, the "frontier" and capitalism. It is a record of more than a century's continuous adaptation to the American environment for the purpose of learning how to change the latter so as to yield more elbow room and more opportunity to a growing population group, labor.

(3) It is essential to underline in this account of the adaptation process the difficulties of characteristically American origin, such as the entrenchment of the institution of private property and free enterprise in this land way beyond the other countries. Hence I have decided not to reduce the space given to the 1900–1933 stretch, in which, except for the few years of World War I, the American labor movement had to battle for its very existence.

(4) Another characteristically American feature has been the mental subjection of the American labor movement, down to the victory of the AF of L over the Knights of Labor, to middle class reform ideologies. The latter were essentially individualistic ("make economic individualism safe for the small fellow") and a factor for weakness in a movement which had to seek to become organizationally stable as a compensation for the lacking cementing influence of class consciousness. Hence the factual material pertaining to the

seventies-nineties had to be fully retained in order not to lose this essentially American flavor.

(5) Although the exposition underlines the FDR "revolution in labor," and a revolution it was, the space given to the New Deal, which to my view has stopped advancing in 1938, is not over large (about 26 pages), and instead of particularizing on its numerous facets, it "paints with a broom." To me, this was a period when the typically American pulls have been mitigated by the combined effects of the Great Depression and FDR's politicianship, which have produced a real geological change in the lay of the land. Yet after the "earthquake" the "face of the land" has not by any means been altered out of recognition.

(6) The chapter on World War II likewise "paints with a broom" and, if anything, with a wider one than the New Deal chapter. The accent through the whole manuscript being on the history-begotten American normalcy, the war years dominated as they were by the President's war powers and by the nation's proneness to war time self-discipline, should not be given too much space.

(7) The decade since Roosevelt was not slighted. It was a "new normalcy" (despite the Korean war) and is thus in the real center of the stream of American history.

(8) The "theory" has been boiled down to one chapter and a short one at that. It brings to my mind that in the Russian translation (1927) the book was prefaced by a long attack on Browder on the four theoretical chapters which, however, the Soviet editor thought better of publishing, so that the joke was on Browder, whose twelve pages of blasting were published.

(9) I felt I had to exceed the size of the old book by somewhat less than 5000 words, considering how much has taken place since 1922. I believe that my transgression is not too flagrant.

With my very best wishes.

Selig Perlman

Perlman to Stephansky, April 8, 1955

Dear Ben and Ann:

Am very glad that the Spanish version of my theory will come out in a few months. My Italian translator has included the paper I am now enclosing, on the ground that it has been more explicit than the 1928 version.

I have just finished reading a 600pp (in English) manuscript for the Yiddish Scientific Society (Yivo) on the background of the American Jewish labor movement in the old country and the early period of it, in my capacity as chairman of their Editorial Advisory Board on Labor History. I opined that neither the drive nor the pathos of the Jewish labor movement here will be understood by the next generation unless this exposition is included: that was the issue on which they wanted my judgment. "Die Zukunft," the serious publication of the "braintrust" of the Jewish labor movement (founded in 1892), is bringing out in November a special issue on the American labor movement in honor of the re-unification [of AFL and CIO] and will use an article of mine on the all-American contribution of the Jewish movement. I am very happy to be dealing with these people who have learned about America the hard way and are not likely to find satisfaction in the vacuities of the economists or even in the platitudes of the industrial relations experts.

I am about ready to send in my added chapters to the 'History of Trade Unionism in the U.S.":

27pp.	Chapter 11 Renewal of the Struggle for Existence, 1919–1933
20pp.	12 Under the New Deal, 1933–1939
12pp.	13 Defense and World War II
26pp.	14 In the Decade After Roosevelt
13pp.	15 In Retrospect and in Prospect
98pp.	

Am enclosing a copy of my letter to the editor of the series.

Yours,

Selig

Perlman to Stephansky, July 21, 1955 [from Tel Aviv, Israel]

Dear Ben and Anna:

[Much of the letter is devoted to Perlman's reading proof of the Italian translation of his *Theory* with the translator; he and his wife meeting with relatives; a lecture he has agreed to give at the Histadrut; and similar matters. Of particular interest are the following:]

This morning the man in charge of the Arab affairs (within Israel) gave me a comprehensive account. "Israel does by its 'minority' as well as any other nation, but not well enough."

I have been sending part of the library John R. [Commons] has left me to Hebrew University.

Yours,

Selig

Perlman to Stephansky, November 29, 1955

Dear Ben and Ann:

I met my class in American Labor History this morning and Father Dempsey, who lovingly watches over my physical condition as he watches what I say in my lectures (I figure he would not mind an even more thoroughgoing program of watchfulness), sadly remarked that I looked quite washed out. However, I have my inner indicator and I know that I am rapidly mending [after influenza]. I am no utopian, however, and I am not looking for the glow I felt last summer when I was breathing Mediterranean Sea air.

Best wishes,

Selig P.

Perlman to Stephansky, March 2, 1957

Dear Ben:

I was greatly impressed by the opus: it reads like a chapter from McCaulay [presumably Thomas Babington Macaulay]. I thoroughly agree that the Kerr-Siegal "innovation" is an intellectual backwardation and that your approach as well as the term "pre-capitalist nationalism" breathe with life instead of wishing upon us another generality which may appear "profound" to some but is in reality empty. It is really a history of the creative work of "great men" who grasped the idea that the "common man" of today yearns for a national identity. Also, these "great men" were not held in check by the traditional frameworks, either material or spiritual, come down from the past. They were "free agents" and free manipulators so long as they held the concrete human being – peon, laborer, military man or state employee – in the center of their vision. This freedom from traditional (foreign) capitalism seems to have anticipated, and did no without distortion, the national self-determination in the several "backward countries" of today.

Sincerely yours,

Selig P.

Perlman to Stephansky, August 7, 1957 [From Tel Aviv, Israel (second trip)]

Dear Ben and Ann:

I have . . . learned from Alma Bridgman that Ben is about to be transferred to Washington and be placed in charge of labor affairs for the entire Latin American region. Heartiest congratulations from both Fannie and myself. You are quickly catching up in prominence with him whom to date I have used to class as my most prominent former student: Senator Wayne Morse.

On the latter point ["to do a bit of 'feeling of the pulse' of this little land as the 'land of promise,' in a modern framework"] it is quite possible to give a positive answer in the sense of "folk" self-respect and dynamism and a not so confident an answer in terms of a solution of the problem of "economic viability." This land is in the state of "perpetual motion," in a state of continuous development and simultaneously in a state of continuous "basic problemism" (a poorly fitting expression, especially verbally). The basic problem of cost inflation is here and deriving added strength from the new avalanche of forced immigration (especially from Poland, Egypt, and some of the other Arabian lands), from the high bargaining power of organized labor and from the development of the economy itself.

At home, they have just established the John R. Commons Research Professorship and given it to me. I am due, if my health holds out, to stay in harness until June 1959.

Yours,

Selig

Perlman to Stephansky, September 30, 1958

Dear Ben:

I hasten to acknowledge the receipt of the Spanish translation of my Theory, etc. Not having heard about it in almost 3 years, I had given it up as one off the good intentions which have failed of becoming materialized.

You probably know that this is my last year as a teacher at Wisconsin; I turn seventy years old on December 9. I am still vigorous and have decided to "burn myself out" in a couple of years rather than to wait for a slower end. My wife sees eye to eye with me on this point, thank God.

The University Press of Southern Illinois (Carbondale, Illinois) has just brought out a very attractive volume by Marc Karson, American Labor Unions and Politics, 1900–1918, with a two and { page Foreward [sic; as in original] by me. It was initiated as a Ph.D. thesis under Harold J. Laski (who as you know is not one of my intellectual favorites). In my Foreward I praise the author's ability but make it plain that I am not endorsing even the tiniest of his "left overs" from brother Laski. The author liked my Foreward [sic; as in original].

Yours,

Selig

Perlman to Stephansky, November 5, 1958

Dear Ben:

I have taken a job for 1959–1960 at the Wharton School at the University of Pennsylvania.

Yours,

Selig

[Perlman died in 1959]

NOTES FROM EDWIN E. WITTE'S COURSE ON GOVERNMENT AND LABOR, ECONOMICS 249, FALL 1955

Taken and Edited by Warren J. Samuels

INTRODUCTION

As indicated in the biographical materials in Archival Supplement 22C, Edwin E. Witte was one of the foremost labor economists, or labor relations specialists, of his day. He was influential in the adoption of labor relations and protective labor legislation, a leading labor-relations arbitrator and expert on collective bargaining, a university professor and administrator, and a writer on various topics in economics and labor. He was also an empirically and pragmatically oriented interpreter of the legal-economic nexus and the history of political-economic policies and relations in the United States. One hesitates to say theorist, he was anything but pretentious, but at the bottom of his legal-economic interpretation was a corpus of legal-economic theory. So, too, was there a corpus of legal-economic theory at the core of his interpretation of government-labor relations. This corpus, and more, was highly evident in his course on Government and Labor, in which, the semester the course was given, he concentrated on protective labor legislation and its history.

Further University of Wisconsin Materials: Further Documents of F. Taylor Ostrander
Research in the History of Economic Thought and Methodology, Volume 23-C, 35–55
ISSN: 0743-4154/doi:10.1016/S0743-4154(05)23203-0

Economics 249
Government and Labor
Fall 1955
Lecture: Protective Labor Legislation Terminology

In Commons and Andrews' *Principles of Labor Legislation* (1916–1936) "labor legislation" meant protective labor legislation, which is still the most important type of labor legislation in volume, both state and national. "Labor legislation" today refers to both protective and restrictive (regulative) labor legislation.

The criterion differentiating "protective labor legislation" and "industrial relations legislation" is not whether they are for or against the interest of labor. The interest is that of the general public, as is the case with all legislation. The basic difference concerns the parties to two types of labor contracts. Protective labor legislation concerns the individual contract and labor relations legislation concerns the contract between the specific groups in the field.

Thus there is value in differentiating between two types of relevant contracts: the labor-management contract, or union agreement, formerly trade agreement, which is entered into by the organized group of workers, the union, and the employer or group of employers; and the employment contract, entered into by the employer and the employee contracting for the actual performance of work.

The labor-management agreement is an agreement determining the conditions of employment and contains nothing about actual employment, though the presence of an agreement does assume employment, but does not require employment by the employer. It merely determines the conditions of employment for those, if any, who are employed. There is no breach of contract if no employment is undertaken or if the workers do not work.

The real employment contract is an individual contract, only small parts of which are actually written. It is essentially dependent upon custom and usage, and to a lesser extent the labor-management agreement; shop rules and prevailing conditions and customs are the primary factor.

Protective labor legislation operates on the level of the actual employment contract; labor relations law concerns the labor-management agreement. The provisions of the statutes cannot be set aside by private agreement; statutes declare contradictory clauses of contracts to be invalid. Workmen's compensation, child labor, safety standards, etc. are all a requisite part of the contract under which the worker is employed and works.

Labor relations legislation, on the other hand, governs the parties and the agreement, and contracts between the parties, on the organizational level.

Historical Review of Protective Labor Legislation

No younger than the employment contract itself is government regulation of the private employment contract. The contract itself is very recent in human history; the private employment contract replaced the master-servant contract and attendant legislation. Just as the law, evolving slowly, tries to apply the most felicitous type of law, that of contracts, already existing to the new institution of the labor agreement, so the law pertaining to the employment contract (workmen's compensation, child labor, safety standards) is still included amidst the laws of master and servant in law books and indices. The different between the master-servant contract and the employment contract of today juxtaposes the superior-inferior status associated with the former, with restrictions on the master or employer's treatment of the servant but still a status arrangement, with the latter which is between relatively equal but, most important, free individuals. The nineteenth century saw the birth of the free employment contract with consequent state interference in the freedom of contract.

In the early nineteenth century, England, shortly before the U.S., enacted the first labor law, concerning compulsory school attendance (1802). Employers of children under ten or twelve years of age were required to provide six weeks of schooling per year; the statute was introduced by Lord Peel, a textile manufacturer, whose son some forty years later was responsible for the repeal of the Corn Laws, restoring free trade to England in that respect.

In the United States, the first similar law was in Massachusetts in 1819; much early legislation was in Massachusetts, for it was in that state where modern industry first developed in America – the same reason such legislation occurred in England before it did in our country. The law provided for schooling of children employed in the textile mills.

Next came laws limiting the hours of labor of children, around 1842; prescribing the minimum age of children for employment, about 1840. Massachusetts and Connecticut were both leaders in such legislation as the first industrialized states, where the problem became important.

By 1860, mechanics lien laws were enacted; indeed the problem still exists today though virtually neglected by students despite its fundamental importance to labor. Today it is usually only the smaller businesses and farmers, both of whom may hire considerable casual or transient labor, and the housewife, who may get into difficulty with her domestic help (and make unreasonable deductions for breakage, accidents, etc.). The logic of the operation of the law is to give the worker a claim on what he has produced until he is paid, which claim clouds the title until payment. The statutes have been extended beyond wages to include material, but not to cover intangible services where no attachable product is involved.

Laws highly important to labor were passed, beginning prior to the Civil War, concerning preference, time, form, and manner of wage payment. Included were such matters as wage assignments, bankruptcy, death (claims against the estate), receivership. Laws concerning the time of payment of wages date from the 1870s and 1880s. Statutes governing the form and manner of payment – including such problems as regular paydays and the worker who leaves the firm between paydays – also date from that period. Another important problem with which the law attempted to deal was the "store order," where the worker was paid not in cash but with a store order which he exchanged for goods at the company store; the law signified that the worker must be paid in cash or by check redeemable in cash. Many of these problems are still with us, in skid row and with migrant farm labor, etc. The presence of many of these issues indicates unequal power; today the rights are taken for granted.

Laws relating to women date from the 1840s when a few ineffective laws attempted to regulate the hours of labor of women. However, the statutes read "in the absence of a contract to the contrary," which was construed by the courts to imply that if the employers ran their plants ten hours a day such custom was a part of the contract. No proscription against working over the maximum time was thus set in the statute.

In the 1880s and 1890s legislation attempted again to limit the hours of labor of women. In Illinois the Supreme Court declared such an act unconstitutional as an infringement upon the freedom of contract. By the turn of the century, statutes limited the hours of employment in particular employments. In Holden v. Hardy a divided court upheld the law as a proper limitation of the freedom of contract as the Utah mine has peculiar attributes and the public has a legitimate concern. The law in question concerned an eight-hour law. However, in Lochner v. New York, the court ruled a ten-hour law in the baking industry unconstitutional as an undue interference with the freedom of contract. In 1908, however, the Supreme Court of the United States sustained the regulation of the hours of labor of women. Brandeis filed a brief on behalf of the National Consumers' League with the court, pointing out the hazards of the baking industry in the Lochner case in which only precedents were argued. Brandeis, in his epochal brief, covered social and economic concepts and the realities of working conditions; also covered were such points as the weakness of women, their additional home responsibilities, and their bearing of children.

Lecture:

In the early period all protective labor legislation was on the state level and continued so until the 1930s. Although the most important single act is the Fair Labor Standards Act of the U.S., the great majority of legislation on this subject is still state law.

There were three major periods of great advances in protective labor legislation in this country. The first major period was the period of the late 1870s and 1880s. Perhaps the major development of this time was the development of state administrative departments charged with the administration of state labor law. Although Massachusetts had the first such department as early as 1868, most came in the 1880s, with Wisconsin's in 1884 being an early state. Today all states have one, and some more than one, labor department. The origin of the department was in the Bureaus of Labor Statistics, originally charged with gathering data and making recommendations to the legislature. By the 1880s and 1890s they became charged with the administration of labor law, particularly of industrial safety statutes. A part of the story was the use for the first time of factory inspectors in connection with safety enforcement.

Although more will be said on this later in the course, the first labor-relations legislation, of both a promotional and restrictive character, came during this time. One law pressed for by the unions was the right to incorporate; however, they did not take advantage of the law they sought to have passed after it became enacted. No real change was effectuated by the passage of the law in the picture of labor; originally they had thought it would bring about a gain in their status if they were able to incorporate, something that did not materialize. Only a few unions have incorporated under the many state laws enabling them to do so. Brandeis strongly advocated their incorporation under those laws.

Also coming in this period were the first laws concerning boycotts and offensive picketing as well as the regulation of private detective agencies (as a result of the Homestead strike). In addition came more restrictive child labor laws, much like those operative today, covering education, hours, age, etc.

In the 1880s starts the system of child labor permits, issued to children of specified age usually by labor authorities of the state, though sometimes by school officials who do not do as good a job (perfunctory).

Also, there was extensive wage regulation, as to time, manner and form of payment. This what the basis on which Samuel Gompers turned sour on labor legislation: a New York law tried to legislate conditions of employment governing home work, as well as a manner of payment law, but was declared unconstitutional by a reactionary New York Supreme Court prone to declaring such laws invalid.

In addition, women's laws, governing maximum hours of labor, were enacted, upheld in several states, but declared unconstitutional in Illinois in the mid-1890s.

The second major period was from 1907 to the outbreak of the first World War, c.1915; this was *the* great period, the period in which the greatest advances in protective labor legislation were made. Wisconsin, replacing Massachusetts, was the leader of states; the reputation of Wisconsin as a progressive state is based on her progress during that time. 1911 was the peak year in Wisconsin and the nation generally.

Enacted were such statutes as present day child labor laws with adequate enforcement machinery, particularly permits, which were coordinated with compulsory school attendance laws, and the modern type of safety and sanitation (including industrial poisons, etc.) legislation.

In this field of safety legislation, John R. Commons made his great contribution to Wisconsin, manifested in the Industrial Commission Act of 1911. Prior legislation was specific and in great volume, dealing in detail as to be proscriptions and prescriptions and describing actual procedures and safeguards. From a study by Commons of Belgium and the rest of Western Europe, the 1911 act repealed all existing safety legislation and substituted for them a general duty of an employer to safeguard against hazards and to "operate a safe place of employment and employment which is safe," governing also the owner of buildings used by the public. The labor department determines, through general and special orders, safe conditions of employment in the many employments in the state. Advisory groups from the areas in which government promulgates general orders and the Commission are empowered to issue special orders allowing modification under certain conditions or on special topics. All orders have the same force and effect as statutes. This new administrative method, while not universal even today, has proven to work, eliminating both the carelessness and the burden from legislatures inexpert in the problems involved in many fields of activity governed by codes and orders. In Wisconsin the idea has been extended in part to the administration of women and child labor laws.

During this great era, laws governing the hours of women were passed in large numbers, and upheld. The first minimum wage laws for women and children, passed during this period, were upheld in state courts during the 1920s. But a divided U.S. Supreme Court, in the Atkins case, held minimum wage legislation unconstitutional. Justice Sutherland thought that minimum wage laws were immoral, a thesis appealing to conservative elements but which drew wrath from the church, Father Ryan in particular, who said church pronouncements were to the contrary. This decision was later reversed in the 1930s.

Modern apprenticeship legislation also appeared. Previously the master-servant relationship in law governed such a condition; the law did not fit the new employee relationship. Wisconsin enacted in 1911 the first such law, a law which sounds regulatory – where, it says, part of remuneration is training on the job, it must be administered by the state – but is not followed as strictly as the language might imply; technical education is merely administered by the state. Wisconsin's example was not followed widely until the 1930s and 1940s. Before, most skilled workers had learned their trade in Europe, and they died off. Skills, therefore, were disappearing and "barn carpenters" were coming into town – poor on house building but offering competition. Thus the impetus for apprenticeship programs, later on to come under state scrutiny and administration.

Unions serve as a market mechanism supplying skills in distant cities where the demand is not strong enough to warrant permanent settlement etc. of similarly skilled workers – e.g. structural metal workers in Madison – called in from out of town through unions.

Similarly, industry location depends on the availability of the required skilled labor. The problem arose for the War Labor Board in World War II concerning the location of war plants. Such a matter appears as a "problem" in a free society, not so apparent as unsolved in a centrally directed and controlled economy.

Lecture:

In the last lecture we dealt in considerable detail the period of great advance from 1907 to 1915 in which the most important legislation can in 1911 and 1913.

Federal agencies only then began to become important; the Labor Department was organized in 1913 with no administrative functions except regarding the immigration laws. It promoted labor legislation in the states and assisted the states in that matter; at that time state legislation predominated even more than now.

Child, women, vocational education, apprenticeship, modern safety, workmen's compensation, and centralized and unified administration of labor law were some of the important improvements made at that time.

Characteristic of the Wisconsin labor department is its order-making power, replacing the multitude of statutory provisions, especially regarding industrial safety, while the U.S. Department of Labor was still not an administrative agency, with research and promotion its main functions.

Workmen's compensation was first thought of as a modification of employer-liability law; later, on the ground of social responsibility and security purposes. Still the last state law on workmen's compensation came in 1948. Some states have separate workmen's compensation departments, outside the labor department.

Also coming in this period are the first modern statewide public employment offices and services. While the first one was in Ohio in the early 1890s, the real beginning was made in Wisconsin in 1911, with the establishment of a real and permanent office system.

The United States Employment Service began in 1907 as an immigration service. The immigration laws since the 1880s have prevented immigrants from having a job prior to entrance, demanded by labor to prevent strikebreakers from coming into the country, although specialized skills were exempted. The decade of peak immigration was the first decade of the twentieth century – the peak of post-Civil War immigration. The minimum funds of the immigrants and the desire to protect them against exploitation culminated in the establishment of an employment service on their behalf.

In 1917 a different employment problem presented itself; the service expanded to include recruiting for farms and war industries, with farming emphasized as the U.S. fed the allies. During 1917–1918, the USES was set up in all the states, with local offices being run by appropriate government bodies in the states already have them, using the one collective name of USES, with the Federal government footing the bill as of the Wagner-Pyser Act of 1933.

In the first World War the beginning of vocational and rehabilitation programs got under way. They were centered in workmen's compensation administrative groups as more were injured in industrial accidents than in the war itself. In 1920, the first Federal aid classified now as "social security" was in this field.

The 1920s period was one of few advances and little improvements, but no retreat. In the U.S., full repeal of any protective labor legislation has been impossible. The period did see, however, improvements in administrative functioning.

This was the period of the high tide of conservatism, with employer groups heatedly anti-protective labor legislation.

The New Deal period was second highest in importance in U.S. protective labor legislation history. Its height was 1933–1938 nationally, and 1935 and, especially, 1937 in the states. Little new legislation showed on the horizon but considerable improvements were made in existing legislation. The U.S. Department of Labor became in this period the main agency promoting state protective labor legislation, in good part due to its very able Secretary, Miss Frances Perkins, the first woman cabinet member. The USDL was able to push legislation where it was most needed, in the South.

The techniques by which the USDL promoted state protective labor legislation included: (a) drafting of model statutes; (b) sending representatives before state legislatures; (c) appeals over the President's signature; and (d) national conferences (which still continue). The Bureau of Labor Standards, in USDL, has the function of developing and "selling" new standards.

The effects of USDL prodding were the improvement of Northern laws and the enactment of laws in Southern states, where they were exceptionally weak prior to the 1930s. Though they have never been enforced to any great extent, some are enforced better than in some Northern states, e.g. North Carolina and Pennsylvania as to child labor, and in some cases more modern laws are at least on the books in some Southern states than in several Northern states.

The prestige of the Administration was considerably responsible for state action.

This period was one of considerable Federal action and value of protective labor legislation, for the first time. The three most important statutes were enacted at the time:

(1) Bacon-Davis Act, enacted in 1932 during the Hoover Administration, covering hours and wages of contract work in construction.
(2) Walsh-Healy Act, enacted in 1935, established the determination of minimum wages in production for government – purchases of commodities on government account, relatively large purchases.
(3) Fair Labor Standards Act, most important Federal law, enacted in 1938, to be discussed in greater detail later.

In addition, the USES became a reality with the passage of the Wagner-Pyser Act in 1933, granting Federal aid to the states for use in the conduct of public employment offices. In 1935 the source of support was shifted to the social security fund administration. Thus the states control the offices and the Federal government pays 100% of the bill, with the state systems linked into a national system.

The Social Security Act of 1935 was the most important general law in social legislation ever enacted. It encompassed largely state administration and control, except for Federal Old Age and Survivors Insurance. The Social Security Act will be treated in much greater detail next semester in a course devoted solely to it.

Also enacted during this period was the Wagner Act.

Halting old controversies concerning protective labor legislation, the Supreme Court of the United States, in 1937, reversed the status of social legislation and the concept of state-national relations. Previously, the Court divided five to four against; thereafter, five to four pro. When Justice Roberts changed his mind – "a switch in time saved nine," for the court-packing bill was in Congress at the time – the Constitution and social legislation changed with him.

Chief Justice Hughes was greatly responsible for the climate of the shift; he had suggested what was to come in earlier majority and minority opinions.

In interpreting Constitutional provisions, the earlier method was to reason on analogy and precedent as to conflict of law – the only way such a case can get before the Supreme Court – i.e. a statute or administrative action vs. the Constitution. The new line of reasoning was to look to the Constitution, not earlier decisions, and determine by necessary inference or explicit mention the issue at hand. No act of the Federal government has been held unconstitutional since 1937.

Minimum-wage Legislation and the Courts: In 1917 the United States Supreme Court upheld an Oregon law on the briefs submitted by Brandeis and Frankfurter after the state Supreme Court had found it constitutional. The Court was tied, 4–4, but a majority vote is necessary to declare unconstitutionality.

In 1923, in Atkins v. Children's Hospital, in a 5–3 decision, minimum wage legislation was held unconstitutional and immoral, as to a Federal law governing the District of Columbia; thereafter it was difficult to enforce any state minimum wage law.

In 1933 new laws were passed; others were still on the books but not enforced; New York tried to enforce it law. In the Trypolda case of 1936, the New York Supreme Court held the state law unconstitutional, basing its decision on the District of Columbia case. The case went to the United States Supreme Court on certiorari and a 4–4 decision upheld the lower court; the ninth justice was ill.

Reversal came in 1937 in Parish Hotel Co. v. State of Washington. A law establishing standards for a living wage and banning the payment of less than a living wage, was in 1934 declared constitutional. Justice Roberts wrote the decision. It cited the case most cited than any other, Nebbia v. New York, in which the state fixed the price of milk, both the minimum price paid to farmers and the maximum price to consumers. The New York Court of Appeals upheld the law, on the ground of an emergency. The United States Supreme Court said that the law was constitutional, emergency or not; that the test was not the status of emergency but due process of law. Roberts upheld the constitutionality of the law, citing that criticism of regulation of price had no basis as it has been continual in U.S. history. The Nebbia case thus questioned whether prices are subject to regulation; the U.S. Supreme Court said yes, that such regulation was in accord with due process of law. Thus, with the Nebbia case upholding the thesis that prices are subject to regulation, wages then became subject to regulation because wages are prices, with no violation of due process.

Federal-State Jurisdiction: The dividing line between Federal and state jurisdiction came to a head over the Fair Labor Standards Act.

Contrary to popular opinion, the power to regulate does not come from the power to regulate interstate or foreign commerce. In 1937 "interstate commerce" was broadened to mean the *effect* on interstate commerce that determines whether the Federal government has jurisdiction.

The Minnesota Rate Case is an example of an earlier case as to affecting interstate commerce. It was concerned with too low intrastate rates burdening interstate commerce, rates which held invalid for that reason.

The original clause was inserted into the Constitution because of the restrictive regulations imposed by the former colonies on interstate commerce after the Revolutionary War under the Articles of Confederation before the Constitution was adopted, i.e. they were concerned with the burdening of interstate commerce.

In 1937 five different cases came before the Supreme Court in connection with the National Labor Relations Act, the Wagner Act. The NRLA was wholly ineffective during 1935–37 because it was enjoined by various district courts. The Liberty League, composed of 58 lawyers, was one group with but one idea: all New Deal legislation was unconstitutional. Despite their objections the Supreme Court held the Act constitutional, and firms had to pay many large bills owed under NLRA and Social Security – all because of their acceptance of the gratuitous advice, in Wisconsin and elsewhere, of anti-New Deal lawyers.

The simplest case concerned the Pennsylvania Greyhound Lines, which was clearly interstate commerce. The Court said, 9–0, that the legislation was not contrary to due process and therefore confiscatory.

The Jones and Laughlin Steel case was the most important. Important in connection with this case is the 1894 Knight case in which it was held, and never reversed, that manufacturing is not interstate commerce even if it is for interstate commerce. In the Steel case the Court, 5–4, said that it was not over-ruling the Knight case, but concluded that consideration must be taken of the *effect* on interstate commerce.

Another important case was the 1938 Consolidated Edison Co. case, involving the largest operating utility, operating exclusive within New York state. The U.S. Supreme Court nevertheless upheld the NLRB who had held that despite the fact that Con Ed sells only in New York, much of the by-products of the power process are sold over the U.S., as well as the fact that many factors of production were bought over the U.S. The U.S. Supreme Court said that the argument over by-products missed the point, 5–4, and that the test is the *effect* on interstate commerce. New York is such a great center that the power industry operating therein is of concern because much U.S. commerce is dependent upon power in New York.

The test is, therefore, "substantiality"; the Court has always upheld were the effect is "substantial"; and the NLRB voluntarily refuses cases on the basis. The implication is that the United States could therefore go further than it has, e.g. safety in coal mines and factories has effect on interstate commerce. The doctrine of substantiality would permit expansion.

[The foregoing was typed at the time of the course and edited in January 2001. The remainder was drafted from the original notes in January 2001.]

The period since 1937–1938, discussed in Witte's 1946 speech, until today, has not seen much change; a little progress, especially in the 1949 and 1955 legislative sessions, and not much retrogression.

Recent Developments

(1) Fair Labor Standards Act: increase in minimum wage rate in 1949 and 1955, no increase in coverage.

(2) Coal Mine Safety Act, 1954: inspection. Still much on advisory level but not only so. Grew out of central Illinois mine disaster in mine condemned time and time again by state inspectors but allowed to operate. Heavy contribution to Illinois governor and attorney general campaign funds. Issue in 1948 campaign. Governor Green kicked out by Adlai Stevenson.

(3) More state and Federal attention to apprenticeship.

(4) Some improvement in Workmen's Compensation and in Unemployment Compensation insurance but no more than keeping up with decreased value of the dollar.

(5) Fair Employment Practices lag (FEPC): main new type was anti-discrimination as to race, creed, and color. Origin in administrative decrees of Franklin D. Roosevelt; set up Fair Employment Practices Commission based on war power. No national legislation though recommended by Roosevelt and Truman. Truman lost Southern democrats in 1948 because of his recommendation of it.

Slowly, states passed legislation, some as early as World War II; one or two a year; less than half of the 48, all in the North, some advisory (Wisconsin), some mandatory. Effect has been good. Considerable effect on public opinion. Five or six in 1955, mostly mandatory type of legislation.

Cannot enforce such laws on penal basis, have to work it out and favorably improve the situation. As with FEP, employer is usually not at fault; fellow workers are at fault and engage in wildcat strikes. Difficult spot is retail store.

In industrial safety field, prosecution is a rarity, used only in extreme cases of failure to cooperate.

Much FEPC and safety work is educational.

Another new type are laws promoting equal pay for women; against discrimination on basis of gender. Almost all are penal laws. Some are very old, but are dead letters. Difficulty is with "equal job." Few women are employed on same jobs as men. Employer usually changes job, e.g. making it unnecessary for women to carry heavy loads as men do, etc. "Same" work seldom exists.

Still must recognize differential against women in employment in U.S., as to time of work, absentee, sickness, percentage getting skilled in a job, etc.

Laws have not changed the structure very much.

Minor law requires employer to pay for any medical exam he requires for employment.

Improvement in some laws, some of which had been suspended during wartime: child labor, hours of labor, etc.

Lecture:

The reasons for lack of interest in protective labor legislation in last twenty years, especially since 1938, and relatively little progress:

(1) Standards of protective labor legislation are now much higher, therefore less concern over raising the standards. Inevitable. Legislative standards are far behind actual practices in many respects in this country, e.g. minimum wage – $1 against $1.60 average in manufacturing. Thus many feel workers are in great prosperity and don't need increased standards. Child labor laws setting 16 years have little appeal to raise them compared to when limit was 12 years.

(2) Lack of promulgating group. Pressure for improvement – for new legislation – most effective when from outside of government, such as American Association for Labor Legislation, 1907–1942, National Consumers' League. Former died out because death of Andrews of UW (see 246 notes), its founder, as is usually the case – had tremendous influence in social security etc. especially until 1930 (died 1942) – in part because people thought all it stood for had been accomplished and in part to presence of government bodies – an incomplete replacement, though. Hard to find money-raising people interested in the program to be active in the drive.

(2) National Consumers' League mainly a women's organization, also having a great promoter, Mrs. Florence Kelly. It originally functioned around the white label given to businessmen following their accepted standards. Good effect, particularly in their special field, women and child labor (c.1900–1930). Mrs. Ely McGee (Cleveland) now has successor to it and also AALL (they say). Background of women's organization, while best we have is still not too effective.

(3) Organized labor has always supported protective labor legislation. Most bills have their origins with them. But only a secondary interest of theirs – always and still. Union members are not principal beneficiaries of protective labor legislation: minimum wages, hours. Their achieved standards are much higher. Protected though by fierce competition from unorganized who benefit from protective labor legislation. Gompers: raise standard of competition to protect organized, despite his desire to keep government out of picture. Much protective labor legislation deals with subjects not incorporated in or lending themselves to collective bargaining (except industrial safety and sanitation and even then of little meaning; John L. Lewis has tried to incorporate them by striking if minor conditions are unsafe; did not get credit because of failure to strike at Centralia mine).

Protective labor legislation is mainly state legislation and national organizations (AFL and CIO) have in the main left it alone. Only in general recommendations have they treated it. The main drive is through industrial councils and state-level organizations which are, however, relatively weak.

(4) A general lack of interest in state government. Washington, DC has attracted complete attention; even though state governments have control over basic law, interest is still in Washington, DC.

(5) Representation in a majority of all states is very unfair to the urban areas and working people, therefore state legislatures are [indecipherable]; and labor, especially organized or industrialized workers, are a small percentage of the population. Also, three-quarters or more have discriminated in representation against urban areas. In New York, it is unconstitutional for New York City, with over one-half the population, ever to control the legislature. In California, senate representation is by counties; Los Angeles County, with four and one-half million out of ten million, has equal number of senators with counties of 100,000 population, one. Legislatures are controlled by rural small town areas usually and still now hostile to labor.

Growing employer hostility to government intervention; an increasing feeling over last twenty years by business groups.

(6) Absorption of labor and general public interest in labor relations legislation – less important though in volume and general importance.

(7) Financial and other weakness of state labor departments, plus pitiful appropriations, politics rather than civil service in majority of states, in North and South, even within one part, i.e. factions.

CIO support is kiss of death in Wisconsin. Most influential group in the past has been the railroad brotherhoods: but (a) dwindling in number; (b) oldest in U.S.; (c) independent; and (d) concentrated living of railroad men.

National Protective Labor Legislation

State legislation older and often the only.

National protective laws:

(1) Fair Labor Standards Act, 1938: Given little or minimal support by labor; passed because of Roosevelt's pushing and insistence upon such legislation; labor even undercut it. The foremost protective labor law and presently of great significance to labor and unions. Amended quite often, materially in 1949, 1955.

Coverage: Production for interstate commerce and interstate commerce, with broad stated exceptions (agriculture, retail). Trend to neither broaden nor narrow coverage, though some broadening of exceptions since 1938, e.g. agricultural labor. Against presidential recommendation, e.g. distribution of products entering interstate commerce in sizeable distribution outlets.

Many manufacturing-process firms thus want to get classified as agriculture; work with farm products. Series of amendments in 1940s, especially supported by "farmers" in California and Arizona, exempting numerous such manufacturing groups dealing with agricultural products. They are corporations dealing with agricultural products, large crop production and hundreds of workers. Still, legislators associate "farmer" with usual small farmer.

"Agriculture" covers now where processing is engaged in on farm property – wine, etc., from California, lettuce packaging, etc.

Cooperatives have gotten great privileges in that respect even though processing is not done on the premises; qualifies as being made up of farmers.

By narrowing of farm exemption means bringing processors under the law.

Little drive this year.

Coverage: manufacturing, not railroads (have own legislation), other transportation forms, finance, mining. Law applies to production for interstate commerce and therefore applies to almost all manufacturing except those sneaking out through agriculture. Applies to stenographer in manufacturing plant; construction areas and services for equipment by manufacturer.

Law presently reads minimum wage of $1 per hour, raised in 1955 from 75 cents. Labor wanted $1.25 – sincerely, says Miss Brandeis. Not too interested in extending coverage, mainly wants to better relations with agriculture – main group in exemption section.

Forty-hour week as basis for payment; no prohibition of work over forty hours. Provide for time and one-half for hours over forty. Union contracts provide for eight-hour day and 40-hour week. Different from other laws prescribing absolute maximum hours – women, children, and certain special occupations and industries. Not time and one-half minimum rate but actual rate of worker. Important effects in beginning: many workers accustomed to work over forty-hour weeks had to be paid time and one-half by FLSA, as Northern employers long did. Previously, many workers had not received extra pay for overtime.

Most important effect is limitation on hours, while still not rigid, in effect on overtime. Minimum wage provisions less important as to influence and effect.

Questions:

(1) Who benefits from protective labor legislation?
(2) What is union and management interest therein?
(3) To whom in management is it valuable?
(4) How do collective bargaining and protective labor legislation fit together?
(5) What is value of protective labor legislation to the public, in whose interest it is enacted?

(6) What limitations are desirable with reference to what government should do, i.e. what should government do through protective labor legislation?

Lecture:

Role of National Government in Protective Labor Legislation

1938 FLSA, amended materially regarding rates in 1949 and 1955. Applies to interstate commerce and production for interstate commerce, with many exemptions usually broadened. No extension of coverage for some time. Hours provisions unchanged from beginning. Employment over forty hours a week must be at one and one-half times regular rate, not minimum rate. Also unchanged materially are child-labor provisions: under 16 in mining and manufacturing, and in other vocations during vacation and with child labor permit, granted by states usually. Twelve-thirteen Southern states have Federal permits; Wisconsin: Industrial Commission. Restrictions issuable for especially hazardous employment, usually 16-year age standard. These are standards comparable to the best states in the Union, ahead of others. Wisconsin ahead in child labor: 17 age, vocational education requirement, hazardous employment. One-dollar minimum wage affects only two million workers, mainly in South and Prairie states; few in Northeast and North. About 30–35 million covered by the law.

Areas of debate

Labor slightly interested except regarding minimum-wage rate. Sees increase in wages above minimum to retain differential. Wage controls employed tapering off principle, increase high rates but less than lower rates. Lower rates always allowed for learners and apprentices.

Imparted concern over failure to extend coverage; lowest wages exist in industries not covered: service and retail trade, particularly women's industries, industries with relatively high labor cost (manufacturing average is 20% labor cost), relatively small firms with high relative labor costs: second largest group of employees, only 30% of working force; large group, in manufacturing, need protective labor legislation least.

Child-labor provisions have worked satisfactorily with little debate. Same with overtime provisions – common in labor contracts, plus 8-hour day, 40-hour week.

Other Federal laws:

Bacon-Davis Act, 1932: Wage rates on all government construction over $10,000 for Federal government and its agencies; same or similar law in states; Wisconsin includes construction and highway building. Early state laws knocked down, after 1930s, upheld. State has some rights as private employer. Unions are very interested in these laws.

"Prevailing wage" – in area of construction, as determined by Secretary of Labor; usually means union wage rate. Included in specification as minimum wage rate. Drastic penalties (contract payment loss). Usually county is the area. Contractors neutral; government pays the bill.

Usually hire union men, but in Southwestern states (Texas, Oklahoma) union labor is not used, though uses prevailing wage rages, freely moving the men around to save cost (from job to job and from trade to trade).

Walsh-Healy Act, 1935: Minimum wage on all production for sale to government over $10,000. Important during wartime: in World War II, production was 60% for government. On a contract, rather than a yearly, basis. Important today, as 15% of total industrial production is used by government. Peculiar in providing for a minimum wage rate to be determined by Secretary of Labor. Usually a common labor rate, often wage as you go from industry to industry, e.g. auto; but no such thing: who or what is the laborer? Usually the unskilled jobs.

"Area" is another problem: often same rate entire country – tested in courts now (textile mills); can have different areas for different industries.

Many often affected by FLSA which is sometimes lower than this rate.

Haus-Cooper Act, 1930: directed against sale of products made by prison labor in interstate commerce, i.e. may only be shipped into state allowing such manufacturing in that state to be sold therein – a decided minority of states now, formerly a majority. Net effect is decrease in employment of prisoners on marketable products; now mainly for government account. Agricultural products an exception despite cry of labor. Successful in eliminating market production.

Coal Mine Safety Act, 1954: First Federal safety law. Earlier safety inspections were advisory by Bureau of Mines, i.e. no mandatory jurisdiction. Result of Centralia disaster. Imposes Federal standards in additional to state standards. Both inspect.

Conditions of labor prevailing in Federal government itself: The Federal government has two and one-half million employees (five times those of General Motors), only one-quarter to one-third in Washington, DC; in the Department of Defense and Post Office, especially. Federal workers in Madison are one-half those working for the state of Wisconsin, greater, if teachers are excluded.

John R. Commons felt that government should be a model employer. The prevalent view now is that it should be equal to that in private employment. In many respects government employment is ahead of private employment, especially regarding lower wage rate groups, whereas the higher rates are lower than private rates. Conditions of employment are generally comparable; hours less than in private work, pensions (U.S. Civil Service) are the best, more sick leave. State and especially municipal and county workers are usually the worst paid. General picture is about equal. The labor relations situation is worse, e.g. unionized government workers, collective bargaining.

Regulatory legislation in special fields: railroads, airlines, migratory labor, immigrants.

Railroads and airlines: Considerable protective labor legislation, in addition to states: safety, sanitation, standards, hours of continuous work (1907 LaFollette law: sixteen hours maximum, plus eight hours off). Federal government could take over the entire field.

Migratory labor: Little direct regulation, as applicable general labor laws exempt agriculture (discussed above). Some special state legislation (New York, California, Wisconsin), especially on work camps. No national legislation. Truman created migratory labor commission in 1951, making many recommendations ignored by Congress. Wetback regulation of wages and housing and insuring payment of wages (Mexicans and Puerto Ricans).

Immigration: Early field of protective labor legislation. Earliest advocated by labor, anti-Chinese immigration on West coast. Labor nativist and anti-Red. Basic 1922 law now limits immigration in proportion to percentage here in 1920, limits South and East European and Asian, none regarding Canada, Puerto Rico, or Mexico. Labor department and Puerto Rican government enable foundry workers to come to U.S. to work where shortages. Organized labor still in favor of restricted immigration. No longer bar Chinese; separate treatment of refugees; new laws for subversives, etc.) Main immigration is from Mexico, British West Indies, and Puerto Rico, also Philippinos to Hawaii. Mexico: illegal (wetback) immigration, legal limits controlled by treaties and laws. Puerto Rican and BWI workers admissible for temporary agricultural and industrial work.

Service Functions

Influence greatest not in regulatory labor legislation but in services and aids, many in form of aids to states. Largest is USES.

USES: Interstate clearance; important in wartime. Most important service to employers is with "rare" specialized labor and for men hard to place – handicapped, older, etc. Federal offices for immigrants; St. Paul, Kansas City agricultural offices for transient labor and school labor on vacation.

Bureau of Apprenticeship: Uniform standards of USDL. Bureau of Labor Standards: trains inspectors, develops and promulgates standards.

Statistical and Research: U.S. Bureau of Labor Statistics: Largest of such in the world. Women's Bureau: Problem studies, research. Children's Bureau (ditto).

Other government agencies: Bureau of Mines (Coal Mine Safety); Department of Agriculture (migratory labor); Justice Department, Bureau of Immigration; ICC (railroad and airlines); Defense Department and Atomic Energy Commission (employers of labor under contract work); Civil Service System (standards, pensions, etc.).

Current Questions and Problems

Fair Labor Standards Act: raising minimum wage rate, broadening coverage.

Walsh-Healy Act: type of order issues, now before the courts.

National safety and sanitation standards: alternatives are Federal legislation and aid to the states.

Regulation or protection of migratory labor: In worst position. Little done now.

Federal aid to states for worker education: Failed because of employer opposition and friction in labor movement over it.

Lecture:

Place and Importance of Protective Labor Legislation

Who benefits from it?

(1) Humanitarian employer: eliminates fear of competition less humane. North vs. South: lower wages, newer mills. As main drive, overstated. Progressive employers hesitant to advocate protective labor legislation. Same ownership

(2) Organized labor: can claim credit if active; stepladder increase to retain differential.

Labor cost depends upon productivity. Sumner H. Slichter: increase in wage rate leads to mechanization which increases standard of living through productivity increase.

John R. Commons: order in which prices increase and decrease: changes in productivity of labor lead first to changes in raw materials and farm products, second to changes in partially finished goods, third to changes in wholesale prices, fourth to retail prices, fifth to changes in wages, and sixth to changes in rents. Retail prices change before wage rates; strikes come when price level increases; increases in wage rates do not lead to increases in prices. Recently, farm and raw material prices have fallen, with retail prices steady; may lead to beginning of downward cycle. Increases in wage rates will lead to increase in prices in this situation. Causes of change: demand and supply in farm products, decline in foreign markets, production in new countries.

Lecture:

Is protective labor legislation needed today?

Have high standards. Collective bargaining is widespread.

(1) Wide areas where collective bargaining has little influence; does not affect all. Labor force (all employed – employees, self-employed, professionals, agriculture, etc) = 68 million, including 3 million military employees; less those not employees = 52 million; less non-industrialized employees (farmers, domestics, public (4 million), retail and service) = c. 40 million. With 15–16 million unionized, less than one-half can rely on collective bargaining (less union members where collective bargaining is absent, plus where non-union workers have collective bargaining agreements). Therefore, largest group is not benefited by collective bargaining

(2) Collective bargaining agreement does not include matters treated by protective labor legislation. Uniformity is necessary and cannot get agreement to change. Workers will not strike for such matters. Little attention paid by unions – rely on laws.

Is protective labor legislation important to unions?

Keeps down competition of "unfair employer," reduces their effects, provides better situation for fair employer. Not large factor at present time; still the legislation does not apply to the lowest wage-rate industries, such as textiles.

Why do unions generally support protective labor legislation?

Organized labor sees itself as representing "all labor" – from Gompers on down; comes close to anyone else.

What should be the standards in protective labor legislation? Should protective labor legislation aim at best conditions, or average conditions?

Are well below best conditions.
Minor issue of what part of protective labor legislation one is talking about.
Would create little disturbance in the economy if brought all workers up to average.
Look at cost to industries of increased minimum wage.

Is more protective labor legislation by national government desirable?

What kind of standards are we likely to get under Federal legislation: Mississippi or California or Michigan? More progress likely through which?

Multiplicity of bills before Congress.

State legislatures less representative than national government – heavily rural areas dominate, often very extremely.

Experimentation comes on state level when each is left to own

Is uniformity desirable or possible? Uniform standard closer to low than high, at least mediocre.

Do have wide differences in conditions. Average per capita incomes in lowest states are less than one-third that of highest states.

Failure of states to make any progress.

Concentration of efforts on Washington, DC.

Cannot get at through Congress.

A "state problem," traditional state problem.

Elements of a progressive state: industrialization, large group of interested people, record of neighboring states.

Politician knows best what public wants, in order to return to office; and must know what the people will think tomorrow.

Lecture:

International Labor Legislation

In brief: (1) Notre Dame speech presents views; (2) later, question ILO director in Washington, DC.

*****

FURTHER DOCUMENTS FROM
F. TAYLOR OSTRANDER

MATERIALS FROM JOHN ULRIC NEF'S COURSES ON ECONOMIC HISTORY, ECONOMICS 221 AND 322, UNIVERSITY OF CHICAGO, 1933–1934

JOHN ULRIC NEF: A BRIEF BIOGRAPHY

John Ulric Nef was born in 1899 and died in 1988 having had, in effect, three careers, all centered at the University of Chicago.

A native Chicagoan, he received his undergraduate degree from Harvard in 1920 and his doctorate from the Robert Brookings Graduate School in 1927. After teaching at Swarthmore College, Nef joined the Chicago faculty in 1929.

Nef became a foremost economic historian, one whose largest domain of interest was the economic, cultural and military history of Western Europe since the end of the 15th century, whose mid-range area of concentration was the comparative economic histories of Britain and France, and whose most intensive field was the economic history of France. Especially important was his early work on the British coal industry and the early Industrial Revolution in 16th and 17th century England. This work suggested that the "Revolution" was a long-time evolutionary process:

> The rise of industrialism in Great Britain can be more properly regarded as a long process stretching back to the middle of the sixteenth century and coming down to the final triumph of the industrial state towards the end of the nineteenth, than as a sudden phenomenon associated with

Further University of Wisconsin Materials: Further Documents of F. Taylor Ostrander
Research in the History of Economic Thought and Methodology, Volume 23-C, 59–78
Copyright © 2005 by Elsevier Ltd.
ISSN: 0743-4154/doi:10.1016/S0743-4154(05)23204-2

the late eighteenth and early nineteenth centuries. (John U. Nef, "The Progress of Technology and the Growth of Large-Scale Industry in Great Britain, 140–1640," *The Economic History Review*, Vol. 5, No. 1 October 193?, pp. 3–24, at 22)

Nef was one of the first economic historians to pay serious attention to technology. He also focused on the recursive relations between political and economic histories within a larger view of the interrelations between religion, science, politics and technology.

Nef was a founder, initial financial underwriter, and administrator of the famous and unusual if not unique graduate-studies Committee on Social Thought at the University of Chicago.

Thirdly, Nef was a philanthropist and patron of the arts, accumulating a major collection of modern art.

Many of the foregoing activities were financed from the substantial inheritances he and his wife received from both their families.

His publications were wide ranging and, in some cases, reissued. Books in economic history (usually broadly comprehended) included: *The Rise of the British Coal Industry* (1932) and *The Conquest of the Material World* (1964). Those emanating from economic history into larger, cultural topics included: *Industry and Government in France and England, 1540–1640* (1940), *War and Human Progress: An Essay on the Rise of Industrial Civilization* (1950), *Cultural Foundations of Industrial Civilization* (1958), *Religion and the Study of Man* (1961), and *Western Civilization since the Renaissance: Peace, War, Industry, and the Arts* (1963). *Search for Meaning: The Autobiography of a Nonconformist* was published in 1973.

Nef was an officer of the French Legion of Honor and received the University of Chicago Medal.

INTRODUCTION TO THE NOTES TAKEN IN NEF'S COURSES BY F. TAYLOR OSTRANDER

The contents of Nef's two courses are different. One covers general European economic history (Economics 221); the other, French economic history (especially in relation to England) (Economics 322). Their focus, however, is much the same: the absence or presence of industrialism, the form taken by industrialism, and the absence or presence of industrial capitalism. The key concept is industrialism – that is largely what happened in history and therefore what is principally examined in Nef's courses. But not only industrialism: Absent industrialism, a story of economic history still must be told.

In this Introduction I comment on topics and points pertinent to both courses. Cited material is identified by the course numbers in which each appears. Material from Economics 322 is commented upon more frequently than material from Economics 221 but that does not imply that the latter lectures or notes are inferior, only the desire to avoid duplication.

Industrialism and Its Enormous Incidents

Most people in the developed countries take industrialism as a given. Not so, of course, people in the non-developed countries. Development is, in one word, industrialization. "[I]ndustrial civilization as we know it," Nef wrote in *The Conquest of the Material World* (Chicago: University of Chicago Press, 1964, p. i), "is a new thing in history." By the end of the eighteenth century "the evolution of European society – especially since the Reformation – had made the triumph of industrialism virtually inevitable" (p. ii). That such did not signify a simplistic determinism but a mixture of free will and determinism in the form of path dependency is suggested by his attribution "to the individual a more active and noble role in the making of . . . not just another 'civilization,' but potentially *civilization* itself" (p. iii) – the last clause raising a different sort of question.

I note the foregoing to introduce three important characteristics of Nef's work, especially his books. One is his focus on industrialization – the economic and cultural sides of technology – as critical to the modern world. The second is his objective, clinical, diagnostic attitude and methodology, given the preeminent status he assigned to industrialization. The third is his therapeutic approach, in two senses. In one sense, he is concerned with the problems caused by industrialization and their remedy. In a deeper sense, he is concerned, not with stimulus and response, but with institutional and other innovations as potential, putative solutions to perceived problems. Examples of all three include, first, the development of the modern state, generated in part by his discussion of the growth in the authority of the prince (1964, pp. 52–61), and as both a cause and a consequence of large-scale industry; and, second, the problem of the relation of the Protestant Reformation to industrial capitalism – whether one is the progenitor of the other or they are mutually recursive, interacting phenomena?

A third example, found in all his books, for example in *The United States and Civilization* (Chicago: University of Chicago Press, 1942), is his sensitivity to the fact of moral and intellectual crisis ("the collapse of standards") as new ways of doing things, new moral rules, and new definitions of reality combat with and slowly replace older ones (Chapter 4). Included is his approach to the problem of the relation of the intellect and passion. It is for him "the control of appetite and passion by the intellect" (Chapter 5), which may be juxtaposed to its Humean opposite, reason as the tool of the passions. Nef's findings suggest that in industrial capitalism one may find both moderating controls on appetite (and passion) and encouragements to appetite (for Adam Smith and Thorstein Veblen, status emulation) that make of new, hitherto unknown products matters of seemingly deep, if transient, desire, thereby stimulating industry and further industrialization. As for the aforementioned "*civilization* itself" theme, the Preface to the 2nd edition of *The United States and Civilization* (Chicago: University of Chicago Press, 1967) stresses the thesis "that there are fundamental values independent of time and common to humanity" (1967, p. viii). Whether Nef is thereby projecting the values of his own civilization, and whether he and his own civilization have gotten values just right, is no easy matter to solve, especially in light of continued criticism of Western civilization from within and from resurgent Islamic civilization largely from the outside.

Further down Ostrander's second page of 322 notes Nef is recorded raising the problem of the *concept* of "Industrial Revolution." Among other things, in 2004 it is now easier to see that the concept, not unlike that of "the Enlightenment" and many others, can be and perhaps typically is, either a short-hand for an amorphous group of factors and/or a reification of some of them. As is suggested some lines further down, the problems of meaning and of implicit theorizing apply to both concepts, "industrial" and "revolution." Even Nef neither unpacks nor identifies what he means by "capitalism," as in "industrial capitalism." We seem to know such things when we see them but find it difficult to put into words or into words eliciting unanimous agreement.

Nef is nonetheless exceedingly careful when it comes to the myriad of elements that constitute, or may be deemed to constitute, the "Industrial Revolution" or "Industrial Capitalism." This may be illustrated by the following lines from 322 (comparable ones are found in the notes from 221):

–Quasi-factory development . . .
  –From 13th Century on.
  –Houses around the warehouse – a semi-factory.
–However, the great majority of workers were under the domestic system – in 1700 – factory an exception, but a more important one than in 1600.
–Dutch loom, stocking frame, wire drawing, blast furnaces – were all used for a century or more before we need to take account of them as an important element.

Every aspect of capitalist industrialization can provide a differentiating characteristic. These include financing of raw materials and of work in process, location of work, organization of work, relation of workers to organizers of work, ownership of plant and equipment, and incremental changes over time in regard to each aspect.

The notes from 322 indicate that Nef did not think that French Crown-supported ventures were an early example of industrial capitalism. The notes continue:

–Started by government – <u>artificial</u> – doomed to fail – begun in regions of <u>little</u> manufacturing – no market.

–Crown went on assumption that you could create industry at the will of the State.

–Crown carried on State socialism on a large scale, yet these ventures never <u>expanded</u> – nor lasted, except by Royal favor – while private ventures expanded, lived.

It is certainly sensible to make those remarks. The question, however, is how probative are they? Several points: Most businesses were/are doomed, eventually, to fail. These businesses were Royal favors, not independent enterprises; saying they were "artificial" adds nothing without a carefully developed, if ultimately presumptuous, account of the respective meanings of "artificial" and "natural," its usual opposite. Much the same is true of "State socialism," though, worse yet, one wonders if the term properly can be meaningfully used in the context of the old regime. Most important, even given the situation as one of Royal favoritism, two further characteristics can be read into the practice: One is that Royal handouts were part of implicit (perhaps explicit) transactions buying loyalty and support or paying for past support. The other is that, the Crown's intentions and views notwithstanding, such handouts were a form of primitive accumulation of capital. To make these points is not to legitimize or praise them, only to interpret their historical meaning. Today's equivalents take the forms of tax breaks, subsidies, and facilitative and promotional provisions in commercial and other law, but they facilitate capital accumulation, primitive or not.

Nef made an important if subtle point when, according to the 322 notes, he said, "For the concept of <u>an</u> industrial revolution was not one which turned people's searches to <u>evolution</u>." Paradigm-, model- or theory-led path dependence explains this, just as the difference between the Fisher version of the quantity theory – P = (MV)/T – and the Cambridge version – K = MTP led to different paths of inquiry. Even though K = 1/V, V led to the study of the efficiency of the banking system turning over money between depositors, and K led to the study of the motives of holding money. So, too, the concept of revolution seems to require suddenness and abruptness, and not the slow development of foundations and beginnings.

It would seem that the term Industrial Revolution must be broad enough to encompass two paths: one long and gradual in development and the other shorter and more rapid in development, the emphasis of the former more on industrial than on revolution, the emphasis of the latter on both. The notes from 322 read:

–If rapidity of change is the criterion of an industrial revolution,
  –Then the industrial revolution of 1750–1830 can not be confined to England.
  –In fact, the rapidity of change was greater in France than in England.
  –And rapidity of change in Wales was greater than in England at this same
    time.

In 322, Nef contrasts de Tocqueville's view, that changes had roots in past, with that of Stendhal, that there was profound change, and concludes that "most changes were well under way by 1750, i.e. de Tocqueville was right that the Revolution continued more changes than it began." One wonders, however, if both views were correct, especially if qualitative changes are included, and if the Revolution is seen as both an accelerant and an inhibitor of changes.

A major theme of Nef's in 322 is the tension between the old and the new France. He argues that "France imposes a civilization of its own on the course of industrialism" and that "The old France is too strong, it moulds industrialization."

One striking twist in Nef's account concerns Germany. He does not have much to say about Germany but what little he does say in 322 has its industrialization come well after mid-19th century. His comparison, in 221, with other societies reads,

–Industrialism in Great Britain was a long, slow process, with its roots in the
  16th century and extending to end of 19th century. Industrialism in Germany
  came very suddenly and rapidly – 60 years. France has hardly yet become
  industrialized.

This discussion is a part of a larger characterization of European industrialism. Nef argues, first, for "A combination of causes leading to the birth and growth of industrialism (i.e. in its sense as dominating)." Several points: First, the "combination of causes" theme is consistent with his general view, which is complicated enough. Second, the requirement found in "in its sense as dominating" further complicates the matter. Industrialism can proceed otherwise equally (however measured or reckoned) in two countries but can be dominant in one and not the other. His formulation leaves open, perhaps even stresses, the possibility of a society that is industrial but which industrialization does not dominate. Third, "we must pay much attention to Medieval society, for in it lie the roots of all those causes whose simultaneous occurrence brought industrialism." But Medieval society itself is the product of a combination of causes – and while it may be difficult to conceive of a society in which feudalism is not dominant, feudalism too had several different forms and its developmental paths differed from area to area. His formulation may leave open, perhaps even stress, the possibility of a feudal society in which the feudal elements do not dominate. Fourth, Nef points out that "there were <u>contrary developments</u> which made the birth of industrialism a mighty struggle." This is a conflictual view of systemic development, often at odds with the honorific and harmonistic rationalizations promulgated by the victors in the struggle.

Ostrander's original 221 notes run 65 pages handwritten. Nef is recorded getting serious and systematic in his definition of industrial capitalism as late as page 57:

–Growth of industrial capitalism in this period [1300–1550], i.e. growth of individually owned units hiring labor, providing capital.

Much of the lectures covered in the remaining pages deal with the definitions of industrialism, industrial capitalism and industrial revolution as well as their relations to each other. Nef weaves together a number of major threads: the domestic system, the factory system, and the three just mentioned. Other threads include the capital and organizational needs of large-scale production; various modes of financing plant and equipment; the several contenders for organizational and control roles; questions of proportion; the gradual disempowerment of artisans and others as workers change from autonomous individual actors to hired hands owning no capital; and the quest by capital to control labor and to acquire labor's products for (re)sale. Compared with such other economic historians as A. P. Usher, Nef devotes less attention to the cumulative development of technology; but by no means totally ignored the subject.

As already indicated the definitions are derived from the experience which they then help explain. Consider the recorded statement:

–Clapham shows that the Industry State did not come till 1880.

What does this mean? The term is no longer used and likely was not used widely a century or so ago. So Clapham defines economic (or legal-economic) reality with that term. It meant something to him, but not, or not much, to us. The reality to which it related was socially constructed, and the term itself was likewise.

As for the terms used by Nef and others, different definitions lead to different perceptions of and stories about economic history.

The dangers of reification and of explanation by use of an abstraction are rampant; also, implicit theorizing and conjectural history can deceive. Paraphrasing John R. Hicks, no one theory, no one definition, no one conception, can answer all the questions that can be put by economic historians.

One can conclude that the matrix of all definitions of a term, rather than the myopic pursuit or use of only one definition of the term, may provide more intelligent interpretation (the term "comparative history" is found in the concluding lines of the 221 notes).

Capitalism

The principal concept coordinate with industrialism is capitalism. In both courses Nef is almost constantly recorded as discussing industrial capitalism. I take up only a few considerations.

Consider the line from the 322 notes that reads, "large plant, large capital." The term "capital" has been given many different meanings in the history of economic thought. By the most common definition used today, the statement is repetitive, inasmuch as capital is defined as capital goods, i.e. plant and equipment. Not so for Nef, who uses "capital" to mean the financing of plant and equipment. A large plant requires a large amount of financing. Capitalism thus means, in part, a system that both uses plant and equipment *and* requires a subsystem through which their purchase is financed.

The 322 notes record Nef saying, "Number of workers, their proportion of the total population, engaged in work in large-scale enterprise is the best test of the growth of industrial capitalism." Several points: "Industrial capitalism" being the combination of two concepts each of which is complex, one would expect a multi-pronged "test" from such a careful and competent scholar. Indeed, one wonders if industrialism and capitalism should be separated. Further, one wonders, given Nef's focus on large-scale enterprise, whether and, if so, how he would treat the modern corporate system, in which size of plant is eclipsed by the multi-product, multi-division, even multi-country corporate firm in which financial considerations tend to outweigh manufacturing ones – financial capitalism today. One supposes that Nef would urge that industrialism provided the material for capitalist enterprise and that capitalist enterprise drove the form which industrialism took. Further, if one focuses on large-scale enterprise, it is a test which combines and to some extent confuses tests of industrialism and of capitalism. Also, if size is so important, the question arises as to whether and if so in what form Nef would consider "competition" to be a fundamental concept for either or both industrialism and capitalism. It may well be that capitalism is – in Frank Knight's terminology – the game being played for power, wealth and honor, with industrialism providing the means. Moreover, the domain is increasingly the entire planet and the game is being played in such a way that the international corporate system is gradually diminishing if not eclipsing the nation-state system.

The State and Its Capture and Use

Shortly after his discussion of capital in 322, we read, "Growing power of State." This was the period of the emergence of the modern state. Hitherto it meant, for our purposes, an area ruled by a king who had achieved that status by winning wars with the other, now lesser, nobility. In time, the meaning of governing a nation meant that it now was doing things that earlier had been done in their areas by the local nobility or, perhaps more likely, not done at all. It also meant that national governments were acting toward each other as local lords or municipalities had been doing, namely, engaging in one or another form of economic protectionism – Mercantilism – and military warfare.

The late eminent University of Wisconsin authority in public finance, Harold Groves, a Quaker, was fond of saying that the central behavioral principle of tax policy was to shift taxes from me to thee. Nef related, according to the 322 notes, that at first industry in England was financed by the landed gentry and the merchant classes. These two groups formed a political coalition, opposing Royal power, the result of which was parliamentary government. Especially strong for the first time in the 17th century, Parliament was driven by middle class interests who also claimed to act for "the people." At this point in the story, the 322 notes read:

–Claiming to act for "the people" – especially under Charles I.
  –But once in the saddle, the House flaunts the interests of the common people, taxed them more heavily than the Crown had when the merchant and landed classes challenged the right of the Crown to tax.
  –People usually sided with House against Crown.

Not surprisingly, in England, for example, one of the sources of the working class and socialist movements and of the Ricardian and Benthamite Left in general, in the third and fourth decades of the 19th century, was precisely the complaint that the middle-class revolution had been touted as being on behalf of all the hitherto disadvantaged interests in society. But that is not what happened. Once in power the middle class pursued its own interests. When the working class and socialist movements became seen as a threat, the two propertied classes, the landed aristocracy and the non-landed property middle class, joined forces in opposition. One specific force in the historical process was thus shown to be class interest; another was the attraction that engendered alliances and coalitions.

Gustav Schmoller's *The Mercantile System and its Historical Significance*, on Nef's syllabus, illustrates two complications of historical processes. Among other things, Schmoller argues that the Mercantilist period was one of both nation-state building and national-economy building. In part, nations now were doing what hitherto municipalities or local governments had been doing, namely, promoting and protecting interests. That substitution phenomenon is one complication. The other is that nation building was begun during the hegemony of the landed property interests; the King was the last local noble left standing, as it were. He beat up on the others and the conquered territory became the domain of the state ruled by the King (of course, actual history was messier than this, but this is the logic of what happened). Eventually, nation building, and national-economy building, continued during the hegemony of the non-landed property-owning middle class. Such development is the logic of power. That the nation state was rationalized as a "necessary evil" is the logic of rationalization – and of the exclusion of others from power. The development of the nation state and of the nation-state system was a major development of the last five hundred years; another was the development of technology for both civilian and military purposes.

Ostrander's 221 notes record Nef making the following point: "Conflict between natural economic development and the aims and policy of the State." In some sense, everyone knows what this means: the power, the aims and the policy of those in official state positions crystallized and their preferences entered the social decision making process. Consider the following: Let economic development, X, be a function of variables A, B, C, D, E. Let government action affecting development be E. The quoted statement amounts to identifying "natural" economic development with the combination, A, B, C and D, to the exclusion of E. There are several problems with this procedure. First, variables A through D may themselves be problematic. Second, underlying variables A through D undoubtedly is a body of law – government action; ergo the distinction between A through D and E is blurred. Third, identifying variables A through D with "natural" economic development privileges both the government action underlying them and A through D per se vis-à-vis E. The privileging arises from the use of a term, "natural," that has for millennia been used for that purpose. It selectively creates a dichotomy of "natural" and "unnatural" or "artificial" that is socially constructed and subjectively given content. It provides a dichotomy when none such conclusively exists, using a primitive term to which varying substantive content is adduced by different readers or auditors.

In both sets of lecture notes, Nef shows sensitivity to the connections and non-connections between the State and industrial capitalism. In the 221 notes we thus read,

–State restrictions did not cause lack of industrial capitalism, but the lack of industrial capitalism was due to lack of the kind of minerals which give rise to it.

–No patents or trade markets [trademarks?]. Rostovtzeff says that lack of patent law, plus State policy in interests of wine and cotton growers – prove that manufacturing had not yet any political influence.

–Importance of State enterprise – reducing the sphere of private enterprise.
Ideological influence here seems minimal if not non-existent. Surely, his later statement,

–Rich men had predominant place in society, and great influence on government. Is essentially, and intentionally, a positive, non-normative statement. Very impressive is Nef's remark,

–State interference is itself a function of almost every other force in the State (just as <u>every</u> historical development is a function of every other).

Methodological and Historiographical Considerations

Nef's courses, especially perhaps 322, create and elicit sensitivity to several points. These include the importance of methodological and historiographical aspects of doing economic history; the problem of determinism; multiplicity of forces; the recursive, over-determined, cumulative causation nature of the material of economic history; paradox, and related problems of causation.

Nef's lectures in Economic History, 322, clearly had two grand objectives. One was to explore the designated subject, French industrial history since the Reformation. The other was to instruct his students in the problems whose solutions (such as they are) constitute the historiographical foundations of doing history.

The reader senses the two-pronged approach, suitable for, actually required by, a graduate course, before he or she comes, on the middle of the second page of 322, to the following:

Course covers two aspects of economic history

(1) France's place in the rise of industrialism
(2) Methodology in Research

On the very first page of Ostrander's 322 notes, we read of the difficulties of understanding a different people, their society and their history; of the paradoxes that emerge in pursuing such history; of the problem of designating the scope of one's subject; and of the problem of establishing the beginning and ending dates of periods, especially when major transformations were "long being prepared for," as was the case of industrialism and capitalist organization in France and elsewhere.

Consider the subject of paradoxes. One example is a consequence of dualisms evident in every society: The problem of order – comprised of the conflicts of freedom and control, of continuity and change, and of hierarchy and egalitarianism – enables quite contradictory propositions each to be true. Another and not unrelated example is a consequence of multiple simultaneous systems of thought. Understanding Adam Smith, for example, is rendered difficult, first, because he stands abreast of several different paradigms: individualism, empiricism, naturalism, secularism, supernaturalism, pragmatism (utilitarianism), historicism, and materialism; and, second, because he attempted a tri-partite model or system of what now would be called social science, namely, the process of forming moral rules, the market system of production and exchange, and the domain of government and law.

A related theme of Nef's in 322 was the interaction of social change and industrial history. Contemporaneous with the transformation of social structure and state was the transformation of the system in which the mass of people earned their living – from a rural, agrarian to an urban, industrial system. The two were in a recursive relationship (over-determination, cumulative causation) in which each was driven by forces internal to it simultaneously with interactive effects on each other. And while each country – England and France – had commonalities, they were different; the social history of each country, Nef reports, is "tremendously complex," and so is his comparison of them.

At the beginning of his second page of notes in 322, Ostrander records Nef pointing out, "Tawney – the important thing for the economic historian is that he ask the right questions." The point – that questions must be asked and (presumably) that they be the questions deeply pertinent to the material under study – is unobjectionable. But the point must be accompanied by other points. One is John Hicks's, that no one theory can answer all of our questions, here meaning that multiple questions must truly be asked and multiple theories used in answering them. Another is Post-Modernism's, that the same material may be amenable to quite different questions and quite different stories. A third is that at the bottom of every historical interpretation is some generalizing theory. Fourth, one must appreciate that the same interpretation and the same generalizing theory can be joined with different supplementary premises or propositions, yielding quite different results. Examples of this include the meaning of the Enlightenment, the putative difference between the Scottish and French Enlightenments, and the role of balance of power in understanding European history. The notion of "the right questions" should not lead one to entrapment in the hermeneutic circle formed by "the right questions" and the approach to history constituting the basis of "the right questions." A fifth, already implicit in the foregoing, is the ubiquitous dualism: historical facts beyond the mundane tend strongly to be theory based and theories themselves are matters of particular readings of facts. A sixth, readily found but easily neglected, is that historical factors both act and interact (as Nef puts it later), implying that a complex and evolving matrix of interaction is the basis of explanation and interpretation. The sixth engenders a seventh, that the more encompassing the matrix of interaction, the greater the tendency for circularity, for the object of inquiry becoming its own explanation.

A chief lesson of Nef's courses was that economic history – possibly a story of development and growth – though not always dramatic, was the result of a multiplicity of factors, of opportunities taken and opportunities not taken, of opportunities not always perceived as such but understood retrospectively. This lesson, one is tempted to say, derives from the material. But it is also a function of Nef's approach to economic history. The story he tells is close to low-level facts, facts made important in part by how he integrates them into his story in relation to other facts and in part by how he theorizes about low- and mid-level relations among variables. These relations are intractable in part because they are recursive relations of mutual interdependence and in part because particular consequences could be the result of very different causes or sets of causes. The story is not, say, how aggregate saving meets aggregate investment, with a resultant warranted rate of growth. That is not to say that a story told in terms of such macroeconomic aggregates is by its nature inferior; only that it is a different (type) of story. Economic history was not economic growth theory. Economic history dealt with economies as they were in detail, not with a pure abstract conceptual economy.

One major thread common to England, France and the U.S. as well as other European nations in the 17th, 18th and 19th centuries was the contest between two modes of life, one rural, agrarian and, especially, fundamentalist in religion, indeed, one focused on religion; the other urban, industrial, and some combination of secular, material and non-fundamentalist in religion, actually, one not, or not very much, focused on religion. How these societies worked out this conflict depended on the complexities of each society and on the conflicts relating to these complexities and the interaction of each's set of conflicts. Each society must continuously work out solutions to the components of the problem of order, namely, hierarchy vs. equality, continuity vs. change, and autonomy vs. control, each of which is multifaceted, etc. Nef himself is interested in the development of industrialism and especially industrial capitalism – and, as we have seen, these too are multifaceted and conflictual phenomena.

The problem is in part one of possible multiple definitions and multiple elements. One illustration involves the question as to which is more important, a novel industrial development operative (1) for an industry, thereby for a significant but not overly large part of the population [what constitutes a "significant part"?] or (2) for large masses of people? Another question is, if capitalism can be defined in terms of variables a, b, c, and d, or one or another combination, what is the interpretive historical significance of their different uneven development in different areas?

There is a tendency (already noted above) in historical work to succumb to some form of determinism. Whatever the appropriate combination of determinism and free will that is appropriate, one topic is the role of social constructionism. Schematically, if X is explained by the historian B to be the result of some set of causes or origins M, even if B is wrong that M led to X, it is useful not to take X as a given, as part of the inevitable natural order of things. Yes, M and X did occur. The key methodological insight is the question, how did X come to be? Instead of postulating a deterministic X, the "right question" involves the process of social construction in which M and X existed and in which M led, putatively, to X. It may be that some other set, N, could also have led to X. This is more complicated and problematic than postulating the natural relations of things but the latter is likely to be simplistic and question-begging.

Extraordinarily impressive is the detailed attention that Nef devotes to archival sources and their use. He is truly teaching both history and how to do history. Amidst the discussion of the use of sources is a group of cautions and lessons relevant to writing in general and writing history in particular. These include:

> Slowness, accept boredom, <u>care</u> – accuracy.
> Is not simple – a struggle.
> <u>Rewrite</u> – <u>rewrite</u>.
> Give best part of time to writing.
> Be in the heat of enthusiasm and close to your documents – <u>then</u> write – at a fell swoop.
> You can't be too short about what is dull, or too long about what is interesting.
> Necessity of <u>élan vital</u>.

The problem of cause and effect, or of propitious conditions, is neatly illustrated in the 322 notes:

> –Rise of royal absolutism hindered the rise of industrialism.
> –Backwardness of industrial capitalism favored the rise of royal absolutism.

Clearly there is no, or not much of, an interpretive problem. Not unlike the Max Weber problem – the spirit of capitalism generating capitalism vs. capitalism generating the spirit of capitalism – the matter is one of cumulative causation built on mutual interdependence. Just as Weber, in his *General Economic History* (translated and edited by Nef's colleague, Frank Knight), articulated a much more complex process, so too did Nef. For example, for Weber accounting was a dual transmission mechanism; for Nef, the honorific status, or its negation (vulgarity), accorded the merchant was a dual transmission mechanism.

A related example is discussed by Nef immediately following the quoted dualism. He argues that in France "the strengthening of [the] merchant class meant the weakening of the royal power – which had been <u>dependent on</u> a weak merchant class." In England, the contest between merchants and King over control was won by the merchants and "<u>their</u> control of Parliament and the King was in large part responsible for the rise of industrial capitalism" which further weakened the power of the King vis-à-vis the merchants. Success, in other words, breed further success in a process of cumulative causation.

What drives the foregoing story is perhaps less the self-reinforcing cumulative causation and more the premise that industrialism and industrial capitalism properly won out. If one can momentarily suspend belief on that point (as to "properly"), then the open-endedness of development-"non-development," cumulative causation, transmission mechanism, and multiple possible paths, appears more plausible.

Economic history shares with economic development (the story of the former is often the story of the latter) not only the foregoing but paradox as well. The well-known Leontief paradox arose because it was expected that U.S. exports would be capital intensive whereas in fact they were labor intensive – because U.S. labor was more productive than labor abroad. More recently it has been argued, first, that modern economic growth, generated by productivity advances began before the institutional reforms of the Glorious Revolution of 1688; and, second, that human capital accumulation in England began when the market return to skill acquisition was historically low. The first paradox parallels the Weber problem; institutional change can generate productivity change *and* productivity change can generate institutional change – the former either because it frees up activity or because it whets the desires that fuel productivity change, the latter because productivity change can reinforce the power and motivations of certain groups so as to generate pressure for institutional change. The second paradox implies, first, that there is more to human capital formation than high returns to skill acquisition and that social and market anticipation and pressure can lead people to invest in human capital formation, say, once they sense the possibility that their children might be able to lead more productive (or some synonym) lives. (See Gregory Clark, "The Condition of the Working-Class in England, 1200–2000: Magna Carta to Tony Blair," University of California-Davis, Working Paper, 2004; abstracts@eh.net, 16 February 2004.) All of which seems to imply that paradox can be a function of incomplete knowledge leading to erroneous expectations.

Nef's introductory lecture in 221, as recorded by Ostrander, beautifully illustrates the socially constructed nature of what Nef presents as European economic history. All that is lacking is for Nef to give, and for Ostrander to record, a name – say, social constructivism, discourse analysis, or historiography – for what he is doing. The reader need only follow the key points of the recorded lecture: The course not only does not cover general history (by implication) it does not cover general economic history. It concentrates on industrialism or industrial capitalism – and it does so through Nef's particular formulations thereof. The purpose of the course is, following Bacon, to cover "everything about industrialism, something about all history." Stressing, after Pareto, that "at any one time, every social phenomenon is related to every other – i.e. no chain of cause and effect," he stipulates, "We will study relationships, not causes and effects." Following

Spengler, he will study only certain periods of history; moreover he will "define Industry (arbitrarily) as manufacturing and mining" but also cover "population, markets, trade, social and cultural backgrounds." The foregoing is described as "Carving reality out of the joints of history." He then examines the meaning of the word, industrialism, he will use, and the problem of "progress." All this may seem obvious but there are other formulations and they, too, can seem obvious – more clearly if the course were taught with a view to comparing different formulations and the different histories that result, and perhaps the matrix formed by those different formulations and different histories. In any event, Nef's constructivist purpose and course design is at least in part transparently implied in Ostrander's notes reading, "Nef's whole theory is against the idea of any Industrial Revolution." More subtle is his combination of technology and institutions (including both organizations and belief system). When Nef is recorded to have said, "– The amount of industrial capitalism that brings about a dominance of it over a civilization must have some relation to what its amount was in early 19th century England," one can appreciate both the historic importance of England and the possibility that while England was the first it may or may not be – say, from the perspective of 2004 – the Weberian ideal type. Again, Nef makes his constructivist design explicit. (Nef's use of statistical data is pointed to by his use of "amount" of Industrial Capitalism.)

Nef urges that industrial capitalism was not everywhere homogeneous, that it does not everywhere develop at the same pace, and that manufacturing is not by itself industrialism. So, too, the use of tools is not the use of machinery; engaging in trade is not necessarily tantamount to participating in a market.

Nef surely must have been aware – apropos of the statement recorded in the notes, "What does survive when a civilization goes down is the great literature – i.e. history must be written as good literature" – that what survives need not be a fallen civilization's great literature. For one thing, it may not have survived; for another, what is "great" is subjective.

One way in which Nef is at his best is his recognition of the interactive, recursive and over-determined nature of the variables that comprise his story – economic, social and political variables, and technological, institutional (including ideational) and practical variables. A brilliant example in the 221 notes is the theme that in agriculture land is very important in economic history: the uses to which land is put [and] the way it is held react on each other, and both have a reaction on political life. Nonetheless, Nef feels compelled to pick sides, as it were: Apropos of Western Europe the notes record the following: "Urbanization is not made possible by industrial capitalism, but the dominating influence of industrial capitalism seems to make possible the overbearing proportion of urbanization." For someone, like this editor, who considers recursiveness the default solution for many comparable problems, albeit remaining open to further study, such seems too narrow and uni-directional, though more valuable than some other approaches.

How accurate *are* the stories told by Nef? Consider his account of ancient Athens recorded in the 221 notes. We read, in part,

–The human scale of values was different in Greek times, than now.

–The Greeks distinctly felt that there was something unique in their own culture; had a faith in themselves.

–Owing partly to their ideals, the leisure which improved technique brought them was turned to artistic, cultural account.

–Every Athenian was an art-critic, drama-critic and literary-critic.

–Ethical emphasis on "the complete life" – rounded, and on "Moderation" – i.e. leisure, relaxation, helped on by climate (relaxing and stimulating), by economic development curbed by State action.

–A society of extroverts, objectivity; the Greeks did not live alone, but out of doors and in companionship always.

–Strict limitation on material drives – which is unusual as accompaniment of a surplus.

–Much use of tools, but little use of machinery.

–Commerce and riches served the State rather than dominated it.

–Gifts to State – political and ethical background.

–Quick disposition of fortunes.

–Out-door life and country life, in Mediterranean climate, but urban at the same time.

–Great surplus available from technical advance.

–Strength of State control limiting materialism. – Greeks recognized that they were living in a civilization of delicate adjustment – to which materialism was the greatest danger – sense of impending fate.

Athenians sensed they were holding back the ordinary march of economic and other forces.

This is an interpretation and Nef may or may not be correct. Athens was also a society laden (as he also says) with slaves and engaged in more or less frequent warfare – recognition of which surely qualifies some of the foregoing statements. Also, the picture may be unduly influenced by certain literary and philosophical writings of a utopian or visionary nature. Here, too, the question of survival of representative material arises.

One point is made in a potentially misleading way in the 221 notes. Noting that in Roman times development was away from small holding to large holding – the villa civilization – the notes record Nef as saying that "There was not real ownership – but a <u>divided ownership</u>. Land was 'owned' and inherited in the family. But there was an Overlord to whom certain obligations were owed – a portion of produce, a dowry for the Lord's daughter – i.e. a feudal system (partly paraphrased)." The problem is that no such thing as "real ownership" existed. Quite aside from changes in the law of property and the economic significance of the rights of other owners of property, within whatever system of property is in place, "divided ownership" exists. It is no less "real" than any other type of property arrangement. For example, subsurface and surface mining and drilling rights may not accompany and likely will supersede the other usual rights of "land ownership." Property with liens under mortgage amounts to divided ownership. Nef seems to be drawing a comparison with the common modern arrangement, but neither is more "real" than the other.

That Nef knows better is indicated by a later discussion in which he is reported to have said, "Trade and financing was well split-up though our preoccupation with seeking to find the exact model of <u>joint–stock companies</u> usually blinds us to the fact."

At another point, the eye comes upon recorded remarks that elicit hope that Nef is using them (as recorded by Ostrander) descriptively and not condescendingly:

–Workmen were more badly off than today.
–But they did not require much – few clothes, little food.

The French Revolution

The bicentennial of the French Revolution was the subject of a symposium in volume 8 (1990) of this annual.

Nef's treatment of the French Revolution in 322 is very useful. It emphasizes the complex nature of the Revolution; the Revolution as a middle-class, or bourgeois, phenomenon, as also an artisan and peasant phenomenon, and as the mode of collapse of the old regime; the Revolution as meaning something different in 1789 than a half-century later; and as a paradoxical phenomenon. The latter, the Revolution as a paradoxical phenomenon, is perhaps less striking in the early 21st century than it was seventy years ago. The idea of meaning as a function of context enables complex, multi-faceted contexts having different interpretations depending upon standpoint and perspective. That such multiplicity can involve paradoxes follows, as we have seen above, readily from that idea. In any event, near the end of the course Nef is quoted as saying,

<u>Politics</u> – democratic government in Revolution was an expression of peasants as well as of middle class.

For perspective, the reader might dwell for a moment on Nef's recorded statement in 322, "All the elements of our present day standard of living are products of the last seventy years." My point is not that, writing these comments in February 2004, the products of today are so different from those of 1933–1934 when Ostrander attended these lectures, though that is true. My point concerns Nef's use of "seventy years." 1934 was seventy years since the Civil War, and 2004 is seventy years since 1934; moreover, the U.S. Civil War comes close to seventy years after the French Revolution. Someone alive in 1934 stood in relation to the fourth year of the Civil War chronologically exactly as someone today stands in relation to the fourth year of the Great Depression, and as someone during the Civil War stood to the French Revolution. If psychology is influenced by demography, at least the most recent of these chronologically equal standpoints must be influenced as to perception by the fact that in the U.S. life expectancy has increased by some twenty years since c.1900.

What then of the heritage of the French Revolution? Nef points to the development for the first time of a class-conscious wage-earning class. This class is Marxian, and "cannot reconcile democracy and private property ... the twin beliefs of Revolutionary and peasant France."

The traditional view is that effective democracy requires widespread ownership of private property and that concentrated ownership of private property negates democracy; democracy becomes plutocracy. Nef points to the "Society of Balzac's novels believed in wealth – but not the wealth of large industrialism." He points to a "new financial element" and "an aristocracy of wealth." There have been "Great changes in the moral life, consequent on the industrial change." But a social conflict has arisen through the "split of capital and labor." Nonetheless, Nef concludes:

–Social and political – even economic equality.
  –Universal suffrage, widespread ownership of land.
  –And a real democracy of social position.
And
  –The old political cleavage between l'ancièn régime and the Revolution has not been broken down by industrialism.
  –The course of industrial history is partly a cause of and partly a result of this political twist.

Editor's Note

Published below from 221 are: (1) the nineteen-page Outline of the Course and Select Bibliography; (2) the mid-term and final examinations; and (3) Ostrander's notes from Nef's lectures.

Published below from 322 are: (1) the eighteen-page "Select Bibliography" distributed to students; (2) Ostrander's notes on Nef's lectures; and (3) the final examination given in the course. Of particular interest is the fact that part of the final examination was given in French.

In some instances, titles in the text of the notes that were seriously incomplete have been completed or replaced using the syllabus and library sources. The reader is cautioned that Nef's use of † in his select bibliography for 322 does not indicate a deceased author but "Indicates a standard work of scholarship."

The two sets of notes constitute masterful expositions of their subject(s). The lectures combined close attention to empirical data with carefully grounded interpretation. The notes can be used to help ascertain how much and what of present-day understanding was already in place when Nef taught his course some seventy years ago. The notes will be of interest to economic historians in various other ways as well. They are samples of what was taught in a leading department, of the state of knowledge and the state of the discipline of economic history at the time. The notes can also be used to learn how Nef handled interpretive differences between writers.

As with Ostrander's other notes from Williams, Oxford, and Chicago, going through these notes almost amounts to going to his professors' classes. They are like going back to school, they help give one an education, not least in being exposed to a group of remarkable professors.

ACKNOWLEDGMENTS

I am indebted to Holly Flynn for assistance in preparing the biography. See Wolfgang Saxon's obituary of Nef, *New York Times*, December 27, 1988, p. A19; and Arthur P. Molella, "John U. Nef (1899–1988), *Technology and Culture*, October 1990, Vol. 31, No. 4, pp. 916–920. I am also indebted to F. Taylor Ostrander for comments on the first draft of the Introduction.

MATERIALS FROM JOHN ULRIC NEF'S COURSE, INTRODUCTION TO EUROPEAN ECONOMIC HISTORY, ECONOMICS 221, UNIVERSITY OF CHICAGO, FALL 1933–1934

1. OUTLINE OF COURSE AND SELECT BIBLIOGRAPHY

Economics 221

INTRODUCTION TO EUROPEAN ECONOMIC HISTORY

or

THE RISE OF MODERN INDUSTRIALISM

Outline of the Course

Part I

Introductory. The main object of the course is to study the manner in which the modern industrial civilization of western europe and america, with its social, political and cultural complements, has evolved. As a preliminary, an attempt is made to set forth what appear to be the principal features distinguishing present day industrialism from economic conditions at other periods of recorded history. The

Further University of Wisconsin Materials: Further Documents of F. Taylor Ostrander
Research in the History of Economic Thought and Methodology, Volume 23-C, 79–154
Copyright © 2005 by Elsevier Ltd.
ISSN: 0743-4154/doi:10.1016/S0743-4154(05)23205-4

early meetings of the course are then concerned with graeco-roman civilization. This subject is discussed because an investigation of some of the differences and similarities between the economic life of classical and western european peoples, considered in relation to the conditions of climate, soil, politics and culture, can contribute to an understanding of the causes for the rise of industrialism in western europe. The remainder of the course is concerned with the economic life of western europe since the eleventh century, when progress towards modern commercial and industrial conditions, as we find them in the principal european countries today, can fairly be said to have begun.

Part II

Graeco-Roman Economic Civilization. No attempt is made to sketch the whole of classical economic history from the homeric period until the fall of rome. Instead two phases are selected for special treatment:

(i) The Athenian city state in the fifth century B.C.
(ii) The Roman Empire, and particularly Italy, in the first century, A.D.

These two phases are selected because they seem to represent the height of the two periods in the classical historical cycle, which oswald spengler has called "culture" and "civilization." on the assumption that the spenglerian pattern of history is on the whole correct, special attention is paid to the resemblances and contrasts between the economic and social life at what are, according to this pattern, the corresponding periods of western european history.

Under each of the two principal heads, the following topics are discussed: (a) the size of the population and its distribution between towns and rural districts; (b) the produce of the land, agricultural technique, and land tenure; (c) the conditions of commercial life, including the methods of financing trade; (d) the place of industry in economic life and the nature of industrial organization; (e) the relation of economic conditions to the social, political and cultural aspects of life.

Part III

The Rise of Economic Civilization in Medieval Europe. After a reference to the controversy over the extent of the reversion to primitive economic relationships during and after the decay of Roman civilization in western Europe, a very brief survey is made of the progress towards modern commercial and industrial relationships, prior to the emergence of what may be called the national economic state in the sixteenth century. This survey is made under two heads:

(i) Economic and social conditions in the twelfth and thirteenth centuries, when Gothic art was at its height in Europe.

(ii) Progress towards a more capitalistic organization of commerce and industry in those parts of continental Europe where economic relationships were most advanced during the fourteenth, fifteenth and early sixteenth centuries.

Under the first head (i), the main emphasis is laid upon conditions in northern France, because the economic life in this region appears to be most characteristic of the feudal period in western Europe. The principal topics treated are: (a) Distribution of population between towns and rural districts; (b) Conditions on the manors with respect to the commodities produced, the markets for these commodities, the systems of landholding, and the material welfare of the country population; (c) Conditions in the towns with respect to the commercial and industrial activities of the inhabitants, the markets for the produce of their labor, the gild merchant and the craft gilds, industrial organization within the latter, and the distribution of political authority and of earnings among the citizens; (d) Relations between economic life and cultural, religious and political life, especially in the towns.

Under heading (ii), the main emphasis is laid upon conditions in the Low Countries, because it was there that industrial units requiring a considerable capital appear to have been most important before the middle of the sixteenth century. First, an attempt is made to estimate the influence of the development in this area of the textile, the metallurgical and the mining industries in changing the distribution of population, the technique of agriculture, the nature of land tenure, the organization of manual workmen, the division into social classes, the manner of living, the nature of religious belief, cultural expression and political institutions. Next, a brief comparison is made between these changes in the Low Countries and similar changes which took place in italy and southern Germany, where economic developments were in many respects parallel. Finally, the question is asked, how far the germs of modern industrialism appear in these three parts of western Europe before the middle of the sixteenth century, and to what extent their appearance seems to be related to climatic, geographical, geological and religious conditions peculiar to Western, as distinguished from Classical, civilization.

Part IV

The Evolution of Industrialism in Great Britain. After a reference to the temporary progress made towards a modern industrial state in sixteenth-century Spain and seventeenth-century Holland, this part of the course is devoted to the economic history of Great Britain from the reign of Elizabeth, which was marked in England by the first great strides towards the technique and organization of industry which we associate with the word industrialism, until the end of the nineteenth century, when modern machine technology and capitalistic production may be said to dominate the life of the country. The history of the rise of industrialism covers a longer time in England than in any other country, and this history can be conveniently divided into three periods:-

  (i) The era dating roughly from the accession of Elizabeth to the revolution of 1688.
 (ii) The traditional era of the "Industrial Revolution," from about 1760 to 1830.
(iii) The modern era, from 1830 to the end of the nineteenth century, when Britain's hitherto undisputed industrial supremacy was seriously challenged by Germany and the United States.

The progress made in each of these periods towards modern industrialism is shown to be reflected in: (a) The growth of population, and especially town population; (b) The changes in landholding and the methods of farming; (c) The growth of markets; (d) The development of banking and finance.

There follows a brief discussion of the possible inter-relations between industrial history, on the one hand, and constitutional, scientific and cultural history on the other.

Part V

The Evolution of Industrialism in Germany. A survey of conditions in the German countries, with respect to topics (a) to (d), as outlined in the preceding part, indicates that, while progress towards a national industrial state hardly began until the nineteenth century, and only became marked during the second half of that century, machine technology and capitalistic production spread during the period from 1870 to 1914 with a rapidity unprecedented, at any rate for Europe. A brief attempt is made to obtain some understanding of possible causes for and effects of the especially rapid development of industrialism in Germany, as reflected in the early history, the geographic conditions, and the modern social, political and cultural history of the German people. For this purpose, special attention is paid to the conclusions reached by Thorstein Veblen, in his book, *Imperial Germany and the Industrial Revolution*.

Part VI

The Evolution of Industrialism in France. A similar survey of conditions in France, with respect to topics (a) to (d), as outlined in Part IV, indicates that, while that country possessed at the time of the reformation, a more advanced economic civilization than England, progress towards industrialism has since been much slower, at any rate until the Great War. Even today France cannot be called an industrial country in the sense that Britain, Germany and the United States are industrial countries. Some attention is also paid in this part of the course to possible causes and consequences of the relatively slow evolution of industrialism in France, and a connection is established between her economic history and her climate and soil, on the one hand, and her social, political and cultural history, on the other. For this purpose, and for the survey of conditions above referred to, special attention is paid to the economic history of france in three periods:

(i)   The seventeenth century
(ii) The last forty years of the ancien Régime
(iii) The half century between the Franco-Prussian War and the Great War.

2. A SELECT BIBLIOGRAPHY FOR PART II OF THE COURSE

(Works which are likely to be of especial interest are indicated by an asterisk.)

(i) *General economic histories.*
Brentano, Lujo. *Das Wirtschaftsleben der antiken Welt.* 1929.
*Frank, Tenney. *An Economic History of Rome.* 2nd ed., 1927.
Glotz, G. *Le travail dans la Grèce ancienne.* 1920. (Translated as *Ancient Greece at Work.*)
Knight, M. M. *Economic History of Europe.* 1927, pp. 30–84.
*Rostovtzeff, M. *The Social and Economic History of the Roman Empire.* 1926.
Toutain, J. *The Economic Life of the Ancient World.* 1930.

(ii) *Studies of special phases or periods of economic and social life.*
Brewster, Ethel. *Roman Craftsmen and Tradesmen of the Early Empire.* 1917.
*Calhoun, G. M. *The Business Life of Ancient Athens.* 1926.
*Calhoun, G. M. "Risk in Sea Loans in Ancient Athens." *Journal of Economic and Business History,* Vol. II (1930), pp. 561 sqq.
Cavaignac, Eugène. *Etudes sur l'histoire financière d'Athènes au Ve siècle.* 1908.
Davis, W. S. *The Influence of Wealth in Imperial Rome.* 1910.
Dill, S. *Roman Society from Nero to Marcus Aurelius.* Last ed., 1925.
Francotte, henri. *L'industrie dans la grèce antique.* 1900.
Friedlander, L. *Roman Life and Manners under the Early Empire.* Trans. Of 7th ed., 4 Vols. 1908–1913.
*Fustel de Coulanges, N. D. *La cité antique.* 1924.
Gardner, P. *History of Ancient Coinage.* 1918.
Gernet, L. "L'approvisionnement d'Athènes en blé au Ve et au IVe siècle." *Bib. Fac. Lett.,* Vol. XXV (1909), pp. 268–391.

Guisaud, Paul. *Etudes économiques sur l'antiquité.* 1905.

Guisaud, Paul. *La main d'oeuvre industrièlle dans l'ancienne Grèce.* 1906.

Hasebroek, J. *Stadt und Handel im alten Griechenland.* 1928.

*Heitland, W. E. *Agricola.* 1921.

Jardé, A. *Les ceréales dans l'antiquité grecque.* 1. *La Production.* 1925.

Knorringa, H. *Emporos. Data on Trade and Trader in Greek Literature from Homer to Aristotle.* 1926.

Lombroso-Ferrero, G. "Le machimisme dans l'antiquité." *Revue du Mois,* Vol. XXI (1920), pp. 448 sqq.

Mahaffy, J. P. *Social Life in Greece from Homer to Menander.* 1874.

*Meyer, Ed. *Forschungen zur alten Geschichte.* 2 vols. 1892–1899.

*Meyer, Ed. *Kleine Schriften.* 1910.

Oliver, E. H. *Roman Economic Conditions at the Close of the Republic.* 1907.

Park, Marion. *The Plebs in Cicero's Day.* 1918.

Riezler, K. *Über Finanzen und Monopole im alten Griechenland.* 1907.

Salvioli, G. *Le capitalisme dans le monde antique.* French trans., 1906.

Ziebarth, E. *Beitrage zur Geschichte des Seeraubes und Sechandels im alten Griechenland.* 1929.

Zimmern, Alfred. *The Greek Commonwealth.* 4th ed., 1924.

(iii) *Studies in related fields of classical history.*

Azambuja, G. De. *La Grèce ancienne.* 1906

Bardon. M. D. *Costumes des anciens peuples.* 1772.

Gardner, Ernest A. *Six Greek Sculptors.* 1910.

*Gibbon, Edward. *The Decline and Fall of the Roman Empire.* Ed. Bury, 7 vols. 1896. Esp. Chs. 2 and 44.

Graesse, J. G. Th. *Orbis latinus.* 3rd ed. by F. Benedict. 1922.

Hehrn. V. *Culturpflanzen und Hausthiere in ihrem Uebergang aus Asien nach Griechenland.* 6th ed. 1894.

Jacquemart, Albert. *History of the Ceramic Art.* Trans. By Mrs. Bury Palliser. 1873.

*Mommsen, Theodor. *The History of Rome.* Trans. By Dickson, 4 vols., 1891.

Sohm, R. *The Institutes of Roman Law.* Trans. By J. C. Ledlie, 1892.

Wallon, H. A. *Histoire de l'esclavage.* 3 vols., 2nd ed. 1879.

[the following items were added in longhand by ostrander, largely as below.]

Cambridge Ancient History, "Economic Conditions in Hellenistic Period" – Rostovtzeff

Beloch – Zeitschrift für Socialwissenschaft, 1898, Population ("Die Bevölherung")

Charlesworth, Trade Routes and Commerce
Brooks Adams (Deflation and Decline of Roman Empire – app. x)
Inge – Society in Rome under the Caesars
Diderot – Encyclopédie – on Roman roads
Rose – Mediterranean and Ancient World
Warrington
Rostovtzeff, Economic History Review, 1930, "The Decay of the Ancient World and Its Economic Explanations"
Westermann, American Historical Review, July 1915, "Economic Basis of Decline of Ancient Culture"
Otto Seeck – Geschichte des untergang der Antiquen Welt. Berlin, 1920.
Huntington, Quarterly Journal of Economics, February 1917, Climatic explanation answer.
Usher, Quarterly Journal of Economics, May 1923.
Liebig
Simkhovitch, "Toward an Understanding of Jesus"
Buckle – History of Civilization, Chapter 2 (Geography)

3. BIBLIOGRAPHY FOR PART III OF THE COURSE

(The rise of economic civilization in medieval Europe).

General Works on the Whole Period:
Boissonade, P., *Life and Work in Medieval Europe*, 1921, Eng. Trans. 1927.
Clapham, J. H., Article in *Cambridge Medieval History*, Vol. VI.
Knight, M. M., *An Economic History of Europe*. pp. 86–254.
Kötzschke, R., *Allgemeine Wirtschaftsgeschichte des Mittelalters*. 1924.
Thompson, J. W., *A Social and Economic History of the Middle Ages*. 1928.

On the Passage from Classical to Western Civilization:
Dopsch, A., *Wirtschaftliche und soziale Grundlagen der europäischen Kulturentwicklung*. 1920.
Dopsch, A., *Die Wirtschaftsentwicklung der Karolingerzeit*. Esp. Vol. II, pp. 133–233.
*Fustel de Coulanges, *Histoire des institutions politiques de l'ancienne France*. 6 vols. 1875– etc.
Fustel de Coulanges, *Etude sur les origines du régime f'éodal au VIe–VIIIe siècles*.
[Histoire des institutions politiques de l'ancienne France: Les origines du systéme féudal *le bénéfice et le petronet pendant l'epoque mérovin gienne, 1890*]

Halphen, L. *Etudes critiques sur le rêgne de Charlemagne*. 1921.

Heynen, R., *Zur Entstehung des Kapitalismus in Venedig*. 1905.

*Pirenne, H., *Medieval Cities*. 1925.

Schaube, A., *Handelsgeschichte der Romanischen Völker*. 1906.

Heyd, W. van., *Histoire du commerce du Levant au Moyen-âge*. 1885–1886.

*Vinogradoff, P. G., *The Growth of the Manor*. 1904.

Economic Society in the High Gothic Period, Especially in Northern France:

(a) *Population*

Cuvelier, J., *Les dénombrements de foyers en Brabant*. 1912.

Jastrow, I., *Die Volkszahl deutsche r Städte*. 1886.

Levasseur, E., *La population française*. 3 vols., 1889–1892.

Beloch, *Zeitschrift für Sozialwissenschaft*. 1900. [Added by hand]

(b) *Rural economic life, especially agriculture*:

Ashley, W. J., *Introduction to English Economic History and Theory*. 2 parts, 1888.

Calmette, J., *Le régime féodale*. 1924.

Coulton, G. G., *The Medieval Village*. 1926.

Genestal, R. *Rôle des monastères comme établissements de crédit étudié en Nomandie au XIe à la fin du XIIIe siècle*. 1901.

Gray, H. L., *English Field Systems*.

Endemenn, W., *Studien über romanisch-kanonistische Wirtschafts- und Rechtslehre bis gegen Ende des siebzehnten Jahrhunderts*. 1883.

*Maitland, F. W., *Domesday Book and Beyond*. 1897.

Meitzen, A., *Siedelung und Agrarwesen der West- und Ost-Germanen*. 1895.

Mispoulet, I. B., *Le régime des mines à l'époque romaine et au moyen-âge*. 1908.

Neilson, N., "English Manorial Forms," in *American Historical Review*, vol. XXXIV, 1929, pp. 725 sqq.

*Sée, H., "Les classes rurales et le régime domanial en France au Moyen-âge. 1901.

*Seebohm, F., *The English Village Community*. 1893.

Seignobos, C., *The Feudal Regime*. Chapter i. 1902.

*Vinogradoff, P. G., *The Growth of the Manor*. 1904.

Vinogradoff, P. G., *English Society in the Eleventh Century*. 1908.

Vinogradoff, P. G., *Villeinage in England*. Oxford, 1892.

Verriest, L., *Le servage dans le comté de Hainaut*. 1909.

Verriest, L., *Le régime seigneurial dans le comté de Hainaut*. 1918.

(c) *Economic life in the towns as centers of commerce and industry*:

Aclocque, G. *Les corporations, l'industrie et le commerce à Chartres.* 1917.

Ashley, W. J. *op. cit.*, part 1, chapter 2.

Cheruel, A., *Histoire de Rouen pendant l'époque communale, 1150–1382.* 1843–1844.

von Below, G. *Entstehung der deutschen Stadtgemeinde.* 1889.

von Below, G. *Ursprung der deutschen Stadtverfassung.* 1892.

Boileau, Etienne (fl. 1255), *Les métiers et corporations de la ville de Paris.* (ed. Lespinasse). 1879.

Bourquelot, C. F., *Etudes sur les foires de Champagne.* 1865.

Des Marez, G., *Etude sur la propriété foncière dans les villes du Moyen-âge et specialement en Flandre.* Ghent. 1898.

Des Marez, G., *La première étape de la formation corporative, l'Entraide, in Bull. de l'Acad. Royale de Belgique.* 1921.

Des Marez, G., *L'Organisation du travail dans une ville du XVe siècle.*

Doren, A. J., *Untersuchungen zur Geschichte der Kaufmannsgilden des Mittelalters.* 1893

DuBourg, Antoine, *Les corporations ouvrières de la ville de Toulouse au XIIIe et XVe siècles.* 1886.

*Eberstadt, R., *Das französische Gewerberecht.* 1899.

Eberstadt, R., *Magisterium und Fraternitas.* 1897.

*Espinas, G., *La vie urbaine de Douai au Moyen-âge.* 4 vols. 1913.

Fagniez, G., *Etudes sur l'histoire de l'industrie et de la classe industrielle à Paris au XIIIe et XIVe siècles.* Paris. 1878.

Genestal, R., *Role des monastères comme établissements de crédit en Normandie du XIe à la fin du XIIIe siècle.* 1901.

Giry, A., *Histoire de la ville de St. Omer.* 1877.

Giry, A., *Documents sur les relations de la royauté avec les villes en France de 1180 à 1314.* 1885.

Green, Mrs. J. R., *Town Life in the Fifteenth Century.* London, 1894.

Gross, C., *The Gild Merchant.* Oxford, 1890, especially vol. i, pp. 282 sqq.

Havelin, P., *Essai historique sur le droit de marchés et de foires.* 1877.

Hegel, K., *Die Entstehung des deutschen Städtewesens.* 1898.

Hegel, K., *Städte und Gilden der germanischen Völker im Mittelalter.* 1891.

Keutgen, F., *Untersuchungen über den Ursprung der deutschen Stadtverfassung.* 1895.

Keutgen, F., *Aemter and Zünfte.* 1903.

Kramer, S., *The English Craft Gilds.* New York, 1927.

Labande, H. L., *Histoire de Beauvais et de ses institutions communales.* 1892.

*Levasseur, Emile, *Histoire des classes ouvrières et de l'industrie*, vol. I of the 1900 ed. – See also his *Histoire du commerce.*

Luchaire, A., *Social France at the Time of Philip Augustus.* Eng. Trans. 1912.

*Maitland, F. W. *Township and Borough.* 1898.

Maurer, *Geschichte der Städteverfassung.* 2 vols., 1870.

Pirenne, H., *Medieval Cities.* Princeton, 1925.

Reinecke, W., *Geschichte der Stadt Cambrai.* 1896.

Salzman, L. F., *English Industries of the Middle Ages.* Oxford, 1923.

Sneller, Z. W., *Le développement du commerce entre les Pays-Bas Septentrionaux et la France jusqu'au milieu du XVe siècle.* 1922.

Unwin, G., *The Gilds and Companies of London.* London, 1908;

Van der Linden, H. *Les gildes marchandes dans les Pays-Bas au Moyen- âge.* 1890.

(d) *On the relation of economic to political, religious and cultural life*:

Adams, Henry, *Mont St. Michel and Chartres.* 1904.

Aquinas, Thomas, *Summa Theologica.*

Abelard and Heloise, *Letters.*

Beaumanoir, Philippe de Remi, *Coutume de Beauvoisis.* 1280.

Coulton, G. G., *Art and the Reformation.* 1928.

Durand, G., *La Cathédrale d'Amiens.* 1901.

Esmein, A., Cours élémentaire d'histoire du droit français. 1892. (Many editions.)

Gierke, O., *Political Theories of the Middle Ages.* Trans. by Maitland. 1927.

Haskins, C. H., *Studies in the History of Medieval Science.* 1924.

Haskins, C. H., *Studies in Medieval Culture.* 1929.

Leach, A. F., *The Schools of Medieval England.* 1915.

*Lethaby, W. R., *Medieval Art.* 1904.

Moore, T. Sturge. *Albrecht Dürer.* 1905.

Norton, C. E., *Historical Studies of Church Building in the Middle Ages.* 1880.

Power, Eileen, *Medieval People.* 1924.

Power, Eileen, (translator), *The Goodman of Paris.* 1929.

Schaube, F., *Der Kampf gegen den Zinswucher, ungerechten Preis und unlauteren Handel im Mittelalter.* 1905.

*Taine, H., *Philosophie de l'art.* 1869.

Taylor, H. O., *The Medieval Mind.* 1913.

Tawney, R. H., *Religion and the Rise of Capitalism.* London, 1925.

Violet-le-duc, E. E., *The Habitations of Man in All Ages.* Eng. Trans. 1876.

[Across from foregoing, handwritten by Ostrander, on back of page 7:

Mâle
Maritain – Scholasticist
Hoskins – Medieval Science
Coulton –]

(e) *On economic development in 14th and 15th century Flanders*:

Bahr, K., *Handel und Verkehr der deutschen Hanse in Flandern*. Leipzig, 1911.

Cuvelier, J., *Op. cit.*

Des Marez, G., *L'Organisation du travail dans une ville du XVe siècle*. Brussels, 1904.

Dürer, A., *Records of Journeys to Venice and the Low Countries*. (ed. Roger Fry), Boston, 1913.

Espinas, G., *Le draperie dans la Flandre française au Moyen-âge*. 1923.

Espinas, G., and Pirenne. *Recueil de documents, relatifs à l'histoire de l'industrie drapière en Flandre*. 4 vols., Brussels, 1906–1924.

Finot. J., *Etude historique sur les relations commerciales entre la Flandre et l'Espagne au Moyen-âge*, Paris, 1899.

Genard. Pierre, *Anvers à travers les âges*. 2 vols. 1888.

Gilliodts-van Severen, *Cartulaire de l'ancienne estaples de Bruges*. 4 vols., Bruges, 1904–1906.

Gilliodts-van Severen, *Cartulaire de l'ancien consulat d'Espagne à Bruges*. 2 vols., Bruges, 1901–1902.

Goris, J. A., *Étude surl es colonies marchandes méridionales à Anvers de 1488 à 1576*. Louvain, 1925.

Guicciardini. L., *Description de tous les Pays-Bas*, 1613. (Partly translated in Tawney and Power, *Tudor Economic Documents*, vol. iii, pp. 149–173.)

Kurth. G., *La cité de Liége au Moyen-âge*. 1910.

*Pirenne. H., *Histoire de Belgique*, vols. 1–3.

Pirenne. H., *Les démocraties urbaines aux Pays-Bas*. 1910.

Pirenne. H., *Histoire de la constitution de la ville de Dinant*. 1889.

Van der Essen, and Cauchie, *Inventaire des archives famesiennes de Naples*. 1911.

Van der Linden. *Les gildes marchandes dans les Pays-Bas au Moyen-âge*. 1890.

(f) *On economic development in Renaissance Italy*:

Ajano, R. B., d' *Die Venetianische Seidenindustrie und Ihre Organization*, 1893.

Arias, G., *I trattati commercialli della republica fiorentina*. 1901.

*Burckhardt. J., *The Civilization of the Renaissance in Italy*. 1878.

*Cellini. Benvenuto, *Memoirs* (Symonds trans.) 1899.

Davidsohn, R., *Geschichte von Florenz*. 1890.

Doren, A. J., *Entwickelung und Organisation der Florentiner Zünfte im 13 und 14 Jahrhundert.* 1897.

Doren, A. J., *Studien aus Florentiner Wirtschaftsgeschichte.* 1901.

Gandi, G., *Le Corporazioni dell' Antica Firenze.* 1928. (Popular)

Gargiolli, *L'arte della seta in Firenze.* 1868.

Renard, Georges, *Histoire du travail à Florence.* 2 vols. 1913–1914.

Sapori, A., *La Crisi della compagne dei Bardi e dei Peruzzi.* 1926.

Schaube, A., *Handelsgeschichte der romanischen Völker des Mittelmeergebiets bis zum Ende der Kreuzzüge.* 1906.

Sieveking. H., *Die Genueser Seidenindustrie im 15. und 16. Jahrhundert in Jahrbuch fur Gesetzgebung.* XXI, 1897.

Yver, G., *Le commerce et les marchands dans l'Ittalie meridionale au XIIIe et au XIVe siècle.* 1903.

4. A SELECT BIBLIOGRAPHY OF BRITISH ECONOMIC HISTORY FROM THE REFORMATION TO THE END OF THE NINETEENTH CENTURY.

4.1. Designed for Part IV of the Course

* Indicates books which are especially recommended.

\# Indicates books which are considered standard works of scholarship.

General works covering the economic history of the entire period.

Cheyney, E. P. *An Introduction to the Industrial and Social History of England.* New York, 1901.

#Cunningham, W. *The Growth of English Industry and Commerce.* 6th ed., 2 vols. (2nd vol. in 2 parts.) Cambridge, 1915–1919.

Usher, A. P. *An Introduction to the Industrial History of England.* London. 1921.

General works covering the economic history of particular periods.

*Ashley, W. J. *An Introduction to English Economic History and Theory.* 4th ed. 1906. Part 2 deals to some extent with the 16th century.

Bowden, W. H. *Industrial Society in England towards the End of the 18th Century.* 1925.

Brentano, L. *Eine Geschichte der wirtschaftlichen Entwicklung Englands.* Jena, 1927. Vol. 2 deals with the 16th, 17th, and 18th centuries.

*Clapham, J. H. *An Economic History of Modern Britain.* Cambridge, 1927. Deals with the early 19th century.

Fay, C. R. *Great Britain from Adam Smith to the Present Day*. London, 1928.
Hammond, J. L. and B. *The Rise of Modern Industry*. London, 1925. Deals
especially with the period of the so-called "Industrial Revolution."
*Held, Adolf. *Zwei Bücher zur Socialen Geschichte Englands*. 1881. Deals
especially with the period since 1760.
Knowles, L. C. A. *The Industrial and Commercial Revolutions in Great Britain
during the Nineteenth Century*. 4th ed., London, 1926. Covers the period from
1789–1914.
Lipson. E. *An Introduction to the Economic History of England*. 1931.
#Mantoux, Paul. *The Industrial Revolution in the 18th Century*. 1st English ed.,
London, 1928.
Toynbee. Arnold. *Lectures on the Industrial Revolution*. London, 1884. Many
subsequent editions. Important for its attempt to relate economic history to
economic theory.

[Across from foregoing, handwritten by Ostrander, on back of page 9:
H. Pirenne – *Medieval Cities*
W. Ashley – *Introduction to English Economic History and Theory*, Part I,
Chapters 1 and 2
H. Taine – *Philosophy of Art* – painting in Italy, and in Low Countries
R. Ehrenberg – *Capital and Finance in the Age of the Renaissance*, Introduction,
Book I, Chapter I; Book II, Chapter I
W. R. Letharby – *Medieval Art*, pp. 135–261
Burckhardt – *The Civilization of the Renaissance in Italy*, Part 4, Chapters 1 and
2; Part 5
Boissonnade – *Life and Work of Medieval Europe*, Part 2, Chapters 1–10
M. Knight – *Economic History of Europe*, pp. 86–254
Stephenson – *The English Borough*
Parrington – *Main Currents in American Thought*
B. Cellini – *Autobiography* (translated by Symonds)
Kingsley Porter – (Gothic Art)
Hulme – "Speculations"
Mâle

Victor Hugo – William *Shakespeare* (Essays on Genius)]

Accounts of travelers, collections of documents, parliamentary reports.
Camden, William. *Britannia*. 1st ed., 1586. The best ed. is that of 1607, translated
from the Latin and enlarged by R. Gough, 3 vols., 1789.
*Cobbett. William. *Rural Rides*. 1830. To be had in 2 volumes in the Everyman
Library Series. New definitive ed. by G. D. H. and M. Cole. 1930.

*Defoe, Daniel. *A Tour through the Whole Island of Great Britain*. 3 vols., 1724–1726. Modern edition by G. D. H. Cole. London, 1927.

English Economic History. Select Documents. Ed. Bland, Brown and Tawney, London, 1914. Covers the period from 1660 to 1840.

*Harrison, William. *An Historical Description of the Island of Britain*. 1577. 2nd ed., 1587.

Kalm's Account of His Visit to England – in 1748. Trans. by Joseph Lucas, London, 1892. Deals mainly with agricultural conditions.

*LeLand, John. *The Itinerary of John Leland, 1535–1543*. Ed. Thos. Hearne, 9 vols., Oxford, 1768–1769.

Meidinger, H. *Reisen durch Grossbritannien und Irland*. 1828.

Misson, H. de V. *M. Misson's Memoirs and Observations in His Travels over England* (1698). Trans. by James Ozell, London, 1719.

Parliamentary Reports of the Early19th Century. For a list of the more important ones, see Eileen Power, *The Industrial Revolution 1750–1850. A Select Bibliography*. Economic History Society, Bibliographies, No. 1, London, 1927.

Pennant, Thomas. *A Tour in Scotland, 1769*. Chester, 1771.

Tudor Economic Documents, ed. by R. H. Tawney and E. Power, 3 vols., London, 1924.

*Young, Arthur. *Farmer's Tour through the East of England*. 1771.

*Young, Arthur. *Six Months' Tour through the East of Scotland*. 1770.

*Young, Arthur. *Six Weeks' Tour through the Southern Counties*. 1768.

Works dealing mainly with agrarian conditions.

*Eden, F. M. *The State of the Poor*. London, 1797.

Gonner, E. C. K. *Common Land and Enclosure*. London, 1912.

*Hammond, J. L. and B. *The Village Labourer, 1760–1832*. London, 1911.

Johnson, A. *The Disappearance of the Small Landowner*. Oxford, 1909.

Leadham, I. S. *The Domesday of Inclosures*. 2 vols., London, 1891.

#Prothero, R. E., (Lord Ernle). *English Farming, Past and Present*. 4th ed., London, 1927. Best general account of the whole subject.

*Tawney, R. H. *The Agrarian Problem in the 16th Century*. London, 1912.

Works dealing mainly with population and migration.

Buer, M. C. *Health, Wealth and Population in the Early Days of the Industrial Revolution*. London, 1926.

#Griffiths, G. T. *Population Problems in the Age of Malthus*. Cambridge, 1926.

Redford, A. *Labour Migration in England, 1800–1850*. Manchester, 1926.

Weber, A. F. *The Growth of Cities in the Nineteenth Century*. New York, 1899 (also for France and Germany).

Works dealing mainly with industry and industrial organization.

Allen, G. C. *The Industrial Development of Birmingham and the Black Country, 1860–1927.* London, 1929.

#Ashton, T. S. *Iron and Steeel in the Industrial Revolution.* Manchester, 1924.

#Ashton, T. S. and Sykes, J. *The Coal Industry of the Eighteenth Century.* Manchester, 1929.

Cole, G. D. H. *A Short History of the British Working Class Movement.* London, 1925.

#Daniels, G. W. *The Early English Cotton Industry.* London, 1920.

#Hamilton, Henry. *The English Brass and Copper Industries to 1800.* London, 1926.

*Hammond, J. L., and B. *The Skilled Labourer.* London, 1919.

*Hammond, J. L., and B. *The Town Labourer.* London, 1917.

#Heaton, H. *The Yorkshire Woolen and Worsted Industries from the Earliest Times up to the Industrial Revolution.* Oxford, 1920.

Jevons, H. S. *The British Coal Trade.* London, 1915.

*Jevons, W. S. *The Coal Question.* 1865. 3rd edit., ed., A. W. Flux, London, 1915.

Kulischer, J. "Die Ursachen des Ueberganges von der Handarbeit zur Maschinen Betriebsweise," in *Jahrbuch für Gesetzgebung,* vol. XXX (1906) pp. 31–79.

Levy, Hermann. *Monopoly and Competition.* London, 1911. Deals with the modern question of cartels and trusts, but is not entirely satisfactory.

Lewis, G. R. *The Stannaries.* Cambridge (Mass.), 1907. A study of tin mining and the tin industry.

#Lloyd, G. I. H. *The Cutlery Trades.* London, 1913.

#Lipson, E. *History of the Woolen and Worsted Industries.* London, 1921.

Rogers, J. E. Thorold. *Six Centuries of Work and Wages.* New York, 1884.

*Unwin, George. *Industrial Organization in the Sixteenth and Seventeenth Centuries.* London, 1904.

Unwin, George. *Samuel Oldknow and the Arkwrights.* Manchester, 1924.

Wadsworth, A. P. and J. de L. Mann. *The Cotton Trade and Industrial Lancashire, 1600–1780.* 1931.

#Webb, S. and B. *History of Trade Unionism.* New ed., 1920.

Works dealing mainly with internal trade.

*Defoe, Daniel. *The Complete English Tradesman.* 2 vol. ed., 1745. An excellent description of internal trade and of the functions of middlemen in the various branches of this trade early in the eighteenth century.

#Gras, N. S. B. *The Evolution of the English Corn Market.* Cambridge, (Mass.), 1915. From the 12th to the 18th century.

Jackman, V. T. *Development of Transportation in Modern England*. Cambridge, 1916. Especially river and canal transportation.

Pratt, E. A. *History of Inland Transportation and Communication in England*. London, 1909.

*Unwin, G. "Commerce and Coinage in Shakespeare' s England," in *Studies in Economic History*, pp. 302 sqq.

Westerfield, R. B. *Middlemen in English Business, Particularly between 1660 and 1760*. New Haven, 1915.

Webb, S. and B. *The Story of the King's Highway*. London, 1920.

Works dealing mainly with foreign trade and the export of capital.

Beer, G. L. *The Old Colonial System, 1660–1754*. 2 vols., New York, 1912.

Bowley, A. L. *England' s Foreign Trade in the Nineteenth Century*. Revised ed., London, 1905.

Hobson, C. K. *The Export of Capital*. London, 1914.

Horrocks, J. W. *Short History of Mercantilism*. London, 1925.

Jenks, L. H. *The Migration of British Capital to 1875*. New York, 1927.

Knowles, L. C. A. *The Economic Development of the British Overseas Empire*. 2nd ed., 1928. Other volumes to follow.

Krishna, B. *Commercial Relations between India and England, 1601–1757*. London, 1924.

Levi, Leone. *History of British Commerce, 1763–1870*. 1872.

Murray, A. E. *Commercial Relations between England and Ireland for the Period of the Restoration*. 1903.

Williamson, J. A. *A Short History of British Expansion*. 1922.

Works dealing mainly with banking and finance.

Andreades, A. M. *History of the Bank of England*. 2nd ed., London. 1924.

*Bagehot, W. *Lombard Street*. London, 1873:

Bischhop, W. R. *The Rise of the London Money Market, 1640–1826*. London, 1910.

Corti, E. C. *The Rise of the House of Rothchild*, and *The Reign of the House of Rothchild*. Both translated by B. and B. Lunn, New York, 1928.

Gregory, T. E. *Select Statutes, Documents and Reports relating to British Banking, 1832–1928*. (Selected, with valuable introduction). 2 vols., London, 1929.

Powell, E. T. *The Evolution of the London Money Market*. London, 1915.

Rees, J. A. *A Short Fiscal and Financial History of England*. London, 1921.

Richards, D. W. *The Early History of Banking in England*. London, 1929. (To be used with caution.)

Robinson, R. M. *Coutts': The History of a Banking House*. 1929

#Scott, W. R. *The Constitution and Finance of English, Scottish and Irish Joint Stock Companies, to 1720.* 3 vols., Cambridge, 1911.

*Tawney, R. H. *Introduction* to Thomas Wilson's *Discourse upon Usury.* London, 1925. Deals with the Elizabethan period.

Works dealing mainly with the history of prices.

Layton, W. *Introduction to the Study of Prices.* London, 1912.

Rogers, J. E. Thorold. *A History of Agriculture and Prices in England.* 7 vols., Oxford, 1866–1902.

Silberling, N. J. *British Prices and Business Cycles, 1779–1850.* Harvard Economic Service, 1923.

Tooke, T. *History of Prices and of the State of Circulation.* 6 vols. London, 1838–1857.

Wiebe, Georg. *Zur Geschichte der Preisrevolution des XVI. und XVII. Jahrhunderts.* Leipzig, 1895.

Works dealing mainly with social reform.

Beer, M. *A. History of British Socialism.* 2 vols., London, 1919–1920.

Cole, G. D. H. *Robert Owen.* London, 1925.

Disraeli, B. *Sybil.*

Gray, B. K. *History of Philanthropy.* London, 1905.

Hovell, Mark. *The Chartist Movement.* Ed. T. F. Tout, Manchester, 1918.

Leonard, E. M. *The Early History of English Poor Relief.* London, 1900.

*Wallas, Graham. *Life of Francis Place.* 2nd ed., London, 1918.

Webb, S. and B. *English Poor Law Policy.* Part I, *The Old Poor Law.* London, 1910.

Works dealing (usually indirectly) with the relations between economic history and political thought, religion, law, literature, natural science, and invention. (Apart from Tawney's book there is no book dealing directly with the relation between economic and other aspects of life.)

Allen, J. W. *A History of Political Thought in the 16th Century.* London, 1928.

Brinton, Crane. *The Political Ideas of the English Romanticists.* London, 1926.

*Buckle, Thomas. *History of Civilization in England.* London, 1857, 1861. Can be obtained in a cheap 3 vol. edition in "The World's Classics" Series.

Dicey, A. V. *Lectures on the Relation between Law and Public Opinion,* etc., 2nd ed., London, 1914.

Gillespie, F. E. *Labour and Politics in England, 1850–1867.* Durham (N. C.), 1927.

Gooch. G. P. English Democratic Ideas in the 17th Century. 2nd ed., H. J. Laski, Cambridge, 1927.

Halvey. Elie. *A History of the English People*. London, 1924.

Lord, J. *Capital and Steam Power, 1750–1800*. London, 1923.

*Macaulay, T. B. *History of England*. Especially the 3rd chapter.

Maitland, F. W. *English Law and the Renaissance*. London, 1901.

Pollock, Sir F. and Maitland, F. W. *The History of England Law*. 2 vols. London, 1923.

Seeley, J. R. *The Growth of British Policy*. 1895. Reprint in 1 vol., Cambridge, 1922.

Simmonds, P. L. *Science and Commerce: their influence on our manufactures*. 1872.

Smiles. S. *Lives of the Engineers*. 5 vols., London, 1874–1891.

Taine, H. A. *History of English Literature*. English ed., 2 vols., London, 1871.

*Tawney. R. H. *Religion and the Rise of Capitalism*. London, 1925.

5. A SELECT BIBLIOGRAPHY FOR PARTS V AND VI OF THE COURSE. THE ECONOMIC DEVELOPMENT OF FRANCE SINCE 1600 AND OF GERMANY SINCE 1815

I. *General economic histories*:

*Clapham, J. H. *The Economic Development of France and Germany, 1815–1914*. 3rd ed., 1928.

D'Avenel, G. *Histoire économique de la propriété, des salaires, des denrées, etc.* 1894–1898.

Dutil, Léon. *L'état économique du Languedoc à la fin de l'ancien regime*. 1911.

*Fagniez, G. C. *L'économie sociale de la France sous Henri IV*. 1897.

*Hauser, Henri. *Les débuts du capitalisme moderne*. 1927.

*Hauser, Henri. *Travailleurs et marchands dans l'ancienne France*. 1920. (Both collections of articles on special subjects.)

Huber, F. C. *Fünfzig Jahre deutsches Wirtschaftsleben*. 1906.

Inama-Sternegg, K. T. *Deutsche Wirtschaftsgeschichte*. 1879–1901.

Kovalevsky, M. M. *La France économique et sociale à la veille de la révolution*. 1909.

Moreau de Jonnes, A. *Etat économique et sociale de la France*. 1867. (Out of date, and of little value.)

Ogburn, W. F. and Jaffé, W. *The Economic Development of Post-War France: A Survey of Production*. 1929.

Pohle, Ludwig. *Die Entwicklung des deutschen Wirtschaftslebens im 19. Jahrhundert*, 1908.

*See, Henri. *L'Evolution commerciale et industrielle de la France sous l'ancien régime.* 1925. (A useful survey.)

Sée, Henri. *La vie économique et les classes sociales en France au XVIII siècle.* 1924. (Treatment of' agriculture.) (See also Sée's *Esquisse* in French, and his more detailed *Französische Wirtschaf'tsgeschichte* in German for attempts to cover the entire field of French economic history.)

*Sombart, Werner. *Die deutsche Volkswirtschaft im neunzehnten Jahrhundert.* 1903.

*Veblen, T. *Imperial Germany and the Industrial Revolution.* 1915.

#Waltershausen, A. S. von. *Deusche Wirtschaftsgeschichte, 1815–1914.* 1920.

[Across from the foregoing, handwritten by Ostrander, on back of page 14:

Tawney – *Agrarian Problem in 16th Century* – Part III
Thomas Wilson, *A Discourse upon Usury*, 1925, Tawney's Introduction – (all but [or best], for each, and life of Wilson) Part II, except #4, Part III
Mantoux – *Industrial Revolution of the 18th Century* – Coal and Iron, Population – Part 2, Chapters 3, 4; Part 3, Chapters 1, 2
Hammond – *The Skilled Laborer*, Chapters 2–3
The Town Laborer, Chapters 1–3
J. H. Clapham – *An Economic History of Modern Britain*, Volume I, Chapters 1, 5; Volume II, Chapters 1–4, 12]

II. *Books dealing especially with population, agriculture and landholding*:

a. *France*

*Augé-Laribé, M. *L'évolution agricole de la France.* 1912.

Bonnemère, Eugène. *Histoire des paysans depuis la fin du Moyen-âge jusqu'à nos jours, 1200–1850.* 1856.

Lascauz, R. *La production et la population.* 1921.

Lavergne, L. de. *Economie rurale de la France depuis 1789.* 1860.

*Lefebvre, G. *Les paysans du Nord pendant la Révolution française.* 1924. (See also his "La place de la révolution dans l'histoire agraire de la France," in *Annales d'hist. econ. et soc.*, vol. i, (1929), pp. 506, sqq.

*Levasseur, E. *La population française.* 3 vols., 1889.

Loutchisky, I. V. *L'état des classes agricoles en France.* 1911.

Loutchisky, I. V. *La petite propriété paysanne à la veille de la révolution.* 1912.

Mounier, L. *De l'agriculture en France, d'après les documents officiels.* 1846.

Romieu, Mme. *Des paysans et de l'agriculture en France au XIXe siècle. Interêts Meurs. Institutions.* 1865.

Roupnel, M. G. *Les populations de la ville et de la campagne dijonnaises au XVIIe siècle.* 1922.
Sion, Jules. *Les paysans de la Normandie orientale.* 1909.

b. *Germany*

Dieterici, K. F. W. *Der Volkswohlstand im Preussischen Staate.* 1846.
Knapp, G. F. *Die Bauernbefreiung und der Ursprung der Landarbeiter in den älteren Theilen Preussens.* 1887.
Wittich, W. *Epochen der deutschen Agrarigeschichte, im Grundriss der Sozialökonomie.* VII, 1922.

III. *Books dealing especially with transportation, commerce (domestic and foreign) and finance*:

a. *France*

*Afanasiev, G. C. *Le commerce des céréales en France au XVIIIe siècle.* 1894.
Biggar, H. P. *The Early Trading Companies of New France.* 1901.
Bijo, T. *La Caisse d'Escompte, 1776–1793, et les origines de la Banque de France.* 1927.
Bonnassieux, L. J. P. M. *Les grandes compagnies de commerce.* 1892.
Chailley-Bart, J. *Les compagnies de commerce sous l'ancien régime.* 1898.
Chemins-Dupontes, P. *Les compagnies de colonisation en Afrique sous Colbert.* 1903.
Chemins-Dupontes, P. *Les petites Antilles; étude sur leur évolution économique.* 1909.
Clark. G. N. *The Anglo-Dutch Alliance and the War against French Trade.* 1923.
Clément, Pierre. *Histoire du system protecteur en France depuis le ministère de Colbert jusqu'à la revolution de 1848.* 1854.
Coq, Paul and Benard, T. N. *Résumé analytique de l'enquète parlementaire sur le régime économique de la France en 1870.* 1872.
#Dahlgren, E. W. *Les relations commerciales et maritimes entre la France et les côtes de l'ocean Pacifique.* 1909.
Franklin, A. L. A. *Les corporations ouvrières de Paris du XIIe au XVIIIe siècles.* 1884.
Franklin, A. L. A. *La vie privée d'autrefois.* 27 vol. 1887–1902.
Guillaumot. *L'organisation des chemins de fer en France.* 1899.
Levasseur, Emile. *Histoire du commerce de la France.* 2nd ed. 1912.

Mantellier, P. M. *Histoire de la communauté des marchands fréquentant la Loire et fleuves descendant en icelle.* 1864–1869.

Masson, Paul. *Histoire du commerce français dans le Levant au XVIIe siècle et au XVIIIe siècle.* 2 vols. 1896, 1917.

Masson, Paul. *Histoire des établissements et du commerce français dans l'Afrique barbaresque.* 1903.

Mims, S. L. *Colbert's West India Policy.* 1912.

Noel, O. *Histoire du commerce extérieur de la France, depuis la révolution.* 1879.

Nussbaum, F. *Commercial Policy in the French Revolution.* 1923.

Pereire, J. *La Banque de France et l'organisation du crédit en France.* 2nd ed. 1864.

Preiset, Ernest. *La chambre de Commerce de Lyon, 1702–1791.* 1886–1889.

Ségur-Dupeyron, P. de. *Histoire des négociations commerciales et maritimes.* 1872–1873.

Theisserone, E. *Etude sur les voies de communication perfectionnées et sur les lois économiques de la production du transport.* 1847.

Thirion, Henri. *La vie privée des financiers au XVIIIe siècle.* 1895.

Usher, A. P. *History of the Grain Trade in France, 1400–1710.* 1913.

Vignon. Etude historique sur l'administration des voies publiques en France. 1863.

Wallon. *La chambre de commerce de la province de Normandie.* 1903.

b. *Germany*

Baasch, E. *Die Handelskammer zu Hamburg, 1665–1915.* 1915.

Fitger, E. *Die wirtschaftliche und technische Entwicklung der Seeschiffahrt von der Mitte des 19. Jahrhunderts bis auf die Gegenwart.* 1902.

Hauser, Henri. *Germany's Commercial Grip on the World.* 1917.

Gothein, Eberhard. *Die Geschichtliche Entwicklung der Rheinschiffahrt im 19. Jahrhunderts.* 1903.

#Lotz, W. *Die Verkehrsentwickelung in Deutschland, 1800–1900.* 1920.

#Reisser, J. *The German Great Banks and Their Concentration in Connection with the Economic Development of Germany.* 3rd ed. 1911.

#Wagner, Adolph. *Finanzwissenschaft.* 3rd ed. 1910.

IV. *Books relating especially to the history of industry and industrial organization:*

a. *France*

Bacquié, F. *Les inspecteurs des manufactures sous l'ancien régime, 1661–1791.* 1927.

Babeau, Albert. *Les bourgeois d'autrefois.* 1886.

*Ballet, Charles. *L'introduction du machinisme dans l'industrie française.* 1923.

Boissonnade, P. M. *Essai sur l'histoire de l'organization du travail en Poitou.* 1900.

Boissonnade, P. M. *Le socialisme d'état: l'industrie et les classes industrielles en France, 1453–1661.* 1927.

Bourgin, G. and H. *L'industrie sidérurgique en France au début de la révolution.* 1922.

* Bourgin, G. and H. *Le régime de l'industrie en France de 1814 à 1830.* 1912.

Decamps, G. *Mémoire historique sur l'origine de l'industrie houillere dans le bassin . . . de Mous. Publ. of Soc. des Sciences des Arts et des Lettres de Hainaut.* 1819.

Des Cilleuls, A. *Histoire et régime de la grande industrie en France.* 1898.

Gauthier, Jules. *L'industrie du papier dans les hautes vallées franccomtoises du XVe au XVIIIe siècles* in *Mémoires de la Soc. d'Emulation de Montbéliard" vol, XXVI.*

Germain-Martin. La grande industrie en France sous Louis XIV et Louis XV. 2 vols., 1898, 1900.

#Godart, Justin. L'ouvrier en soie à Lyon. 1899.

Gras, L. J. *Histoire économique de la métallurgie de la Loire.* 1908.

Gras, L. J. *Histoire économique générale des mines de la Loire.* 1922.

Guéneau, Louis. *L'organisation du travail à Nevers aux XVIIe et XVIIIe siècles (1660–1789).* 1919

Hauser, Henri. *Ouvriers du temps passé.* 1899. (Relates mainly to 16th century.)

Havard, R. and Vachon, M. *Les manufactures nationales.* 1889. (Refers to the Beauvais and Gobelins tapestries.)

Hottenger, G. *L'industrie du fer en Lorraine.* 1927.

#Lespinasse, R. de. *Les Metiers et corporations de la ville de Paris.* 1879.

Levainville, J. R. *L'industrie du fer en France.* 1922.

#Levasseur, Emile. *Histoire des classes ouvrières en France.* 2nd ed. 1901.

Levine, L. *The Labor Movement in France.* 1912.

Levy, R. *Histoire économique de l'industrie cotonnière en Alsace.* 1912.

#Martin St. Leon, E. *Histoire des corporations de métiers.* 3rd ed. 1922.

Philippoteaux, A. *Origines et débuts de la draperie sedanaise, 1575–1667.* 2 vols. 1924, 1927.

Poulin, Abel. *Etude critique sur la petite et la moyenne industrie en France.* 1919.

Reybaud, L. *Le coton.* 1863.

Reybaud, L. *Le laine.* 1867.
Rouff, Marcel. *Les mines de charbon en France au XVIIIe siècle.* 1922.

b. *Germany*

Baumont, M. *La grosse industrie allemande et le charbon.* 1928.
Ehrenberg, R. *Das Haus Parish in Hamburg.* 2nd ed. 1925.
Ehrenberg, R. *Die Fugger – Rothchild –Krupp.* 3rd ed. 1925.
Ehrenberg, R. *Die Unternehmung der Brüder Siemens.* 1906.
Fitgel, E. *Die wirtschaftliche und technische Entwicklung der Seeschiffahrt von der Mitte des 19. Jahrhunderts bis auf die Gegenwart.* 1902.
Gothein, Eberhard. *Die geschichtliche Entwicklung der Rheinschiffahrt, in 19. Jahrhundert.* 1903.
Gothein, Eberhard. *Wirtschaftsgeschichte des Schwarzswaldes und der angrenzendén Landschaften.* 1892.
Hue, Otto. *Die Bergarbeiter.* 1910, 1913.
Meerwein, G. *Die Entwicklung der Chemnitzer bezw. Sächsischen Baumwollspinnerei von 1789–1879.* 1914.
Walker, F. A. *Monopolistic Combinations in the German Coal Industry.* 1904.
Wiedenfeld, K. *Ein Jahrhundert rheinischer Montanindustrie, 1815–1915.* 1916.
Wiedfeldt, O. *Statistische Studien zur Entwickelungsgeschichte der Berliner Industrie von 1720 bis 1890.* 1898.
Wirth, M. *Die Industrie der Grafschaft Mark und der französischen Schutzzollgesetzgebung,* 1791–1813. 1914.

V. *Books on topics allied to economic history*

Benda, Julien. *Belphégor.* Eng. translation, 1929.
Caillaux, J. *Les impôts en France.* 2 vols. 1911.
Chéreel, A. *Dictionnaire historique des institutions, moeurs et coutumes de la France.* 8th ed. 2 vols. 1910.
Dawson, W. H. *The Evolution of Modern Germany.* 1908.
D'Avenel, G. *Le méchanisme de la vie moderne.* 1896–1905.
Esmein. (See bibliog. for Part III of the course.)

Fagniez, G. C. *La femme et la société française dans la première moitié du XVIIe siècle.* 1912.
Grant, E. M. *French Poetry and Modern Industry, 1830–1870.* 1927.
Kessler, Count Harry. *Walter Rathenau, His Life and Work.* 1928.
Lichtenberger, André. *Le socialisme au XVIIIe siècle.* 1895.
Maurras, Charles. L'avenir de l'intelligence. 3rd ed. 1905.
Norman, C. *La bourgeoisie française au XVIIe siècle.* 1908.

*Taine, H. *Les origines de la France contemporaire*. Eng. trans. 1878–1894. (Esp. the vols. on the ancien régime.)
Tolstoy, L. *What is Art?* 1898.

[Across from foregoing, handwritten by Ostrander, on back of page 18:

J. H. Clapham – *Economic Development of France and Germany*, Chapters 1, 3, 8, 10 and Epilogue
T. Veblen – *Imperial Germany and the Industrial Revolution*, Chapters 3–8]

VI. *Literature contemporary with the period written about:*
Arnould, A. M. *De la balance du commerce et des relations commerciales extérieures de la France, etc.* 1716. 2nd ed. 1795.
Banfield, T. C. *Industry of the Rhine.* 2 series, 1846, 1848.
Boisguilllebert. *Le détail de la France sous le règne présent.* 1695. New ed. 1707.
Boulainvilliers. *Etat de la France, extraits des mémoires des intendants.* 8 vols. 1752.
Boulenger. *Calculation et description de la France.* 1575.
*Chaptal de Chasteloup, J. A. C. *De l'industrie française.* 1819.
Chevalier, Michel. *Des interêts matériels en France.* 1838.
Laboulaye, C. de. *De la democratie industrielle. Etudes sur l'organisation de l'industrie Française.* 1849.
Gournay. *Tableau genéral du commerce, des marchands, négocians, armateurs . . . de la France, de l'Europe et des autres parties du monde.* 1789, 1790.
Mercier, L. S. *Tableau de Paris.* 1782 ed. in 8 vols.
Molinari, G. de. *Conversations sur le commerce des grains et la protection de l'agriculture.* 1886.
Russell, A. *A Tour in Germany.* 1825.
*Young, Arthur. *Travels in France.* 1793.

6. MID-TERM AND FINAL EXAMINATIONS

6.1. Mid-Term Examination

Hour Examination   November 17, 1933

(1) Discuss the nature of the source materials available to the economic historian for estimating the extent of industrial capitalism in Italy in the first century

A. D. How do they limit our knowledge of the subject? Illustrate these limits with special relation to the treatment of the subject in Tenney Frank's "Economic History of Rome."

(2) Compare Taine's theory of art with that of Oswald Spengler.

(3) Discuss and compare the role played by the State in limiting the freedom of the wealthiest financial class in Attica in the 5th century B. C., in Italy in the 3rd century A. D., and in some town of northern France in the twelfth century A. D.

(4) Restate Lucian's precepts to make them applicable to the writing of economic history. How far are these precepts satisfied by the chapters that you have read in Zimmern, in Rostovtzeff, in Gibbon, and in Ashley?

Final Examination   December 22, 1933
Please answer <u>any two</u> of the four questions.

- What is the ordinarily accepted meaning of the term "Industrial Revolution"? To what extent does the concept provide a satisfactory picture of the rise of "Industrialism," as the word has been used in this course?

- "In the ancient (i.e. Classical) world and throughout the Middle Ages common men were without rights or privileges. They did the drudgery of the world's work as peasants, slaves or serfs, but received little more recognition or consideration socially and politically than the beasts whom they tended and with whom they worked." How far is the view expressed in this passage borne out by your study of (a) the slave in 5th century Attica? (b) The craftsman in a town in northern France in the 12th century, (c) a peasant holding his land by free tenure at the beginning of the 14th century.

- In the light of your knowledge of cultural, social and economic conditions in nineteenth-century Great Britain, write an explanation, after the manner of Veblen in his <u>Imperial Germany</u>, of the relatively slow progress of "industrial capitalism" in that country as compared with Germany during the second half of the nineteenth century.

- "Art and literature . . . have nothing to fear in the long run from steel and steam and electricity." (G. G. Coulton) Discuss this proposition in the light of your knowledge of the economic conditions which appear to have accompanied the great periods in the history of the arts with which you are familiar.

7. OSTRANDER'S COURSE NOTES

ECONOMIC HISTORY (221) <u>NEF</u>
<u>First three weeks</u>
    Spengler – Decline of the West – <u>Introduction</u> <u>Dial</u> 1924

Zimmern – The Greek Commonwealth – Part I, II Chapter 8, III Chapters 1, 2, 7–12, 15–17

Tenny, Frank – An Economic History of Rome – Chapters Chapters 13–14

Rostovtzeff – Social and Economic History of the Roman Empire – Chapters 5 and 6

Gibbon – Decline and Fall of Roman Empire

Juvenal – Satires – 1–4

Lucian – How History Should be Written

–This course does not cover "general economic history" – agriculture, commerce, banking, etc.

–But concentrates on Industrial Organization – Industrialism – Industrial Capitalism.

–Economic history is taking a new turn – as shown by Tawney's (London) and Clark's (Oxford) appointments as professors of economic history.

  –Marshall – defines Economics – "the study of man in the ordinary business of life."

  –Cannan – Economics = "having to do with material things in life." But can not be rigidly marked off.

  –Unwin – 1909 – Economic Historian is concerned with collective aspects of life – the motives of groups, rather than individuals or "the economic man."

    –He ought to enter every where where that clue leads him – i.e. he becomes more of a sociologist. (Cf. Tawney, Economica, 1932)

    –Bacon – "know everything about something, and know something about everything."

    –I.e. the purpose of this course: everything about industrialism, something about all history.

    –Pareto – at any one time, every social phenomenon is related to every other – i.e. no chain of cause and effect. [In margin: Cf. Harpers [Magazine, article by] Bernard DeVoto]

    –We will study relationships, not causes and effects.

    –We shall study certain periods of history, after Spengler – and define Industry (arbitrarily) as manufacturing and mining.

    –Also population, markets, trade, social and cultural backgrounds.

      –"Carving reality out of the joints of history."

–We shall seek how Industrialism has come to dominate Western civilization.

–What we shall mean by Industrialism, in this course.

  –Different from Capitalism – we live in the midst of it [arrow indicating "it" is Industrialism].

  –Dependent on Industrial Capitalism [arrow to "Plant" on next line].

1/<u>Plant</u> – <u>privately owned</u>, but <u>not by workers</u>, workers away from home, hired in open market.

   –Not public ownership, not <u>aesthetic</u> labor.

   –What of aesthetic labor in 15th century printing?

   –What is proportion of aesthetic to monotonous labor? – Industrial capitalism requires more of latter.

–<u>Industrialism</u> only exists when the economic system is <u>dominated</u> by Industrial Capitalism. [Two vertical lines in margin alongside this point.]

   –What matters is the <u>quantity</u> of <u>Industrial</u> <u>Capitalism</u>.

   –Nef's whole theory is <u>against</u> the idea of any <u>Industrial Revolution</u>.

–<u>Machinery run by power</u>

   –Has existed for centuries – 14th-15th; but use of non-human power, then of

2/<u>underground fuel</u>, has been more recent.

   –Again a matter of degree.

   –Use of coal in 16th century speeded up <u>Industrial Capitalism</u>. –The <u>amount</u> of Industrial Capitalism that brings about a dominance of it over a civilization must have some relation to what its amount was in early 19th century England.

3/ As well as <u>underground fuel</u> – in extensive use for glass, iron, steel – in a certain amount is imp[ortant].

4/ Development of <u>natural science</u> in a <u>new predominance</u> – <u>exact</u> science is new – in course of last two centuries (Cf. Pope – <u>re</u> Newton).

5/ Importance of the city, over against country.

6/ New abundance of <u>things</u> in houses of all classes.

7/ New growth of credit condtions – predominance of wealth in unequal distribution is nothing new.

–Should we assume a constant <u>rise</u> in History – 19th century "progress-belief" – Wellsian <u>present</u> climax – "historical Coué-ism" – or should we study History <u>via</u> great civilizations – parallel.

   –As Spengler – (civilization plus cycle) = Civilization but each entity [arrow to parenthetic "civilization"] has some <u>distinct</u> and individual characteristics.

[In top margin: Spengler – Man and Technics]

   –Loss of faith in industrialism – in our civilization.

   –Veblen said we never had really <u>believed</u> in our civilization.

   –Each Civilization goes through the same course of cycles, but each subsequent Civilization is different because of the others that have existed.

–We do not accept the pessimism, or ideological approach, of
Spengler.

Greco–Roman Economic Organization

Time

–Beginnings in 9th or 10th centuries B. C. – Homeric period in Greece,
some new national life-legends, trade, etc.
–Ending sometime in reign of Diocletian (d. 305) in Third Century A. D.
(cf. under Hadrian, 117–136 A.D.).

Area

–Shores of Mediterranean – Northward into Euroope.
–Greek supremacy until Second Century (end of 3rd Punic War).
–Not only a product of Greek and Roman experiences.
  Contemporary
    –Phoenician influence – 8th and 7th centuries [B. C.] – Empire to west
    of Mediterranean – Carthage's influence longer.
    –Etruscan – invaded Latin in 10th century [B. C.] – brought an Oriental
    influence, advanced civilization.
  Earlier
    Egyptian – peculiar domination of the State over all activities of life –
    State socialism coming from Pharaohs – influenced Rome.
    (Persian)
    Creton, Mycenian influence on Greek culture.
  Domination of Attica – 6th century. Battle of Marathon 480B. C. until
  Peleponesian War. [In margin: Greek supremacy]
    Roman Empire – 1st and 2nd centuries A. D. Roman Empire [In margin:
    Roman supremacy]

We shall stress these two epochs; thus leaving out the Hellenic civilization, 4th,
3rd, 2nd [centuries B. C.] of great development, factory system, much materialism
– taken over by Romans.
  Sources
    –Abundance of writings → books, of monuments → works.
    –Classical civilization must always remain a mystery – as far as detail is
    concerned.
    –We have mostly literary writing; not treatises on Economics (which exist
    for any period after 12th century [A. D.]).
      –Even historians did not deal with Economics, were not enough
      conscious of Time.

–Plays (Aristophanes) – Plato, Aristotle – furnish our best information.
–Secondary sources – Heitland "Agricole" – derived from belles lettres.
   –What does survive when a civilization goes down is the great
   literature – i.e. history must be written as good literature.
–Monuments – coins, implements, etc. – affording much information
   directly, indirectly.
   –Direct – Roman baths at Bath [England] – Aqueduct at Nîmes
   [France].
   –Indirect – style of painting, what is shown on Greek vases.
–We have been extremely fortunate in the practitioners who have elected
   to study either the works or the writings of Classical civilization.
   –The histories are often great literary events. Mommsen (Rome), Fustel
   de Coulanges (Early Roman, Early France), J. Beloch (population), R.
   Sargeant (slavery), Wolff (population), Facts and Factors of History,
   Andréades.
–Population much greater in Athenian period than Homeric.
   –10th–5th centuries [B. C.]= increasing population tending to
   concentrate in "agglomerations" (not like medieval, modern cities).
   –Pressure on means of subsistence, necessitating imports.
   –City-States – in geographical compartments. Attica, a city-state; Athens
   the principal town.
      –Did the Athenian citizens live in Athens or out in the country.
      –Some slight congestion in center of town, but no city walls in the
      mediaeval sense – town becoming city slowly.
      –Difficult to arrive at population of Athens – but figures available for
      Attica: 200,000–400,000.
         –70,000–100,000 were slaves.
         –Free men outnumbered slaves! (new finding).
         –How then could the slaves have done all the manual work (as
         Calhoun said) – i.e. manual labor was not considered lowly or
         undignified.
   –Greek peninsula (excluding Epirus, Macedonia) – population about
   1,000,000.
   –Greater Greece – population 2,500,000–4,000,000.
   –Population living outside of Greece another 3–4,000,000 – i.e. nearly
   8,000,000 Greeks – Athenians a small proportion.
   –Attica – small proportion engaged in farming, larger proportion in trade
   and commerce, importing.
   –Interlocking commerce between cities, by land, was lacking; not so by
   sea in North.

–City government supreme; outdoor life, at least for six months.

–Population growth due to economic surplus, getting away from the land.

–States became politically conscious as they developed.

–Greek population after 5th century did not grow in Attica or Greece.

–Did not greatly decrease after Peleponesian Wars but remained nearly stable.

–Decline came later – 2nd century A. D. – i.e. economic life declined.

(1) Greece and Athens reached height of their national economic development in 5th century [B. C.].

–When economic organization grew, after 5th century, it grew more rapidly in other parts of the Mediterranean world. [Double vertical lines in margin alongside this statement.]

(2) Outdoor life generally, not crowded in "cities."

(3) Much normal work by free men.

Agriculture – land is very important in economic history: the uses to which land is put [and] the way it is held react on each other, [and] both have a reaction on the political life.

–In Attica, 5 B. C. – still mostly individual holdings, i.e. a "Commonwealth."

–Most of available soil under cultivation.

–Most crops consumed away from farm.

–Growth of population seems to have culminated in the 5th century.

–In Homeric days, pasturage more important than arable land.

–Aristocracy grew – horses, oxen, goats, sheep.

–Ox became unit of value; sheep gave wool; goats gave milk.

–Hunting in bands – meat plentiful – fish looked down on.

–After Homeric days – meat less plentiful, cereal more important (barley first, then wheat).

–In Homeric days – very little exchange – self-sufficient farms and villages. First specialization came in pottery and forging (iron imported).

–After Homeric days – increasing exchange; land put to different uses.

–Pasturage declined relatively to proportion of arable land; but not much increase of cereal-growing; not much improvement of agricultural methods (Greeks did not know of rotation of crops).

–Old plow-share still used.

–But marked improvement in arboriculture – especially olive and wine, but also figs and other fruits.

–Honey – the sweetening of classical days.

–Most famous for wine and olive oil.

–Long waiting for results of olive tree cultivation – 16–40 years.
   –Destruction in war much more serious than, say, in North France.
   –But labor is much more necessary in North France, than in Greek olive
      groves.
   –Tendency to large-scale farming in Greece.
–There was a great deal of industrial capitalism in classical days, but it did
   not predominate.
[In margin on top of page: "Revolution" is a bad word in History – should be
avoided.]
–A good deal of trade expansion – importing of food from abroad – growth
   of trading villages and much more exchange within the country. Decrease
   of plentiful meat; fishing gains in prestige. Relation of Greek civilization
   and Mediterranean water.
–Exporting of wine and oil, manufactured goods, mining ores.
–Tendency to specialize in production of certain goods, but these were not
   the goods of subsoil derivation to nearly so great an extent as in Western
   Europe. Not iron – not coal.
   –Subsoil development was mostly in finer metals.
–Most Greek crops "just grew" – did not serve to develop – by ceaseless
   drudgery – the Inventive Man.

Land Holding:
   –Importance of small peasant was not nearly so great in Homeric day, as in early
      Western European days.
   –Land held by law, usually tenant farming – number of farmers; large scale
      farm; the ordinary farmer working the land did not have much independence.
   –The development of agriculture – olives, wine – did not contribute to the power
      of small farmers.
   –Introduction of coinage had serious effect on peasant.
      –Small cultivator did not know the value of money and was gyped by
         middleman. Did not get enough to carry him through the winter. Borrowed
         from middleman – high rate of interest. Same rate as charged for risky sea-
         voyage was carried over.
   [In margin on top of page: Public Economy of the Greeks – [Buckle]
   –Was the "monetary revolution" the real explanation of this state of affairs?
      [Arrow from "monetary revolution" to the following:] Introduction of coinage,
      exchange.
   –But it was a gradual revolution; was it not more the failure to adjust himself to
      new conditions? Not enough capital.
   –7th–6th centuries [B.C.], lands coming in to fewer hands – traders.

–Reforms of Solon – freeing of debtors from <u>slavery</u>, forbidding of mortgaging family and self. Philosophy and religion preached the bad effect of riches.
–Thus land went back to small owners – and the citizen who owned a small amount of land was the normal.
  –The decline in their status that had been going on the 7th and 6th centuries was nearly ended in the 5th century [B.C.] – due to philosophy, religion and laws.

<u>Commerce</u>
–Greeks had almost no land communication, at least no land transport, no roads.
–Some individual peddling; some carting of stone for buildings.
  –I.e. mining of heavy <u>base minerals</u> had not brought need for large-scale transportation.
  –Chariots were numerous – for city passengers.
–Grain trade – needed to import to support population.
  –Bringing <u>commerce by sea</u>.
  –Extension of Greek <u>colonies</u> brought need of <u>more ships</u> – outlet for civilization and <u>markets</u> for Greece.
–Kind of commodities traded by Attica.
  –<u>Imported</u> grain; sea-food; some fruits, some wines – <u>luxury articles</u>: ivory, tapestry, timber, copper, tin.
  –<u>Exported</u> figs, wines, fruits, olives, honey, manufactured goods – reworking of imports or original.
Grain trade = imported grain was a very considerable portion of the total consumption – over a half – and due to the importance of grain in their diet, Athens was very dependent on her foreign supplies.
  –Athenian traders had control over the sale of grain – but not over its production or over any industry, i.e. <u>Commercial Capitalism</u> (not Industrial).
  –Improvements in ships-of-trade, till, by 5th century they had large freight vessels of 360 tons displacement – three rows of oars.
    –But only a summer season of sailing, April to October (in both size and length of season, Greeks were not behind 15th century Europe) – four round trips to Egypt in one season.
    –Different standards of weight. But growing importance of Athens and introduction of coinage there – led to a more universal standard of weight and currency.
    –<u>High</u> risk rates and insurance premiums.
    –Small units of entrepreneurship: owner-captain.
    –Large risk led to some <u>partnership</u> of traders who <u>hired</u> ships. – Borrowed capital: came from a <u>special</u> class of traders; never more than one-half of capital but 20–30% interest charged.

–Rise of a money-lending class – rise of some form of banking. Private banking can not be proved before 4th century. Public monies were put into temples, or city treasuries. (Journal of Economic and Business History, Westerman, 1920) [William Linn Westermann (1873–1954) published several books on ancient Greece and Rome. *The Journal of Economic and Business History* was published at Harvard from November 1928 to August 1932. Westermann reviewed William Stearns Davis, *The Influence of Wealth in Imperial Rome* (New York: Macmillan, 1910) in American Historical Review, vol. 16 (1911), pp. 591, 592.]

–Banking seems to have arisen in a sort of pawn-banking. Most private money kept in the sock. [Arrow from first sentence to next one.] Deposits and cheques but no bank rates on bills of exchange.

–Considerable fortunes were being built up – wealthy men, making money from commerce and finance. But fortunes played much less a role in the City-State than in any later civilization – due to slight development of banking. Farming of taxes. State borrowed from temples. Interests of State were different from interests of wealthy men. – Influence of wealthy men was very small – owing to their independence from the state.

–Posion – most important banker of 4th century [B. C.] – but had at most $20,000 [equivalent].

–(1) State didn't have to borrow; a- Tradition of private benevolence to the state. b- State had large income from ownership of property – mines (Laurian), etc. (royalty).

  –Fortunes were made by people of relatively humble origins – by sea-commerce. This class was in a state of flux.

  –Trade in capital did not dominate.

    –The State was not in the position of having to borrow from private sources. c- Tribute being collected as tribute (or defense fund) from the Allied States.

      –Taxes "farmed out" – not corrupted.

      –Because of the lack of necessity of borrowing from monied class – the Greek State was unusually free from domination by the wealthy, trader class and often acted in opposition to their interests.

      –In early 5th century – State asserted its ownership over minerals. – Gave it much wealth and power.

      –State asserted some regulation over trade – as in grain trade; ships licensed to leave Athens only on condition that grain be brought back and put in State warehouses; two-thirds sold locally.

        –To prevent merchants from exploiting their control of a vital trade.

–Were these laws carried out? Probably quite well. – Small area to police.

Summary

(1) –Owing to widespread sea trade – it became profitable and necessary to invest large capital – thus a rise of a banker, capitalist, trader class.

(2) –But the State did not depend on this class, nor did they have unequal influence on the State – Zimmern says trader was looked down on.

(3) –Conflict between <u>natural</u> economic development and the aims and policy of the State.

Industry

–German historical school claimed that <u>commercial</u> capitalism <u>begets industrial</u> capitalism.

–There is <u>more</u> to the coming of industrial capitalism than a "Commercial Revolution."

–Greek experience does not carry out the German argument.

–Greek Industry

(a) <u>More specialization by artisans</u> (contrasted to potter and smithy of Homeric days) – in new lines; more specialization in old lines. Streets set aside for one trade.

(b) More <u>specialization by geographical position</u>. Corinth – horse equipment. Attica – pottery, etc.

(c) <u>Improvement of technique</u> – coming from impetus of quality rise, rather than quantity rise (although in iron – a furnace led to quantity).

–Yet, <u>not yet a "technical revolution."</u> (Zion, circa 1607 16th century machines).

–No windmills, horse wheels, water wheels.

–As in mines; adits, not pumps, to get rid of water.

[In margin: Cf. <u>Agricola</u>, translated by Herbert Hoover]

–This is a large reason why industrial capitalism was relatively so absent.

–Textile industry occupies very small place.

–As compared with rise of industrialism in moyen âge Europe, Greek has:

–Less large units, less capitalism; less invention, less <u>power</u> machinery.

(1) –Metallurgy:

–Iron ore was made into pig iron, then bar iron.

–Work shops were owned and operated by workers, and product sold by them.

–Bucher: <u>household, guild, domestic, factory</u>.

–Idea of <u>stages of advance</u> is largely breaking down – but the terms are still descriptive of institutions.

–Domestic: worker is no longer owner of material he works with.

–Factory is being used to cover all industrial capitalism, not only power-driven machinery.

–<u>Some</u> connection between domestic system and the rise of factories.

–Not much domestic system in Greece.

(2) –Building – luxurious public buildings; low standard of comfort in private buildings. But public buildings could not fit in with industrial capitalism because of lack of private control and planning.

[In margin at top of page: (<u>History of building operations</u> – very important for economic historian – yet little touched on – much needed – even for a small period.)] [Double vertical lines in margin alongside.] [This comment was important to Ostrander. He was writing his paper on Elizabethan building at that moment – intended to be submitted for the Wells Prize – and thinking of it as a thesis subject.]

(3) –Textiles – unimportance of clothing and hangings.

–Simplicity of costume (reaction against rich clothing of Near East – formerly imported) – no hats, little change of fashion and style (all related to the climate; etc).

–All this has its bearing on the relative backwardness of industrial capitalism. Household economy dominated, or at least persisted.

Domestic system did not develop (– usually does so first, in textiles).

[Double vertical lines in margin alongside preceding two sentences]

(4) –Sculpture and masonry – done under <u>guild</u> system. Number of persons in Greek 5th century who were dependent on selling their services into a domestic or factory system – was very small. An economy of <u>small artisans</u>.

(5) –<u>Mining</u> – silver mines of Laurian.

–Greeks had advanced beyond the most primitive in their mining technique – shafts of 250 feet.

–Slave labor – joint-stock companies to furnish capital, and take profits.

–Role of the State was very important (and kept the mining from becoming as important as it became in later common law countries and from being the usual spur to industrial capitalism).

–How the State theorized its ownership of minerals, we don't know; – a <u>regale</u>.

–State took a royalty – regulated the manner of exploitation. I.e. it stepped in to regulation of free enterprise in <u>mining</u> as in <u>wheat</u>, and had its effect on the progress of industrial capitalism.

The Cultural and Social Life, against this Economic (and Political) Background
  –Aristophanes, Euripides, Sophocles, Phideas, Socrates, Thucydides.
    –Aristotle, Plato, Praxiteles lived partly in 5th century.
    –A large total of the great men of all ages lived in that period of great activity
    in Attica.
        –400,000 population in Attica, large proportion slaves, thus the average
        man in Athens would have known by sight more men of genius than
        perhaps ever lived in the world at one time since.
  –Men in all fields, several men who spread their interests over many fields.
    –Aristotle and Plato embraced the whole sphere of knowledge.
  –Sculpture and public buildings – mostly built between 447–431 [B. C.].
What made this cultural development possible?
      –Taine – genius does not rise above from the lowlands, but must be
      surrounded by foothills, and by a few nearby high peaks.
      –What was the background of that culture?
      –While the Athenian appears to us poor – uncomfortable – still, in
      Athens, an economic equilibrium had produced a large surplus, which was
      available for non-economic expenditure.
      –This due to skillful production, to silver, to tribute.
      = a considerable improvement in manufacture of objects, yet without losing
      the skill of personal touch, no machinery.
        –And new technique brought new goods, etc., but the standard of living
        did not rise greatly – a surplus that might have been spent on themselves,
        was spent on public buildings.
      –The human scale of values was different in Greek times, than now.
      –The Greeks distinctly felt that there was something unique in their own
      culture; had a faith in themselves.
  –Owing partly to their ideals, the leisure which improved technique brought
  them was turned to artistic, cultural account.
      –Every Athenian was an art-critic, drama-critic and literary-critic.
      –Ethical emphasis on "the complete life" – rounded, and on "Moderation"
      – i.e. leisure, relaxation, helped on by climate (relaxing and stimulating),
      by economic development curbed by State action.
      –A society of extroverts, objectivity; the Greeks did not live alone, but out
      of doors and in companionship always.
  = Strict limitation on material desires – which is unusual as accompaniment
  of a surplus.
      –Much use of tools, but little use of machinery.
      –Commerce and riches served the State rather than dominated it.
        –Gifts to State – political and ethical background.

–Quick disposition of fortunes.

–Out-door life and country life, in Mediterranean climate, but urban at the same time.

–Great surplus available from technical advance.

–Strength of State control limiting materialism. – Greeks recognized that they were living in a civilization of delicate adjustment – to which materialism was the greatest danger – sense of impending fate.

Athenians sensed they were holding back the ordinary march of economic and other forces.

Roman Empire

–All the economic tendencies at work in 5th century – went on much faster in 4th and 3rd centuries [B.C.]. But the locale of their working-out shifts from Attica and Greece, to Italy and Rome.

–We skip the Hellenistic Period.

–Why did not industrial capitalism ever occupy the same place in the ancient world that it occupies in the "modern world"? [Double vertical lines alongside this question.]

–Period of Caesar 27 B. C., Augustus 138 A. D. Rome of the Empire.

–Rome was little more than Italy until fall of Carthage, 146 B. C., most of imperial expansion took place between then and [blank]

–Economic civilization of 1st century A. D. Rome was very little Roman. Before Punic Wars, industry and commerce were very secondary in ancient world. Only in agriculture, primary and independent. Rome was a good borrower.

–After Carthage – Rome acquired all that civilization; then the period of expansion, absorption of alien cultures, and blood – debasement of the language, then importance of trade and industry, great influence of rich men.

–Population – All figures are guesses.

–Of whole Empire – 300,000,000–400,000,000.

–Montesquieu thought the population of this area was [arrow to amounts on preceding line] and had declined ever since.

Gibbon claimed 120,000,000. Delbrück, 65,000,000.

Beloch states 100,000,000 (in 3rd century [A. D.]).

–Cf. Rome

–Montesquieu thought Rome had 6–7 million.

–Beloch – 700–800,000.

–Cf. Alexandria – 300,000, Antioch, 250,000, Ephesus, Carthage, Lyons – over 100,000.

–Great number of towns with population of 25–50,000.

–Population of Empire was increasing all through 1st, 2nd centuries A. D.

   –<u>Rate of increase</u> fell off seriously, well before 3rd century A. D.

   –Declining population in Greece after 2nd century <u>B.C.</u>

   –Still the increase in the Roman <u>Empire</u>.

Increasing <u>urbanization</u> of the population – especially in Italy – evident in Gaul, Britain, Africa.

   –These cities differ from Athens – had definite city-limits – no longer the city-country mixture.

   –Still, the urban population was not a large proportion of the whole – it was as great as in Europe in 18th century.

–Western Europe area estimated at 50,000,000 population at height of Empire – about the same as the same area in 16th century.

–Urbanization is not <u>made possible</u> by industrial capitalism, but the dominating influence of industrial capitalism seems to make possible the overbearing proportion of urbanization.

–<u>Agriculture</u>

   –In each sphere (products, technique, tenure) there are <u>three</u> well-marked stages-

   –The second stage roughly corresponds to the Empire.

–Metals played a small part in the life of the Romans – metals cost five times as much as now, labor one-fifth as much.

   –Lead must have been less expensive than iron – less fuel needed to work it. Fuel was very scarce – becoming more so.

   –Italy – the heart of the Empire – had few mines.

   –"Mining was a group of tiny hills in a sea of fields and meadows."

–<u>Agricultural Products</u>

   (1) –Italy possessed, as compared with Greece, a particularly fertile farming soil (richer than to-day, richer at first than in Empire).

     –It was not parceled up into small areas by natural barriers – only the single range of Appenines.

     –Wheat, barley, millet, lentils, beans.

     –Wine and olives in much abundance.

     –Wood and charcoal were main fuels – infinitesimal use of coal.

     –Draft animals occupied an increasing place in Roman Empire – as goods exchange increased – meat not a large item of food.

     –Many more articles of food than in Greece.

       –Fruits, vegetables, etc. – more luxury of food, more balanced diet – many dishes on table.

–Lack of coal and iron and meat has important effect on the <u>kind</u> of civilization.

   –We know the effect of coal on civilization.

   –What of effect of tobacco and sugar.

–Increasing emphasis on growth of arable crops.

(2) –But after Punic Wars –middle 2nd century [A. D.] – Rome becomes increasingly dependent on corn and wheat from abroad.

   –Giving way to increasing production of <u>wine</u> and <u>oil</u> (olive) in Italy.

   – Rostovtzeff argues: This struggle for mastery of oil and wine over wheat was <u>cause</u> of Punic Wars.

   –Giving necessity for longer periods of production – more capital – <u>concentration of riches</u> to an extent unheard of in Greece – absentee landlordism.

(3) –Increase of <u>pasture farming</u> – rejection of small tenants – discouraging of olive and wine growing in provinces.

   –Some overproduction of wine and olive oil.

      –Particularly in 3rd century [A. D.].

      –Low prices, depression.

(4) –Thus farms are turned back into grain cultivation – small farms.

   [Single vertical line in margin alongside preceding four items; additional single vertical line alongside the fourth item.]

–<u>Technique</u>

   (1) –Even at very early date the <u>Latins</u> were superior to the Greeks in technique of agriculture.

      –Perhaps unsurpassed again until 18th and 19th centuries.

      –<u>Crop-rotation</u>, surprising yield by scientific cultivation; <u>good plowing</u>;; but they knew little of fertilizer. Use of lime and chalk was slowly introduced from Gaul. Also (even if Italy had much limestone) they had no surface coal to make lime with.

   (2) –No important advances over Greece in arboriculture – wines, olives.

      –But Roman conquest spread <u>their</u> scientific methods of corn [wheat] growing, and <u>also</u> the best methods of arboriculture of Greece, and the best methods of cultivation of any conquered district were spread to all other districts.

      –Raising the standards of farming, of scientific agriculture – throughout the Empire.

   (3) –But a lowering of this high standard during the latter 3rd century – due to exhaustion of land (Liebig), carelessness, forgetfulness – paralleling the revision in products.

      –Effect of intensive cultivation on history of Rome.

–Growing population, need for much wood, as fuel, heat, material – great pressure on fuel resources (coal unknown) – but Italy also exported wood to other parts of the Empire.

–Professsor T. Frank, argues that the deforestation of Italian uplands was the cause of the exhaustion of the soil in the plains.

   –Natural irrigation, soil renewal, moisture supply – ended.

   –Dried up in summer – wheat production no longer possible – turning to olives and wine.

–Professor Rostovtzeff – argues that this shift was due to economic interests; it being more profitable to raise olives and wine than corn – conflict of interests.

   –Why did Italy then go back to corn growing – how could it?

Tenure

–Development was away from small holding to large holding – the villa civilization.

(1) –There was not real ownership – but a divided ownership. Land was "owned" and inherited in the family. But there was an Overlord to whom certain obligations were owed – i.e. a feudal system. [Arrow from "certain obligations" to:] –portion of produce; dowry for Lord's daughter.

  –It may be that the position of the peasants was enlarged in the Etruscan period in order to strengthen the Etruscan rule.

   –So that by 3rd and 2nd century B. C. the position of the peasant was one of individual ownership, little use of slaves; agriculture the respectable occupation.

(2) –But after Punic Wars, in 2nd, 1st B. C., 1st A. D. [centuries], the peasant seemed to be forced off the land. Growth of pasture farming and of arboriculture both weakened the position of the small tenant.

  –Both these new forms of cultivation were most economically carried on in large units.

–Effect of the Wars? – peasants were used as soldiers – were given new lands in conquered provinces; but did the soldiers like to go back to farming?

–Or effect of the introduction of a money economy?

  –Ignorance of peasants in dealing with middleman?

  –Or need for large capital to carry on the new forms of cultivation and crops.

–<u>Villa system</u> – work done by slaves for a new owner – who owns the land used in this system? – Sometimes an old over-lord.
  –More usually, a new man from a city, who had made his money elsewhere, wanted to invest it for steady profits.
  –The old tenants drifted to the cities, to form the new proletariat.
  –Not self-sufficient for the usual purpose.
  –Taken charge of by a foreman – whose only interest was to make as large a profit as possible.
    –Tendency was to reject the small farmer from the lands.
    –Tendency was away from self-sufficiency.
      –Although a great deal of small-scale production – decentralized production.

Land tenure in four provinces:
  –Sicily-when conquered, Italy used it as a granary, collected grain as a <u>tribute – eased balance of payments</u>.
  –Kept the island in a primitive state.
–Asia Minor-had had a very archaic land system.
  –Monarch had theoretical right to most of the land – but overlords had actual right – paid monarch a revenue. Temple lands, free cities [exempt].
  –Romans "farmed out" the taxation on these overlords.
    –Groups of traders farmed the taxes – foreclosed often.
    –Thus these traders came into possession of large estates. Breaking down of feudalism.
    –Incomes came back to Rome to their owners – eased balance of payments.
  –Carthage-much land confiscated by Roman State.
    –Gracchii gave these lands to the landless proletariat of Rome – who were clamoring for land.
      –But Italians did not want to leave Italy – they sold their claims to tax-free lands to traders – who made a few large estates.
  –Egypt – Romans inherited a <u>royal business enterprise</u> – a State monopoly. Rome kept control of this land.
  –Increasing bourgeois control of land – owned by city rentiers – for income.
  –Very difficult and costly long distance land transport – but locally, many goods exchanged.
  –Bourgeoisie got their large incomes from commerce and land-holding, not industry.

–In late 2nd century [A. D.] Italian villa system broke down – overproduction of wine and olive oil – crisis.

–Deflation of money throughout this period.

–Bourgeois were getting more and more in debt to the Emperors – who were getting more land – they hired it out to small leaseholders.

–Decline of scientific agricultural technique.

–Two fortunes were estimated at 20 million dollars – the largest – (very different from Greece – and from Elizabethan times – 2 million largest).

    –Example: Trimalchio – nouveau riche – Steward of rich man, inherited his money – invested it: in wholesale wine market, in lands, in trade, in banking. – i.e. not at all in industrial capitalism.

Towns and Cities

–Wealthy city merchants developed refined and very comfortable lives – a luxury unparalleled until very recent times.

    –Surplus to support city life – due to rich soil, and tribute, and freedom of action of traders.

    –Cities got most of this surplus – spent on private comfort, or public monuments.

    –Even in Augustan age (turn of century 1st to 2nd [A.D.]) the cities were being built as monuments to luxury and comfort.

        –Huge public works: aqueducts, arenas.

        –Sport carried on in professional manner.

        –Art galleries – temples (sorry imitation of Greeks).

        –Society reluctant to forego the forms of culture – but itself unable to create it. [Single vertical line in margin alongside these two lines.]

        –Straightened streets – Sombart uses this to illustrate the importance of standardization, by which he meant industrialism. [In margin at top of page: Standardization does not bring about industrial capitalism.]

        –Connection of the straight line and standardization [led] to decline of art (Cezanne: "Not a straight line in nature").

        –Main element in the city became the rich man's home – luxurious – [but] little glass. [In margin at top of page: Humphrey Clinker Smallet]

        –Apartment houses like modern ones.

        –Bathing arrangements [as at Bath, England] unparallel[ed] until a century ago – private baths in houses, lavish public baths.

–Heating – hot room – hot water led through pipes – giving a continuous, even, heat.
–Luxury of food and garment.
  –Some attempts at refrigeration (snow).
  –Wonderful furniture.
  –But no radical change in clothing from Greek – textile industry in a minor place.
  –Much collecting of art – especially Athenian.
    –Sophistry, Philistinism.
  –Heavy rents.
–Brilliant exterior of cities concealed the fact that the majority of the population were very poor. However their homes and habits of life have not come down to us – not substantial in any way – no tombstones, houses, art pieces, etc.
  –<u>Many</u> domestic servants (cheap labor and expensive machinery – if any).
  –Many transport workers, artisans, traders, etc.
–Workmen were <u>more</u> badly off than today.
  –But they did not require much – few clothes, little food.
    –Government gave a <u>dole</u> – (bread, grains, etc.) – plus many free public works.
    –Did <u>not</u> have one-tenth of the workers' income in 1916 – T. Frank.
      –Are really <u>incomparable</u> items, was more than that any way.
–Rome- was like Washington – and also other cities, i.e. income derived from outside the city – little industry inside it.
  –A top-heavy structure, tribute pouring in to form basis of luxurious city life.
  –Overproduction of wine and olives brought crisis.
  –Decline of the city incomes, decline of the city.

<u>Commerce</u>
  –Principal Roman contributions were in <u>land transportation</u>.
    –Roads – in 18th century, Diderot's time, roads in Europe were more backward than in Roman times.
    –Followed the terrain – through hills, over valleys.
    –Layers of cement.
    –Built at great cost. (Appian Way, $350,000 per mile) – borne by central government – but side road cost borne by cities.

–Rome to Carthage (6000 miles around Mediterranean Sea). [circa 3000 miles at most; must be km.]

–100 miles a day – change of horses.

–Reflection of need to carry commodities and passengers.

   –But the military importance was probably greater in Roman times (Roads led to frontier).

–Little attempt to improve wagons and carts.

   —River and canal traffic – several attempts at river deepening – Tiber (Ostia to Rome) ([by]Nero).

   –Canals connected Rhine and Meuse, Rhone and Moselle.

   –Not much facility in Italy for intra-regional river transport; but a great deal in Gaul and Rhineland.

–Sea-Traffic – regular yearly trade with China.

   –Lack of harbors in Italy – artificial harbors.

   –Lack of compass hindered.

   – [blank]

   –Little passenger travel – had to carry own food.

   –Little precision and schedule of sailings, Romans were not artists in seamanship.

   –No advances in speed of sea travel.

   –Much importation into Italy – little exportation.

   –Balance made up by tribute – and specie.

   –Drain of specie to India and China – new mining but inevitable deflation – increasing trade.

      –Made up by inflation, by currency debasement.

      –Value of gold in terms of silver rose.

      –Increasing value of money added to the crisis of falling prices of olives and wine through overproduction.

–Commercial Capitalism, but not yet Industrial Capitalism.

   –According to Rostovtzeff.

–Other historians dispute this – admit the existence of flourishing sea trade in luxuries but deny any very great commerce in necessities of life.

   –Nef agrees with them – that trade in bulky goods was mainly local. Aside from wheat imports into Italy – most commodities were produced locally in the colonies – great amount of local trade.

      –Elaborate structure for financing commerce (unlike Greek conditions).

      –Large warehouses: – paper transactions in goods.

–Retail shops – although still many artisan-shops and peddlers; and products of domestic servants – department stores were still absent.
   –Major portion of trade carried on by people who were connected in some manner of financial organization.
      –Trade and financing was well split-up though our preoccupation with seeking to find the exact model of joint-stock companies usually blinds us to the fact.
   –No elaborate joint-stock banking – but groups of men organized into partnerships for banking.
      –Transfer of money by paper offsetting lending, some discounting – no credit structure.
   –No economic science.

Summary of Commerce

–Absurd to speak of Roman Empire as a household economy – in spite of the place of the domestic servant in production. It did not dominate.
   –Elaborate trade in goods – but little extensive commerce in heavy, bulky goods.
   –Much banking – but not yet any extensive credit structure.
   [Single vertical line in margin plus braced markings pointing to preceding two points, with comment, "Seem to be characteristics of modern industrial capitalism."]

Industry – Factory existed but did not dominate.
   –Increasing of State ownership in mining – less industrial capitalism.
   –Industrial capitalism in Roman Empire was no further advanced than in Europe in middle 18th century.
   –Mining and manufacturing are both covered by industrial capitalism.
   [In margin at top of page: Bucher – believe[s] that development must be through a set course – Household, Guild, Domestic, Factory.]
   Domestic system was backward – for this reason the Germans have said there was no factory economy.
      –Building – must have been very important-must have had a good deal of industrial capitalism.
      –Mining – no coal or iron – thus it did not have the same relative importance it came to have later on.
         –State controlled them greatly – and mining towns.
         –Minerals were the property of the State.
            –Republic had not claimed those minerals in a province which were found after the conquering of the province.

–But under Empire – a larger claim made by the State.

–As to extraction of such minerals – by private companies – State puts up many regulations and restrictions – and State came to extract them itself.

–State restrictions did not cause lack of industrial capitalism, but the lack of industrial capitalism was due to lack of the kind of minerals which give rise to it.

–Great fortunes did not seem to originate in mining or manufacturing – though large fortunes were invested in them.

–No patents or trade marks. Rostovtzeff says that lack of patent law, plus State policy in interests of wine and cotton growers – prove that manufacturing had not yet any political influence.

–Large capitalistic industries did exist, but they did not dominate. Forces tending to large-scale industry under private control were present. –Importance of State enterprise – reducing the sphere of private enterprise.

Cultural Aspects

–In Greece – Beauty and Creation – la gloire glory.

In Rome – Comfort, Standardization, [blank] glamour.

–Two ideals of civilization: some majesty of government in Rome – but not the same as in Greece.

–Sculpture in Rome – lack of originality, of composition – imitation.

–Greek sculpture was all composition, all creativeness, all originality.

–Important contributions to materials and building construction.

–Feeling of inferiority in art – collections of Greek art.

–Yet, a different civilization, and no envy of Greek.

–Self-satisfaction.

–Originality in historical satire and literature.

–Literature is always associated with aging of a civilization.

–Diderot – anticipated Spengler.

–Lucien and Juvenal – art no longer possible – thus a bitterness in place of pride of achievement.

–Thus a decline in literature after 2nd century [A.D.].

–Forgetting of old masters – "the load of a long artistic and literary past is a very heavy one to bear." (Nef)

–Does modern subjectivism give literature an indefinite future?

–Or is subjectivism a mere loss of disciplinary form – i.e. decline?

–As argued by M. Benda-Belphiégor [?] and Irving Babbitt.

–When art goes, civilization goes. (Cf. F. L. Wright)

–Romans had achieved a great measure of political stability by beginning of 4th century [A. D.]. – No danger of <u>war</u>. [Alongside in margin: Unlike our condition to-day.]
–Romans had more leisure than Greeks (5th century [B.C.]).
   –Great surplus – but still no original art – i.e. art is the result of a <u>balance in life</u>.
–Riches were general – and more sought after.
   –Rich men had predominant place in society, and great influence on government.
      –Is art possible where artist is not the chief figure in the civilization? Can artist share his position of prominence with the financial magnate? – he did not have to in Greece. Proxitiles and Hericles equal.
–What is the explanation of the <u>decline</u>?
   (1) Is it the <u>failure of industrialism to develop</u>? (Can you ever find <u>one</u> cause of decline?)
      (a) Bucher: Roman economy failed to emerge from <u>household</u> economy – a statement of fact – wrong assumption.
      (b) Frank: Slave labor gave cheap labor no incentives.
         –Rostovtzeff points out that period of <u>greatest</u> progress of industrial capitalism was Hellenistic period of greatest slavery. – Nef: Slaves due to lack of industrial capitalism.
      (c) Rostovtzeff: <u>State playing too large a role</u> (influence of his expulsion from Russia?). [Emphasis mark in margin.]
      (d) Fabvre (Geographic Influence on History) – bearing of overproduction of olives and wines on the problem. Underdevelopment of minerals. – Both due to geographical features – warm climate, absence of natural resources (coal, located in one place – necessity of transportation).
         –Cold in Gaul led to a more elaborate industrial capitalism – need for textiles, thus need for large capital, factories.
      –State interference is itself a function of almost every other force in the State (just as <u>every</u> historical development is a function of every other).
      –But influences of geographical conditions are fixed (natural resources and climate).

(2) Otto Lusk – <u>Depopulation and race–suicide</u>.

–Concentration in cities leads to sterility of urban population.

–But Roman Empire did not have any great proportion of its population living in cities.

  –In 18th century we perhaps had an equal proportion of our population in cities as in Roman days.

  –But instead of depopulation – we had largest growth of population ever known.

  –Evidence of a taller race (i.e. a stronger?).

(3) <u>Exhaustion of the soil</u> – Liebig and Simpkovitch.

–No manure; but it would have affected only grain growing – not olive and wine growing.

–And would not have applied to colonies.

–Usher claims the Romans did <u>not</u> exhaust the chemical element of the soil – what Simpkovitch said.

–This theory is also a depopulation theory – explaining why population fell – no subsistence.

–Frank might explain exhaustion as due to <u>deforestation</u> – again it would apply only to Italy.

–Huntington – 100 year cycle of favorable weather 450–250 B. C. [sic].

  –Then a long cycle of unfavorable wealth – several centuries.

  –But what proof? – only applies to Italy (?).

(4) <u>Political causes</u>

Gibbon: Christianity weakened the peoples, so that barbarians conquered.

  –Tied up with 18th century agnosticism. Breakdown of religion always liberated peoples. But increasing dominance of religion spelled doom to a people. Voltaire.

  –How explain progress of Europe 900–1500 A. D. when Christianity was supreme.

  –Nef: Christianity may be a <u>partial</u> cause.

(5) <u>Rostovtzeff</u>: <u>Supremacy of the state's</u> interests over those of the individual citizens.

–Westermann takes this view too.

–<u>Bourgeoisie made a caste</u>, no longer recruited from below, no more spirit of enterprise.

–State insisting on enterprise catering to <u>its</u> purposes – and carrying on enterprise on its own – both also ended spirit of enterprise.

–State more and more levying <u>uncollectible taxes</u> – on proletariat and farmers.

–Tax farmers themselves <u>responsible</u> – so that wealth was being turned over by rich to the State.

(6) Nef: <u>Danger of excess production</u> of unbalanced nature; <u>danger of loss of culture</u>; State control does not seem to have altered things much. The causes of decline were there anyhow.

<u>Medieval Europe</u>

–A much longer period than Gothic Period.

–Often used to cover period from 400 to 1500.

–Nef uses it to cover period from 1000 to 1500.

  –For period from 500 to 1000 was <u>not</u> one of economic development – probably reversion.

  –I.e. "Dark Ages" (400–1000), and "Medieval Period" (1000–1500), and "Gothic" (1100–1300).

–Nef will consider this Gothic period, and thus Northern France, although that was not the region of greatest economic development; which was North Italy and Netherlands.

–Northern France offers most typical example of a feudal society at late stage of development.

–"Renaissance" 1300–1550 – <u>Belgium, Bavaria, North Italy</u> – all small city-states.

  –Great changes in economic organization

–Whatever our definition of the beginning of the Middle Ages, they come to an end in middle of 16th century.

  – A combination of causes leading to the birth and growth of <u>industrialism</u> (i.e. in its sense as <u>dominating</u>). But we <u>must</u> pay much attention to Medieval society, for in it lie the roots of all those causes whose simultaneous occurrence brought industrialism; <u>also</u>, the heritage of the Medieval period is an integral part of <u>our</u> cultural fabric; and also, there were <u>contrary developments</u> which made the birth of industrialism a mighty struggle.

  –Industrialism in Great Britain was a long, slow process, with its roots in the 16th century and extending to end of 19th century.

Industrialism in Germany came very suddenly and rapidly – 60 years. France has <u>hardly</u> yet become industrialized.

–Apart from late 18th, early 19th century Germany, and France – great cultural development has usually been associated with industrial <u>activity</u>.

<u>French Gothic Period</u>

–Separation of Western from Byzantine civilization and from Russian civilization; Western <u>core</u>, borders on North Sea and Channel; boundaries: Pyrenees, and line of Turkish conquest (between Vienna and Budapest).

<u>Dark Ages</u> – how much retrogression? When and where did the <u>origins</u> of Medieval civilization come?

<u>Geography of the Western Core</u> (around the borders of North Sea)

–Much more <u>even climate</u> than in New York or Chicago – small range of fluctuation of summer and winter temperatures.

–Much moisture and cloudiness. Four seasons, instead of the <u>six months</u> each of winter and summer of Mediterranean lands.

–Many <u>rivers</u>, navigable – in contrast to Italy and Greece.

–Well stocked with mineral wealth – especially <u>iron and coal</u>.

–Abundance of timber; rolling, pleasing, varied countryside.

–<u>Machine civilization of Western Europe a product of natural resources, of environment, not of the spirit of the people</u>.

–<u>Soil is the natural mother of a culture, but subsoil is the natural matter of science and industry</u>.

[Double vertical line in margin alongside the first underlined sentence; single, alongside the second.]

"Dark Ages"–Split over this period among historians.

–Pirenne, Halphen, Stephenson vs. Dopsch, Palzelt.

–Shrinkage of population everywhere – especially in cities and towns.

    –Rome 500,000 in 2nd century, 50,000 in 6th century.

    –Thus the town culture decays, artisans and trade go.

    –The towns become more fortified places – Burg [German], Bourg [French] – usually given to Bishops and the Church.

    –Roads decay; reversion to barter economy, no money.

    –Luxury and comfort decline – also rich bourgeoisie goes.

–All signs of industrial capitalism disappear – standardization goes.

–Rural communities less affected – only artisans are to fill rural needs.

–Growth of feudalism – both Count and Bishop have a <u>right</u> to certain <u>proportion</u> of crops – but give nothing in return – thus no trade in towns.

–No trading class – thus no city life.

–Decline in skill of agriculture, decline in land under cultivation.

–Tendency for end of free-farmers, who turn into cultivators or serfs. Land becomes inherited – passes into overlordship of a noble or of Church (probably one-third of all).

–Manorial system – divides ownership by Lord and tenants.

–Franc alleu (freehold, in a way) remnants of old system. Outside the system – no overlordship.

–More common in South France and Italy – less need for protection.

–These changes take place constantly from 3rd century on.

–But unequally; e.g. never great retrogression in Po Valley.

–There was retrogression; but due to what, and how long? [In margin: Boissonnade]

Catholic historians incline to view of a sudden end. Decline, but a coup de grace given by barbarians.

–Very little known of this period. Most of these men take their inspiration from accounts of Gregory of Tours.

–Though these were eye-witness accounts – somewhat in the nature of atrocity stories; can not be trusted too far.

–Decline was going on even before Barbaric invasion and at a good rate.

–As for political institutions – the Barbarians used much of what was there – no break with tradition. [In margin: Fustil de Coulanges]

–But, Dopsch and Pirenne point out that commercial life did not end with Barbarian invention [sic: invasion], but continued in some importance through Merovingian invasion.

–Evidence of commerce from Gaul to Marseilles, from Marseilles to the East.

–Pirenne has a rival coup de grace theory re the Mohammedan conquest – this ended the Roman freedom of the Mediterranean – ended trade with the East.

–Disappearance of coins in this period.

–Nef does not go all the way with Pirenne, re the decay of town life. But he does think the lowest point was reached in Carolingian time.

–Dopsch finds German tribes had some industrial life of their own – asserts a renaissance of industry and commerce came about in Carolingian times. Argument mixed up with nationalism – Germans anxious to prove the purely Aryan origin of modern civilization.

–Pirenne asserts that the industrial revival came at a later time, as a result of contacts with the East.

–Nef admits influence of contact with East, but also recognizes the original, Western character of much culture.

    –But he sees <u>possibility</u> of decline right up to 1000 [A. D.], nothing proved either way. But certain advance after 1000.

–Trade routes from East to Venice, over Alps; to Marseilles and up Rhone valley; through Russia, down Baltic – lasting all through 11th, 12th, 13th centuries.

–Growing trade between growing towns on a local scale in Western core – more local trade, much water traffic.

–Pirenne claims a growth in population – leading to <u>famine</u>, trades grew out of such dire necessity.

–Why such a growth of population? – Pirenne does not answer.

–But trade in grain due to famine would have been a <u>sporadic</u> trade.

–Necessity of a <u>continuous</u> trade, to build up the <u>fau</u>burgs around the bourgs. But grain trade was carried on by husbandmen, who were traders only in part.

–Development of early art Renaissance <u>from the soil</u> of Western Core is explained in terms of <u>history</u> (intellectual) and <u>natural resources</u>.

    –Letharby: – Romanesque architecture is essentially a product of the East, coming by way of Venice.

    –Learning – a renaissance in (11th and) <u>12th centuries</u> – explained by contact with East – through <u>Venice</u> and <u>Spain</u>.

    –Naturally, a leaning on the past; but also a new, original, indigenous creation.

    –Marked revival in 10th and 11th centuries – in <u>art, learning, economics</u> – becoming swifter in 12th and 13th.

    –Going back to Classical culture, but via the East, rather than via the culture that had been on this same soil.

    –Contacts with Near East – where economic development had not receded, but progressed, during Dark Ages.

    –But the creative impulse of the Gothic North.

    –Freshness of outlook combined with rich heritage.

<u>The Gothic Period</u> – Period of great <u>unity</u>.

    –The <u>same</u> problems of existence; the single faith of the Catholic Church; no nationalism; all compartments of arts, science, and learning, and economics were brought together.

–<u>Population</u>: 1100–1300 – still on uncertain ground – studied best by poll taxes and hearth taxes.

1328, hearths in France counted: 20–22 million people (Colville)

1577, 20 million population (Black Death)

1700, 23 million population. Increased rapidly <u>only</u> in last two of six centuries.

   –Slowest growth of any State in Europe. 100% increase in six centuries – (England 600%).

   –Was population increasing or decreasing during 10–12th centuries?

   –During High Renaissance France's population grew very rapidly.

      –<u>Is this typical of Northern Europe? Yes.</u> [Arrow from "grew" to:] economic activity.

   –Unsafe to say that German population was increasing <u>faster</u> than French – but it probably was about the same.

   –England and Wales. Domesday Survey (1087), Poll Tax (1377), Ashley guessed 1,500,000. [Arrow pointing to Domesday Survey]

      –Poll tax a good standard. <u>1377</u>, Chalmers, 2,300,000, Rogers, 2,500,000, Beloch, 2,600,000.

      –Increase of 1,000,000 in three centuries. But the <u>Black Death</u> came in <u>1348–50</u>.

   –How can we estimate the size of the population of England at end of 13th century? Most people estimate the size of the diminution due to Black Death too high. (Size of Black Death – Doctor's thesis).

   –Seebohm: states that one-half of <u>population</u> died, i.e. population of England in 1340 5,000,000. But little evidence of enough cultivation to support that number.

      –After a <u>huge</u> diminution of population it tends to recuperate very rapidly, then to slow up. But we find that it did not recuperate very rapidly.

   –Rogers: estimates population of 1340 to be nearly as high as 1377 – was never right.

   –Nef guesses 3,000,000.

Distribution of population – between cities and villages.

   –Pirenne – abstracting burgs and episcopal towns – the <u>towns</u> or cities were trading centers dependent on the surplus of the surrounding country.

   –Villages, fiefs, seigneuries – were self-sufficient.

   –Size of the Medieval town – only <u>Paris</u> was very large.

      1200: 100,000 population; 1300: 200,000 population; 1328: 240,000

   –Probably too large, but in every way this was an exception.

–Not another place in Europe (except for North Italy) had a population over 50,000.

–Florence, Venice, Milan, may have been over 50,000.

–What was the size of the average town?

  –As French cathedral towns in valley of Seine and its tributaries not one had a population of over 25,000 people

  –Probably, a better guess would be 5,000–15,000.

    –Rouen in 1325 (approximately) had 14,000 – was larger than most.

    –Flemish towns – Ypres, 12,000.

    –Germanic towns: Nurembourg and Kölm [Cologne] larger – 20,000.

    –England – London only city to have over 15,000 people – 1340 – 35,000.

      –Fewer towns than on more developed continent.

  –Typical town of the period: – on the continent, 2,000–15,000. In England, 2,000–6,000.

–Paris: in a cup-shaped valley. Seine winds through it.

  –Very fertile country – good quality. Ile de France.

  –But by vast network of rivers flowing into the Seine, it taps all the rest of France.

–Except for Paris: – no tendency for growth of metropolis, for one city to grow at the expense of another. Almost all towns had a similar size.

–Communal development very possible – layout of all much the same. Economic development very similar.

–Proportion of population in towns – in France in 1200, about one-tenth of population in towns.

  –Living in villages, seeing few people (Tawney, Coulton) but coming to see more people – going to towns.

  –Even meeting foreigners. (Cf. "Crowley" – Gros).

  –Peasant never again so important – was not very connected with outside world, but increasingly so – important change.

Agriculture: – growth of population could only have been possible with an increase in the productivity of the land – (a) Due to increase of land under cultivation (reclamation, drainage, deforestation). (b) Improved methods.

  –Much of reclaimed land had been farmed formerly by Romans.

  –France was so fertile that it fed its larger population without bringing timber shortage: forests adequate 1300.

    –Well stocked to begin with.

  –Scarcity of heavy fuel-consuming industry to use up forests.

–Backwardness in industries of glass, iron, salt, etc.

–Though this was a period of great economic change – these wood-consuming industries did not come yet.

–Improved <u>technical</u> knowledge of cultivation.

–Improvements in land tenure – so that peasant applied himself more to cultivation.

–Increase of <u>variety</u> of commodities; <u>vegetables</u>.

    –More kinds of animals raised and consumed.

      –More red meat eaten. More varieties of fowl.

      –Increase in fish consumption – fishermen.

    –Introduction of flax and hemp, saffron, teazle.

      –Elaborate <u>cloth</u> industry growing up in North France, Flanders and West Europe as a whole.

      –No tobacco, coffee, little sugar.

–France so fertile, that each village could produce a wide variety of products – "spots of fertility." North France more fertile.

–Wheat – very little capital needed – but <u>continued</u> application to the job necessary (different from Mediterranean arboriculture – bringing different methods of peasant control and working.

–Unimportance of <u>mining</u>.

–<u>Other countries</u> were less fertile, and could not absorb or provide for increased population as easily as France.

    –Pressure on land supply in Italy, Flanders, Germany.

    –Need of irrigation, need of land reclamation.

Land Tenure – <u>end of 11th century</u>. North France, England.

    –All cultivatable land owned by one or another Manor, fief, or seigneurie; the noble or abbeys who owned it – owed allegiance to some overlord.

      –Much land held by the Church.

      –Other land held outright by the Royal House.

      –Some holdings of land outside the feudal system (nulle terre sans seigneur [no land without a lord]) – Franc-Alleu – a lord without a sovereign.

    –What was the economic system <u>within</u> the Manor. It was the same whether land owned by Church, by King, by free lord, or by seigneur.

      –Theoretical plan of a Manor (not good). [Diagram, within text-of-notes area, showing:]

        –Demesne was originally only the Lord's house.

        –Open field in strips.

        –Three fields, two cultivated, one barren.

        –Village street with houses.

–Villagers owned land by strips – one or one-half acre.

–Tenants' holdings called <u>Virgates</u> – thirty acres, ten in each field, or Half-Virgates, 15 acres – also smaller.

–Cultivation done in common – steward in charge with bailiff under him – and foreman.

–This system did not apply to any of Europe but North France and England.

–Three fields not strictly true; pasturage often mixed in with cultivation.

–Villagers lived in a group. Land worked in common. Villagers in some form of servitude – had right to take timber for fuel or building, stone, marl, etc.

–Domestic servants for Lord's demesne.

–Villeins – tenants – (servile) – no selling his land; men bound to soil. Produce-rent – proportionate.

–Freemen – no servitude – services commuted – increasing in 12th and 13th centuries.

–Economy of the Manor – self-sufficient.

–Food, beer (made at manorial brewery), sheep furnished clothing.

–Some division of labor – as <u>smith[y]</u>, one of first.

–Very little outside contact; except for trade in <u>salt, grinding stones, iron</u>.

   –France had abundant iron, in small scatterings.

One of the great changes of the 12th and 13th centuries was the breakdown of this self-sufficiency – it was not sudden, had its roots in 11th century.

–12th and 13th century: <u>Changes affecting the Manor</u>: growth in population, rise of towns, <u>rise of prices, metallic currency</u>.

–Breaking down its outward aspect, the terms on which land was held, peasant status.

   –<u>Growth of population</u>: <u>Growth of land under cultivation</u>.

      –Impossible to increase the <u>number</u> of manors – all land distributed; thus the expansion came with<u>in</u> the old manor.

      –Some of new population went to towns, rest remained in the country.

         –Who could be hired to cultivate the Lord's demesne.

         –But usually settled on the Manor, on new lands, and in a new form of servitude.

         –No more need for services in kind to Lord.

         –He was glad to rent out this new land on a "freehold" basis, getting <u>money</u> rent.

   –But, with increased hired servants working the Lord's demesne – he needed less services from serfs – thus they could become free, by commutation of rent by money payment.

Growth of Towns:
  –Serf could go to town, make payment to lord and become free (an example to serfs or the farmer – to pay and become free).
  –Furnished a market for surplus crops – were not self-sufficient, exchange of crops and manufactured goods.
  –Growth of artisans in towns – more serfs coming in, at first to supply needs of townspeople, but then to furnish a surplus of goods to exchange with surplus of crops.
  –Also furnished a market for exchange of crops – so that peasant became more specialized.
  –Old Lords were not good business men, were bought out increasingly.
    –Tenants paid money instead of goods – sold the goods themselves; lords did not have to carry on large-scale sales of produce.
  –Increase of metallic currency – money economy – worked in direction of emancipation of serf.
  –Rise of prices – 1300–1500 a period of stable prices, 1500–1600 rapid rise. In favor of serf.
    –In a sense a repetition of the introduction of money in Greece – but that worked to disadvantage of peasant.
  –Why did not the same thing happen in Middle Ages?
    –Peasants did not get into debt, were not confused by money.
    –But the change was not paralleled by a change in the kind of cultivation from corn to olives and wine.
    –Peasant kept on raising corn.
    –Where there was a change in crop, a change to mining, etc. – the small free owner was wiped out.

  Effects on Fiefs of these changes in 12th and 13th centuries.
    –Self-sufficiency broken down – increasing exchange of goods with towns – still not carried to any modern extent – so that necessities were still provided by the manor.
    –Outward aspect changed – outlying farmhouses built – more houses – still the village the center of life.
    –Increasing specialization of labor – more artisans in village.
    –Coal out-croppings begin to be used, over Europe.
    –Social side of Manor becomes more complex, more people, new modes of life.

Land Tenure – beginning of 14th century

England	France
(1) Servile tenure	(1) Tenure servile

(2) (Free) Tenure

   –Free holder

   –Customary tenants

   –Copyholders

   –Tenants at will

(3) Leasehold tenure

(2) Tenure roturière

   –Censitaries (bail à cens) [freeholder]

   –Holders under: bail à emphytiose

   –Holders under: bail à champart

   –Métayers

   –Fermiers

(3) Bail à rent

–Not all synonymous terms – especially [#2] is nearly the same, but subdivisions are different.

–General tendency was away from #1 into #2.

England:

   Free holds not very numerous until mid 16th century – held land by charter – inherited land – fixed annual rent.

     –Value of land rising, deflation [sic: inflation] relieved from payment.

     –Precarial [free] – obligations to work some days for lord – [words indecipherable] – commuted their obligations.

     –Owed annual rent to Lord. How did they become free men.

   –Rise of prices brought damage to landlord – impetus to get rid of other men.

   –Free hold – passed on from father to son.

   –Censitare – in France, were not owners of land, but were partners in ownership of land – paid a cens, or censive to overlord – owed payment also when land changed hands (like English copyholder's fine) – [arrow from "land" prior to "changed hands" to:] called lods et rentes.

     –Tended to approach the out and out freeholder – comes to be regarded as outside the manor.

     –Cens can not be put on cens – by law.

     –But rent-leasing got around this.

     –Had to give corvées – services – had rights to common holdings.

     –Subsoil rights? Right to minerals in England was whittled away from freeholder – placed in hands of Lord. – But in France – belonged to the Crown.

   –Position of small holder was being strengthened all through this period.

   –Bail à emphytiose – almost a lease (not very different from bail à cens) – many varieties of land holding – especially in Brittany.

   –French overlord rented out land under bail à champart – different from feudal system – lord gets a fixed proportion of produce.

     –Metayage, Fermage, lord contributes share of capital, still gets fixed proportion of produce – sometimes get money proportion.

–Lords shared in increase in value of land and produce (unlike early feudal system).

–Land was inherited under these last three systems.

–In England land "enclosed," villages and manor system ended – land rented out to capitalist farmer.

–Agricultural wage earners – as a new class appear – not sharply differentiated from other peasants.

[End of explanation of land tenure comparison]

Effects of all these changes on the material welfare of peasant – marked improvement – and in social status.

–Improved productivity – good share went to peasant.

–Gradually rising wages 1100 – 1450 – for those who earned them.

–Black Death (1350) visits country districts as well as urban – scarcity of labor.

–Status improved – left serfdom, became freemen.

–But this was not so very important as we think.

–Yeomanry came to be considered indispensable to the nation – for war, for food. – Cf. Physiocratic doctrines.

–Increase in cleanliness, in education.

–Catholic School of "The Golden Age of the Peasant."

  –Coulton opposes this; but admits some rise of his position. [Arrow to "admits" from] (prejudice vs. Catholics).

  –600 word vocabulary; cruel, clean?

  –Peasant was not better off than today – but may not have been as badly off as Coulton pictures.

Town Life – 12th and 13th centuries

  Commercial activity

    –Depended on immediate countryside for supplies.

    –Division of labor among artisans.

    –Geographic specialization – importing much from country.

      –Manufacturing more and more to export to country.

    –Sea towns had monopoly on fish.

    –Towns exerted efforts to get industries within the towns – to make it impossible to set up industry outside.

      –But they did not wholly succeed.

        –Village artisans (smithy, lime, etc.).

        –Royal establishments – not centered in towns.

      –Frequent struggles between towns and abbeys.

    –Peculiar aspects of Northern France led to these self-centered towns – dependent on the immediate neighborhood.

–Great fertility and variety of products.

–No need to trade far from town.

Industrial activity

–But some <u>trade on a wide-spread scale</u> – as <u>subsoil products</u>.

  –Dependent on value in relation to bulk, i.e. <u>tin</u> more traded in than iron (also iron more widely found).

  –<u>Tin; calamine; iron</u> in England, not France. <u>Salt, alum</u> (from Near East, also some local).

–As <u>luxury articles</u> – spices from East (came in through Italy), etc.

–As <u>textiles</u> –

–Made in towns – shift away from silk to wool.

–Early tendency for textiles to concentrate in certain parts of Europe. Flanders, North Italy.

  –This concentration already apparent in 13th century.

    –Why did not England have this textile trade?

      –England was a backwater country – industrially undeveloped.

  –Major portion of raw material came from English.

  –Why manufacturing in North Italy? – important market.

    –Proximity to alum – natural skill in textiles, coming from skill and technique of the East.

  –Products of Flemish and Italian clothes merchants were traded in at much distance from origins – traded in even in the East.

  –Typical town of this period (12th and 13th centuries) did not make more cloth than necessary for its own account.

    –Cloth sold to Church, and high people – not so much to common people.

    –Most cities had to import cloth.

    –Only the <u>finest</u> cloth had an international market.

    –Commoner cloth made in each town.

  –Transportation: by sea, river, land.

    –To end of 13th century traffic by land and river was more important in Northern Europe – as shown by the fairs of Champagne – much traffic across Alps.

    –Barges poled, or pulled by men or horses, – but few <u>bulky</u> goods, needing barges.

    –Packhorses – <u>bad roads</u>, thus few wagons. 18 miles per day.

    –Innumerable local tales – smuggling – goods carried easy to conceal (bearing on study of any medieval statistics).

    –Fairs held in small villages.

    –Palace of Jacques Coeur – Bourges Cathedral.

–<u>Cathedral</u> is the expression of the 13th century, the expression of the 15th century is the private <u>Palace</u>. [Double vertical line in margin alongside this sentence.]

  –Change from collective to private.

  –Change to private luxury.

–Amounts spent on merchants' homes were not great compared with 15th century.

  –Although Dante (1265–1321) thought Florence too much ruled by money.

  –This was not typical of Northern Europe.

–International trade <u>affected</u> the life of the inland towns much less than we would expect, from the considerable size of such trade.

–Also true of sea towns – increasing trade, traffic in grain (relieving famine) – wool, cloth, spices.

  –Direct sea traffic from Mediterranean to Baltic or North Sea was unimportant.

  –Deep sea navigation was more difficult than in Mediterranean – though a great extension of it was brought about by invention of Mariners' compass.

–Financing of trade

  –<u>Fairs</u> of Champagne etc. – interregional.

  –Controlled by <u>merchants and traders</u> from Flanders and, especially, Italy.

    –They brought goods to the fairs, and changed money – little uniformity.

  –<u>Credit</u> playing an increasing role – given by merchants and traders who came to fairs – from Bruges, etc. – Genoa, Lucca, Florence.

  –No such independence in North Europe for traders and financiers as was possessed by those of Italian cities.

    –Colonies of merchants from the South are being set up in North. Hence the medieval town.

    –Did not gain control over the artisans of the town or the supply of materials.

  –And sea towns, merchants controlled fish trade and grain supplies.

  –Cathedral building brought a large impetus to forming of a market – for wares of townsman.

    –Glaziers, sculptors, masons, carpenters, decorators.

    –A collective effort – individual submerged.

    –Prevented merchants from becoming as wealthy as they might otherwise have done.

–Church controlled the building of cathedrals – no opportunity for private <u>investment</u> and financing of industry – no chance to control artisans.

–And wealth of trading class was tapped to a large extent by the Church.

   –Traders were believers and religious men to a greater extent than ever since.

      –Prohibition of usury, high profit, etc.

      –So that their wealth was taken by Church so much that not much was left for investment in other lines.

      –Most of traffic in goods produced in a 13th century town was disposed of direct[ly] to consumer – so that it did not enter into the calculations of the trader.

Municipal government

–Rise of independent tribunals in 12th century – outside of the lord's court or bishop's courts: – Echevins.

–Also a local municipal council – the same thing, but usually separate.

–Towns in feudal fiefs belonging to the Royal Crown – tended to lose their powers rather than gain them – especially after 14th century.

–Other towns belonging to lesser lords tended to gain many new rights.

–<u>Patricians</u> – those who held land in the town.

   –Governing class recruited from this class – included not only traders but artisans – also landowners. [In margin: Ashley]

   –After expansion of the 12th and 13th centuries a new element in the towns – many new artisans, not holding land.

   –13th-14th centuries – increasing travail en jurande.

      –Guilds – formed by professional and manual workers – little distinction between intellectual and manual work – both workers were regarded as artisans. Both did artistic, intellectual and manual work.

      –A great deal of unpleasant work had to be done, much more unpleasant work wasn't done because of their standard of living. [In margin: Cf. <u>Cordes</u>, Southern France]

      –All workers were not formed into guilds – maybe majority were not – this was <u>travail libre</u>.

   –Struggles in towns – dominance of traders, craftsmen – rebellious.

      –In France order <u>quickly</u> reestablished by power of Crown.

         –French King very powerful – acted as arbiter to his own advantage.

      –In Holland and Germany – order not so quickly brought but when it was – craftsmen were apt to be in a better position than in France – abuses of traders had gone further.

–Conflicting forces in municipalities – during 12–13–14th centuries
  –Municipal government's acts were mainly in interest of craftsmen and democratic majority.
  –Struggle for rights from feudal lords – by charter and privilege.
    –Commercial codes over prices, weights and measures, quality, cornering supply.
      –Applied to small market – locally traded goods.
  –Taxes had some rough proportion to ability to bear them.
  –Towns contributed to Cathedrals which were antagonistic to rise of industrial capitalism.
  –Town expenditure for sickness, deaths, etc.
  –A sense of solidarity in the town structure.
    –Probably the basis for this was laid in early days when everyone in the town was struggling against the Lords, to get rights.
    –Conflicts grew up later – craftsmen trying to keep rights.
  –Agrarian forces played almost no part in town life.
    –Growing control by trading element could be used against Lords and farmers – <u>germ of control by financial circles</u>.
    –Except in France – Crown was becoming supreme.
  –<u>Craftsman</u> – able to maintain economic independence.
    –Was a workman, a foreman, an employer, provider of capital, a shopkeeper.
    –Most craftsmen either worked for public authority, or were independent of traders for their raw materials.
    –Market small but sure – little fluctuation.
    –System of regulation applied to very different situation from our own.
    –Most craftsmen worked for Cathedrals – hired by a "public body" – not industrial capitalism.
      –Trend for manual labor to fall into more and more disrepute.
    –Number of crafts increases; vertical subdivision of labor.
      –Increase in "stages" of production.
      –Weavers in 12th century – a powerful guild. But by 1300, weavers employed by a group of independent cloth traders.
      –Local supply, in a town, of cloth used for all but the best materials. Rich textiles imported.
      –<u>Textile</u> making very complex – needed many steps, many kinds of wool – capital needed to buy it.
        –Domestic system grew up in this industry.
          –Subdivision of labor, etc. – Much capital required, and coordination of different steps.
        –These things were not true of other medieval industries.

–Nearest approach was in metallurgical industries. (Dinant)

   –Iron, bar iron, charcoal, blooming forge – usually carried on outside the town.

–It was extremely rare to find industrial capitalism in towns or countryside of 12th and 13th centuries.

   –Metal working on manorial system, forges owned, provided by Lord – workers [were] agricultural workers.

   –Capital provided too small in importance.

   –Textile workers were the exception, and not majority of workers.

   –Liège – center of textile trade.

–Craft guild organization – majority of Parisian workers in guilds, but not a majority of Lyonaise workers in guilds.

   –Hauser thought this represented a decline from a former Golden Age of guilds. – But this is not now considered true. More workmen in France belonged to guilds in 16th than in 13th century.

   –Also free workers and guild workers were not very different. [Arrow from "free workers" to:] was completely regulated by the municipality.

      –No necessity of a chef d'oeuvre (Ph.D), no masters, no restriction of outsiders.

   Origin [of towns]

      –Pirenne: – economic needs of craftsmen, need for protection from traders and rich monied class (Nef). Eberstadt – worship of some saint brought sense of union.

         –Regulation of competition between guilds.

      –Growth of division within the craft – apprentice, master, servant, etc. – long enough to teach mastership of the task – much skilled labor, still very low [?].

      –Ruby glass – degenerated by child labor.

   Apprenticeship-

   Journeymanship-

      –Access to mastership, based on accomplishment.

      –Long period of working next to master before arriving.

      –Examen before a jury, written and oral – also a chef d'oeuvres.

   –Close connection between life in crafts and life in new universities.

      –Manual and intellectual work intermingled and on same social plane.

Classic form of guild in 12th and 13th centuries.

–Different form in 14 and 15th centuries, again different in 15th and 16th.

–Although guilds lasted, although more people belonged to them in later centuries, – yet the most typical and original form was in 12th and 13th centuries.

–The delicate balance was already beginning to break down in 13th century.

–Classic guild found its best expression in the building of Cathedrals.

–Break-down features:

(a) – Mastership becomes exclusive – based on other considerations than ability – birth distinction (heredity), wealth distinction (huge fees).

(b) – Journeyman had been paid a wage, to distinguish him from apprentice.

–But as more and more paid workers were taken on – journeyman class became too large to expect any large proportion to become masters.

(c) – Growth of new industries – new large capital, large machines, wage earners were that for life.

–Thus a rise of Journeymen Guilds – at end of 15th century.

–To keep up wages, conditions, etc.

–Seeds of modern industrial conflict were here. – Cf. Hauser, Hammonds.

–But [the] Webbs tried to show that no connection existed between early journeyman's guilds and later trade unions.

–Wages of the time – (Thorold Rogers, Coulton).

–Rogers

–Before 14th century:

–Carpentry gets £4 a year	£48 @ modern rate
–Mason £4–10shillings a year	£54 @ modern rate
–Tiler £6 a year	£72 @ modern rate

–based on 300 days' work per year

–Corrected for modern purchasing power – X 12.

–Not bad salaries – food cheap, wood plentiful.

–Riches not the same criterion of success as now.

–Status of peasant rising all through 12th and 13th centuries.

–Craftsmen in town moved about among equals. His inferiority to nobles and knights could hardly have been important to him.

–Material standard of living low – but not low with respect to their wants.

–Along with and as a part of Gothic architecture went the rise of Universities.

–A vast proportion of scholarship and craftsmanship found its way into Cathedrals.

Cultural Background – Gothic art means more than the Gothic arch.
  –Cathedrals were possession of all the townsmen.
    –Could hold them all, were made by them all.
    –Collective enterprises of all people, not only at one time, but for four or five generations.
    –Collective learning of the time – art the expression of learning. "Bible of the poor."
      –Learned with eyes from art of Cathedrals.
  –Abélard, St. Thomas Aquinas – their work developed in this milieu of great unity of all aspects of life.
    –Adelard of Bath.
    –Renaissance of the 12th century in learning. (Classicism)
    –England had its own renaissance as well as following France – it has been claimed that it began in England (Durham Cathedral).
  –Science – much interest in practical application of science to industry and life (different from Greek science).
    –Most invention of the time borrowed heavily from the East.
    –Important inventions of the time (12th and 13th centuries).
      –Water wheel (just coming in) – gave rise to a whole industrial system based on the wheel principle – in 15th century.
      –Introduction of zero from Arabia.
      –Paper – from China.
      –Gunpowder (13th century).
      –Compass – 1300. (From China; Arabic improvements.)
  –Cathedral towns were the centers of study of these new inventions.
    –The whole of life, including science, was merged with art.
    –No attempt to divide knowledge into compartments.
    –No disharmony between need for beauty and need for knowledge.

–Economic conditions essential for development of this art.

–Necessity of financing the Cathedrals – tremendous expense. 1170–1270, 80 Cathedrals, 500 churches. $3,000,000,000 (Adams).

(a) – Willingness to put aside this large a proportion of the national income. Surplus due to advance in effectiveness of labor.

   –This must have represented a very considerable proportion of all the productive activity of the period. Huge sums needed in advance.

   –Coulton claims that it was not a society of artists – but of very good workers. Marks on stone were made to claim piece-wage; some were due to pride in workmanship. – Most information in his book taken from 14 and 15th century in England.

     –Claims mason was on same level as peasant.

   –Letharby says Gothic builders were guildsmen craftsmen, creatures of towns, much free movement (Romanesque builders were attached to soil).

   –Coulton says highest flights of art were impossible but lowest depths also impossible.

   –It was a period of collective art of high standard.

   –Coulton won't glorify this age because it was a Catholic age – he hates Catholicism.

(b) – A large degree of collective inspiration.

(c) – Wide diffusion of technical skill – increased effectiveness of labor went on after 13th century; power to produce beyond the necessities of life had been increased leading to surplus, but why was this surplus used in the creation of the totally uneconomic, unproductive Cathedral?

   –Coulton: creation of art demands a balance of surplus and community ideals.

  –Use of surplus in art required a stable standard of living – not rising; rough equality, requiring a lack of hired-wage system.

(1) – Sense of political equality – due to struggle for rights.

(2) – Strength of Catholic religion as universal faith.

   –The Church – influence of its secular functions, new orders.

(3) – Geographic conditions of Northern France.

[Explanation of points 1, 2, 3 above:]

(1) – City Council represented the citizens as a whole – was anxious to spend money on what the citizens as a whole enjoyed – the Cathedral.

   –A rough sort of income tax – equality of wealth.

(2) – Role of Church –

   –Feeling that great wealth was a hindrance to entrance to heaven; disrepute of usury.

–I.e. large revenues from gifts of nobles and wealthy.

–But most revenues came from the Church's large land holdings – seigneur for large properties.

  –Being a strong collection agency, could centralize funds and deal in large ideas.

–Church could get people to work on basis of equality, for nothing – tremendous power of the Faith.

–Cathedral stood at center of town, was the focal point of the whole town's activity.

–Cult of the Virgin; <u>transcendental</u> belief in and regard for the mysteries of life (birth, love life, death).

  –Coulton – tries to throw mud; says Church did not enter into the thing in the spirit attributed to it.

  –Was not the whole religious enthusiasm more a product of the people than of the Church?

(3) – Soil and natural resources of North France.

  –Luxurious soil – every necessary commodity.

    –Curb on strength of trader – town could control locally produced commodities (trader who intervenes between producer and consumer always benefits – gets craftsman or producer in his power (hires him), and gyps the consumer. – True of any industrial system.

In the Low Countries and North Italy, neither of these two (2 and 3) were present. – In these parts – individualism led to a more <u>vital</u> art, more representative – new sensuousness in music, literature.

–12th and 13th centuries were a period of regulation.

13th and 14th centuries were a period of the rise of liberty, of individualism.

  –Individual masterpieces, but no collective art. (Attica had combined both individual and collective masterpieces.)

<u>1300–1550</u> – Netherlands, Northern Italy, Southern Germany.

  Holland and Catholic Low Countries separate.

–Growth of industrial capitalism in this period, i.e. growth of individually owned units hiring labor, providing capital.

–Textile, metallurgical, mining – industries.

  –In these three, we find industrial capitalism emerging in its most typical form, at a later period.

  (Nef suggests their importance has been overstressed.)

  –In areas of Ypres, Bruges, Ghent – textile manufacturing dominates the town life, dependence of those towns for grain supplies extends to <u>wider area</u> than was common at the time – river valleys.

–At a later date these towns declined, new textile villages grew up; England refused to export raw wool (only cloth); this influenced them too. Spanish wool used then.

   –English wool was better than Spanish.

   –Thus direction away from quality – towards quantity.

–Growing use of flax – locally produced.

   –Most beautiful tapestries of any time produced in 14th century Flanders.

–Entering period of relative freedom – in 14th century.

   –Antwerp much freer than Bruges – new market for English cloth.

–Metallurgy – wood and water needed – new industrial villages in the country – shift away from Dinant [French town], etc.

   –Gunpowder, cannon provided a stimulus to industry.

   –New use of coal – valleys of Somme and Meuse were well stocked with iron and coal, as well as wood and water, and cheap transportation for food.

–Mining – expansion in late 15th, early 16th centuries.

   –Outcroppings of coal used up, necessity of sinking shafts.

   – Liège – old Gothic Catholic town.

      –Important coal mines were found under the old town.

      –Almost the only example of such an old town having new life brought to it in this way.

      –Thus miners were organized into crafts.

         –Yet there was a peculiar contradiction between a medieval craft and the status of the coal miners.

         –Before middle 16th century, mines were in private hands; in Liège industrial capitalism slowed up.

–New industries: – Printing, sugar-refining, brewing, glass-making, soap, gunpowder.

   –All brought rapid increase of industrial capitalism.

   –Great amount of expensive capital needed.

Effect of industries on Low Countries.

   (1) – Industrial villages grow up rapidly.

      –Very different from older Gothic town.

      –Partially they were used to escape old craft regulations.

      –Not walled-in, haphazardly formed.

      –Labor supply came from leisure and surplus of agriculture.

         –The Domestic System tended to concentrate in small towns.

–The town a perfectly hit or miss affair, looking like a spiderweb.

–New groups moving in to increase population.

–Decline of population of old towns, but great increase or rise of villages, population rise in them.

–By 1600, one-quarter or more of population lived in towns (in Gothic France, one-tenth of population lived in towns).

   –Town a bad word: had no charter; were <u>agglomerations</u>.

   –Spinning done in them, some other work.

(2) – Growth of a metropolitan market.

   –Antwerp grew tremendously, to disadvantage of Bruges.

   –New discovery, silting up of Bruges harbor.

(3) – Craftsmen revolted against merchant domination.

   –Usually won.

   –New industrial villages were not usually based on craft guilds, neighboring craft towns tried to assimilate new village trades, but usually failed.

–Effect of industrial development upon organization of industrial activity.

   –Gradual and continued weakening of power of craftsmen – <u>losing</u> independence, direct contact with market, ownership of tools, raw materials, locus of working.

   –Gradual and continued strengthening of power of capital.

   [In margin, braces encompassing preceding two points.]

   –As shown by the course of <u>textile</u> industry.

     –Growth of <u>domestic system</u>.

     –Regulation often difficult, embezzlement possible.

     –In textile industry, craft guilds were all in power of capitalists; textile workers were <u>segregated</u> into <u>sections</u> of the Flemish town – like the modern slums, set apart by its poverty from the rest of the town.

     –14th century: – important revolt of textile workers.

     –The international merchants took the place of the drapers as the leading power in the system.

       –Drapers became only contractors, capital advanced to them by Italian, Spanish, Jewish merchants.

       –Weavers attempted to monopolize certain privileges – internal jealousy – also led to economic dependence of workers.

     –These textile operations requiring <u>most</u> capital and large equipment (pulling, calandering, etc.) tended to develop a small <u>factory</u> system.

–Embryonic form of industrial capitalism – but not even a majority of textile workers concerned.
–In country, merchant could extend his power over as large a field of activity as his means permitted. – But in towns, old guilds made rigid rules re this.
–Few factories, these clustered about merchant's warehouses; but no factory system in case of tapestry, finer cloths, woolens.
  –[Arrow from "tapestry" in preceding line, to:] though 30–60 ateliers were grouped in a single unit, under a single foreman.
–In England at this time, early 16th century, there seemed to be large textile factories.
  –Deloney – 60 looms, 200 men in a row – not a power factory.
  –Still, practically all weaving done in domestic system.
–Progress of factory in connection with rural industry of 1300–1550 – slight – merely finishing processes, tapestry, etc.
–Extension of industry into country.
  –Allowed merchant to extend his market and his control.
  –Led to breakdown of old system of journeyships.
  –Led to villages whose raison d'être was avowedly industrial – spread capitalism (not industrial capitalism).
  –Wider markets, more scattered industry.
  –Precarious status of worker in country – unemployment.
  –But worker usually had a plot of ground.
  –Offered a sort of bulwark against the success of industrial capitalism and factory – was an alternative.
–The Domestic System encourages the control of workmen by capitalists, but does not encourage the introduction of factory system.
  –In fact, where domestic system was well founded, the factory system came last.
–Metallurgical industries – had always been in the country, by the mines.
  –Increase in capital needed for smelting.
    –Blast furnace substituted for blooming forge – greatly increased output.
    –Increased amount necessary for capital to start with.
    –Bellows driven by water power – expensive change of damming rivers, etc.
    –Forge making pig iron – much larger.
      –Bellows, and hammering done by water power.
    –History of blast furnaces remains to be written. (Beck)
    –Real progress between 1500–1600.

–Striking growth in output of metal, accomplished here.

–Requirement of considerable capital: <u>Mining</u> industry was the first to come to the place where it needed much more capital, where industrial capitalism came to dominate.

Industrial Capitalism

–Wage owners [sic: earners] work away from home, under private ownership of the means of production.

–In Belgian provinces, from 1300 down to 1550, especially 1450–1550, a great spread of industrial capitalism.

  –Metallurgical, mining, textile, printing, gunpowder, brewing.

–Striking increase (multiplication many fold) of workers employed in private industry.

  –Still they are the minority of all workers – although some textile processes were done under industrial capitalism, the major portion (spinning and weaving) were carried on under the <u>domestic system</u>.

  –In <u>finishing</u> metallurgy, much domestic system.

  –The domestic system is still the <u>predominant</u> system, in spite of rise of industrial capitalism.

  –A great many <u>artistic</u> considerations remain to influence even industrial capitalism.

  –This holds it back from reaching industrialism.

  –Period of <u>greatest advance</u> in industrial capitalism was this period, and Belgium, South Germany, North Italy was the locale of this advance – "precocious provinces."

  –It was in Great Britain, at a later date, that we first get <u>industrialism</u>.

–Conditions making for failure of <u>industrialism</u> in these precocious provinces, were mostly absent in England.

  (a) – Catholic religion.

    –Protestant spirit is peculiarly fertile ground for rise of capitalism: <u>Max Weber</u>.

    –<u>Tawney</u> claims that conditions making for <u>industrial capitalism</u> force a <u>compromise</u> by religion – religion is not primary, but economic conditions are.

    –Land holding of Church a detriment to industrial capitalism.

      –Little development of enterprise on its land, if it was developed it was not private.

        –Land of Church in England changed hands at Reformation – not on continent.

    –Taxation by Church soaks up some of supply of capital.

–Precocious provinces were all Catholic.

(b) – Lack of natural resources (especially in Italy) – iron, coal.
   –Whose presence seems to lead to inventiveness.
   –Whose bulk leads to transportation improvements.
   –Minerals in South Germany, were of smaller bulk (silver, copper) – belonged to Emperor, rented out, reverted.

(c) – Political events.
   –Italy had been a half way house between North Europe and Near East; lost this.
      –Fall of Turkey.
      –North Europe begins to break into Italy's new trade.
      –Discovery of New World.

(d) – Facilities for carrying bulky commodities.
   –Not good in Catholic countries.
   –Exceedingly fortunate in England – broken coast line – coal could be carried by water from mines to cities.
   –Canal building on continent hadn't gone far enough – didn't go through coal section.

(e) – Restrictions on enterprise on continent, not in England, revee\rse of Anglo-German status in 19th century.

(f) – Constant warfare on continent.
   –<u>Destructive</u>; shifting frontiers, especially important when industrial centers were along that frontier.
   –England free from wars on her own territory.
      –Union with Scotland in 18th century helped.
   –Not ceased on continent, till 1800. [Sic: line has no definite meaning]

(g) – Strength of the State of absolutist governments on the continent was hostile to growth of industrial capitalism.
   –England developed Constitutional Parliamentaryism led by <u>new</u> (economic) classes.
      –Attempts at government monopoly failed, just when they were spreading – successfully – on the continent.

–For these several reasons, industrialism came first in England.
   –Tawney uses "capitalism" to include the domestic system: control of workers by capitalist, control of materials and market.
   –But the workers' position is <u>very</u> different.

–Nef uses Industrial Capitalism in a more restricted sense – to cover factory and mine.

–1760–1832 In England –

–Remarkable growth in population – increased urbanization.

–Agrarian revolution: enclosures – complete breakdown of old system of land tenure.

–Steam in factory.

Industrial Revolution – a <u>speeding up</u> of all the developments of Industrial Capitalism.

–Not a qualitative change; but a quantitative change.

–Toynbee: Industrial Revolution "a speeding up of evolution."

–English and American economic historians now generally agree that old conception of industrial revolution must be "profoundly modified," to say the least.

　–The coming of industrialism can not be explained by the factory system of England of 1760–1830.

　–The study of 1900–1930, and 1500–1800, has brought a new shift of emphasis.

Chairs: Clark-12th century. Tawney, 16th century. Clapham, late 19th century.

Oxford   London   Cambridge

[New professorships for specializing economic historians.]

–Macaulay wrote about 1830 – wrote of the Industrial Revolution of 1760 to his own time.

　–People came to write of Industrial Revolution of 1760–1830 – instead of continuing it to their times.

–Clapham shows that there was large development of domestic system in England in 1830.

–But, in 1760–1830, spinning and weaving, the factory system conquered.

　–Textiles <u>were</u> the most important industry.

　–But factory system had by no means taken over all of industry (or a majority).

　–Clapham shows that the Industry State did not come till 1880.

　　–Due to developments of later and different kind from "Industrial Revolution" developments.

　　　–Steam railways and transportation (shipping).

　　　–Iron and steel in all construction – buildings, ships, factories, bridges, etc.

–Tremendous development of the dependence on export of manufactured goods and coal, and import of foodstuffs.

–1830–1880 – development at least <u>as fast</u> as in 1760–1830.

–Measured by growth of Industrial Capitalism, of population, of output.

–In this period, U.S.A., Germany, Belgium come abreast of England [and] begin to surpass.

–Still, it may be argued that the growth of Industrial Capitalism from 1800 on is due to a <u>change</u> in <u>the rate</u> of development, a speeding up – that took place in 1760–1800.

–But a study of 16th and 17th and early 18th centuries invalidates this view. (Nef)

–The <u>form</u> of Industrial Capitalism is never claimed to be a product of the "Industrial Revolution."

–We are coming to realize that 1550–1640 was also a period of rapid <u>speeding-up</u> of development.

–Still a hypothesis – proofs: –

–Rate of annual increase of <u>coal</u> production was higher than thee rate of annual increase in 1760–1830, was the same as rate of annual increase in 1830–1880.

–Coal is not all industrial but it reflects the growth of much Industrial Capitalism. Change in: –

–Salt; glass; brewing; soap; – making for <u>quantity</u> production; centralized in a factory.

–New industries: alum, copper, saltpeter, gunpowder, suger, pipes, shipping (increase in coal output reacts on shipping).

–Mostly carried on by Industrial Capitalism.

–Public to private building. (Is this evidence of Industrial Capitalism in building?)

–Spread in blast furnace type of production of iron.

–Spread of zinc, wire, copper production.

–Increase in capitalistic working up of metals.

–This time (1600–1650) was a period of change in textile production second to none (Wordsworth).

–Decided movement from country to industrial village.

–Growth of population.

–Increasing changes in all aspects of industry.

The coming of industrialism to England was a long process – from Reformation to 1900.

–Opens up opportunity for <u>a more intelligent analysis of ordinary history</u> (and other aspects in history) <u>against</u> <u>this</u> <u>background of economic interpretation</u>.

–Industrial history and all other aspects of history react on each other.

  –Comparative history; giving

    –<u>unity</u> in historical study.

FINIS

NOTES AND OTHER MATERIALS FROM JOHN ULRIC NEF'S COURSE ON FRENCH INDUSTRIAL HISTORY SINCE THE REFORMATION, ECONOMICS 322, UNIVERSITY OF CHICAGO, SPRING 1934

COURSE BIBLIOGRAPHY

A Select Bibliography of French Industrial History Since the Reformation, together with some of the principal works which deal with other branches of French History

[†] Indicates a standard work of scholarship.
[*] Indicates that the book is considered to be of special value because of the author's historical insight and literary gift.

I. Works covering the whole, or the major portion of the whole period.

Bibliographies
See the bibliographies of general history by Hauser, Molinier, etc. and those in
Lavisse, Ernest, Histoire de France depuis les origines jusqu'à la révolution. 9 vols. 1900–1911.
Langlois, Ch. H., and Stein, H. Les archives de l'histoire de France, 1891.

Further University of Wisconsin Materials: Further Documents of F. Taylor Ostrander
Research in the History of Economic Thought and Methodology, Volume 23-C, 155–239
Copyright © 2005 by Elsevier Ltd.
All rights of reproduction in any form reserved
ISSN: 0743-4154/doi:10.1016/S0743-4154(05)23206-6

Monod, G. Bibliographie de l'histoire de France, catalogue méthodique et chronologique des sources et des ouvrages. 2 vols.

Schmidt. Les sources de l'histoire depuis 1789 aux Archives Nationales. Paris, 1907.

For recent works, see especially the bibliographies in the following periodicals, Economic History Review, Annales d'histoire économique et sociale, Revue historique.

General works of reference

Biographie Universelle. 52 vols. Paris, 1811–1828.

Chéruel, A. Dictionnaire historique des institutions, moeurs et coutumes de la France. 8th ed., 2 vols. Paris, 1910.

Esmein, A. Cours élémentaire d'histoire du droit français. 15th ed. Paris, 1925. Excellent sketch of constitutional history to 1789.

Jourdan, A. Recueil des anciennes lois françaises. 29 vols. Paris, 1822–1823.

Langlois, Ch. V. Manuel de bibliographie historique, 1901–1904.

For general history, see Lavisse and the much earlier work of Michelet, and also Charles Seignobos, A History of the French People (trans. Phillips), 1934.

General economic history

Germain-Martin, H. Histoire économique et financière de la France. 1927. Popular.

Hauser, Henri. Les débuts du capitalism. Paris, 1924(?).

Hauser, Henri. Travailleurs et marchands dans l'ancienne France. Paris, 1920. (Both of these are collections of essays, several very valuable, previously published in periodicals.

Sée, Henri. Esquisse d'une histoire économique et sociale de la France depuis les origines jusqu'à la guerre mondiale. Paris, 1929.

Sée, Henri. L'Evolution commerciale et industrielle de la France sous l'Ancien Régime. Paris, 1925.

Sombart, Werner. Der moderne Kapitalismus. 4th ed., 1922. While it covers a larger area, it is indispensable as the best general treatment of the subject.

Sée, Henri. Franz\ösische Wirtschaftsgeschichte. 1930.

Industrial History

†Beck, Ludwig. Geschichte des Eisens. 5 vols. Brunswick, 1884–1903.

Boissonnade, P. Essai sur l'organisation du travail en Poitou. 2 vols. Paris, 1900. From 11th century to the Revolution.

Couffon, O. Les mines de charbon en Anjou. Angers, 1911. Slight.

Dubois, P. Histoire de l'horlogerie depuis son origine jusqu' à nos jours. Paris, 1849.

Franklin, Alfred. Les corporations ouvrières de Paris du XII ^{e} au XVIIIe siècles. Paris, 1884. Popular.

Godard, Justin. L'ouvrier en soie. Paris, 1899. Reliable monograph on the weaving industry of Lyons, 1466–1791.

Gras, L. J. Various histories of the industries of Forez of which the most important is Histoire économique générale des mines de la Loire. 2 vols., St. Etienne, 1922. See also Essai sur l'histoire de la quincaillerie et petite métallurgie à St.-Etienne, 1904; Historique de l'armurerie stéphanoise, 1905; Histoire de la rubannerie et des industries de la soie à St.-Etienne, 1906. These are the works of a local engineer and antiquarian and from the point of view of the scholar they leave a good deal to be desired.

Hayem, Julien (Ed.). Mémoires et documents pour servis à l'histoire du commerce et de l'industrie en France. Numerous series. Paris, 1911. Contains many valuable studies, dealing with commerce as well as industry.

†Lespinasse, R. Les métiers et corporations de la ville de Paris. 3 vols. 1886–1897.

Levainville, J. R. L'industrie de fer en France. 1922. A sketch, especially useful for the 19th century.

†Levasseur, Emile. Histoire des classes ouvrières en France. 2 vols. Paris, 1859. New edition, rewritten, and greatly enlarged. 4 vols. Paris, 1901.

Lippmann, E. O. von. Geschichte des Zuckers. 2nd ed., 1929. Not very satisfactory for France.

†Martin Saint-Léon, Etienne. Histoire des corporations de métiers. 3rd ed. Paris, 1922.

Mellottee, Paul. Histoire économique de l'imprimerie. Paris, 1905. Valuable, but hardly fulfills the promise of its title.

Pariset, E. Histoire de la fabrique Lyonnaise. Lyons, 1901. Leaves much to be desired.

†Pouzet, Ph. Les anciennes confréries de Villefranche sur-Saône. Lyons, 1904.

Prinet, M. L'industrie du sel en France-Comté. Besançon, 1900.

Quenedey, R. L'habitation rouennaise, étude d'histoire, de géographie et d'archéologie urbaine. Rouen, 1926.

†Rébillon, A. Recherches sur les anciennes corporations ouvrières de Rennes. Paris, 1902.

Vincent, Ch. Histoire de la chaussure, de la cordonnerie et des cordonniers célèbres. 1861. Out of date.

Agrarian history

Babeau,   A.   La vie rurale dans l'ancienne France.   Paris,   1883; Le village sous l'ancien Régime. Paris, 1878. Both   popular,   unscholarly works, of some value especially on the side of manners.

Bloch,   Marc.   Les caractères originaux de l'histoire rurale française.   Paris, 1931. Best general synthesis of agrarian history.

Bonnemère, Eug. Histoire des paysans depuis la fin du moyen-âge jusqu'à nos jours, 1200–1850. 2 vols. Paris, 1856. (Several subsequent editions.) Of little use to the modern scholar.

Chénon, Emile. Les dénombrements de la propriété foncière en France avant et après la Révolution. 2nd ed. Paris, 1923. Valuable for legal aspects of various kinds of land tenure.

Roupnel, Gaston. Histoire de la campagne française. Paris, 1932.

†Sée, Henri. Les classes rurales en Bretagne du XVIe siècle à la Révolution. 1906.

Commerialhistory

†Dahlgren, E. W. Les relations commerciales et maritimes entre la Franceet les côtes de l'Océan Pacifique. Paris, 1909.

Jeulin,   P.   L'évolution du port de Nantes, organisation et trafic depuis les origines. Paris, 1929.

†Levasseur,   Emile.   Histoire du commerce de la France.   2   vols.   Paris, 1911–1912.

Malvézin, T. Histoire du commerce de Bordeaux. Bordeaux, 1892.

Mantellier, M. Histoire de la communauté des marchands fréquantant la Loire. 3 vols. 1864–1869.

†Masson,   Paul.   Histoire des établissements et du commerce dans l'Afrique Barbaresque (1560–1793). Paris, 1903. Algeria, Tunis, Tripoli and Morocco.

Pigeonneau, H. Histoire du commerce de la France. 2 vols. Paris, 1885, 1889. Out of date.

Other aspects of economic and social history

d'Avene1, G. Histoire économique de la propriété, des salaires, des denrées et de tous les prix en général; 1200–1800. 7 vols. Paris, 1894–1898. A much criticized work.

Babeau, A. Les bourgeois d'autrefois. Paris, 1886. Popular.

Baudrillart, H. J. L. Histoire du luxe privé et public. 4 vols. 2nd ed. Paris, 1880–1881.

†Levasseur, E. La population française. 2 vols. Paris, 1889, 1891.

Moreau de Jonnes, A. État économique et sociale de la France. Paris, 1867. Out of date.

II. Works dealing with the Sixteenth Century and especially the period 1547–1614

Bibliography
The bibliography in P. Boissonnade, Le socialisme d'état, 1927, while not a scholarly job, is voluminous and will be found useful for the late 16th and early 17th centuries.

General surveys
Boissonnade, P. Op. cit. Not altogether satisfactory.
Fagniez, G. L'économie sociale de la France sous Henri IV, 1589–1610. Paris, 1897.
Febvre, Lucien. Philippe II et la Franche-Comté. 1912.
*Hanotaux, G. La France en 1614. 1913 (in Nelson ed.).

Industrial history
Claudin, A. Histoire de l'imprimerie en France au XVe et au XVIe siècles. 4 vols. Paris, 1900–1921. Little for the economic historian.
†Coornaert, E. La draperie-sayetterie d'Hondschoote. Paris, 1930. Covers the period from the late 14th to the early 18th century.
Coornaert, E. Une industrie urbaine du XIVe au XVIIe siècle; l'industrie de la laine à Bergues-Saint-Winoc. Paris, 1930. A much slighter work than the above.
Gauthier, Jules. L'industrie du papier dans les hautes vallées franc-contoises du XVe au XVIIIe. (Mem de la Soc. d'Emule de Montbeliard, vol. XXVI.) Also of use for a later period.
Hauser, H. L'ouvrier du temps passé. Paris, 1899.
*Hauser, Henri. Les débuts du capitalisme. Paris, 1924 (?); Travailleurs et marchands dans l'ancienne France, Paris, 1920; and Les origines historiques des problèmes économiques actuels. Paris, 1930. These are all collections of essays containing valuable matter for the historian of industry; but the subjects are no means limited to industry or to the late 16th and early 17th century. The second collection contains an excellent essay on State interference in economic life.
Michel, F. Recherches sur le commerce, la fabrication et l'usage des étoffes de soie, d' or et d' argent et autres – principalement en France. 2 vols. Paris, 1853–1854.

Agrarian history
Bézard, Yvonne. La vie rurale dans le sud et la région Parisienne de 1450 à 1560. Paris, 1929.

Raveau, Paul. L'agriculture et les classes paysannes dans le haut Poitou au XVIᵉ siécle. 1926. Also valuable for history of prices.
See also Febvre, op. cit. for Franche Comté.

Monetary history
Harsin, Paul. Les doctrines monétaires et financières en France du XVIe au XVIIIe siècles. Paris, 1928. Also valuable for economic thought on the question from Malestroit to Forbonnais.
Hauser, Henri. Introduction to La réponse de Jean Bodin à M. de Malestroit. Paris, 1932; and various articles in the collections already mentioned.
Liautey, André. La hause des prix et la lutte contre la cherté en France au XVIᵉ siècle. 1921. Deals mainly with price regulation by the State.
Raveau, Paul. "La crise des prix au XVIᵉ siècle en Poitou," in Rev.Hist., CLXII (1929), 1–44, 268–293. And see also his book already cited.
Romier, L. Le royaume de Catherine de Médici. 2nd ed., Paris, 1922.
See also d'Avenel, op. cit., and for works on the price revolution which do not deal primarily with France, G. Wiebe, Zur Geschichte der Preisrevolution des XVI. und XVII. Jahrhunderts, Leipzig, 1895; E. J. Hamilton, various articles, especially the one in Economica, Nov., 1929, and his forthcoming book, American Treasure and the Price Revolution in Spain; and J. M. Keynes, A Treatise on Money, 1931, vol. ii, 152 sqq.

Commercial and Financial History
Ehrenberg, R. Capital and Finance in the Age of the Renaissance. Eng. trans. 1928.
Germain-Martin. La monnaie et la crédit privé en France (1558–1668). 1909 (from Rev. d'his. des doctrines écon. et soc).
Girard, Albert. Le commerce français à Seville et Cadix au temps des Habsbourg. Paris, 1932.
†Usher, A. P. The History of the Grain Trade in France 1400–1710. Cambridge (Mass.), 1913. Also for 17th century.
Vigne, Marcel. La banque à Lyon du XVᵉ au XVIIIᵉ siècle. Also of use for later periods.

Constitutional history and political thought
See Boissonnade, Socialisme d'état, and Hauser's article in Travailleurs et Marchands. J. W. Thompson's Wars of Religion in France, is suggestive in spite of its faults.
*Allen, J. W. Political Thought in the Sixteenth Century. London, 1928.

Picot, Georges. Histoire des Etats généraux, considérés au point de vue de leur influence sur le gouvernement de la France de 1355 à 1614. 4 vols. Paris, 1872.

Contemporary literature

On economic subjects, see especially the writings of Bodin, the two Laffemas, Montchrétien, Francois Grimaudet. For a description of the country see Boulenger, Calculation et description de la France, 1575. For contemporary descriptions of economic life, see L. Gollut, Les mémoires historiques de la République Sequanoise (1592), new ed. Arbois, 1846; T. Coryat, Crudities, hastily gobbled up (1611), new ed. 2 vols., Glasgow, 1905; Montaigne's Journal de voyage, 2 vols., Paris, 1774; Froumenteau, Le secret des finances de France, 1581. For the relations between economic and political life see Loyseau's works, especially the Traité des ordres, Sully's Mémoires, C. Le Bret, Souveraineté du roi, 1632, and Richelieu's Testament politique.

III.   Works dealing with the Seventeenth Century and especially the period 1643–1715.

Bibliographies

Boissonnade, P. Colbert. Paris, 1932. A continuation of Le socialisme d'état (see above).

Sagnac, Ph. "Histoire économique de la France de 1669 à 1714, essai de bibliographie critique." Revue d'histoire moderne. Vol. iv (1902), pp. 5–15, 89–97.

General surveys

Sagnac, Ph. in Lavisse, Histoire de France, vol. viii, 215 ff., 232 ff.

*Voltaire's Siècle de Louis XIV is still perhaps the best general work on the period as a whole, though it is not strong on the economic side. See also G. N. Clark, The Seventeenth Century, Oxford, 1929.

Industrial history

As the State took so active a part in carrying on and regulating industry, works on industry generally have a bearing on constitutional history, and vice versa.

Boissonnade, P. Articles on industry in Languedoc in the age of Louis XIV in the Annales du Midi for 1902, pp. 5–49; for 1905, pp. 329–330; for 1906, pp. 411–472.

Boissonnade, P. "L'état, l'organization et la crise de l'industrie languedocienne pendant les soixante premières années du XVIIᵉ siècle" in Annales du Midi for April, 1909.

Boissonnade's <u>Colbert</u> deals with many industries, especially those controlled by the State.

Clément, Pierre. <u>Histoire du système protecteur en France</u>. 1854.

Clément, Pierre, (Ed.) <u>Lettres, instructions et mémoires de Colbert</u>. 10 vols., 1861–1862. Valuable for all aspects of economic history.

Des Cilleuls, A. <u>Histoire et régime de la grande industrie en France</u>. 1898. Out of date.

Dumas, F. <u>La réglementation industrielle après Colbert</u>. Mém. de L'Acad. de Toulouse. 1906, 1909.

Frémy, E. <u>Histoire de la manufacture royale des glaces</u>. Paris, 1909. Incomplete and unsatisfactory; also deals with 18th century.

†Germain-Martin. <u>La grande industrie sous le règne de Louis XIV</u>. 1899.

Granat. "L'industrie de la draperie à Castres au 17ᵉ siècle," in <u>Annales du Midi</u>, 1898–1899 (D.C. 607.A61).

Gueneau, L. <u>L'organisation du travail à Nevers au XVIIᵉ et XVIIIᵉ siècles</u>. 1919. Also for 18th century.

Hovard, H. and Vachon, M. <u>Les manufactures nationales</u>. 1889.

Nef, J. U. <u>The Rise of the British Coal Industry</u>. 2 vols. London, 1932.

Sagnac, Ph. "L'industrie et le commerce de la draperie en France à la fin du XVIIᵉ siècle et au commencement du XVIIIᵉ," in <u>Rev. d'hist. mod. et contemp</u>. ix (1907), 24–40.

Wadsworth,	A.	P.	and	Mann,	J.	de	L. <u>The Cotton Trade and Industrial Lancashire</u>. Manchester, 1931. Also for 18th century, and especially for the introduction of textile machinery into France.

Agrarian history and the history of population

Roupnel,	Gaston.	<u>La ville et la campagne au XVIIᵉ siècle, étude sur les populations du pays dijonnais</u>. Paris, 1922. A valuable work.

Commercial and financial history

As is true of industrial history, it is difficult, in dealing with seventeenth century France, to separate these subjects from constitutional history. Therefore, see also under the latter.

Biggar, H. P. <u>The early trading companies of New France</u>. Toronto, 1901.

Clark, G. N. <u>The Anglo-Dutch Alliance and the War against French Trade</u>.

Decharme,	P.	<u>Le comptoir d'un négociant au XVIIᵉ siècle, d'après une correspondance inédite</u>. 1910.

†Masson, Paul. <u>Histoire du commerce français dans le Levant au XVIIᵉ siècle</u>. 1896.

Mims, S. L. Colbert's West India Policy. New Haven, 1912.

Prato, Giuseppe. Problemi monetari e bancari nei secoli XVII e XVIII. Turin, 1916.

Social history and the history of manners

Berry, Mary. Comparative View of the Social Life in England and France, from the Restoration to the Present Time. New ed. 2 vols. London, 1844.

Cruttwell, Maud. Madame de Maintenon. 1930.

Fagniez, G. La femme et la société française dans la première moitié du XVIIe siècle. 1924.

Normand, Charles. La bourgeoisie française au XVIIe siècle. Paris, 1908.

Strange, T. A. French Interiors during the 17th and 18th Centuries. 1903.

Constitutional history

See also above under commercial and industrial history.

Beaulieu, E. P. Les gabelles sous Louis XIV. Paris, 1903.

Boissonnade's Colbert (see above) is the latest study. See also the article of Hauser on state regulation of economic life, referred to above. While largely out of date, Felix Joubleau's Études sur Colbert ou exposition du système d' économie politique suivi en France de 1661 à 1683. 2 vols. Paris, 1856, may be consulted in addition to the books mentioned here. See also Hayem, op. cit.

Clement, P. Lettres, instructions et mémoires de Colbert (see above).

Depping, G. B. Correspondence administrative sous la règne de Louis XIV. 1850–1855.

Esmonin, E. La taille en Normandie au temps de Colbert. Paris, 1913.

Germain-Martin and Bezancon, M. Histoire du crédit de la France sous le règne de Louis XIV. Paris 1913.

Harsin, Paul. Crédit public et Banque d'État en France. Paris, 1933.

Heckscher, E. F. Mercantilism. 2 vols. English edition announced for early publication. The best work on the subject. Morini-Comby is not to be recommended. But G. Schmoller's The Mercantile System and its Historical Significance (1884), Econ. Class. Ser. (Ashley), 1896 is still important for the period.

Jubert, Paul. "La juridiction et l'inspection des manufactures à Rouen de 1670 à 1699," Soc. D'émulation du commerce et de l'industrie de la Seine-Infer., 1931, pp. 22–82.

Monin, H. Essai sur l'histoire administrative du Languedoc pendant l'intendance de Basville. 1884.

Pasquier, J. L'impôt des gabelles en France aux XVIIe et XVIIIe siècles. Paris, 1905.

Roux, Pierre. Les fermes d'impôts sous l'ancien régime. Paris, 1916.
Sagnac, Ph. "Le credit de l'état et les banquiers à la fin du XVIIe et au commencement du XVIIIe siècle," in Revue d'histoire moderne et contemps. 1908.

Religious history
See the Catholic Dictionary and the Catholic Encyclopedia.
Cans,   Albert.   L'organisation financière du clergé de France à l'époque de Louis XIV. Paris, 1909.
Gazier, Cécile. Histoire du monastère de Port-Royal. Paris, 1908.
*Sainte-Beuve. Port-Royal. 3rd ed., 7 vols., 1867–1871.

Intellectual and cultural history
Bray, R. La formation de la doctrine classique en France. 1927.
Brunetière, H. Evolution des genres dans l'histoire de la littérature. 3rd ed., 1898.
Lancaster, H. C. A History of French Dramatic Literature in the Seventeenth Century. Part I dealing with 1610–1634 appeared in 1930.
Ornstein, Martha. The Rôle of Scientific Societies in the Seventeenth Century. New York; 1913.
Palmer, John L. Molière: his life and works. London, 1930.
Robinson, Howard. Bayle, the skeptic. 1931.
Sée, Henri. Les idées politiques en France au 17e siècle. 1923.
Sée, Henri. "Molière, peintre des conditions sociales," in Rev. d'hist. econ. 1929.

Contemporary literature
For economic thought, mention may be made of Sieur de la Gouberdière, Nouveau règlement général sur toutes sortes de marchandises et manufactures qui sont utiles en ce royaume. 1634. This is a defense of mercantilist doctrine. A study of the French literature on this subject, such as Viner did for early English thought in Journ. of Pol. Econ., 1930, still wants doing. The first two treatises which seriously questioned the mercantilist doctrine, Boisguilbert, Le détail de la France sous le règne présent, 1695 (see also his Traité des grains) and Vauban's Projet d'un dîme royale, 1707, are of special importance. Reprints will be found in Eng. Daire, Economistes financiers du 18e siècle, 1848. On the question of usury, Bossuet's treatise is especially important. See also De Vourric, De l'usure et les moyens de l'éviter, Avignon, 1688; L. Thomassin, Traité du negoce et del'usure. Paris, 1697. In addition there are many books, which can hardly be regarded as contributions to economic thought,

which deal with economic conditions. Preeminent among these for the information they contain are Jacques Savary, Le parfait négociant, Paris, 1673 (for a good article on Savary, see Hauser's Débuts) and Savary des Bruslons, Dictionnaire universel de commerce, 1723–1730 (with important references to industry). See also Jean Eon, Le commerce honorable, 1646, Piganiol de la Force, Nouvelle description de la France, 1717; Samuel Ricard, Traité général du commerce, 2nd ed., Amsterdam, 1705. Boulainvilliers, Etat de la France, 3 vols. London, 1727 contains a number of mémoires of intendants, submitted to Louis XIV, which give much information on economic conditions.

IV. Works dealing with the eighteenth and early nineteenth century (especially 1740–1848).

Bibliographies

Boissonnade, P. "Les études relatives à l'histoire économique de la Révolution française," in Rev. de Synthèse hist., X and XI (1905). Also published separately in 1906.

Sée, H. "The Economic and Social Origins of the French Revolution," in Econ. Hist. Rev., III (1931), 1–15.

General surveys

Attention should be paid to the great works in general history, especially *de Toqueville, L'ancien Régime, Taine, Origines de la France contemporaire (esp. *L'ancien Régime), *Michelet, Révolution française, and the more recent works of Aulard and Mathiez. Jaurès, Histoire socialiste de la Révolution française is very valuable on the economic and social side. On the strictly economic side there are several surveys.

Braure, M. Lille et la Flandre wallonne au 18ᵉ siècle. Lille, 1932. Contains survey of economic history, but the treatment of the subject leaves something to be desired.

†Dutil, Léon. L'état économique du Languedoc à la fin de l'ancien Régime, 1750–1789. 1911. Highly recommended.

Kovalevskii, M. M. La France économique et sociale à la veille de la Révolution. 2 vols. 1909, 1911.

Sée, H. La France économique et sociale au XVIIIᵉ siècle. 1925. A good sketch and guide.

Sée, H. La vie économique en France sous la monarchie censitaire. 1927.

For all phases of economic development in the period consult the Collection de documents inédits sur l'histoire économique de la Révolution française.

Industrial history

Hayem, op.cit., is especially useful here.

†Ballot, Ch. L'introduction du machinisme dans l'industrie française. 1923.

Bardon, A. L'exploitation du bassin houiller d'Alais sous l'ancien Régime. Nimes, 1898.

Bondois, P. M. "L'industrie sucrière française au 18e siècle," Rev. d'hist. econ., 1931, no. 3, 316–346.

†Bourgin, H. and G. (Ed.). L'industrie sidérurgique en France au début de la Révolution. 1920. Documents with an introduction.

Boyé, Pierre. La Lorraine industrielle . . . 1737–1766. Nancy, 1900. Sketchy.

Choulguine A. "L'organisation capitaliste de l'industrie existait-elle en France à la veille de la Révolutioon?" Rev. d'hist. écon. et soc., X (1922), 184 ff.

Dauphin, V. Recherches pour servirs à l'histoire de l'industrie textile en Anjou. Angers, 1913.

Depitre, E. "Les prêts au commerce et au manufactures, 1740–1789," in Rev. d'hist. écon. 1914–1919.

Depitre, E. La toile peinte en France au 17e et 18e siècle. Paris, 1912.

Depors, H. Recherches sur l'état de l'industrie des cuirs en France. Paris, 1932.

Germain-Martin. La grande industrie en France sous le règne de Louis XV, 1715–1774. 1900.

Grar. Ed. Histoire . . . de la houille. 3 vols. Lille, 1847–1851.

†Levy, Robert. Histoire économique de l'industrie cotonnière en Alsace. 1912.

Leseure. Historique des mines de houille du département de la Loire. 1901. Out of date.

Martin, Gaston. Capital et travail à Nantes au cours du XVIIIe siècle. Paris, 1932.

McKay, D.C. The National Workshops. London, 1933. On the eve of 1848.

Mozoyer, L. "L'exploitation forestière et conflits sociaux en Franche-Comté, à la fin de l'ancien régime," in Ann. D'Hist. econ. et soc., 1932, 339ff.

†Rouff, Marcel. Les mines de charbon en France au 18e siècle. 1922.

Sée, H. "Les forêts et la question du déboisement," in Ann. de Bret., XXXVI (1924).

Sée, H. "Études sur les mines bretonnes au XVIIIe siècle," in Ann. De Bret., XXXVII (1926).

Sée, Henri. "L'influence de la Révolution sur l'evolution industrielle de la France" in volume in honor of Giuseppe Prato.

Tarlé, E. L'industrie dans les campagnes à la fin de l'Ancien Régime. 1910.

Agrarian history
For a statement of the problems involved and work published on the subject prior to 1929 see Georges Lefebvre, "La place de la Révolution dans l'histoire agraire de la France," in Ann. d'hist. écon. et. soc., i (1929), 506 ff. See also the following.
Lavergne, L. de. Economie rurale de la France depuis 1789. 1860.
Lefebvre, Geo. Les paysans du Nord pendant la Révolution française. 2 vols. 1924.
Lefebvre, G. Questions agraires au temps de la terreur. Strasbourg, 1932.
Luchitskii, I. V. L'état des classes agricoles en France à la veille de la Révolution. 1911.
Luchitskii, I. V. La propriété paysanne en France à la veille de la Révolution, 1912. (Principally in Limousin.)
Luchitskii, I. V. La petite propriété en France avant la Révolution et la vente des biens nationaux. 1897.
Mounier, L. De l'agriculture en France, d'après les documents officials. 1846.
Remondière, L. A. Les charges du paysan ayant la Révolution de 1789. 1894.
Sée, H. La vie économique et les classes sociales en France au XVIIIe siècle. 1924. Also valuable for social history.

Commercial and financial history
†Afanasiev, Geo. E. Le commerce des céréales en France au dix-huitième siècle. 1894.
Bijo, T. La Caisse d'Escomte, 1776–1793, et les origines de la Banque de France. Paris, 1927.
Biollay, Léon. Le pacte de famine. 1885.
Bonnet, Pierre. La commercialisation de la vie française du premier empire à nos jours. 1929.
Courtois, A. C. Histoire des banques en France. 1881.
Garnault, Emile. Le commerce rochelais au XVIIIe siècle. 3 vols. 1887–1888.
Manger, J. B. Recherches sur les relations économiques entre la France et la Hollande. 1923.
†Masson, P. Histoire du commerce français dans le Levant au 18e siècle. 1911.
Pariset, E. La chambre de commerce de Lyon, 1702–1791. vol. I, 1886.
Ramon, Gabriel. Histoire de la Banque de France d'après les sources originales. Paris, 1929.

Social history and the history of manners
Brinton, Crane. The Jacobins. 1930.
Ducros, L. French Society in the 18th Century. 1927.

Mathiez, A. La vie chêre et le movement sociale sous le terreur. 1927.
Thirion, H. La vie privé des financiers au 18 siècle. 1895.

Religious history in its economic aspects
  Groethuysen, B.   Origines de l'esprit bourgeois en France. I. L'église et la
  bourgeoisie. Paris, 1927.

Constitutional history
  Grandsire, Geo. L'impôt sur le revenu en Lorraine au 18ᵉ siècle. 1927.
  Harris, S. E. The Assignats. 1930.
  Marion, Marcel. Les impôts directs sous l'ancien régime, principalement au
  XVIIIᵉ siècle. Paris, 1910.
  Marion, M. Histoire financière de la France depuis 1715. 2 vols. 1914.
  Nussbaum, F. L. Commercial Policy in the French Revolution. 1923.

Intellectual history in its economic aspects
  For the principal economic thinkers of the period prior to the Revolution, see
  Gide and Rist, Histoire des doctrines and also
  Espinas,   Alfred.   La philosophie sociale du XVIIIᵉ siècle et la Révolution.
  1898.
  Lavergne, L. G. de. Les économistes français du 18ᵉ siècle. 1870.
  Lichtenberger, A. Le socialisme au XVIIIᵉ siècle. Paris, 1895.
Weulersse, G. Le movement physiocratique en France. 1910.

Contemporary literature (almost too voluminous to refer to particular items)
  Of the innumerable writers on economic theory, reference may be made
  to the following (some of whose works are to be found in Eugene Daire,
  Mélange d'économie politique): Duhannel de Monceau, Le Trosne,
  Mirabeau, Necker, Quesnay, Roland de la Platière, Turgot, Vincent de
  Gournay. See also the works of Condorcet, especially Du commerce des blés,
  and those of Condillac, especially Le commerce et le gouvernement
  considerés relativement l'un à l'autre. Of books dealing more exclusively
  with the economic condition of the country, reference may be made
  to A. M. Arnould, De la balance du commerce, 3 vols. 1795; Coyer,
  La noblesse commercante, 1756; De Jeze,Etat et tableau de la ville de Paris,
  1760; La France agricoles et marchandes, 2 vols., Avignon, 1762; Ange
  Goudar, Les interêts de la France mal entendus, 3 vols., Amsterdam, 1756
  (verbose and badly composed); Gabriel Jars, Voyages metallurgiques, 3
  vols., 1774–1781 (dealing mainly with foreign countries); L. S. Mercier,
  Tableau de Paris, new ed., 8 vols., Amsterdam, 1782; and above all, Arthur
  Young, Travels in France, 1787–1789, 2 vols., 1794, a book which has been
  quarried in by nearly all historians of the period.

V. Works dealing with recent history, especially since the advent of the Third Republic.

General surveys

Clapham, J. H. The Economic Development of France and Germany. 3rd ed. Cambridge, 1928.

d'Avenel, G. de. Le mécanisme de la vie moderne. 7th ed., 5 vols., 1922.

Ogburn, W. F. and Jaffé, W. The Economic Development of Post-War France. New York, 1929.

Industrial history

Blanqui, J. A. Des classes ouvrières en France en 1848. 2 vols., 1849.

Block, Maurice. Statistique de la France. 2nd ed., 1874.

Clerget, P. Les industries de la soie en France. 1925.

Coq, Paul and Benard, T. N. Resumé analytique de l'enquête parlementaire sur le régime économique de la France en 1870. 1872.

Dunham, A. L. The Anglo–French Treaty of Commerce of 1860 and the Progress of the Industrial Revolution in France. 1930.

Foville, A. de. La transformation des moyens de transport. 1880.

Guillaumot, G. L'organisation des chemins de fer en France. 1899.

Laboulaye, Ch. P. S. de. De la democratie industrielle. Etudes sur l'organisation de l'industrie française. 1849.

Levainville, Jules. L'industrie du fer en France. 1922.

Levasseur, E. Questions ouvrière et industrielles en France sous la Troisième République. 1907.

Lorwin, Lewis L. The Labor Movement in France. New York, 1912.

Lévy, Robt. L'industrie cotonnière en Alsace. 1912.

Louis, Paul. Histoire de la classe ouvrière en France de la Révolution à nos jours. 1927.

Olivier, M. La politique du charbon. 1922. (Deals with the war period.)

Passey, F. Les machines et leur influence sur le développement de l'humanité. 1866.

Pelloutier, F. L. E. Histoire des bourses du travail. 1902.

Picard, A. Les chemins de fer Français. 1884.

Reybaud, L. Le coton. 1863.

Reybaud, L. La laine. 1867.

Rousier, Paul de. Les grandes industries modernes. 5 vols. 1825–1828.

Villain, G. Le fer, la houille et la métallurgie à la fin du XIXe siècle. Paris, 1901.

Agrarian history

Augé –Laribé, M. L'évolution de la France agricole. 1912.
Augé –Laribé, M. Grande ou petite propriété? Montpellier, 1902.
Augé –Laribé, M. Le paysan après la guerre. 1923.
Barral, J.-A. L'agriculture du Nord de la France. 2 vols. Paris, 1867–1870.
Baudrillart, H. J. L. Les populations agricoles de la France. 3 vols. 1885–1893.
Foville, A. de. Le morcellement. Etudes économiques et statistiques sur la propriété foncière. 1885.
Graffin R. Les biens communaux en France. 1899.
Grandeau, L. N. L'agriculture et les institutions agricoles du monde au commencement du XXe siècle. 5 vols. Paris, 1905–1912.

Commercial and financial history
Chatin-Ollier, L. La politique douanière et la stabilité dans les relations commerciales. Paris, 1925.
Colin, A. V. C. La navigation commerciale au 19e siècle. Paris, 1901.
Courtois, A. C. Histoire des banques en France. 1881.
Dupont-Ferrier, P. Le marché financier de Paris sous le Second Empire. 1925.
Franklin, A. Les magasins de nouveautés. 1894. (And a number of other useful works by the same author.)
Vilogeux, Maurice. Quelques aspects de l'évolution des prix au siècle dernier et en notre temps. 1927.
Weill, Georges J. Histoire du movement social en France, 1852–1924. 3rd ed., 1924.

COURSE NOTES

322
Nef
Seignobos – History of France
{Sée   Esquisse d'une histoire economique et sociale de la France
{Hauser
    [Charles Seignobos, A History of the French People (trans. Phillips), 1934.]
    [Sée, Henri. Esquisse d'une histoire economique et sociale de la France depuis les origines jusqu'à la guerre mondiale. Paris, 1929.]
[Line connecting to Sée and Hauser] Two outstanding French economic historians.
  –Hauser, especially, is lazy about looking up archives and manuscripts.
  –Sée, qui a la peur, doesn't get too much of a chance to do it. (Research showed more workmen to have been joined in guilds in 16th century, than in 13th century.)

–It <u>is</u> premature to make a general economic history of France – and especially one with social, political, and cultural aspects.
–Difficult for a foreigner to deal with history of France.
   –Mental and physical self-sufficiency is difficult to understand.
   –We lack their tradition of tradition.
   –One must know a <u>people</u> in order to know their history.
   –French history full of paradoxes, especially to foreigners.
–The Frenchman – a paradox.
   –Loose morals <u>versus</u> horror of Anglo-Saxon loose talk among men <u>versus</u> love of the family.
   –Lack of race prejudice.
   –Intellectual honesty?
   –I.e. two apologies – one for treating France at all, one for treating so large a block of France.
   –But – our excuse is that France is a valuable study in <u>comparison</u> with other countries and that French historians don't usually make such a comparison, and that the American, having no national prejudices involved, [sentence not completed]
<u>Industrialism</u> – did not occur in any European country till late 18th or early 19th centuries – at earliest.
–Though it was long being prepared for in the growth of Industrial Capitalism.
–Industrial Capitalism has made less progress in France than in other countries; industrialism has not been so severe in its impact. France is more similar to its condition four centuries ago, than any other country.
   –"France has survived into a world to which she does not belong, and for which she has no spiritual dominance" (Roger Hinks).
   –Is like an old lady –
   –The modern economic historian must find a new synthesis to take the place of a discredited old synthesis.
      –Sombart's general plan is not successful.
      –<u>Tawney</u> – the important thing for the economic historian is that he ask the right questions.
      Harsin – Comment on écrit l'histoire – very good on methodology.
      Webbs – Method in the Social Sciences
      [André] Siegfried – France, A Study in Nationality [1930]
      Phillip Carr – The French at Home
      Fords – The Mirror of France
      Wendell – The France of Today
      Curtius – The Civilization of France
      [Single vertical line in margin alongside list from Harsin through Curtius.]
Course covers two aspects of economic history

(1) France's place in the rise of industrialism
(2) Methodology in Research

    Anatoux – France in 1614 (1614, last meeting of the Estates General until 1789) (was the model for Clapham's Chapter I – "The Face of the Country")
    Fagniez – L'économie sociale de la France sous Henri IV, [1589–1610] (1897) (chapter on L'industrie was written as a magazine article thirteen years before – i.e. the book was uneven, not connected)

The term "Industrial Revolution" has been traced back to the 30s and 40s of last century.

    Beales – in <u>History</u> – has treated the <u>concept</u> "Industrial Revolution."
        –At London School of Economics pass students are taught there was an Industrial Revolution, lower students that there was not.
    Toynbee gave great advocacy to the idea.
    Marx gave support to the idea – though did not subscribe entirely.
    Lord Macaulay gave support to this idea by his <u>sharp contrast</u> of <u>his</u> times, 1849, with early conditions in England.
    Held –? [sentence not completed
    1760 (accession of George III) is usually taken as <u>the</u> date for the beginning of the [Industrial] Revolution.
    1832 is a favorite date for the end.

–What got into the popular mind was that in this period the factory system was, if not born, at least given its complete modern form.

    Heaton goes further than Nef in stating the exaggeration.
    Ashley's Introduction to Toynbee.
    –All Toynbee meant by "Revolution" was a <u>speedingup</u> of <u>Evolution</u>.
        –Changes become "<u>portentously rapid</u>" (Macaulay).
        –Ashley was a fellow student at Oxford with Toynbee. It was probably <u>his</u> notes which were used in the book.
    –Even this concept of "Industrial Revolution" is modified by Nef – supported byUsher – who claims that this was only <u>one</u> of a <u>series</u> of <u>speeding ups</u>. [Multiple vertical lines in margin alongside this point.]
    –The <u>rate</u> of industrial change was probably much faster between 1830–1880, than in the former period (Clapham).
    –Heaton points out that the changes in England before 1830 were very slight.

–Montaux, Held, Toynbee, [the] Hammonds are all trying to solve the problem, "How did modern industrialism come about?"
–Nef proposes a new formula for an attempted answer – a more fruitful method.
    (1)- Study the causes and developments of industrialism over the whole of Western Europe and North America.

(2)- Give up idea of revolutionary change – substituting idea of a constant flow or process of development of industrialism with varying <u>rate</u> of advance.

(3)- Use 1560 as the date at which we begin our study of the rise of industrialism – though not denying that the development had already begun.

   –Reasons for choosing this date.

      a. Beginning of a long rise of prices – "profit inflation" – Hamilton (Earl J.) and Keynes.

      b. Rise of Protestantism

         –A spirit of enterprise was its corollary which led to capitalism (Max Weber).

         –Answered by Tawney and recently by [D. H.] Robertson (same answer).

         –Aside from dogma, there <u>was</u> still an effect – especially in England, due to the transfer of mineral lands from the Church to the Crown.

      c. (1550–1688) Establishment of Parliamentary government – giving the merchant class a large hand in government.

      d. First use of coal instead of wood.

      e. Rise of Natural Science – still a good deal of magic, but rise usually dated from this period.

These factors began to act and interact. (Sombart – war, luxury, the Jews and rise of industry.

Measurement of the degree of industrial capitalism in nation at any time.

   –Possibility of quantitative measurement.

      (a)- Proportion of persons working in defined sort of factories – comparisons of countries – data totally lacking before 1800.

      (b)- Nature of work done – "Rise of factory system" does not include mining, thus we use "Rise of industrial capitalism." [Double vertical lines in margin alongside this point.]

-a- Only rough approximations are possible before 1800.

   –Clapham says [word indecipherable] they are out of the question for the period before 1800.

   –Nef thinks you can so estimate – has done so in his book – without any serious criticism.

      –Does it by laying all cards on table – taking reader into his confidence – "I don't know anything about all this" but lets see what we can do – mention all the contrary possibilities, and qualifications (huge number of volumes on <u>printing</u> – by collectors, not economic historians – not on other industries).

c- Compare rates of growth of various <u>commodities</u> in various countries.

d- Compare rates of growth of <u>population</u> – not very good-extremely rough.

e- Compare rate of <u>urbanization</u> – cf. Adam Smith, who connects growth of towns to growth of opulence.

–[name indecipherable] calls this the best piece of economic history ever written.

f- Compare <u>shipments of goods</u> from sea-ports, and down rivers.

–We <u>do</u> have statistics of <u>tolls</u> and <u>taxes</u>.

–Especially for 18th century France – figures of trade between Paris and Rouen.

–In England more records yet – labor involved colossal.

–Giving, not total output, but a guess at the rate of change of total output. [Single vertical line in margin alongside this point.]

France Today

–Judged by these broad means – the progress of industrial capitalism has been much slower in France than in U.S. – between 1530 and 1930 – or than in other countries of Western Europe.

–Today – France is much less industrialized than her immediate neighbors.

–Criteria – <u>Ogburn and Jaffé</u>: per capita coal production, iron and steel production, steam engine use, proportion of population engaged in industry.

[André] Siegfried [Ostrander lines out the following:]

11% of manual workers were employers of labor 3[%] in England

–Percentage of industrial workers not absolutely dependent on their industrial work – is not taken care of by these figures.

France in 1530

–How compare France and other countries in their relative industrialization in 1530?

–France at least <u>as</u> developed as her neighbors.

–England was <u>behind</u> France except in textiles and woolens – England in an economic backwater until Elizabeth.

–France not behind the whole Germany, though some sections of Germany much more advanced than any part of France.

Direct Approach

–Not much <u>industrial capitalism</u> existed anywhere in <u>1530</u>.

–It existed to the <u>largest extent</u> in <u>mining</u>.

–Though even much mining done still on old methods.

–Though probably, most <u>miners</u> were <u>probably</u> working under industrial capitalism.

–Especially in <u>copper and silver</u>. (Strieter)

–Though this was so small, absolutely, that it didn't take many workers.

–Iron, lead, coal – great development after 1500.

–Turning of population away from the quest for the precious, to the quest for the basic. [Single vertical line in margin alongside this and preceding line.]

–Not more than 30,000 miners in all Western Europe (not including husbandmen).

–Next greatest industrial capitalism in metallergy.

  –In smelting, especially.–Finished products done by handiwork.

   –Smelting of iron – "Geschichte des Eisens" – Ludwig Beck [*Die Geschichte des Eisens in technischer und kulturgeschichtlicher Beziehung*, Braunschweig: F. Vieweg und Sohn, 5 vols, 1884–1903]

    –Blast furnace – required stone building, water power to run bellows – needed large outlay of capital. [Single vertical line in margin alongside this line.]

     –Antedates 1500 – but very rare before 1600.

     –Spread in England in 17th century.

     –Output of metal still very small.

–Manufacturing

  –Textiles – Industrial capitalism confined to finishing processes, fulling callendring.

   –Rest of textile industry – carried on by domestic system or individual craftsmanship.

  –Shipbuilding – crane used from an early day – state ownership predominant.

  –Building – still backward for private dwellings – except in Holland.

   –Much public building.

  –Glass, soap, alum – rising industries – the first signs apparent in 1500.

–1500, industrial capitalism was still in its infancy over Europe.

  –France was abreast of rest of Europe – but this does not infer much re her industrial capitalism. [Double vertical lines in margin alongside these three lines]

Indirect Approach

  –Rate of growth of industrial capitalism in France has been slower since the 16th century than that of any other European country – even Spain.

   –J. Beloch – article on population. [Possibly: Baudrillart, H. J. L. Les populations agricoles de la France. 3 vols. 1885–1893]

   –1530 population in France nearly 20,000,000

    1930 population, 40,000,000 [Single vertical line in margin alongside this comparison]

   –1530 – England and Wales – not quite 4,000,000

    1930 – England and Wales – approximately 40,000,000

–1530 – Germany, Austria, Holland, Belgium, Poland had [blank]
    1930 [blank]
–1530 – Scandinavia – less than 1,000,000
    1930 – today, 10,000,000 or over
–Population is not a final proof – but, when added to other proofs, it piles up evidence.
–Not much emigration from France to any country.
–Its population history is peculiar – greater stability than in other countries – this is incompatible with any great development of industrial capitalism.

Conclusions of Course: Effects of this slow rate of industrial progress on all sides of French life.
(1)- General impression of a toy–like industrialism.
(2)- Identical machinery of industry in other countries, but treated in a different way – lighter, more artistic.
(3)- French laborer has a hang-over of craftsmanship so that he can use his hands on a wide variety of things.
(4)- Less regimentation and routine, more DIRT, than in U.S.
(5)- The whole paraphernalia of modern industrial life and its offshoots is somehow lacking.
(6)- The face of the country is not that of an industrialized country (as in England, Germany, U.S.).
    –Natural scenery and Gothic splendors are most obvious and less spoiled by modern change (Cordes).
(7)- The state of the demand is not one that adApts itself to the products and methods of industrialism.
    –If these products are not desired by the masses – how is industry to attain any real advance? (F. T. O.)
    [In margin alongside preceding two lines: "Big problems in rise of industrialism – how do demands grow?"
    –Family businesses in textile industries.
    –Inconspicuousness of machinery of ind[ustrialism].
(8)- A good deal of domestic industry remains.
    –In sum – a greater number of parts live together harmoniously than in other countries – and all seem to fit, to belong.
(9)- A country of small holdings, of peasant ownership.
    –Just as French modern literature has a natural kinship in French ancient literature – or paintings.
    –Paris has always cemented the bonds of the whole country, and the bonds of age are united in the same way.

–"The Gothic died gracefully in France." Henry Adams.

–Frenchmen understand the traditions of their own and others' lives – cf. [Archibald] MacLeish.

(10)- French life and history and national culture is full of paradoxes.

–French volatility, though considered a mark of weakness, of instability, has not proved to be such – as proved by war experience – the real truth is a basic stability.

–1550–1789 – a period of exceptional stability.

–Germany not able to be a State.

–England having two important revolutions.

–We are accustomed to think of France since 1789 as unstable.

–de Tocqueville – "L'ancien régime" emphasized the similarity of old and new France – a continuation of an earlier development.

–M. Mandelaine – idea of equality has always been connected with monarchy – as it is today.

–Coty – wants a Fascism of Industry
Daudet – wants a royalty – equality not allied with industry.

–The change from monarchism to representative government was accomplished in two short revolutions.

–In England (1642–1649, 1688) – but has taken a century – (or more) to effect in France.

–This slowness may be viewed as partially a result of her slowness to take on industrial capitalism.

–Just as her stability in monarchism in l'ancien régime may have been partially a result of lack of industrialism.

a- We will trace the industrial development over four centuries.

b- We will trace the interaction of industrial development and the rest of French civilization, acting on each other.

–Cf. Pareto on causation in social sciences.

–Most interpreters of international civilization – as Sombart, G. N. Clark (17th century) etc. – have overstressed the similarities of nations, Nef will stress the dissimilarities between nations.

Problem of Research in French Historical [Research]

–In Western history – one is expected to unearth new documents (in classical history, one has to rehash the same old few documents).

a- Problem of proper selection among an overabundance of material.

b- Problem of how to treat materials once selected, and why to select them.

–Resources of France have been scarcely scratched.

1- One may write a monograph, or, a synthesis – supposedly, covering everything that bears on the subject; one can, perhaps, treat all the printed material. [Arrow pointing from "monograph" to clause beginning "supposedly."]

   –But one gets closer to this ideal by limitation of the period covered.

      -a- Geographical limitation.

      -b- Time limitation.

      -c- Topic limitation.

   –Necessity of narrowing along all three lines.

   –Danger of limiting too much.

   –Problem is not only to narrow the particular subject; but to broaden the setting in which it lies and to paint in that setting. [Single vertical line in margin alongside second half of sentence; also in margin: "Nef's point a new one."]

   –We must extend our acceptance in order to include amateur, non-professional, non-technical, historians.

      –As M. [Paul] Raveau (business man till 65 – history on agriculture published at age of 87).

      –M. Pirenne is of this opinion also

     –This can be of great value.

     –But it is not a principle to hold up for imitation by young students.

   –Professor Usher thinks the mass of materials is so great that we must proceed by monographs – all any one can handle.

 2- Syntheses

   –M. [Henri Sée] – the more you know, the less you know you know.

(Cf. A[natole] France, L'Ile de Penguin } satires on the

V[irginia] Wolf, Orlando} writing of history

     –Is not a mere agglomeration of monographs, a waste-paper basket of fields. [F. T. O.]

     –It is a general survey of forces acting through all fields. [Double vertical line in margin alongside this sentence.]

Bibliography (sources and technique)

  Manuscript material – France

     –National government, smaller government authorities, private persons.

     –Or, classified by depositoriess (our method).

   –Paris (long a center of centralized government)

Archives Nationales – greatest archives in a city which is the greatest city for documents.

     –Government closely connected with national political life – also with economic life – was an entrepreneur – great collection of economic documents   – F_{12} – but many other series.

–All series have calendars which are to be found here in Chicago to the extent they are in print.

1- Find most important series for your uses, ask for that.

　–Calendar of Conseils de Commerce

　　–Bonnaisieur [?] – 18th century – unpublished cards.

2- Get help of officials.

　–Boislisle – Correspondence entre Contrôleur-Général et Indentends et leurs résponses – printed – covers 18th century.

3- Never assume that officials are correct – when they answer (especially by letter) – "They haven't got it."

Bibliotèque Nationale

Ministère des Affairs Etragères ([Alfred] Espinas)

Ministère de Marine

Ministère des colonies – int[?] for U.S.

Bibliotèque Massoral de Lorcinal [sp]

Archives Départmentales – in capital of each Department

　–Have never been as fully indexed or adequately catalogued.

　–Almost impossible to cover all Departments for agriculture.

　–Difficult to write a history of <u>industry</u> for whole of France – for so many Department archives have to be consulted.

　　–Only M. Rauff has done it – we need more historians of more industries – for France. [Double vertical lines in margin alongside this point.]

Archives Municipales

Archives Communales

Private manuscripts – French noble families were not industrialized, thus few manuscripts of economic importance. Cf. Taine (exception of coal in few cases in last 60 years.)

　–Revolution put an <u>end</u> to nobility – documents went to pieces.

　–Records of business houses. Schneider-Creussot, Ansin.

Cf. collections of documents, collections of public acts.

　–Hayem – documents on French economic history, Mémoirs et documents.

　–Bourgin – documents.

　–Proceedings of local archeological societies – journals.

　　–Annals de Bretagne →from 1885.

　　–Annals du Midi – from 1890.

　　–Have articles on economic history and publication of documents

　–Periodicals – Annales historiques

　　Revue historique

　　Revue d'histoire

Literature to tell us of living conditions – especially Restoration Drama.

–Molière – but direct information re living conditions is less available for France – what literature there is tells us other things about France.

–Hauser – D'histoire économique dans l'ancienne France. [Henri Hauser, *Les débuts du capitalisme*, Paris, 1924 (?); *Travailleurs et marchands dans l'ancienne France*, Paris, 1920; and *Les origines historiques des problèmes économiques actuels*, Paris, 1930.]

Methods of attacking any set subject.

Card indexes

Sources de l'histoire de France

Lavisse, Histoire de France, [*Histoire de France depuis les origines jusqu'à la révolution*. 9 vols. 1900–1911.] Histoire générale

Pirenne – for Belgium

Soulier and Martin, Bibliographie des Traaveaux sur la France, 1500-.

Lavisse – Bibliography for history of working class.

Boissonnade – Le socialisme d'état, 1927 and Colbert, 1932. Bibliography in back – especially for 17th century.

Martin – Bibliographie critique de l'industrie en France to 1789.

Sée – Franz\ösische Wirtshaftsgeschichte. Bibliography. 1930.

Economic History Review – Bib[liographical] articles – and lists of new publications.

Revue Historique – lists of books and criticisms.

–Full cards – one for each book – full information.

–Short sentence of its place – page references.

Study and use of documents – literary style

    –Scientist –Artist

    –Dating, analyzing – interpreting, proving (forgery).

    –Background of writer, who was he?, what did he know?

    –Clear distinction between quotations (quotes), summaries (no quotes) and remarks [in square brackets].

    –Slowness, accept boredom, care – accuracy.

    –In quoting, accuracy and fairness in summarizing.

    –Bulletin of Institute of Historical Research, Vol. I, "Report on Editing Historical Documents." [Single vertical line alongside in margin.]

        –For problem of editing a document written in old English.

    –Translation should always have the original in a footnote.

–Problem of the utilization of notes.

    -1/- Have a purpose in mind before attacking any set of documents – Outline (possible to refer to Bibliography, if one has been made up, instead of repeating whole title for every card.

-2/- Put title at upper left (or reference to Bibliography).

–Put the number of the section of your outline it seems to pertain to.

–Use one card, or page, for each subject.

-3/- Make only scanty notes of anything in your own library – or of books that will be permanently to hand.

Literary Style – necessary to longevity.

–Especially necessary for a general synthesis.

–Is not simple – a struggle.

–Where creation is concerned nothing is too trivial for intensive care. [Single vertical line alongside in margin.]

–Rewrite – rewrite.

–Give best part of time to writing.

–Be in the heat of enthusiasm and close to your documents – then write – at a fell swoop.

–Don't put in footnotes, or take care of accuracy at the first writing.

–But go back, afterwards, to fill in [with] care, accurate quotations, etc.

–You can't be too short about what is dull, or too long about what is interesting.

–Make the gathering of material go hand in hand with writing – it is only as you write that you know what you want to write.

–Make the essay have separate lengths from the amounts of notes.

–Necessity of élan vital.

Larousse – for biography; for names of places.

Biographie Universelle – up to 1820 – for persons.

Vidal-Lablache – maps.

Levasseur – Maps for economic historian.

Price changes – Raveau L'Arsenal (hasty, inaccurate)

      Hamilton (Cf. Keynes [*Treatise on Money*])

Economic History of France

I– Industrial history of the late 16th century and turn into 17th century as typified by conditions in the reign of Henri IV – 1598–1610 – but covering the whole period 1540–1610.

Fagniez – Industrial conditions in reign of Henri IV. [Fagniez, G. L'économie sociale de la France sous Henri IV, 1589–1610. Paris, 1897.]

Levasseur – 1852, 1902 "Histoire des classes ouvrières" [See Select Bibliography, Part I]

Sée – "L'Evolution commerciale et industrielle de la France sous l'Ancien Régime"

Hauser – "L'ouvrier du temps passé" – printing and silk

Boissonnade – "Essai sur l'organisation d'veuvre en Poitou" (1300–1789) (difficult to follow chronology).

Godard, J. – "L'ouvrièr en soie"
     –silk industry, in Lyon down to 19th century
     –two chapters on 16th century – scanty material used well

Pariset – "Histoire de la soie" (not good) [Pariset, E. Histoire de la fabrique Lyonnaise. Lyons, 1901]

Coornaert – "La draperie en Hondschoote" – very able work covering one tiny Flemish-French border town [Coornaert, E. La draperie-sayetterie d'Hondschoote. Paris, 1930.]

Phillipoteaux – "L'origin de l'industrie Gedonaise"

Febvre, Lucien – "Histoire de la Franche-Comté" – attempts to write l'histoire intégrale – good on metallergy. [Febvre, Lucien. Philippe II et la Franche-Comté. 1912.]

Gras, L. J. – series of books on industries around St. Etienne – the important coal field. – Not accurate. [See Select Bibliography, Part I]

[Single vertical line in margin alongside preceding eleven items.]

–Secondary material on 16th century is very slim.

–Most general knowledge about industry in 16th century is based on Hauser – who thinks that a substantial industrial revolution – on a small scale – took place between the end of the 15th and end of the 16th century.

   –This industrial revolution was not confined to France, but in France it was only a part of a general industrial revolution that took place in Northern Europe – especially in Pays-Bas.

     –Which opinion is based largely on Marx (who has concept of an Industrial Revolution, 16th to 19th century, as well as of a "period of a manufacturing century."

       –"In this passage," says Hauser, "Marx was talking like a real historian."

       –This view of Hauser's is supported by many French historians.

       –But what real foundations does this theory rest upon?

         –Hauser has never written a general economic history, has written on commerce, workers, but not on industry.

       –Hauser – in "L'ouvriers" – proves that there was industrial capitalism in printing. [In margin: Printing]

         –As many as fourteen men under one roof, and several cases of 6–10 men – (small capital – eight men to one press).

       –Less successful in proving industrial capitalism in silk – (Hauser misreads an authority – a glaring mistake). [In margin: Silk]

–All he tries to prove is that there was some <u>mechanisation</u> of silk-throwing. [In margin: Zonca – History of Inventions (Italian, <u>1607</u>, in British Museum).

  –re Toulouse – though not <u>any</u> evidence to support this.

  –At Lyons – there is <u>no</u> evidence of such a machine <u>before</u> 1600 – but evidence that <u>no</u> factory existed there.

–Hauser mixes in talking of the <u>domestic</u> system in silk – but this is not an industrial revolution.

  –A confused, and poorly substantiated point, in all.

–Fagniez and Levasseur – make much of the artistic goods – do not differentiate between the artisan and the artistic.

  –They were not different for the King – and one comes to this first, in research.

  –The question is, what substitution of industrial routine for artistry.

  –And we must look to the industrial conditions of the factors which affected the activities of the <u>mass</u> of people.

  [Single line in margin alongside preceding two points.]

–<u>In England</u> – in Elizabeth and James I – the London valley became a metropolitan corn market for a great area. [In margin: Food]

  –The city dependent on distant supplies of food – sharing great area of exchange – and <u>specialization</u> in fuel – wood – as to geography.

–Turning <u>to France-</u>

  –We see a tendency for grain supply to widen out about towns. (Cf. Usher on grain.)

  –But, not further than the river valley in which the town was situated.

  –Comparison of Paris and Lyons.

  –The expansion of such marketing exchange and supply territory – had not caused Paris to draw on more than the immediate valley bottom – exceedingly rich.

  –Changes in agrarian conditions – bad, but extensive cultivation – the same.

  –Most remarkable change in food supply was in <u>variety and number of commodities</u> and in <u>cooking</u>.

  –I.e. a survey of fundamental foods – leads us to no proofs of any great <u>change</u> during the 16th century – which is in contrast to the English experience at the time.

    –<u>Printing</u> – usually only two presses under one roof, this required about eight men – only about 2000 men engaged in printing over the whole of France – after a century of the invention.

    –It was an artistic trade anyway.

–Not to be compared with <u>mining</u>.

–No great broadening out of cultivation or extension of the area of cultivation.

–<u>Salt</u> (pumping soliferous water into huge iron pans, round, 20′ in diameter, walls 2 to 4 feet high – then bail it.)

  –In England, 1560–1610 – high level of industrial capitalism in salt manufacturing – a single pan was very expensive to get – needed several workers. [In margin: Coal became the fuel – in Elizabethan times]

  –Some works had <u>several</u> pans – and a few hundred men working (Southshield, 300).

  –Privately owned – seemingly joint-stock, some exchange of stock.

    –Men, recruited from vagabonds, lived in loft above works, miserable state.

–France a larger salt producer than England.

    –Very important salt exports to England from France (and Portugal) – before 16th century.

    –This probably did not fall off during 16th century.

–No reason to suppose that per capita salt consumption was decreasing – or that export to England fell off – in fact exports to Baltic States and Ireland.

–But, in France no evidence that any industrial capitalism in salt manufacturing existed.

  –Main salt works at Saint-Toine, Agincourt (from Bordeaux to La Rochelle – on coast) – on Mediterranean near [Lunel?].

  –Salt mainly from sea water – but not boiled – the heat of the sun did the evaporation. (Mediterranean – less salt, more sun)

  –Peasants living along the shore did the work – wooden troughs – got some capital (under various forms – fermage [leasing] and métayage [sharecropping]) from seigneur – gave up some proportion of product in return.

  –These hundreds of small peasant producers – no large-scale plants – or <u>wage</u> workers.

  –<u>Brine</u> works – <u>Salinas</u> and Alsace-Lorraine (in Franche-Compté, not France then) – wood used for fuel.

    –Iron pans not used till coal used, lead pans used with wood.

    –The <u>pans</u> were <u>owned</u> by the Dukes, or some agents.

–Principal explanation of difference is in national differences.

  a- English could not count on much sun – especially for <u>quantity production</u> of salt.

  b- Relation of salt to French Crown may have had some effect.

–In England, the capital came from salt traders who bought out the small dealers.

–In France, a growing proportion of the salt trade was coming into hands of the Crown.

–Salt tax – gabelle.

–In some Departments the Crown set up warehouses and set up quotas for parishes – which they had to take – more than they used – thus not practicable to buy contraband salt.

–Brittany, Alsace-Lorraine, Franche-Comté – exempt; rest of France divided into pays de petite gabelle – Rhone Valley, and pays de grande gabelle – rest of France.

–In former – Crown always interfering in private trading.

–Salt illustrative of two permanent factors in France, hindering industrial capitalism:

–Geographical aspects.

–Crown policy.

Shipbuilding – large yards throughout Middle Ages – usually in hands of Royal power or Lord.

–But in Holland and England – shipbuilding especially for merchant ships – coming into private hands.

a- Expansion of foreign trade – Dutch the leaders – and supplied other countries with ships – "Their ships, except they stir, the people starve." [Name indecipherable. ***Pope??? – original p. 19].

b- Progress of deep-sea fishing – Dutch in the lead, fish used more in diet.

–England made some attempt to compete.

c- Coastline carrying of coal – called for very heavy ships.

–But nothing in these gave an incentive to France to increase or change its shipbuilding.

–Self-sustaining interior – decline of Mediterranean commerce (producing silk at home – end of Levant trade in silk).

–Many fish in rivers – but less importance of coastline – stopped interest in fish.

–No coastline shipping of coal.

–State retained a dominant role in shipbuilding.

–As a whole, shipbuilding not expanding.

–Fewer ships outfitted in France than in England or Holland – though the population much larger.

Mining

Fuel

–No timber crisis in France in this period – plenty of timber, except in <u>Paris</u>
– but this solved by floating timber down rivers – 1566.

–Thus no shift from wood to coal.

–Coal okay for smithy – but no substitution of coal for wood (a) in hearths
and kitchens, (b) in industries where no technical change was necessary.

  –Except for Lyons – but even here miners only scratched the surface [for
  coal].

–In great contrast to England.

Metallic Ores

  (J. Streider – traces the origins of modern capitalism to mining.)

–First half of 16th century was a period of great activity and progress in
Central Europe, Tyrol, Bavaria, etc.

Iron

  –France, as she is today, is more richly stocked in iron than her neighbors.

  –However, a large part of that iron is in Lorraine, and other border regions
  which were won from Germany.

    –Louis XIV won them; from 1870–1914, lost.

  –But some important iron deposits in the rest of France – especially near
  Lyons.

    –Many small seams dug by peasants, under seigniorial regime.

Rest [of metals]

  –Way behind other central European mining.

  –Beaujolas – lead – late <u>15</u>th century – under public management.

–Mining not developed. This has large influence on the development of
industrial capitalism – mining remains primitive in France.

Metallurgy

  –As separate from the <u>extracting</u> of minerals from the earth; especially as that
  was in early days a simple, <u>single</u> operation.

  –Involves a number of operations and <u>some</u> development of technology.

  –Replacement of old forges by the <u>blast furnace</u>.

    –Forges had predominated down <u>to</u> the 16th century.

    –Blast furnace had been used slightly before.

  –Blast furnace <u>required</u> larger <u>capital</u>, needed huge <u>bellows</u>, which require
  some mechanical power, usually had a <u>hammer</u>, this also needed some non-
  human power, e.g. water.

    –In England – an extraordinary increase of blast furnaces in England
    between 1540–1630 – archeological records.

  –We know little of the use of blast furnaces in France in 16th century – but
  we suspect it was underdeveloped. (Geschichte des Eisens, Beck, 5 vols.).

–Absence of material, does not <u>prove</u> a backwardness of development.

–Impression that failure to develop was due to scattered, small iron ore mines.

[Single vertical line in margin alongside preceding sentence.]

    –Except for Poitou, and <u>Chantelleroux</u> – no evidence, except for these two, of concentration in any one center.

–Still some overemphasis on artistry as against solidity.

–Forez – now heavy industrial center, was a center of arms manufacturing. (L. J. Gras)

    –St. Etienne (capital) – <u>a simple, industrial agglomeration</u>" without a past.

    –Resembling cities in Low Countries – in 16th century (later) and Eastern Frontier.

–Crown exercised a good deal of <u>control</u>, and some ownership here.

<u>Textiles</u>

–Required machinery, power, capital, markets.

–Hauser's proof of labor struggles is not evidence of any <u>new</u> phenomena or even of any new <u>growth</u>.

–No important industry in which the development towards industrial capitalism.

–Except printing, a <u>new</u> industry, greatest growth between 1475 and 1525.

–Capitalistically organized.

–But not a key to further industrial development.

    –Except very indirectly.

    –Levasseur says printing was <u>not</u> regarded as a métier méchanique.

    –Entrepreneurs were not so much traders as <u>savants</u>– who had a beautiful product, rather than <u>profits</u> as an aim.

    –Industrial history of the period: <u>emphasis</u> laid on craftsmanship and art.

    –More so than in any other European country.

    –Since 13th century – France had lagged behind Low Countries, Italy, South Germany in its development of the post-Gothic cathedral. <u>Individualistic,</u> renaissance art.

    –In 16th century France concerned with <u>adapting</u> the Italian influence with its close cooperation of craftsmanship and art.

    –The influence of this technique was very strong on Francc – way into 17th century.

        –All through 16th and 17th centuries France was <u>assimilating</u> this influence and adapting it to their uses.

        –Pottery, books, glass, gold, engraving instead of blast furnaces, coal, etc. as in England (an overemphasis).

    –French laying foundations for an industrial craftsmanship which would enable them to carry their Gothic and the Italian artistry into our own day.

(Boissonnade – speaks of French industry as aided by Colbert – when he means French craftsmanship – typical among writers)
–Humanizing influence of Italy, subsoil richness, strength of autocratic government under Henry IV.
–All served to divert France from the course of that economic upheaval which was engaging all the interests of England and Italy.

Population
–Historians look for evidence of industrial change in growth of population and of urbanization and individual villages – doubtful assumptions to make.
–Population: In England and Wales there is some good evidence to support this contention (3 million – 4.5–5 million).
   –1558–1625 – period of most rapid growth of English population between 1350 and 1760. [Double vertical line alongside in margin. Further in margin: 1564–1605, population of London –quadrupled, based on houses of London.]
      –a great growth of population is generally admitted.
      –In France – Religious wars depopulated.
      –Some increase under Henry IV, and peace.
      –But no evidence that population was much greater in 1610 than in 1560.
      [In margin alongside preceding two lines:

         1324   22,000,000
         1560   20,000,000 (Black Death)
         1610   20,000,000 (Religious wars)]

–Many marks, indeed, of severe depopulation.
   –One Italian estimates Paris population to have decreased from 400,000 to 200,000 during Religious wars.
      –Impossible to use figures, but likelihood that population did not increase.

Urbanization
–In England no evidence of importance has been found to show increase of population in old (usually cathedral) towns.
   –I.e. London not typical of old towns.
      –But the growth of new industrial towns was very marked in England and Low Countries. [In margin: Wordsworth and Mann (cotton).]
         –Pirenne: hasty, straggly origin of these towns, spread out – no walls only walls [at] the market.
   –Especially textiles – peasants recruited for work in factories – peasant houses converted to shops, but large addition to peasant population in villages.

[In margin at top of page: Cf. Tawney – Agriculture 16th century – footnote (c. 180); Nef footnote (c.100)]
  –Metal workers, salt workers, (living over pans).
  –Mining or coal industry.
–In France, no growth of <u>old</u> cathedral towns.
  –Some growth of industrial villages – as St. Etienne – but not nearly so many of these as in England and Low Countries.
    –Was population increase due to a rise in the birth rate? or due to a reduction of the death rate? – Recent studies incline to the latter.
      –Was food supply more adequate due to increased incentive than industrialism.
    –I.e. there seems to have been some connection between industrialism and population.
      –Which came first? Industrial capitalism or population growth? – or both!

Monetary History
  Prices: D'Avenel, <u>History of Prices</u> – many inaccuracies.
    P. Raveau, Le Livre Tournois [Tours]
      La Crise des Prix (Recent History, 1929)
    Earl J. Hamilton, several journals – summarized by <u>Keynes, Treatise</u>, Vol. II, p. 148
    Harsin, <u>Doctrines monetaires et financieres</u>
    Romier, Le royaume de Catherine de Médici
    Lyautey, La housse des prix et [incomplete title]
–Cf. Monetary history of France and England 1500–1610.
–More popular view – widely held by historians – that increase of industry was connected with the great rise of prices – especially if a profit inflation took place.
  –1545 – discovery of Bolivian silver mines – enormous imports of silver into Spain and great increase of [silver] specie all over Europe – (Harsin – tenfold).
  –At same time the early industrial revolution.
  –A great temptation to
    this coincidence as an <u>explanation</u> of the rise of industry.
      –Hamilton, Keynes – profit inflation connected with rise of national strength and wealth in England and France in 16th and early 17th century.
      –S. Chase – in "Mexico" – takes it for granted that modern industry was founded on a silver inflation. [Stuart Chase, *Mexico: A Study of Two Americas*, New York: Macmillan, 1931]

–But very vague reasons supporting this view.

–We shall ask (on basis of study so far) – how did it occur that profit inflation and rise of prices affected England and France indiscriminately – yet the industrial history of the two countries was so strikingly dissimilar? [Double vertical line in margin alongside these four lines.]

    –Level of general prices in France <u>began</u> to rise about 1515.
    –Period of most rapid rise was 1555–1590.
    –Rise of a like size in 1895–1919, world prices.
    –Total rise was about $2^1/_2$ times.

–In England – rise began later, 1530, steepest rise was in 1560–1590 – further from Spain.

–In order to get his figures of profit inflation by taking costs of production to be the same as <u>wages</u>.

    –<u><u>But</u></u> at this time a very important extension of capital cost and plant cost came in.

    –Plant cost was mainly for <u>timber</u> – a great shortage of this in England – but no shortage in France.

    –Thus we would have to correct the French profit inflation by this – on one side and the English profit inflation by this – on the other side.

    –Making the French profit inflation even <u>greater</u>, comparatively.

–Thus we must conclude that monetary changes were <u>not</u> the <u>cause</u> of the rise of industry.

    –Though generally held, and thus it is misinterpreted in the popular eye, today.

<u>Commercial History</u>

    Levasseur, <u>Histoire de Commerce de la France</u>

    Usher, The History of the Grain Trade in France 1400–1710 (internal trade: important)

    Fagniez, L'économie sociale de la France sous Henri IV, 1589–1610

    Masson, Mediterranean trade

    [Single vertical line in margin alongside preceding references.]

Holland

    –Ships from all over the world, and from German river trade.

    –Some exchange of cereals for manufactured goods between Holland and Germany.

England

    –Same kind of trade beginning.

France

–Efforts by Henri IV to improve interior transportation – deepening of streams [Alongside in margin: in Poitiers, [and] near Paris], building of roads, building of canals (Languedoc; Loire-Seine [name indecipherable] begun – not finished before 17th century ended.

–Grandes routes (Routes Nationales) – bridges

　–Impressed peasants under corvée, King as feudal lord.

　–Used peasant stone, without paying, also by feudal rights.

　–Great vexation among peasants, unpopularity, obstruction.

　–Even then, no decent roads about Rouen, e.g. [line incomplete]

　–Everywhere traffic by road was hampered by old feudal taxes and tolls.

　–In general, traffic over a single route was negligible.

–Most supplies of grain for French localities weree brought in from immediate locality – pack horse (exception, Mont de Marsan to Bayonne but this was for export).

　–Blatier – trading in grain.

　–Other markets – wine and [line incomplete]

　–Wood – to be had in abundance everywhere (except where iron works were spendthrift for charcoal).

　–Woolens and textiles

　–For nobility – dependence on shipments from long distances.

　–For common people – dependence on local suppliers – from flax (homespun).

　　–No expansion of demand into luxury products.

–Self-sufficiency of all small provinces or localities.

　a- Abundance of nature in locality.

　b- Lack of that abundant water means of transportation – that was so important in England and Holland.

　　–No transportation of heavy goods.

　　–Emphasis, in what industry there was, was on artistic sides of luxury goods for nobility.

　　–Slight development of banking – except around Lyons – where industry was most advanced.

Agrarian History

　a Land holding on eve of 16th century.

　b Land holding changes during 16th century.

　c Comparison of history of 16th century in France and England

　d Reasons for difference.

　　Bloch, M. – Les caractères originaux de l'histoire rurale française, 1931

　　–Best agrarian history of any country.

–Supplements, rather than replaces, the various monographs.

Esmein, A. – <u>Cours élémentaire d'histoire du droit français</u> 1890s – 15 ed.

    –Chapter on kinds of land tenure from legal point of view.

Chénon, E. – <u>Les dénombrements de la propriété foncière en France avant et après la Révolution</u>

    –First chapter <u>very</u> valuable for l'ancien regime (basis of Nef's notes).

    –None of these bear any specific relation to 16th century.

    –With respect to 16th century, more specifically:

Raveau, P. – <u>L'agriculture et les classes paysannes dans le haut Poitou au XVIe siècle</u>

                 –Chapters II-V.

Febvre, L. – <u>Philippe II et la Franche-Comté</u>

    –Perhaps outstanding economic historian (Chapters 7–11)

Sée, H. – <u>Les classes rurales en Bretagne du XVIe siècle à la Révolution</u>

    –Important for 16th century.

Sée, H. – <u>La vie d'un Aumênier en France en Moyen Âge</u>

    –Sée's first work and definitive.

Bézard, Y. – <u>La vie rurale dans le sud et la region Parisienne de 1450 à 1560</u>

    –17th and 18th centuries.

Thesis – Agrarian history has an important relation to industrial, political, and commercial history.

    –Other researchers show that Raveau's study may be made the basis of generalizations for a wider area than Haut-Poitou.

    –North and North East [In margin alongside the first lines of the following.]

        –Most land east of Brittany – population in villages of a few houses, two or three large fields – in each of which the peasants had some strips. In rest of Seigneurie mostly forest, etc. – the peasant had certain rights of gathering wood and stones, etc.

–South and South West

    –Peasants lived in compact villages, not open field system, compact holdings, held their land by <u>hereditary customary</u> tenure. All kinds of cultivation carried on by peasants – rather than by wage earners working for lord or a lessee.

    –Peasant owed dues in money and in kind, but former had <u>mostly</u> replaced the latter – and money dues were of a <u>fixed</u> nature.

        –Though <u>some</u> servile obligations lasted till Revolution – where they [had] lasted [from] 15th century.

        –Around Paris and some other provinces, no serfdom after 15th century.

1 – <u>Serfdom</u> – owner bound to land under legal theory, not in practice.

        –Specific tasks, and [sentence incomplete]

–Certain number of days per year.

–Mostly disappeared except in two provinces in central France, leaving [sentence incomplete]

2 – <u>Customary</u> tenure – many varieties

    –Tenure roturière [inheritance] – mostly predominant.

    –A holding created, passed on from father to son – indefinitely.

    –But some short-term holdings which were regarded as roturière.

    –Sometimes some services remained due, or some share in produce.

    –Lords willing to sell their seigneurial rights to peasants for cash – were hard up for money.

  a – Censive – most important kind of <u>roturière</u>. [In margin: bail à cens [lease contract]]

    –Many francs-alleux [freed of payment] had been changed into censire by principle "no land without its lord."

    –Could not be turned back to the lord, unless the tenant abandoned it.

    –Censiteur could not lease any part-or create a censive within a censive.

    –Peasant owed lord the right to hunt on his holding (this not a vassal, who was lord of his holding).

    –Owed a <u>cens</u>, usually collected once and for all.

    –Owed a <u>sur-cens</u>, annual rent, paid every year – not large.

    –Owed a payment in case of death of lord.

    –In case the land was not passed on or sold, in hereditary progression <u>lods et ventes</u> (1/12th of sale price).

      –Paid by purchaser of land.

    –In 1789, censiteur was regarded as a peasant proprietor – a full fledged land owner.

  b – <u>Emphytéose</u> perpetuele (allodial lands). [In margin: (bail à emphytéose)]

    –Holder <u>regarded</u> as having definitely alienated the land from the lord.

    –Rare in North, more common in South.

    –Peasant paid a <u>canon</u> or <u>pension</u>.

    –And had to pay a share of the sale price if he sold his land.

    –Lord had right to take back his land, if the peasant decided to sell – actually not used.

  c – Emphytéose temporelle (non-allodial as well as allodial lands)

    –Easier to renew lease.

  d –Locataire perpétuelle – common in Languedoc.

    –Could be made as part of land within the fief or censive.

  e – [missing]

    –In Poitou, Anjou, Nivernais, in South, Centre, Alpine region.

    –Tenant plants trees, and pays annual return <u>in</u> fruit.

–At the end 5–7 years one-half went to lord, one-half went to tenant in perpetuity.
    –An arrangement for planting vines and fruit trees.
    –A permanent holding seldom able to get back [by] lord.
f – domaine congé – lord had right to reject the tenant, provided he paid for improvements – never exercised.
g – domaine quevaise – could only hold one in a seigneurerie.

–During the 16th century in England.
    –Much land formerly farmed was turned into sheep pasture, many forests turned into sheep pasture.
    –Enclosures.
    –New industry – breaking down manorial traditions.
        –More land being put under cultivation.
    –Dissolution and confiscation of Church lands.
        –Bought by merchants, from Crown.
    –Old ecclesiastical and noble owners were being replaced by new merchant owners from towns and cities, especially London.
    –Had such an effect on peasants as to be called an Agricultural Revolution by Ashley and Tawney.
    –Land rented out to capitalist farmers – peasants who held land by copyhold were ejected, and the land "enclosed."
    –Also the forests, etc., which had been used in common were enclosed.
    –For the first time there was a divergence of the history of agriculture in the two countries.

–In France – changes in 16th century.
    –Holders of fixed payments were getting away with a lot – by rising prices.
    –Lords were going into debt and mortgaged.
    –Holdings being bought up by merchants.
    –But – ecclesiastical holdings not changed.
        –And there was not often more land brought into cultivation – any that was was leased out.
        –Seldom any permanent ejection of the tenant, although the form of tenure was changing to metayage fermage.
    –At first sight metayage and fermage were worse – but they became, in practice, about perpetual – so that a peasant became almost a proprietor.
    –Relatively little land brought newly into cultivation.
        –No increase in population – nor in sheep raising.
    –I.e. peasant proprietorship was being maintained in France, at the time he was being wiped out in England – disappearance of yeomanry.

–Mainly due in both cases to the rise in prices.

–But the monetary factor can not explain the underline differences between the two developments.

Review of 16th century –

–Contrary to the view of Hauser the progress towards capitalism and towards a development of the domestic system was not one which could be called an industrial revolution.

–Certainly was not a development on a scale comparable to England.

–This difference of great importance.

–On France's side it was rooted in the whole economy and polity of the nation.

–An[d] in geographical and natural phenomena.

–Monetary history could hardly have caused both the industrial progress in England and sluggishness in France.

–Due to its equal change in both countries.

–But there were differences between the two countries.

   1 – Population

   2 – Commerce

   3 – Agriculture – in France the maintenance, in large proportion, of hereditary ownership, as contrasted to diminution of that in England.

   –Connected (a) to population stability

   –and to (b) industrial history

      (1) through population.

      (2) by religious differences.

   4 – General History

   a/ Social

      –Industrial history related to non-economic aspects of general history.

         –Rapid rise of both industrial capitalism and of domestic system tended to concentrate wealth and power in the hands of the mercantile classes – as the supply of essential commodities became more and more centered in their hands. [In margin: This came about in England.]

         –The strength of the feudal landed aristocracy was losing its raison d'être – the trader found his main object of wealth in stock, goods, notes, not in land.

         –In France, the mercantile classes were not in as much prestige in 1614, as in England.

      –A reflection of industrial development.

   b/ Religion

      –Related to the position of the Church, and to the [sentence incomplete]

      –Church – Religious matters of great import still.

–The Age of Religious Wars.

–Henri quatre [or IV?]: "elle est vièrge, comme je suis catholique" [She is virgin, as I am Catholic.].

–It was still politically expedient for the King to be Catholic.

–While, on the other hand, the Catholicism was changed.

–Royal Absolutism – served to restore in some part the loss of some faith in religion.

[Brace in margin alongside second through fifth items.]

–Max Weber – relation between certain forms of Protestantism and the rise of industry – of importance.

–The strength of religion was still strong in France.

–Thesis: spirit of Protestantism = spirit of enterprise = spirit of industry.

–Many monks have disputed this thesis.

> –Robertson (Capetown) urges that the spirit of both Protestantism and Catholicism are the same, in their attitude towards industry.

–Tawney has a sounder approach, that there is a scrap of truth in Weber's thesis, which element, once present, gathers snow while rolling.

–The relation of religion to industry is not so simple as Weber would have us believe.

–Its effects are not negligible, but are only some among many.

–Outpouring of books, discussion of Usury in 16th and 17th centuries in England may be due to rise of industry. [In margin: Cf. R. H. Tawmey and Thomas Wilson]

–Whereas in France practically no books on this subject were written at this time – only in the 50 years before the Revolution, when industrial advance was great, did an outflow of books occur on this same subject.

> –Due to a lack of rise of industry and lack of need of a more liberal philosophy.

–I.e. we may conclude that the change in religion is as much a result of industrial activity as a cause.

–However, it may have acted as a sort of brake on progress.

c/ Royal Power

Hauser	Poivoir publique et la [title incomplete]
Boissonnade	"Le socialisme d'Etat"
Hanotaux	Chapters on royal power, growing
Esmein	Chapters on royal power, growing

–Estates General called in 1614, last time till 1789.

–With advent of Henry IV, French political theory based its hopes on a strong royal absolutism – as against former insecurity.

  –Joined by centralized powers.

    –King's officials and Crown took a direct interest in municipal elections, naming men, forbidding statutes, etc.

  –And direct taxation – this came into control of funds to govern with.

  –And this money was its, to use as it would.

  –In England and Holland – republican governments were in control of expenditure of money, and a conflict was going on over the position of royal power in municipal affairs – in which the Crown was usually unsuccessful.

  –This power, in France, was one of the main causes of the failure of industrial capitalism to develop.

    –Rich men were being created but their interests were not different from those of the Crown.

    –Interested in collection of taxes.

    –Exploiting their connection with Crown.

  –The Crown, interfering directly and indirectly with industrial life – by regulations over gilds – at just the time when, in England, they were breaking down.

  –Sovereign's strength due to the lack of thriving industrial development – at same time a <u>cause</u> of that lack. [Double vertical line alongside in margin.]

d/ <u>Cultural</u>

  1550–1625 – certainly not a very brilliant period.

  –Only painters, the <u>Le Naim</u> brothers.

  –<u>Jean Bodin</u>, the only political thinker – shortcomings as an artist, but brilliant.

  –Only one great man in literature – <u>Montaigne</u> – but a great gap between him and his contemporaries – a solitary figure – little or no contact with contemporaries.

  –Main flow of thought.

  –Italian influence, and the Court.

  –I.e. industrial history and culture the outgrowth of the <u>same</u> cause.

    –<u>Henri Etienne</u> – printing.

  –It was a period of barrenness in the arts – too much traditional weight, fixity.

  In England – drama and poets.

  In Low Countries – schools of painting.

  [Brace coupling preceding two lines.]

  –Were both outgrowths of a new approach towards existence.

AgeofLouisXIV – 17th century
  Lavisse – Histoire de France, Vol. 8, 215, 232. Sagnac.
  Best survey of industrial history in France at end of reign of Louis XIV.
  Sée, H. – L'Evolution commerciale et industrielle de la France sous l'Ancien
  Régime. Part I, Chapters 7 and 8.
  Levasseur – History of Working Classes. Book VI.
  Voltaire – Le siècle de Louis XIV.
    –First attempt at l'histoire intégrale.
      –Lack of materials or knowledge of where to go for them prevented its
      completion.
    G. N. Clark – The Seventeenth Century.
      –Sketchy, but general.
      –More success at l'histoire intégrale.
    Martin, G – La Grande Industrie sous Louis XIV – best on Royal
    manufacturings
    Boissonnade – Le socialisme d'état
      –Colbert
      –First, goes down to Colbert.
      –Second covers the author's hero.
      –Good bibliography.
      Cf. Annales Soc. and Econ. Febvre's review
      ("Industry" covers art, Gobbelin efforts)
Bondais Colbert | R. d'H. eco. 1929 | Societé Nivernaisede letters, science and art,
1925
    Sagnac L'industrie et le commerce de la draperie, Rev. d'hist. Mod. Et
    contemp.

No century has been more neglected than this one, in France, England, Germany
– as to its economic life.
    –It is generally assumed that it was a century of advance in commerce, of
    delay in industry (cf. G. N. Clark).
    –Clark based his statement on [name indecipherable] Industrial Organization
    in the 16th and 17th centuries.
      –Clark says that small enterprises proved a barrier to the growth of large-
      scale enterprise.
      –This is doubtful, as [name indecipherable] showed.
      –Example of pin-making [above the line: belt-making]. – Why was an
      establishment with 20 employees incompatible with industrial capitalism?
      –Also, there were commercial capitalists in the large cities, who actually
      stimulated the rise of large-scale industry.

–Certain types of commercial capitalisms were hostile to rise of industrial capitalism – as [name indecipherable] showed.

–But, other types were sponsoring the rise of industrial capitalism – by lending large amounts of capital – many enterprises were much more developed at end of 17th century than at beginning. [Brace alongside preceding point and first line of this point.]

–I.e. Clark's opinion will have to be considerably revised.

–Comparison of France and England in 17th century.

–Was France showing a strange resistance to the forces of "modern" development?

–Lack of much quantitative material for comparison (population in France 20–22 million, in England 5–6 million).

–So larger output in France does not necessarily mean the industry has a larger place in the national life.

–What proportions of industry were capitalistic, domestic, private? – Little evidence.

–How far was industry privately controlled?

–If industry was government controlled – was it a forerunner of industrial capitalism? – Boissonnade, yes.

–What of the effect of the kind of product?

–A large shop, many hands, making artistic product.

–Versus a small mine or forge, less hands, more industrial capitalism.

Mining

–Coal occupied much less place in France than in England, Low Countries, Germany.

–Was a much more striking divergence than under Henry IVth.

[Brace alongside preceding two points.]

–Last half of 16th century – and until after middle of 17th century – no complaints, to speak of, of a shortage of wood.

–But, in the last thirty years of the reign a chorus of complaints went up.

[Brace alongside preceding two points.]

–1701, a royal investigation by Comptroller-General.

–Coal had been known, in parts, for centuries, but had been despised for its smell, smoke – and forbidden to be used in Paris, even by smithies.

–1709, the Contrôleur-Général sent to Intendants forreports on coal mining and its extent.

–Result was to show the slight development of mining.

–One, Turgot, said the supply in his Department was not enough for smithies and nail makers.

–Another man, near St. Etienne, said the coal was nearly exhausted, but that it replenished itself!

–Usually just a scratching of the surface by the local peasants who owned the land and had 200 francs to sink a pit.

–Yet most of the fields we know to-day were known – except the field in North France – near [statement incomplete]

–Total output probably 100,000 tons.

–But in England and Wales and Scotland, about two million tons.

　–All larger mines employed 200 or more men.

　–Pits sunk to depth of 100–200 feet.

　–One mine produced 50,000 tons.

　–Coal used in industry, in houses, etc.

–In France, one fertile field of source of industrial capitalism was not tapped.

–Also this mining segregated the miner as the textile worker was not.

–As soon as coal was utilized in England, wider markets, concentration of industry and large-scale production were all encouraged.

–Timber crises, but lack of coal mining, had important repercussions on French economic life.

–Timber crisis, unrelieved by coal substitution, brought a reduction of industry.

–After 1780s – a depression and reduction of industry.

1- Edict of Nantes – skilled workers usually Protestant, had to emigrate.

2- Royal inspection and regulation – Colbert's system not a serious handicap, while he ran it, but he died in 1783, and his successors did not handle it so well.

[Brace in margin around preceding two points, and: "Usual explanations"]

3- But we must not forget the high price of fuel – which made it nearly impossible to make profitable sales – and just at this time, a high tariff was put on coal's importation.

　–Great distress among all lines of industry and their workers.

　–In England – 1800 – problem of overproduction of coal.

–In France – 1800 – problem of finding any fuel which would make production possible.

Lead and Copper – advance in England, but Colbert's attempt to stimulate their production in France, failed.

Bar and Pig Iron – stationary output in England from 1625 to1720.
←(25,000 tons Ashton; 17,000 tons, Scrivener wrong.)

　–After great activity under Elizabeth and James I.

–In France we have no comparable study or figures.

–We have a complete survey of France for 1788.

–None of the big furnaces existent at that time was mentioned in an earlier study of the end of Louis XIV.

–We have nothing but a <u>guess</u> that the output in France was not much more than in England – though it would have had to be three times as large, in order to be comparable [per capita].

–Sagnac, having seen the Intendents' report of 1709, said coal mining was by all means the most important of any kind – we know how much England was in advance of France in coal mining.

–In respect to mining, France was very backward, at the end of the reign of Louis XIV – more backward than England, Germany, Low Countries.

<u>Manufactures</u> – <u>Metallurgy</u>

–Necessary to distinguish raw from finishing processes – for wood was essential to the first, but not for the second.

–<u>Smelting</u> – substitute of blast furnace for old Catalonian furnace, made two steps of the process of smelting – used more wood.

  –Anchors were made direct from pig iron.

  –Blast furnace required the technique of industrial capitalism – it dominated by end of 17th century.

–<u>Finishing</u> processes, did use coal, yet were usually small-scale, non-industrial capitalist – steel was made by large-scale methods.

  (Catalonian forge – hammered hot iron, not molten iron – but some molten iron came with better bellows – the blast furnace developed slowly. Pig iron was first made, then made into bar iron by the blast furnace, before, bar iron made directly.

–France less behind England in the smelting than in the finishing process.

  –Not so much progress in France in 1550–1625 as in England. But during 17th century, a parallel progress.

–St. Etienne, Navarre, Normandy, Alsace-Lorraine had [statement incomplete]

  –Forge sold for 500 Livres Tournois [money minted at Tour later became the Royal money] – replaced by a blast furnace which was rented for 1,200 L. T. <u>per</u> year.

  –About 20 feet high, these furnaces, square, bellows at bottom, water wheel for working bellows.

  –Soon a mountain of slag, piles of wood, charcoal operations.

  –Ideal site was where water power, thick forests, iron ore were together.

  –Became increasingly connected to forges.

  –I.e. good examples of industrial capitalism.

–Who supplied the <u>capital</u>?
  –Usually the seigneurs of the fiefs on which the ore was found.
  –But their capital was usually found to be too small – so they had to call on mercantile classes.
    – Who gradually came into possession of the furnaces – either by taking them over for debts – or by leasing them on very favorable (to him) terms. [In margin: Example from Navarre, Mozorin [?]].
    –Who bought up small forges, or supplied raw iron, and if they fell behind in their deliveries, he took over their forge.
    –I.e. the development of industrial capitalism.
–Finishing processes were not as developed as in England (Cf. Nef., M. Tiqué [?]).
  –Who imported (Lipson thinks) again as much from Sweden, American colonies, (Spain) (not from France, to any degree) as they produced at home.
  –I.e. nearly 50,000 tons worked up.
–In England and France, a few capitalists were controlling a great number of workers by the domestic system.

Textiles
  –Material had to pass through a number of stages of different kind of work.
    –Encouraged the domestic system in towns (as it had since the 13th century – at least).
    –Not the same as industrial capitalism – large plant.
    –Yet it is important for us as an example of a sort of <u>quasi-capitalism</u>.
      –Especially where it is large scale and handles standardized raw materials.
    –Also, some large plants. [In margin: Wordsworth and Mann. Ballot-Industrial Revolution in France]
      –<u>Dutch loom</u>, (Leyden) 1620 – introduced widely by 1700.
      –<u>Stocking frame</u>
      –<u>Silk throwing</u> – water wheel
        –Discovered in Italy in 16th century.
        –No important factories before 17th century – did not get to England before 1721.
    –Quasi-factory development with respect to fulling, <u>callandering</u>, <u>dyeing</u>.
      –From 13th century on.
      –Houses around the warehouse – a semi-factory.
    –However, the great majority of workers were under the domestic system – in 1700 – factory an exception, but a more important one than in 1600.
    –Dutch loom, stocking frame, wire drawing, blast furnaces – were all <u>used</u> for a century or more before we need to take account of them as an <u>important</u> element.

–Municipal regulations and guild regulations had prevented the worker from capitalist exploitation to anything like the extent it might have been.
–<u>Rural</u> domestic system could be carried on much more ruthlessly than in towns.
  –This began, in England, in 14th century (Cotswolds).
  –A movement to extend the town and guild regulations to the country by Crown statute for municipality.
  –Weakest (in Lancashire) where the mediaeval guild had been weakest.
  –Strongest (in Northern France) where the mediaeval gild had been strongest.

<u>Textiles in private hands</u>: 17th century.
  –New demands for clothing – linen began to be worn next the skin.
    –Working towards an increase in the quantity and complexity of clothes worn.
    –Also more frequent changes of style.
    –Greater demand for fine silk and linen, for a large court and nobility, than in England.
    –Also exportation of fine textiles to England, where (only) French cloth was used by upper classes.
    –Thus an increase of production.
    –But a depression 1685–1715 in France, which had no counterpart in England (especially in woolen industry).
    –It has been ascribed to revocation of Edict of Nantes, and Royal interference.
      –We must add – timber shortage.
      –Wool in Picardy, Champagne, Normandy, Languedoc.
      –Wood had to be imported into all these areas.
      –Necessity for mixture of wools in manufacturing.
      –France depended on England for coarse and Castille for finest wools.
    –English forbade the exportation of wool, and attempted to shut off the Spanish supply – neither perfectly successful.
      –But did cut down the supply a lot.
      –England had plenty of wool, France had a shortage.
    –The Domestic System dominated in all the country [sic: countries] into which the woolen industry rapidly spread.
      –Centered in Loire, Somme, Picardie, Champagne.
    –In older towns (Rouen) no such expansion into rural areas as in North and East of Paris – nor in South of Paris (royal manufacturing).
    –All along the roads leading into Beauvais, Amiens, etc., the Domestic System was spreading – <u>the nuclei were old mediaeval villages</u>.
      –They remained villages, – the peasant continued to till the soil to supplement his income.

–(Some development took place in Lancaster but agriculture played a less[er] part.)

–Hundreds, sometimes thousands of workers doing every phase of textile production.

  –Usually under the control of a single trader.

  –Near Lille one trader had 3000 workers working for him.

  –But the workers did not always go to the same trader – flax (doubt cast on figures).

–In England the same nucleus around an old mediaeval town was not present.

–Some people say the guild regulations were so easily controlled by a strong capitalist – that the effect of guild regulations in curtailing trade was not so much (an English school) – Pirenne would not subscribe.

–But – at this time, the Crown, in France, was backing up old guild regulations and making new ones.

  –Whereas in England, the Crown influence was not so great. The guild regulations were easily broken.

Three types of Royal Industry

  1–Manufacturing Royal – Crown-owned plant, its agent paid the worker (at Beauvois, still).

  –Rugs and tapestries.

    –Savarannies [?] } old, reestablished by Colbert

    –Gobelins }

    –Beauvais – established by Colbert.

  2–Manufacturing Royal – right to use Royal arms.

    –Established by lettres patentes, to a person, or group (really agents of Crown).

    –But much financial support given by government, salaries paid – capital supplied.

  3–Manufacturing privilégiés – no use of Royal arms.

    –Set up by Colbert's successors. He opposed these on grounds that they would destroy private initiative.

      –Colbert was never sure of just where he stood – in his own mind.

      –Used phrase "laisser aller."

      –But constantly stood for royal manufacturing.

  –Relation of 1 and 2 to modern industrial capitalism:

    (1) Purely artistic, an offshoot of the Court.

      –M. LeBrun, director, artistes.

      –Large scale production of a nearly standardized kind of interior decorating.

      –Prevented good development of furniture etc. industry.

(2) It has been argued that (2) were the origins of the factory system.

    –Combination of domestic and factory system – workers worked in their own houses, had looms there, yet the whole thing was within fair walls – a factory? [Diagram in margin of "Ville Neuvette" (soldiers uniforms): four working areas – quadrants – with separating hallways in each direction.]

    –Sée thinks this was an exception.

    –Sagnac thinks it was more common – Carcassonne, Abbeville, etc.

–Nef does not think this can be used as a first example of industrial capitalism – Sée agrees.

    –Started by government – <u>artificial</u> – doomed to fail – begun in regions of <u>little</u> manufacturing – no market.

    –Crown went on assumption that you could create industry at the will of the State.

    –Crown carried on State socialism on a large scale, yet these ventures never <u>expanded</u> – nor lasted, except by Royal favor – while private ventures expanded, lived.

    –Were artistic (in England – utilitarian).

<u>Glass</u> – windows, mirrors, vessels.

    1/- Blown glass – artistic – for nobles.

    2/- This expanded, on small scale, especially in Northern Italy, in 15th and 16th centuries.

    –In Venice glaziers were made nobles.

    –Other places only nobles allowed to be glaziers (Altori).

    3/- But in England glass manufacturing was lowly, larger scale.

    –In France the Crown imported Italian glaziers – who were made gentilhommes-vivriers [?] – but were not very successful – initiative [lacked initiative].

    –And could not work so well with sheet glass.

    –Paternalism prevented the accomplishing of just the ends it desired.

    –In England coal used – favored the manufacturing of cruder forms of glass.

    –France ill-adapted to Venetian activity artistry also, by lack of use of coal, ill-adapted to large-scale, crude, sheet glass manufacturing.

<u>Pottery</u> –

–Naverre – a factory set-up – workmen gathered together, paid wages, a number of rooms, for manufacturing, storage – owner lives in the same house.

    –Semi-factory conditions.

       –Artistic emphasis.

       –The workers have a respected place in the community.

–The owner worked with hands next to men.

Summary-Geographical conditions, Crown interference, natural resources [were at work as] in 16th Century, to brake the rise of industrial capitalism.
   –Were still at work in 17th century – but some even stronger.
   –France making some headway in industrial capitalism.
   –Large plant, large capital.
   –But either artificially stimulated by Crown, or artistic elements predominated.
   –Crown influence through guild backing kept textile production from spreading.
   –France lacked coal and wool – had high tariffs also.

General European Situation:
   –Tobacco, coffee, expansion of brick, multi-room houses.
      –An age of growing opulence among the middle orders – Voltaire.
      –The 17th century not one in which industrial expansion lagged behind commercial expansion.
         –Large-scale enterprise, capitalists, or joint-stock.
         –Industrial capitalism – affected only a small proportion of workers.
         –But domestic system became predominant, widespread.
   –In France these lines of development were less sharp.
      –Growing power of State.
      –Intellectual revolution – are more evident in France than in the rest of Europe. [Brace in margin alongside preceding two points; also: Clark's points – of significance in 17th century France.
      –Industrial history not to be understood mainly in terms of constitutional and intellectual history:
         –Understanding of the France of Louis XIV – Cf. Mme. de Sévigny, Saint Simon.
         –Abundance of food and drink – delicacy, (furniture).
            –Wood becoming scarce in all provinces, and not yet used.
         –But these other factors are of some importance:
         –Louis XIV finished many things, began nothing.
         –Great autarchy – monarchy absolute.
         –Merchant and trading classes not excluded from government – they provided the royal officials.
            –Increase of Crown functions – Crown sold offices, took on to itself the best ability of middle classes.
               –Décre de Poulet – original payment, then 1/60th of that each year – could then hand down to their children the office.
            –Richelieu molded the office of Intendent in economic life into one of great importance. (Cf. John Law.)

–Royal authority was coming to dominate in France – new administrative areas.

   –Prévôté – prévot – military and financial functions, public and private sénéchal baillé – to administer feudal estates. – judicial functions.

   –Receveurs royals (generalities)

–13th century – these powerful.

   –17th century – Intendents becoming all-powerful.

   –Sous-délégués – acted for Intendents in Departments, which had no legal position until Revolution – could be changed.

   –Intendents and sous-délégués were recruited from merchant classes – but did not retain their outstanding position as merchants.

   –For England, cf. Stubbs, Maitland, Webbs (local government).

   –Louis XIV – royal authority taken to furthest extent – longevity in highest office.

      –Depression and oppression could not make of any other man in the country a big opposition figure.

      –Men who founded the Revolution were sympathetic to the things they were condemning, when laws had ruled them.

   –No representative assembly – royal rule in every corner of the land.

   –Pays d'états – had their provincial assemblies, which met after 1614.

   [In margin: Especially Provence, Languedoc]

   –Their right to review taxes was being turned into a formality during Louis XIVth regime.

   –A majority of these were turned into pays d'élection – governed by decrees, etc.

      –Parle le ment – self governing bodies, not representative assemblies – Parle le ment de Paris, Toulouse, etc.

      –Could refuse royal assessments, and could initiate taxation – but only pending a royal edict on the same subject, if it were not covered by previous royal enactments.

   –This scope constantly limited as Crown extended.

   –Their members were chosen by the Crown – usually stood to make a good profit out of Crown support – but occasionally rebelled – le Fronde.

–Conseils souverains – instituted in 17th century.

   –Highest courts of appeal – tried cas royales – any thing pertaining to royal authority, or public interest – or tried any cases of conflicting jurisdiction.

   –Practically all cases dealing with industry were handled by royal courts under one or the other of these.

–Parle-le-ment, together with Intendents, possessed the most <u>minute</u> control over provincial matters.

–Comparison with England. 1688 – Parliament had won right to initiate legislation, to pass on taxes.

   –Civil War had resulted in the suppression of many courts.

   –Privy Council only <u>nominally</u> composed of <u>King's</u> advisers.

–<u>A complete difference of constitutional history</u>, during 17th century.

–What   was   the   result   of   this   on,   or   the <u>relation of this to, industrial development</u> in the two countries?

   a- What result did government regulation have on industry in France.

      –Colbert and Crown wanted to have the country developed industrially.

      –But Crown had a multiplicity of objectives of its policy.

         –Could hardly be expected to carry out with single-minded purposiveness this industrialization.

         –E.g., <u>Souliers</u> – wanted better transportation, but fundamentally opposed to the expansion of industry.

         –Especially of <u>silk</u> industry.

         –Thought agriculture should remain the basis of France's economy.

         –Colbert – wanted private industry, but set up public industries to rival them.

         –Wanted to have the use of coal spread – but encouraged industries which did not use much coal.

         –Wanted manufacturing but [with] a heavy protective tariff.

         –Is the best path to industrial development <u>via</u> government paternalism.

         –When the State was the entrepreneur, the private entrepreneur had no place.

         –Certain Crown policies under Louis XIV.

            (a) Aesthetic purposes as end of industry – absorbing capital and labor which might have been absorbed in other lines.

            (b) To extent <u>travail en joindre</u> – the guild organizations.

               –Partly for the income derived from them.

               –which were no longer bulwarks against the spread of Domestic System.

               –But industry tended to concentrate in old centers.

               –And some handicaps <u>may</u> have been imposed – not proved yet.

            (c) To extend transportation and communication facilities.

               –(1) Water, (2) roads, (3) elimination of local tolls on water and road ways.

(1) Water – <u>Canal de Brière</u> (Loire to Seine) (1640) – <u>Canal de Languedoc</u> (Mediterranean to Atlantic

–Rivers deepened for barge traffic.

(2) Roads- Soulier had idea of national road system – after death of Henry IVth, these languished – had never been popular – Crown labor, stones, wood.

–Neither Richelieu nor Mazarin did anything.

–Colbert reconstructed the Administration des Ponts and Routes – but died.

–Then wars occurred, nothing more done, except military roads to East.

[In margin: cheval [?] (for fermes) Dictionaire Historique]

(3) <u>Tolls</u> elimination – something done, but this ran into conflict with Colbert's tariff policy.

–Could enforce the tariff policy only in Central France (les cinq grandes fermes indecipherable])

–Rest of France refused to submit to Colbert's tariffs, and kept their own policy of tolls and tariffs.

–<u>Something</u> done – encouraging industry.

–State of roads was no worse in France than in England but canals better in France (no canals or river deepening in England in 17th century).

–Would not have been done at this time by private enterprise (in late 18th century-early 19th century – private enterprise in England did do great things).

–At end of 17th century England was the largest free trade area in Europe – thousands of miles of coastline.

–Royal policy did not prove an aid to, or substitute for, private initiative and enterprise.

(d) Tariff policy deprived the French producer of <u>coal</u> and <u>wool</u>.

–Partly the cause of the great depression during the last years of the reign [Louis XIV].

–Crown policy – economically suicidal.

–Were a serious handicap to French industry.

–But England was not dependent on foreign trade, and her tariffs didn't have the same effect.

(e) Wars – fought with increasing ferocity in latter years (Cf. <u>Krieg und Kapitalismus</u> – Sombart).

–But they did not make Crown dependent on private traders.

Relation between industrial history and Constitutional history – as cause and effect.
  (f) Taxation and industrialism
    –Interference of private accumulation restricts the growth of industrialism.
    –Crown virtually independent of local authorities in the laying of taxes – for
     its great wars.
      –Problem of royal power – how get money? – In England by representative
       assembly, in France by direct action.
    –Taille – an old feudal tax, its scope widened and broadened by Louis XIV.
      –Taille Personelle – fell on third estate.
        –Was an extension of old taille seigneurelle, so nobles who had assessed
         that, considered they were exempt.
        –Also certain towns escaped.
        –And the church.
  –Taille Real
    –The total amount desired was decided, and proportions assigned to
     généralités where local collectors assigned it to smaller district.
      –These men had to turn in so much, kept over that all they could collect.
      –Very iniquitous.
    –Church and nobility almost exempt.
  –Taille capitation – head tax, extended the taille to urban dwellers – like the
   taille, designed to hit income.
    –Collected differently.
    –Everyone liable – but ecclesiastics and nobles soon wriggled out.
      –Church fixed on a lump sum, 4 million livres then (1710) purchased
       permanent exemption for 24 million livres.
      –Nobles obtained piecemeal reductions, and exemptions.
        –Most nobles were pensioners of the Crown – cut those, without paying
         more.
  –Dixième – a property or income tax, fell mainly on land, sometimes on
   manufacturing plant.
      –Nobility and clergy got reductions.
      –Problem of assessment – a tenth of some assessment was the tax.
    –All direct taxes collected by the royal government through its authorities.
    –Aides, Gabelle, Internal and External Customs
      –Indirect taxes, were "farmed out."
      –Special privileges went to nobility and clergy re their wine production
       and consumptions
      –Gabelle, on salt – upper orders relieved, lower classes had to pay for a lot
       of salt they didn't want.

–Tax farmers could screw up taxes on third estate, but not on nobles and clergy.

–Tendency was towards the complete exemption of the Church and Nobility.

–Some towns and townsmen exempt.

–Royal establishments and workers escaped all or some taxation.

–This an added handicap to private industry.

–Those who were taxed were taxed as heavily as any persons in Western Europe down to the present.

–There were special war taxes, should have been dropped at the end of wars, but were kept on through 18th century – contributed to the top-heavy structure of taxation, leading to Revolution.

–In England, the Bank of England was set up to help with National Debt.

–In France, the setting up of such a bank failed.

  –Bank of England had contributed to the control of the government by merchants and traders.

–War finance was reducing the capital available for investment in private industry (opposite of English experience).

  –These methods could not have been adopted if direct representation had been in existence.

  –The only line drawn in England was between very wealthy and not so wealthy – no such class exemption.

–Capitalist industry had been expanding in England, but not in France.

–Greater prestige of English town merchants than French town merchants.

  –The term merchant must not be confused with the term bourgeoisie – in France.

  –The mercantile classes did not have the higher ranks in bourgeoisie.

  –To say that France was in power of some plutocracy – means only that noblesse du roy [roi] were in domaine over positions.

  –Some merchants came into this class, but soon lost their merchant interests, because of the sameness of their interests with the Crown.

  –England had a different reputation and place for its interests.

  –Merchants – equaled money merchants, grandes fabricants, manufacturers.

  –In England an effective line could not be drawn between nobility and merchants – nor was there anything corresponding to the separation of noblesse du pays, and noblesse du roi.

  –In France, the merchant was considered a vulgar being.

  –Some efforts (Vauban and Richelieu) were made to give him a special position.

–Rise of royal absolutism hindered the rise of industrialism.

–Backwardness of industrial capitalism favored the rise of royal absolutism.

Merchants, continued – Vauban and Richelieu wanted to strengthen industry in France.

> –Thought – probably correctly – that the favoring of a merchant class would hasten this.
>
> –But they failed to see that the strengthening of merchant class meant the weakening of the royal power – which had been dependent on a weak merchant class.
>
> –In England, Crown threats to enforce its monopolies and decrees were met by a boycott, or refusal to send coal to London, deliberately done by merchants – shortage was blamed by people on King.
>
> –The merchants feared the Royal control and monopolies.
>
> –They won out and their control of Parliament and the King was in large part responsible for the rise of industrial capitalism.

–In France, landed families first lent capital for industries on their land – but town merchants loaned to them.

–In England landed families also loaned capital for first industry – but went into debt – merchant classes loaned money – landed gentry and merchant classes formed a coalition – by marriage and interest. [In margin: Cf. Nef, Tawney, Thomas Wilson, Hamilton, Bray]

> –Which coalition was unfavorable to Royal power by its strength.
>
> –Representative government, the result.
>
> –Based on middle class interests, reached its high point in 17th century England. [Double vertical lines in margin alongside this point. Further out in margin: Cf. Macaulay (Walpole's letter to Sir Horace Mann, 1838).
>
> > –Claiming to act for "the people" – especially under Charles I.
> >
> > –But once in the saddle, the House [Parliaments] flaunts the interests of the common people, taxed them more heavily than the Crown had when the merchant and landed classes challenged the right of the Crown to tax.
>
> –People usually sided with House against Crown.
>
> –In France – the investments in industry were smaller – so that merchants did not have as great a chance to obtain control.
>
> > –This due to smaller importance of industry in France.
> >
> > –So that the Royal power came into its greatest heights in the 17th century.

Both industrial history and Royal absolutism explain the intellectual history and cultural history of the 17th century in France. [In margin: Voltaire, G. N. Clark]

(a) <u>Practical slant</u> to philosophical and scientific efforts in England was lacking in France.

–French philosophy and mathematics were supreme and turned towards morality and theology.

–French theologists first, scientists second – England the opposite.

(b) French: form, <u>order</u>, judgment, discipline – was <u>supreme</u> in France – classicism.

  –Looking back to classic form, but creating a new classicism – as it looked back to old theology and created a new one.

  –In England natural scientists held sway. [In margin: "Cf. Nef and Hessen <u>in</u> Science at the Crossroads (<u>Carver</u>)" – with arrow pointing to this line:] –A new <u>religion</u> – the religion of <u>production</u> – <u>saving souls by reducing labor</u>.

    –Newton, Boyle – prayed, etc., but had another kind of belief that rationalized his experiments.

    [In margin: Cf. Schnabel – <u>music and art</u>. Art and the milieu: 1. Artist needs <u>echo</u> of milieu. 2. Artist needs opposition of milieu. 3. Arts do either in varying degree, according to their nature.]

    –<u>Receptivity</u> of the two countries towards new scientific developments was different.

      –Cf. Marquis of Worcester

      –Richelieu had shut up <u>de Cous</u> for insisting on force of a jet of steam. [In margin: Muirhead, with arrow to this line]

      –The age of <u>salons</u> – Mme. de Savigny – the spirit of politeness had no sympathy with the dissecting of dead bodies, the study of smelly test tubes – as in England.

–Malbranche, <u>La chercher de la vérité</u> (<u>versus Locke</u>).

  –Science – diversions for an honest man but not equal to study of man and his relations to man. Pascal.

  –Bossuet – man's solution of his problems is religious, not to be solved by material comforts, etc.

  –<u>Science</u> as well as <u>capitalism</u> is intimately connected with religion. [Single line of emphasis in margin alongside this line.]

  –The sense of stability, the disciplined order were vital to philosophy and to the court and royal power.

  –"Alert and <u>satisfied</u> good judgement"

–The Arts – Classical School

  –Equilibrium between judgment and imagination.

  –But first place was given to <u>reason</u> – <u>lo raison</u> – restraint.

  –No <u>gigantic</u> work – you never can quite let yourself go.

[In margin: Cf. Lowes Dickinson "Conventions and Emotions in Poetry"]
check whether to delete both s'sorig p.90
–Molière – excesses of his characters were never quite shared by the author.
   –Last lines of Le Misanthrope. [Arrow to next line.]
      –Perfect reason shuns extremity, is wise and sober.
   –Don Juan – stricture on Church – one example of letting go, got Molière
   into trouble.
–Corneille and Racine – could never let themselves go.
   –Works of art were produced for Court – had to fit into the Court form –
   music, poetry, painting.
      –All excessive feeling is against excesses and extremity. [Double vertical
      line in margin alongside this point.]
      –Most art was produced for the Court.
      –Artists were patrons of Court.
      –Claude Lorrain – Poussin.
      –Art had a Church and Court audience and paintings went to decorate
      nobles' homes.
      –In England – bourgeoisie were the patrons of art (Pepys bought a
      Holbein).
         –Classicism, but with an entirely different emphasis than in France.
            –Dryden and Pope were shocking to the French, for their disregard
            of rule.
         –Cf. Taine, History of English Literature.

Summary
   –The late 16th, 17th and early 18th centuries had a lasting effect on the whole
   subsequent development of France.
      –Les grandes siècles are always looked back at with reverence, and broken
      with reluctance.
      –France offered resistance to the rise of industrial capitalism.
         –This helps explain the grandes siècles – and helps explain them [sic].
1715–1789
   –Bibliography – a different problem than formerly – almost too much secondary
   work to be easily handled.
   General. [Comments, originally in left margin, have been placed with citation.]
      de Tocqueville – L'ancien régime.
      Taine – Les origines de la France contemporaine.
      Michelet –
      Modern works

Jaurès – Histoire socialiste de la Révolution française. [In margin: Good in economics.] [*Histoire socialiste, 1789–1900, sous la direction de Jean Jaurès*, 13 vols., Paris, 1901–1908]

Aulard

Mathiez – works on economic aspects of French Revolution. [Albert Mathiez, *Annales historiques de la Révolution française*, vol. 1 (1924-)]

Economic History.

Kovalevskii, M. M. The Conditions of Economic Life on the Eve of the Revolution [La France économique et sociale à la veille de la Révolution. 2 vols. 1909, 1911]. Out of date.

Sée, H. [Sée, H. "The Economic and Social Origins of the French Revolution," in Econ. Hist. Rev., III (1931), 1–15. See also L'évolution Commerciale et industrielle de la France, sous l'ancien Régime, Paris, 1925.] Opens subject.

Dutil [Léon Dutil, L'état économique du Languedoc à la fin de l'ancien Régime, 1750–1789. 1911.] Good.

Braure [Maurice Braure, Lille et la Flandre wallonne au 18e siècle. Lille, 1932] Only partly economics.

Industrial History

Sée – "L'influence de la Révolution sur l'évolution industrielle de la France" in volume in honor of Giuseppe Prato.

Sée – "The Economic and Social Origins of the French Revolution," Economic History Review, vol. 3, no. 1 (January 1931), pp. 13–38. Old.

Ballot, C. – L'introduction du machinisme dans l'industrie française. 1923. Especially good for textiles.

Rouff, M. – Les mines de charbon en France au 18e siècle. 1922. Good gastronomy also!

Bourgin, H. and G. – L'industrie sidérurgique en France au début de la Révolution. 1920. Documents mostly – good introduction.

Levy – Histoire économique de l'industrie cotonnière en Alsace. 1912. Relates title to geography.

Martin, Gaston, Capital et travail à Nantes au cours du XVIIIe siècle. Paris, 1932.

Germain-Martin, P. La grande industrie en France sous le règne de Louis XV, 1715–1774. 1900.

These recent works show that the economic historian must draw a line at about 1740.

–Rapid increase in output 1740–1789.

–In output of coal and iron.

–In spread of large privately owned establishments.

–It is difficult to trace the <u>evolution</u> of the new position France is found in, in 1789.

–For the concept of an industrial revolution was not one which turned people's searches to <u>evolution</u>.

–Kovalevskii did this.

–Great increase in literature having to do with industrial subjects – not all of it was printed.

<u>Mining</u>

–Literature was especially prevalent in case of mining – were full of sketches – even of <u>English</u> works.

–Introduction of a <u>whole vocabulary</u> of mining and industrial terms into French.

–Most were English in origin.

–Showing that the French were turning abroad for their inspiration.

a- Output of coal – Rouff shows weakness of former estimates – though he does not himself offer an estimate. [In margin: Levasseur, 200,000 tons per annum in all France in 1789.]

–Nef has composed an estimate – based on Rauff.

Fouray [incomplete]

Languedoc – 50,000 tons per annum.

–Chief change was in North – where coal was discovered, probably in 1717 – practically in Belgium – on Scheldt River – coal carried down into Belgium.

–Bétune

Vallencienne.

–One collery nearb produced 200,000 tons per annum in 1780s – Anzin.

–600,000 tons in North of France, probably.

–or 850,000 tons in North and Lyons (nine-tenths of total).

–or <u>about 1,000,000 tons per annum for the whole country</u>. [Double vertical line in margin alongside this sentence.]

–Probably a 12–18 fold increase after 1740 – and a 20 fold increase after 1709. [In margin: <u>Rate of expansion</u> much greater than in England during this same century (England in 1550–1780 – 15 fold expansion.]

–<u>Total</u> output in England about ten times as great – with one-half the population.

–Thus coal was not playing a role in French life comparable to what it had played in English life at that time, or even in 17th century. [In margin: Main coal bed hardly affected the life of industry <u>in</u> France.] [Double vertical lines in margin alongside this point.]

–Arthur Young did not notice this growth.

b- Change in the forms of enterprises producing coal.

–Large mining plants – producing in single colleries as much as 200,000 tons per annum – and several instances of 50, 80, 100 thousand tons per annum. [In margin: More than any single mine in England.]

–Private capital.

–Large numbers of workers (100–4000 (Anzin).

–FF2,000,000 investment in biggest mine (Anzin).

  –Shares of stock – joint stock. Societé annonyme. Limited liability. Societé en note collective Societé en commendite. Partly unlimited, partly limited liability.

  –Colleries of late 18th century were very directly the ancestors of modern industrial capitalism.

c- Definite change in relation of government to <u>industry</u>.

  –Every peasant felt [it] right to dig for coal in his own territory, and to keep others out – in early times.

  –But Crown gave large grants of coal territory to noblemen.

  –Shortage of wood. Cf. Rouff, Sée (Bretagne), Mozoyer (Frenche-Comté).

  [The works cited are: Mozoyer, L. "L'exploitation forestière et conflits sociaux en Franche-Comté, à la fin de l'ancien régime," in <u>Ann. d'Hist. econ. et soc.</u>, 1932, 339ff.; Rouff, Marcel. <u>Les mines de charbon en France au 18ᵉ siècle</u>. 1922; and Sée, H. "Études sur les mines bretonnes au XVIIIᵉ siècle," in <u>Ann. De Bret.</u>, XXXVII (1926).]

  –Generally admitted – Tristram Shandy – wood scarcer in France than in England.

  –Disturbed, the State granted coal lands with plenary possession to private people.

    –State confined its activities to enforcing its concessionaire's rights against peasant's rights.

    –A thing it had never before done.

    –A part of the general change of government attitude towards industry in 18th century.

    –Especially in connection with mining.

  –Uses for coal in 18th century France – mainly industrial.

    –For glass manufacturing.

    –For blast furnaces (latter part of century).

    –For forges.

–Major portion of country was still dependent on wood, or imports of coal from England – but import tariff, as well as <u>high</u> export tax in England.

  –Biggest [coal] beds on Belgian frontier, Lyons next, small veins at Creusot and Naverre, for local industries.

–Coal could not mean much to most industry.
Iron Mining
  –Expanding markedly.
  –Being combined with iron production.

Metallurgy
  Iron
    –Messers Bourget estimate production in 1788 – total per annum 150,000
    tons (130,000 pig iron, [of which?] 90,000 bar iron).
    –Le Creusot and La Cheveté (near Dijon) did not begin to produce till after
    1750 – some with many small plants.
    –Yet not the same rate as in case of coal – 5–10 fold expansion in century.
    –For one thing, its expansion before this century was greater than in case of
    coal.
    –However, it bears out the conception that France underwent considerable
    industrial change in 18th century, especially 1750–1789.
    –1788 – England had an iron production one-half that of France's, with one-
    third the population.
    –Yet as to its metallurgical industry England was way in advance.
    –Copper, tin and lead smelting industries were highly important in England
    – very small in France.
    –And counting in the finishing processes of all lines.
    –With importing of bar iron of 40–50,000 tons per annum into England.
    –Little importation of iron into France.
    –Thus the position of England relative to France was much more favorable
    in metallurgy.
  –Yet not nearly as great an advantage to England as in case of coal.
    –The rate of growth seems to have been more rapid in French metallurgy as
    with French mining of coal, than in England (three-fold increase in output,
    two-fold increase in imports, during century) – in France – five-ten fold
    increase.
    –Integration of metallurgical processes into a single plant.
    –Two cases in France at end of 18th century – were as developed as anything
    in Europe up to modern times.
  Le Creusot – 10,000,000 Francs investment – joint stock.
    [In margin: Set up by John Wilkinson (English)-engineer, financier.]
    –Several steam engines, driving bellows, hammers, drills, railways – 6 to 10
    miles, bringing coal from mines, owned by company.
    –To engine works, glass works, smelting, bar iron production.
    –Cheapness of coal, and coincidence of coal and iron made Creusat famous.

–Has had continuous history down to present day – bought by Schneider.
La Charité – established 1756.
   –For manufacturing of edge tools and implements.
   –1,000,000 Francs investment in joint stock.
   –250–350 laborers.
–Aside from these two, manufacturing of iron [was] carried on in small forges, or by domestic systems.
–One can not, then, say that the iron industry was <u>dominated</u> by large scale methods.
   –As <u>was</u> the case, at this early time, in the coal industry.
[Single vertical line in margin alongside preceding three lines.]
   –No mine producing as much coal in England at this time as Anzin, and no metallurgical plant in England as highly developed as Creusot in France, at this time.
      –Generalizations from this??
         –England gets stuck in small units.
         –Continent goes on to larger units. (Cf. Veblen [probably *Theory of Business Enterprise*, 1904])
      –But the primary factor leading to large scale production – coinciding of coal and iron in the same area – was already providing a brake on the development of industrial capitalism – even in the 16th century.

<u>Manufacturing</u> Textiles
   –Considerable increase in cotton production.
   –New domestic market and demand for wool and cloth.
   –Third Estate – 90–95% of population – was probably never so well off as at eve of Revolution.
      –One sign of this was the increased demand for clothes – on part of all classes.
         –Lower class for cotton and wool.
         –Upper class for silk, but falling.
         (Fashion and passion on part of many noblemen and upper class of sympathy for common man!)
         –Upper classes were dressing less ostentatiously – more simply – throwing off silk, velours, satins, etc.
            –Shift to coarser fabrics.
            –<u>Production</u> of silk was falling.
            –End of <u>artistic</u> side of textile manufacturing.
            –Growth of <u>new</u> industries with no hindering traditions.
      –I.e. effect of manners on the cloth industry.
         –Cruder goods demanded but in greater quantities than former fine goods had been demanded.

–Textile growth in 18th century was mainly in the direction of a spread of rural domestic system – which has put its stamp on French industry until this day.

–Printing – was carried on under conditions of industrial capitalism in large factories.

–Large areas of land for bleaching.

–Large buildings for drying, tables, tools.

–Large presses for printing.

–Long-time operation, requiring purchase of large supply of raw materials.

–Both factors led to need of large capital.

–And to development of industrial capitalism.

–Several plants with number of workers varying from 800 to 2300 – Mulhouse, Lyons, Rouen, Nantes, Bourges, Orange.

–Large establishments more prevalent in cotton manufacturing than woolen manufacturing. (Cotton had been manufactured all over Europe from 16th century on – Cf. Wadsworth and Mann.)

–It was not a new manufacture, but the expansion of growth and size was fastest at this time, and probably a greater expansion than in England at same time.

–Its large scale rise was new.

–Spinning and weaving were the last strongholds of the domestic system.

–Forces of habit predominant.

–Attempt of some capitalists to introduce English spinning jenny and waterframe met with resistance and struggle. (Cf. Ballot, and Wadsworth and Mann.)

–Down to Revolution this resistance lasted.

–1789 – England way ahead of France as to textile machinery.

–Attempts to introduce English machinery were usually abortive.

–Development of large-scale industries in France.

–Scarcely less marked than in England.

–If rapidity of change is the criterion of an industrial revolution, then the Industrial Revolution of 1750–1830 can not be confined to England.

–In fact, the rapidity of change was greater in France than in England. [Three vertical lines in margin alongside preceding three lines.]

–And rapidity of change in Wales was greater than in England at this same time. [In margin: Cf. Dodd.]

–Other indications of the increased rapidity of change in France 1740–1789. (Coal, iron, textiles)

–Population – What support do we find here, for the view that France was undergoing a remarkable industrial change?

[In margin: Cp. Trevelyan, Queen Anne, Appendix I]
-1700- <u>20–22 millions</u> (modern area)
    1700–1715, Wars of Spanish Succession – some <u>depopulation</u>? Probably not.
      1800 killed in 1704 – English soldiers
      5000 dead from action and wounds
      (250,000 per annum killed in 1914–1918 – English soldiers)
        –English population had increased 7 fold but deaths in war increased <u>fifty fold</u> – yet there was not even then a serious depopulation.
      –Other wars in 18th century.
-Improbable that population <u>grew</u> from 1700–1740, i.e. population 1740, 20–22 millions.
-But no doubt that the population grew 1740–1789.
    1789, population 26,000,000 (Levasseur)
    1801, population 27,300,000 (government census)
    1805, population 29,000,000 (government census)
-Increasing efficiency of census coverages; danger of Napoleonic statistics – bluffing, guessing, audacious lying of Napoleon's advisers harassed by his desire for figures.
-Our tentative conclusion, greatest growth, in France, of population since the end of the 13th century – began about the middle of the 18th century, lasted about a century, was then played out–England and Wales, 1750–1809 (Mantoux) – six million to nine million.
    –Macaulay, Tawney, Mantoux – all make much of population growth as evidence of the <u>industrial revolution</u>.
    –Population increase in France was nearly as much as in England 1750–1850 – it nearly doubled (France reached 35,000,000 by 1870).
    –But the effects of this industrial growth were different in the two countries.
      –In France, those effects were confined to relatively small areas, near coal or iron mines.
      –No traffic in bulky goods, reflecting growth in industrial development.
        –Traffic on Seine remained mainly <u>wine</u> and light commodities.
        –No concentration of power in hands of Paris wholesale merchants.
    –The industrial changes did not soak into the bones of Frenchmen.
    –The English methods were imported from England into France – were <u>artificial</u> in their new setting – regarding inventions with the eyes of a child – as curiosities.

[In margin: Comparison of U.S. and English sport]
–Industrialization was greater in England than in France.
–Natural conditions
–Industrial history
    –Human "geography"
–In France these factors affected the results –
    –Natural conditions
    –The course of French history
    –Human nature of a national sort.
    –A new element – industry – was introduced into French life in the
    half century before the Revolution – and profoundly.
    Fragonard
    [In margin: Where Nef gets his material]
    Stendhal – Racine et Shakespeare
    Jaurès, Histoire socialiste de la Révolution française
    Taine – Les Origines de la France contemporaire, vols. 1 and 2
    Sorel, G. The Illusion of Progress [Georges Sorel, Les illusions du
    progress, 1927]
    Sée, H.

1789–1815
This period – most marked change in political structure ever known in such a
time.
    –Great changes in economic and industrial life – steam engine.
    –Change of clothing – silk court robes to long trousers.
    –Religion – the new agnosticism.
    –New movements in art – romanticism in ideas.
    –Began many things but finished little (Michelet: Louis XIV, ended many
    things but began nothing).
        –Blazed new trails.
        –Participated in most changes of the age.
        –Also was a furnace for the forging of many new ideas which were to be
        worldwide in their effect.
    –French industrial history is not to be separated from the whole history.
        –How reconcile picture of rapid change with a history of less change than
        in other countries.
        –de Tocqueville, changes had roots in past, versus Stendhal, profound
        change.
        –Changes in merchants' position can be traced back to 1730, and most
        changes were well under way by 1750, i.e. de Tocqueville was right that
        the Revolution continued more changes than it began.

–Yet many changes were not finished till 1870, or not yet.

–The old France holding back the new France.

–Rousseau was on both sides of the fence.

–Stendhal was both a romanticist and a classicist, in the same work – did not see the inner conflicts of his position.

–Many paradoxes – are all reflections of <u>one</u> great paradox – the old and the new France.

–Even the Revolution did not end this paradox.

–Radical change in industry, yet an <u>artificial</u> change – again the paradox.

Social

    Mercier   <u>Tableau de Paris</u>, 1770–1780, 7 vols.

Financial

    Babeau   <u>Les bourgeois d'autrefois</u>

    Harsin   <u>Crédit public et Banque d'État en France</u>

    Bijo   <u>La Caisse d'Escomte, 1776–1793, et les origines de la Banque de France</u>

    Marion, Marcel   <u>Histoire financière de la France depuis 1715</u>, 2 volumes, 191

[Single vertical line in margin alongside list.]

–French merchants –

  –Great improvement in their position during the 18th century.

      –Cf. John Andrews, 1785.

      –Cf. Voltaire – when it was still bad.

   –Stendhal said (1840) the betterment began about the 1820s.

    –Voltaire had not seen it by 1740.

     –Leading to presumption that it came after 1750.

  –Refinements not confined to court, but could be bought by well-to-do merchants.

    –Houses larger, more rooms, collections of paintings, etc.

    –La cuisine bourgeoise conquered la cuisine classique of Louis XIV.

    –Even before 1789 the Court had ceased to be the sole arbiter in matters of taste.

  –Bourgeois class composed of:

    –Financiers, money changers [Above the line: lenders], wholesalers, employers of workers under domestic system.

    –Noblesse du roi were learning to govern and investing in industry.

  –Government pillaged the Caisse d'Escompte – opposed to interests of many bourgeoisie who owned shares in the bank.

    –In the Revolution the government officials tended to side with the peasants for the first time.

–Opposed to Crown for its Bank policy.

–And for its hindrance of the growth of private enterprise, in which they had invested heavily.

–And because they had never been accepted as real court officials by the Court – tended to throw their lot in with bourgeoisie.

–In the cleavage that was arising in 18th century between classes, the noblesse du roi tended to throw their lot in with revolutionaries.

–But social history of France, 1750–1815, is tremendously complex.

–Make-up of classes attacked and classes attacking was vitally different from the two sides in the English Revolution of the 17th century.

–France – attacked [were] Nobility and Church and Crown.

England – Nobility not on side of Crown to same extent.

> –Church had had its teeth drawn by Henry VIII and Church lost most of its landed property.

France – Church still a large landholder – and one not likely to <u>sell</u> its land.

> –Still opposed usury and economic activity.

English nobility – says Taine, found new tasks to perform when their old ones had disappeared.

> –Due partly to the tendency since 16th century for the noble and merchant classes to coalesce – intermarriage, younger noble sons going into trade.

> French nobility – Nobility becomes scarce – more and more a <u>closed</u> group – little contact with merchants – who were thought to be lower.

Sharper conflict between merchant class and nobility and Church in France than in England.

–Royal absolutism had been carried on for nobility and clergy, and had driven the merchants to side with the <u>artisans</u> and peasants – who were <u>all</u> over-taxed.

> –Peasant holdings becoming more extensive.

> > –Almost no clergy, nobles, merchants worked their own land, or rented it out to large capitalistic farmers (cf. G. Lefebvre, "La place de la R<u>é</u>volution dans l'histoire agraire de la France," in Ann. d'hist. écon. et. soc., i (1929).

> > –A synthesis.

> –But rented it [land] to small peasants to work it themselves in parts.

–I.e. merchants not opposed to peasants, and had same interests.

–Craftsmen in town had chief interests in cheap food and fuel.

> –In England, 17th century, artisans tended to side with Crown against traders.

> –In France, Crown had no interest in artisans' cheap food.

> > –Crown came to be blamed instead of traders for hardships.

–Social changes and industrial history – interacting.

–Much in social changes to encourage industry – new wealth, new capital to invest, new wants.
–But revolutionary movement depended on artisan and peasant.
  –No encouragement to growth of a large landless proletariat.
–Interdependence of peasant and artisan – partly because there had been no development of large scale sheep farming.

Revolution –
  –Church and nobility lost privileges.
  –Government was founded on personal property, not privilege.
    –Of great aid to the bourgeois[ie], but they did not win out fully until 1871.
    –The peculiar history after 1789, until 1870, was a proof of the underlying paradox.
    –The government could not lose its paternalistic approach.
      –Guilds – requests for their abolition in 1789; Sée says they came from town merchants.
  –A diminution of State interference in economic affairs had begun by 1750, but the end of it had not arrived by 1800.
  –Agriculture – tenure, improvement of cultivation.
    –In half century before Revolution small holdings by peasants were on the increase.
    –By selling Church and government lands, the Revolutionary government was only carrying an already existent tendency – and the land tended to get into the hands of large holders, wealthy merchants.
    –Cultivation began to be stimulated and improved under Louis XVI – to introduce new crops, new methods, etc. Waste land improv[ement].
      –Crown even suggested the enclosure of waste or common land.
      –But peasants, small holders, were opposed to improvements of any kind. (Why?) Conservative, land value.
      –When industrial and agricultural interests conflicted, the industrial interests had to give way every time – both before and after Revolution!
Religion: – 18th century, a great outpouring of books on usury, written by priests.
    –Nef opposed to Robertson, thinks he interprets Groethuysen incorrectly. Nef cannot reconcile the text of Groethuysen with the opinion of Robertson.)
    –Controversy illustrates the relation of the church to individual life.
    –Protestantism had bolstered up the place of the English merchant.
    –Jesuits would accept some compromise of the doctrine of poverty.
(Robertson discusses only Jesuit doctrine – which much more favorable to usury than the Jansen doctrine – both are found in Groethuysen.)
    –Jansenites were more strict than Jesuits.

–Neither went so far as to claim that poverty was disgraceful.

(Nef disagrees with Tawney, in his implication that Catholic divines had this doctrine of the "New Medicine for poverty.")

–The Protestant divines, and the Church of England, <u>did</u> go to the extent of looking <u>down</u> on poverty.

–The Catholic Church did not make open war on sharp trade practices, but set itself definitely against two main tenets of an industrial bourgeois[ie]:

(a) That he had to accept his <u>place</u>, given him by divine authority – it was above the poor, but <u>below</u> the nobility.

(b) That loaning money for large scale enterprise was bad.

–Bourgeois[ie] could not be both good Catholics and good financiers – led to rise of agnosticism.

–The Church also objected to the rise of natural science, and this also led to estrangement from the industrial bourgeoisie.

–Tawney does not mention this aspect – though it supports his case.

–Weber's case is untenable, it explains every thing in terms of rise of Protestantism but doesn't explain that rise.

–Bossuet and Pascal (17th century) were mainstays of later Catholic theology – Bossuet wrote a violent essay against usury. (Robertson doesn't consider this.) [In margin: Renon – Souvenir d'un enfante de jeunesse [?]]

–Although the Church lost much of its land by the Revolution, it did not change its attitudes toward usury, wealth and natural science.

–Thus it opposed a brake to economic progress during the 19th century.

Intellectual and Artistic History

<u>Natural Science</u> – one can often date the growth of the new attitude from the publication of Bouffin [?] work, 1749, Levoissier [?].

–Science mainly attractive to intellectual curiosity.

–But for the first time in France, the scientist was getting prestige, in intellectual society.

–And this must have affected the growth of science.

(Cf. Sorrell and Biography of Turgot) [Spelling of "Sorrell" is questionable. Possibly Gustave Schelle, *Euvres de Turgot et documenets le concernant, avec biographie et notes* (5 vols., 1913–1923); Pierre M. M. H. Ségur, *Au couchant de la monarchie: Louis XVI et Turgot, 1774–1776 (1909)*; W. Walter Stephens, *The Life and Writings of Turgot* (1895); Charles Gomel, *Les Causes financiers de la revolution française* (2 vols., 1892–1893).]

<u>Philosophy</u> – enthusiasm of great men for progress of science had an effect in popularizing scientific knowledge – led to belief in <u>progress</u> – one of the intellectual bases of industrialism.

–Taine – Diderot, Voltaire, Bouffin, Montesquieu, Rousseau, etc. <u>made</u> the Revolution – by their writings – one time in the world when the ideas had an effect.

–The attitude of all these men toward science was itself a revolution from the attitude of the thinkers of Louis XIV's time towards science.

–The surgeon – considered as little better than a butcher in 17th century – becomes admitted to polite society in 18th century.

–Yet, the philosophers were paradoxical in their attitude towards science.

–Science and philosophy were no longer dominated by the Court. [Single vertical line in margin alongside this point.]

Literature – Romantic movement – as consciously conceived by Stendhal – was aimed at new bourgeoisie – write novels, could be read <u>all over</u> France.

–Revolt from rules of Corneille and Racine.

–Stendhal looked to Shakespeare (became the idol), England and Germany for guidance.

–A definite attack on French classicism (and by a classicist – Stendhal).

–Hugo – Hernani

Painting – Delacroix, Jerièl [?] – Romanticism – Shakespearian subjects.

Music – Berlioz – followed German romanticism.

–Not as much romanticism, not as much escape in France as in England.

But the same conflict between the old and the new as in industry.

–Stendhal – both sides.

–David and Ingres represent classicism.

–The new forms are opposed, and their success tempered, by the old traditions which hang on.

–Paradoxical nature of French history of this period explained by the fact that industrialism was a strange plant in foreign soil.

<u>19th and 20th Centuries</u> – 1815–1930

–Their significance for the general history of industrialism.

–The period beginning with about 1850 will come to assume a place of *far* more rapid development in the world than anything known before – after Civil War – Franco-Prussian War.

–Industrialism spread to U.S., France and Germany.

–And to all the corners of the globe – Japan, India, etc. (Cf. Tawney, Land and Labor in China).

–All the elements of our present day standard of living are products of the last seventy years.

   –Although prepared for by at least 300 years of growth.

   –France in 1870 – on all counts, France was markedly behind Great Britain, Eastern U.S. – on a par with other countries.

   –But today France is way behind Germany, Belgium, Japan, U.S. – and her rate of growth has been slower than any other country except, perhaps England.

Transport and Communications – the principal factor in the industrialization of the last century (cf. Knowles – Industry and Commerce in 19th Century)

   –The Railway Age in France

      –Both steam engine and wagon way were both first used in England.

      –The English were as usual ahead of France in the combination railroad.

      –English engineers and English capital (Cf. Jenks – Export of Capital to 1879) – export of capital on a large scale not known before 19th century – due to an overflowing of large profits of industrialism.

         –English navvies to lay ties and rails and run trains.

         –Great inflow came in 1850s.

      –The first railroad was from Paris, through Rouen, to Le Havre – English colony at Rouen; English influence on French life.

      –The railroad, thus, was also an importation, an artificial growth.

      –1850, France 2000 miles, England 7000 (France twice the size of England).

         –Most of French lines built after 1845.

      –1842 – a program of railroad construction.

      –Lines radiating from Paris.

      –Represents the skeleton of the system that exists to-day.

      [In margin, rough scheme of rail lines radiating from Paris to Strassbourg, Marseilles, Toulouse, Bordeaux, Brest, Le Havre, and Belgium.]

      –This program [cf. diagram] was almost entirely of a political impetus [Double vertical lines in margin alongside this point] – controversy between old France and new France over ownership – public versus private ownership.

         –A compromise was effected: the roads to be built by private capital and to be in private hands.

         –But, the State to lay down their plan of route, to regulate rates, and to be able to buy the roads at will.

      –1870 = 12,000 miles – Paris-Calais, [time reduced from] 25 hours to 5 hours.

      –The speed of movement, in two decades, had been increased as much as in two centuries before.

–Since 1870, France's railroad building much faster than Germany and Switzerland, Belgium and Holland, and England.

–But, all those countries had done more in the way of building <u>before</u> 1870, than France had, <u>per</u> the size of the country.

–But, as a whole, the place of the railroad in France is not as developed as in other countries.

–There <u>are</u> fast trains – too fast for passengers, and for specialized forms of freight (Prunier oysters).

–But the facilities for carrying freight, especially heavy freight, are not up to other countries in speed or cost.

–<u>Intermediate</u> passenger services are <u>terrible</u>. "Le petite train."

(Proust is best introduction to French economic history of the period.)

–Thiers – his spirit seems to linger on <u>re</u> railroads (1875).

"We must give Davis this plaything but it will not carry a passenger or a package."

–Inland Navigation – a complete system by 1850, but different sizes.

–Freyciet [?] program – standardized them.

–Freight increased over canals, relative to railroads – up to war – (20% of traffic by canal – after 1850 (1926, 13%).

–Not true of England or U.S.

–Motor Cars – large influence in internal transportation.

–Shares first place with England for largest number of cars per capita

–1926, one car per 53 – first in Europe.

–First large development of autos began in France – before the U.S.

–But, more attention paid to beauty of body than to engine – U.S. styles come from France now.

–Roads – behind England and U.S. – development comes later.

–Toy-like character of French cars.

–Steam Boat

–Never dominated internal transport – houses for canal boats.

–No large shipbuilding trade – one tenth of English tonnage 1913, one third of German.

–No coal for ballast in outer trip.

–Bad ships anyway – except food and beauty – one sunk in Indian ocean on first trip. l'Atlantique. Paris' mishaps.

–Telephone and Telegram

–Quite extensive wiring, but poor usage.

–They neither have been <u>accepted</u> for everyday use – the plaything element.

–Influence of Steamship and Communications on the extension of the market is tremendous.

–Influence of <u>this</u> on industrial capitalism and its growth.

[Double vertical lines in margin alongside preceding two sentences.]

   –All forms of the new transport created new opportunities for large-scale industry.

      –1901 – 300,000 workers in transportation industry.

      1930 – 400,000 workers

   –Number of workers, their proportion of the total population, engaged in work in large-scale enterprise is the best test of the growth of industrial capitalism. [Double vertical lines, and, to their left, double horizontal lines in margin alongside this point.]

   –Great and rapid increase in the number and proportions of workers in transport and communication industries after 1850 – a new "revolution."

   –Yet, the rate and size of growth has been greater in other industrial countries.

   –The State, in France, controls a large amount of the transport industry:

      –<u>All</u> canals, in 1870 took over telephone and telegraph, five state railroads (one sixth of railroad workers), subsidies to C. G. T. [Compagnie Générale du Transport].

–Interference of government in all phases of transport and communications.

–Also, a huge amount of tiny handicraft or individually owned transport services.

   –Private taxis

   –Vegetable wagons – horses

   –Bargemen

   [Vertical line in margin alongside preceding three lines.]

   –In these the ideas of trade or <u>craft</u> and <u>skill</u> remain (Anatole France – taxi drivers – "All trades have their geniuses, you are one in yours").

   –French labor, even when connected with large transport industries, are singularly independent (engineer an owner of a Paris store).

   –Railroads have extended the market, but they have done it less than in any other country.

      –Railroads all converge on Paris – more political than economic (cf. Marshall).

      –Country thus cut up into segments, with their apex at Paris.

      –Paris reaching out to surrounding countries [countryside] for food supply – since 13th century.

–Foreign trade not very important to France.

   –Imports grain, wool and silk (nine tenths), coal (one half).

Industries
  Coal   1789 – 1 million tons
                                    1852 – 5 million tons
                                    1869 – 13 million tons
                                    1913 – 41 million tons
                                    1926 – 52 million tons (including Lorraine)

–50 fold increase in France while a 25 fold increase in England.
–Capitalistic enterprise in coal not new to France in 19th century.
–But a great increase in the number of laborers employed in mining – much more than proportional to the doubling of the population.
–1901 – Mining, 190,000 workers (all kinds).
    –500 men to an enterprise.
    –No softening of the coming of industrial capitalism by French artistry (Zola, Germinal [1885]).
    –60% come from Nord.
–Still coal had much less influence on French internal economy than England or other countries.
–The coal is poor, and is not available to the whole country – all in Nord.
–Also, only in Lorraine (won by war) are coal and iron found together.

Metallurgy – Iron and Steel
  –Large establishment is dominant.
  –France has more iron than any other European country – but poorly placed relatively to coal.
  –1880 – a turning point (1870 the same for British metallurgical industries – Ashton).
  –Concentration of steelworks and blast furnaces become general.
  –Lorraine added by Peace Treaty – doubled the pig iron produced.
  –Cf. Ogburn and Jaffé – progress of French metallurgy since the war very fast.
  –But the finishing industries are still highly individualized – the domestic system and individual system dominate.

Others
  –22 million gainfully employed.
      6 million employed in industrial occupation
      4 million employed in industrial occupation for wages
      700,000 employed in industries of 500 men or more.
  –Textiles
      –Persistence of domestic system.
      –1901 – average of less than four per factory.

–Since then a tendency to concentration, especially in <u>woolen</u> industry.

–French leadership in textiles is based on artistic skill rather than mass production.

   –Artistic element is hostile to concentration or to routinization of work.
   [Double vertical line in margin alongside this point.]

–Cleavage between capital and labor.

      Levine
      Siegfried, André – France: A Study in Nationality.

–Up till 1870, French socialism was <u>French</u> – since then it has been Marxist.

–Social effects of introduction of industry under Third Republic.

   Cf. Proust and A. France – "M. Bergerac."

   –This progress of industry seems incredibly rapid to a Frenchman – they are <u>shocked</u>!

   –Yet it has not nearly caught up with progress in other countries.

   –Communists (not Marxist) and l'Action Française are both opposed to mechanization.

–Only a few industries are large scale, and they are concentrated in one small Northern section.

–France imposes a civilization of its own on the course of industrialism.

   –The old France is too strong, it <u>moulds</u> industrialization.

   –The old ideal of artistic work and the old tradition of government interference continue.

–Industrial development of last century took place all over the world.

   –But with less speed, rate, magnitude in France, than anywhere else.

   –Although the progress – the rate – was slower in England even than in France – England's head start still left her ahead.

–<u>Agrarian History</u>

      Augé-Laribé (two books) – a scholar and a farmer. [Single vertical line in margin alongside foregoing.]

   –Main trends in agrarian history:

      –Yield per acre of all crops increases.

      –Area of grain cultivation fallen off by one seventh since 1860 – but an increase of total yield has been found.

      –1840–1870 a period of more rapid improvement than the period 1870–1925.

      –Reasons for this increase must be traced back to last half of 18th century.

         –Some growth of scientific farming.

            –But in no cases as much as in England, Germany, U.S., etc.

            –Thus the increase per acre of yield has risen even faster elsewhere.

–Less competition of agricultural produce from abroad due to tariffs, which subsidize the inefficient farmer.

–There are facilities of speed and direct transportation.

–Yet for most sections there are local markets with local areas serving them.

–Due to an aversion to standardization because of its effect on taste.

–No parallel to the moving of lettuce – growing from New England to California following refrigerator car.

–In France, a barrier to refrigerated transportation – because of the effects of ice on the product.

–Thus there are local wine markets, and the wines are not exported.

–Also, the railroad system is not adapted to cross-country travel of freight any more than of passengers.

–The growth of metropolitan centers has not destroyed the agricultural tradition.

Population and Urbanization

1806 – 75% of population rural,1906 – 55% of population rural

–But these figures do not represent the facts.

–A tendency for farmers to collect in towns of over 2000 and go out to work.

1866 – 8.2 million agricultural workers.

1906 – 8.8 million agricultural workers

–An increase greater than that of the whole population.

–But this is due to the increase of number of women counted as working in the fields.

1926, 8.6 million agricultural workers

? 1926, 20.2 million gainfully employed

–Thus not the same tendencies – as in other countries – no end of old forms of tenancy.

–Peasant proprietorship interferes with any concentration.

–Of these 8.6 million, five million were actually the owners of the plots they worked.

–Count out their wives and see how large a proportion it is.

–Count out the metayer who do not own, but nearly do.

–Area in which agricultural exploitation in 1908 were:

over 100 acres: 40 million acres

under 100 acres: 70 million acres

–the latter area has increased since the War.

"Le nouveau riche, c'est le paysan" – Augé–Laribé

–As a result of the war.

–He bought up the large land holdings that were thrown on the market.

–Wage labor has not produced as much as peasant labor on French farms.

–I.e. the land settlement made in the Revolution has not been overturned.

–Influence of this agrarian history on industry.

  –It has been an important bulwark <u>against</u> industry.

    –E.g., English industrial growth paralleled by <u>enclosure</u>, spread of large holdings – a new wage earning class.

    –No surplus of labor – cheap.

    –Not so much dependence on industry – more independence in depressions.

<u>Politics</u> – democratic government in Revolution was an expression of peasants as well as of middle class.

  –Peasants could affect the economists who preached free trade.

  –Yet French agrarian history was to some extent a result of slow development of French industry.

    –Transport system worked out without reference to industrial needs – farming persistence of local markets.

    –Industry concentrated – has not molested the peasant owner.

    –Ownership of minerals in hands of State, not of landowner.

      –Thus no incentive to <u>buy out</u> the peasant surface land owner in order to exploit minerals.

<u>Social History</u> – in relation to industrialism in the Third Republic.

  –A reflection of the progress of industry – as well as of the slow rate of that progress.

  –<u>A wage-earning class</u> – for the first time under Republic, it became large enough to become class conscious – in auto, mines, chemicals, perfume, textile, metallurgy industries.

    –No sense of a <u>trade</u>, no land ownership.

    –A "heinous kind" in eyes of Siegfried.

    –Is Marxian – cannot reconcile democracy and private property.

    –Which has been the twin beliefs of Revolutionary and peasant France.

    –Society of Balzac's novels believed in <u>wealth</u> – but not the wealth of large industrialism.

  –A new <u>financial</u> element.

    –An aristocracy of wealth.

  –Great changes in the <u>moral</u> life, consequent on the industrial change.

  –But, a social conflict, for the <u>new</u> theme is only one of several themes.

    –A dual nature.

      –Social strata based on the revolt of the Revolution.

–Social strata based on the split of capital and labor. (E.g., in February riots [1934]. Fascists and Royalists combined, socialists and communists also – craftsmen and peasants hold to democracy – which says that their rights are those of the middle class.

–Industrialism has not yet permeated through society to the same extent as in other countries.

   –The sense of the métier – a job to do well – has not gone.

–Social and political – even economic equality.

   –Universal suffrage, widespread ownership of land.

   –And a real democracy of social position.

Constitutional Aspects

–Egalité – never meant equality of income; but in other spheres.

–Difficult to understand the complex political structure.

   –Parties of Left – Communists are different from Marxists.

      –They are chosen from peasants who don't believe in the end of private property.

      –Parties of Right – Royalists, peasant conservatives, finance (Poincaré stood against inflation, for the peasant's good – and against the financial bien.

   –Party lines are not drawn along purely economic lines, and do not mean as much to the party member as in U.S.

   –The old political cleavage between l'ancién régime and the Revolution has not been broken down by industrialism.

   –The course of industrial history is partly a cause of and partly a result of this political twist.

Art, Literature, Science

–Increase of wealth, in money and time.

–Has brought a higher standard of living.

–Tendency to departmentalization of thought.

   –Industrialism has made mankind more specialized in its efforts to make a living.

–A strengthened authority of science, with a consequent crisis in morals and in art.

–No longer a homogeneous group of rich who provided a definite critical audience.

   –Thus he paints more and more for his own intimate circle of friends, or for himself alone.

   –Cézanne – led a lonely life – could not get discussion.

–Proust – hiding himself away.

–Beaudelaire – and other poetry (Coleridge and escape from industry in England).

–Art losing its universality, no longer had power to speak to a multitude – or to make people <u>do</u> things as a result of seeing it.

–But other artists go to France – because of its relatively greater sympathetic setting for art than the rest of the world.

[In margin: cf. Return from Exile]

–Largely due to the slow and slight degree of industrialism.

–Frenchmen are still "many together."

–Craftsmanship still rules.

–Respect on part of all classes for the great artist.

–Nef thinks it is the <u>place</u> given to the artist which determines whether or not there shall be <u>art</u>.

–Escape and revolt will last a while, but is not a lasting form of art.

FINAL EXAMINATION

(Original plus translation)

ECONOMICS 322

Examination   June 12, 1934

Discuss in detail the uses which might legitimately be made of the following passage by the writer of a profound study of economic life and thought in France at the end of the reign of Louis XIV. In answering the question make full use of your knowledge of (a) historical criticism; (b) French economic and general history.

Extract from the "Mémoire du sieur des Casaux du Hallay, deputé de Nantes, sur l'état du commerce en général." Presented to the Conseil de Commerce, 4 March, 1701.

Il y a une chose essentielle dans le royaume, à laquelle il est important de penser; c'est la diminution des bois et forêts. Tous les bois et forêts qui étoient sur le bord des rivières et qui pouvoient se charger avec facilité, sont presque finis et épuisés; il n'en reste plus guère qui ne soient fort élongnés dans les terres, dont le charroi coûteroit trop pour pouvoir s'en server: en sorte que le bois de construction et de bâtiments de terre et de mer, aussi bien que de chauffage, est extrêmement rare et cher, et le va encore devenir d'advantage dans la suite. Il est à craindre que cela n'aille à un point qui nous obligera d'en tirer de la mer Baltique.

Il s'est fait une grande destruction de bois pour l'usage des sucreries dans le royaume, depuis l'établissement du droit sur le charbon de terre d'Angleterre, dont elles se servoient avant. Nous avons des mines de charbon de terre en Anjou, en Auvergne et ailleurs; mais, comme Mme. la duchesse d'Uzès a eu la permission du Roi de disposer de toutes ces mines du royaume, elle a remis ces droits à des gens qui ont fatigué les propriétaires et les ont obligés d'abandonner ces mines. Ils se sent rendus seuls maîtres du débit de ces charbons; en sorte qu'ils n'en font tirer qu'autant qu'ils en peuvent débiter à un haut prix, qui empêche les raffineurs de s'en pourvoir et les oblige à brûler toujours du bois. Cela peut passer pour une espèce de monopole très préjudiciable.

Il seroit donc très utile que le Roi eût agréeable de retirer le privilège donné à Mme. d'Uzès, de permettre à tous les propriétaires des mines d'en tirer ou faire tirer par qui bon leur sembleroit, et même de diminuer des droits dus au Roi pour les passages, afin d'en faciliter le transport et la consummation, et arrêter celle des bois que les sucreries consomment.

Au reste, il y a quantité de communes ou terres incultes et inutiles dans royaume provinces qu'on pourroit, sans inconvénient, semer et planter en bois, soit tout, ou partie, si S. M. avoit agréeable d'en donner la propriété à ceux qui en voudroient faire la dépense. Cela opéreoit un prompt usage de ces terres; et comme il est dû des droits et des rentes sur quelqu'unes de ces communes, aux seigneurs de qui elles relèvent, il faudroit permettre à ceux qui les prendroient d'en franchir le fond et d'en server la rente aux lieu et place des communières qui en sont actuellement détenteurs, auxquels il y en a peu qui servent.

Ce mémoire prouve assez combien le commerce est gêné dedans et dehors, pour qu'on ne s'étonne plus que les négociants réussissent si mal et se rarement. Le commerce est le domain du Roi de plus beau et plus convenable, dont des négociants font l'utilité, ainssi que la décoration. Quand la maison d'un négociant se retire, ce domaine diminue: c'est un arbre utile qui, arraché d'une terre, ne se rétablit pas.

Les négociants ont lieu d'espère que, par rapport aux intérêts du Roi et à ceux du public, Monseigneur voudra bien leur accorder l'honneur de sa protection et engager S. M., par sa bonté ordinaire, à les regarder d'un oeil de compassion.

On connoîtra mieux dans deux ou trois ans d'ici la conséquence de ce qui est représenté dans ce mémoire. L'État y est plus intéressé qu'on ne pense; on en conviendra pour peu qu'on rappelle combine il sort d'espèces du royaume pour fournir au commerce des Indes orientales et du Lavent, ainsi qu'aux laines d'Espagne, aux soies étrangères. Le grand secret seroit de pouvoir réduire, s'il étoit possible, notre commerce, notre luxe, notre consummation, à ce qui se peut faire par les matières de notre cru, ainsi qu'à ce qui peut provenir de la permutation de nos propres effets, et fournir et faire entrer en espèces dans le royaume, accroître nos colonies et nortre navigation. Ce sont les vues particulières de ce mémoire et les principes solides auxquels on croit qu'il est important de s'attacher, et, sur ce pied-là, de donner aux négociants une liberté sans bornes, avec une protection et une attention particulière.

Et quant aux droits du Roi sur le commerce, il est très assuré que, s'ils étoient moins forts et mieux réglés, les produits en seroient plus considérables, tant parce que les commis et les fraudeurs cesseroient, que parce que le commerce se multiplieroit. C'est un principe incontestable, dont on a la prevue, puisqu'on voit que les nouveaux drois ne rendent pas.

Translation of French text of Nef's 332 examination paper:
By Ruth and Taylor Ostrander September 19, 2004
Memoir of Sire des Casaux du Hallay, Deputy of Nantes
On the State of Commerce in General
Presented to the Council of Commerce, 4 March, 1701:
Extract:

There is something essential in the kingdom which it is important to consider: that is the diminution of woods and forests. All the woods and forests, along the banks of rivers and easily accessible, are almost finished and exhausted; there remain almost only those that are far away in the countryside where cartage costs too much to be able to be used: with the result that wood for construction of buildings and ships, as well as for heating, is extremely scarce and costly, and will become even more so in the future. It is to be feared that it will reach a point where we are obliged to obtain it (timber) from the Baltic Sea.

There has been a great destruction of woods for the use of the sugar mills in the kingdom since the establishment of (export) taxes on English coal that they used before. We have coal mines in Anjou (site of Nantes), Auvergne and at other places, but as Madame the Duchess d'Uzès has had the permission from the Ling to have at her disposition all these (coal) mines of the kingdom, She has given these rights to men who have overtaxed the proprietors and obliged them to abandon the mines. They have made themselves the only masters of the sale of these coals, in such a way that they will only extract from the mines what they can sell at a high price which hinders the (sugar) refiners from obtaining that coal and obliges them always to burn wood. This can be seen as a kind of very detrimental monopoly.

Thus it would be very useful if the King would agree to take back the privilege given to Madame d'Uzès to allow all proprietors of the mines to extract coal from the mines or have it extracted by those whom the consider capable Of doing it, and even to diminish the rights due to the King for taxes in order to facilitate transport and consumption, and stop the use of wood which the sugar mills consume.

Besides in the provinces there is a quantity of communes or infertile and useless lands in which, either all or in part, one could, without inconvenience, seed and plant woods, if His Majesty were agreeable to give the ownership of them to those who would take on the expense. This would bring about a prompt use of these lands; and since taxes and rents on some of these communes are due to the Lords from whom these lands would be taken over, one should permit those who would undertake the task (of running the mines) to pay the rent instead and in place of those who are actually the landowners, of which there are few who pay their obligations.

This Memoir quite proves how much commerce is hindered, inland and outside, so that one is not astonished anymore that merchants succeed so badly and so seldom. Commerce is the realm of the King, most great and honorable, whose merchants are of value and an embellishment. When the merchant's shop shuts down, its sphere diminishes: a useful tree pulled out of the earth will not reestablish itself.

The merchants have reason to hope that with regard to the interests f the King and of those of the public, Monseigneur would well give them the honor of his protection and engage His Majesty by his usual goodness to regard them with an eye of compassion.

One will know better in two or three years from now the consequence of what is presented in this Memoir. The State has more interest in it than one thinks; one hardly recognizes this when one recalls how much cash leaves the Kingdom to support trade with the East Indies and the Levant, as well as for the wool of Spain, the silks of foreign lands. The big secret would be to be able to reduce, of it were possible, our commerce, our luxury, our consumption, to that which can be provided by the materials of our creation, as well as being exchanged for our own money, provide our needs and help build up our hard cash within the Kingdom, to enlarge our colonies and our navigation. These are the special views of this Memoir and the solid principles to which one believes it is important to attach oneself, and, on this footing, to give to the merchants a freedom without limits, with protection and particular attention.

And as to the rights of the King over commerce, it is very certain that if they are less strong and better regulated, the products would be more considerable, so much so because the sellers (scalpers)and defrauders would cease, because the commerce would multiply. This is an incontestable principle, of which one has proof, because one sees that the new rights (of the Duchess) do not work.

MATERIALS FROM CHARLES O. HARDY'S COURSE ON MONEY AND BANKING, ECONOMICS 330, UNIVERSITY OF CHICAGO, 1933–1934

CHARLES O. HARDY, A BRIEF BIOGRAPHY

Charles Oscar Hardy (1884–1948) was a well-known though perhaps not leading monetary and financial economist of his time. He was and is important enough, however, to be remembered and studied a half century later (see Frank G. Steindl, *Monetary Interpretations of the Great Depression*, Ann Arbor, MI: University of Michigan Press, 1995; J. Ronnie Davis, *The New Economics and the Old Economists*, Ames, Iowa: Iowa State University Press, 1971; and Allan H. Meltzer, *A History of the Federal Reserve, 1913–1951*, Chicago, IL: University of Chicago Press, 2003). Educated at Ottawa University, Kansas (AB, 1904) (a private university affiliated with the Baptist Denomination) and the University of Chicago (Ph.D., 1916), he taught at both schools as well as at the University of Iowa. He was Vice President of the Federal Reserve Bank of Kansas City, had a long-term association with the Brookings Institution, and was a frequent advisor to government agencies. Working when the gold standard was in effect, he discerned instability as the likely consequence of excessive gold stocks and resultant credit expansion. An advocate of central-bank monetary management, he worried over

Further University of Wisconsin Materials: Further Documents of F. Taylor Ostrander
Research in the History of Economic Thought and Methodology, Volume 23-C, 241–269
Copyright © 2005 by Elsevier Ltd.
ISSN: 0743-4154/doi:10.1016/S0743-4154(05)23207-8

limits to its power to create monetary stability because of shifts in the balance of trade and in long-term investment, and called for major reform of the gold standard. Subsequently, he advocated activist monetary and fiscal policy. Hardy also contributed to the development of the theory of risk and uncertainty, a field dominated by his colleague, Frank Knight.

Hardy was author, co-author, or editor of the following books in the field of money and banking: *Interest Rates and Stock Speculation*, 1925; *Credit Policies of the Federal Reserve System*, 1932; *Is There Enough Gold?*, 1936; and *Consumer Credit and its Uses*, 1938. Hardy co-authored an early book on forecasting: *Forecasting Business Conditions*, 1927; and a candidate for defining macroeconomics: *Prices, Wages, and Employment*, 1946. In the field of public finance Hardy published: *Tax-Exempt Securities and the Surtax*, 1926 and *Do We Want a Federal Sales Tax?*, 1943. He published *Risk and Risk-Bearing*, 1923 and *Wartime Control of Prices*, 1940. His first book was *The Negro Question in the French Revolution*, 1919.

I asked Robert Dimand, a leading historian of monetary economics, to describe Hardy's status as a monetary economist in the 1930s. He responded that he

knew him primarily from his reviews of Keynes's *Treatise on Money*: an AER review of the first volume, and a JPE review article on the second volume (the applied volume). Hardy noted that "Keynes says much that is new, much more that is new to those who don't read German, still more to those who do not read either German or D. H. Robertson. . . . In analyzing the causes of discrepancies between the rate of saving and the rate of formation of capital, Keynes follows closely in the footsteps of Wicksell, whose work he brings almost for the first time to the attention of readers of English." Hardy also corrected Keynes's handling of Fisher's real interest/nominal interest distinction, pointing out that past price changes matter for the relationship only to the extent that they influence expectations of future price changes. The other striking feature of Hardy's career is that, at the University of Chicago until 1922 and then at Iowa State, he wrote *Risk and Risk-Bearing* (U. of Chicago Press, 1923) while his colleague Frank Knight was writing *Risk, Uncertainty and Profit*. In addition to his review article on Keynes, Hardy was also chosen to write review articles in AER on Hansen's *Fiscal Policy and National Income* and in JPE on Schumpeter's *Capitalism, Socialism and Democracy* and on Henry Simons' *Economic Policy for a Free Society*, which suggests that that he was held in high professional regard, especially among the editors of JPE at Chicago (particularly to be entrusted with a review article of Simons' collected papers soon after Simons' death). Yet he seems to be a shadowy figure in the literature.

Hardy's professional position was unusual: his doctorate was in history, rather than economics, with a dissertation (later a book) on *The Negro Question in the French Revolution*. From 1923 to 1942 or 1943, Hardy was at the Brookings Institution, and then successively economic adviser to the Alien Property Custodian, vice-president of the Federal Reserve Bank of Kansas City (1943–1946), and, from 1947 until his death in 1948, staff director of the Joint Congressional Committee on the Economic Report of the President. Brookings published his major work, *The Credit Policies of the Federal Reserve System* (1932), which led to his directing the research staff of a Congressional inquiry into Federal Reserve policies and practices. Despite his non-academic affiliation from 1923, he was an editor of the University of Chicago's JPE. Since his long career at Brookings, Hardy makes only two fleeting appearances in Charles Saunders's *The Brookings Institution: A Fifty-Year History* (Brookings, 1966): as a critic of the New Deal, especially the NRA as an attempt "to substitute centralized authority of one sort or another for what is left of free competitive enterprise" and as writing a Brookings study on *Wartime Control of Prices* (1940) at the request of the War Department. Malcolm Rutherford's recent HOPE article on W. Hamilton and institutionalism at Brookings does not cite Hardy. Joseph Dorfman (Vol. 5, pp. 550–551) mention Hardy only for his 1927 book with Garfield Cox (of U. of Chicago Business School) on *Forecasting BusinessConditions*. Craufurd Goodwin's paper on Moulton and Pasvolsky of Brookings, in Rutherford's volume of selected papers from the Vancouver HES meeting, does not mention Hardy. The main biographical source is Simeon Leland's memorial note on Hardy in the May 1949 AEA Papers and Proceedings. Irving Fisher listed Hardy in the preface to the 1935 first edition of Fisher's *100% Money* as a supporter of 100% reserve requirements (i.e. a supporter of the Chicago plan for banking reform).

I would describe Hardy in the 1930s as a leading student of monetary policy (as distinct from monetary theory – although his reviews of Keynes demonstrate a solid grasp of theory). (Dimand to Samuels, March 17, 2004)

I am obligated to Gloria Creed-Dikeogu, Myers Library, Ottawa University and to Robert W. Dimand of Brock University, for help in preparing this biography; and to Marianne Johnson for help in preparing the table in the notes.

HARDY'S LECTURES: SOME COMMENTS

The notes record a particularly suggestive, complex account or theory of public-sector decision making. Government, Hardy says, has monopolized money in search of profit from coinage. That implies a monarchical government treating the Treasury as its private bank account. This supports the theory that government is a function of self-interest. That government takes on the responsibility for banking as the main source of money, supports the theory that government, if it is not driven by some benevolent approach to the public interest, nonetheless does tend to be concerned and a function of something more than self-interest. That government socializes bank losses implies that government can be driven by both forces – self-interest, in protecting bank owners and depositors, at least to some extent, and public interest, in protecting the major source of money.

Ostrander queries: "–Was the whole impetus towards the Gold Exchange Standard wholly a matter of the desire to earn some interest on reserve funds? [In margin: F. T. O.]" Here, too, would be some combination of self-interest and public interest in the adoption of a monetary and banking standard.

At one point the notes record two insights into the economic role of government:

–Commodity money is tied to something "independent."
  –It vs. managed money depends on one's confidence in the ability of managers.
–Hardy does not believe in laissez-faire, but neither does he believe in monopoly. But State can not spend all its time <u>enforcing</u> competition.

The first may obfuscate the considerable role of management (discretion) in all systems. The second suggests an uneven contest, between firms – already active in efforts to control government – persistent in their efforts to bend competition to their will, i.e. control markets, and governments which only sporadically attend to competition. An alternative view is that the language "can not spend all its time" is highly misleading: what is required is a competition-enforcing agency with a suitable budget and strong antitrust legislation, coupled with an administration and a management whose philosophy is one of strong enforcement.

From the standpoint of seventy years, the situation in monetary theory was, to put it mildly, jumbled. If something could be thought of and generalized, someone was likely to do so, even to make it a center of gravity in a more or less a priori account. How monetary theory was to be structured, what was the end of monetary policy, what were the actual relations among which variables, including means and ends, and so on – on all these and other questions academic and non-academic authorities disagreed. In some respects, in retrospect, they appear to have operated in a world of fantasy. But the present-day situation in monetary theory, as well as the more-encompassing macroeconomic theory, is no less confused. That historically huge deficits and, at times, low interest rates have meant neither inflation nor boom is, from the perspectives of conventional monetary and fiscal theory, inexplicable.

The notes record "–Hardy surprised that so many – Bradford, Robertson, <u>etc.</u> have accepted a <u>neutral</u> money rather than stable money ideal." Several points: First, a, if not the, classical position held that money *is* neutral with regard to the level and possibly the structure of production (in respect to the latter, not all industries are equally responsive to changes in interest rates, liquidity, etc.). Second, there is an idealist element in all monetary theories, not least the classical ones. Third, for some authorities, stable money meant neutral money, at least typically. Fourth, ideals are <u>ought</u>, not <u>is</u>, propositions. To say that <u>ought</u> propositions have no proper place in monetary theory is consistent with positivism in theory but not in practice. Fifth, the questions whether, how, and to what degree, i.e. when money is neutral in either respect, remain open.

The more or less frequent references to Keynes's work, the reader must remember, are to the *Treatise on Money* and not his *General Theory*.

An interesting, if frustrating, feature of Hardy's lectures, and those of Knight, of course, as recorded by Ostrander (and, as will be seen in future volumes, by Glenn Johnson), is a frequent apparent failure to explain *why* one alternative, said to be better than another(s), *is* better. Hardy's recorded treatment of various price indexes is better than most but is still a bit incomplete in its explanations – though possibly Ostrander felt no need to record them.

The notes conclude with two remarkable statements within inches of each other. The first is an attribution to Say:

–Say – if production is geared to an unequal distribution you may have poverty, but not disequilibrium.

The statement treats two conditions – unequal distribution and equilibrium – as if they were analytically in the same category and subject to potential trade-offs. But distribution (of any structure) is a category of normative economic performance whereas equilibrium is a hypothetical technical condition – hypothetical because the economy is never in equilibrium, and technical because it is only an analytical tool not a category of normative economic performance. Additionally, there is no single, unique equilibrium, rather a set of possible equilibria.

The second statement is an expression of the over-production theory of downswings:

–Cycle in production of capital goods: too much production of them, falling return, depression.

Inter alia, an interesting theoretical aspect of over-production theory is that both it and under-consumption theory are analytically opposite theories of business cycles. In part, too many capital goods and consumer goods are produced because of what transpires on the production side, vs. insufficient purchasing power on the consumption side, because of unequal income distribution; and in part, too little saving to take the capital goods off the market, vs. too much saving to permit adequate purchasing power to take the consumer goods off the market. An interesting empirical aspect of the two theories is that the same evidence was used by both sides to support their respective theories: evidence of unsold goods.

When F. Taylor Ostrander had Hardy's course, Money and Banking, during 1933–1934, a distinctive topic on the agenda was "Plans of Monetary Reform." A one and one-half page mimeographed outline with that title was distributed to students and is published below. The reader is impressed with its comprehensiveness; its inclusion of public works; and its list of authors, including some among the most radical economists. In square brackets are several annotations by Ostrander. The outline is presented substantially as in the original, including varying citation formats.

In the text of the notes, it is not clear whether Ostrander's question marks indicate disagreement with Hardy or worry about his misrepresentation of what Hardy said (Ostrander says, "unlikely" the latter).

Ostrander's term paper in the course was entitled, "Foreign Exchange Restrictions in the Post-Boom Years (1929–1933).

Published below, in addition to Ostrander's class notes, are the outline, "Plans of Monetary Reform;" a set of quotations distributed by Hardy in the course (one can only speculate as to the precise motivation behind the inclusion of each quotation); and, because of the attention given by Hardy to Keynes's *Treatise on Money*, Ostrander's notes on Hardy's A. E. R. review of Keynes's book and on Hardy's related J. P. E. article – in effect, Ostrander's view of Hardy's view of Keynes. This last concern is a serious one. The history of economic thought is a history of interpretations, interpretations of original materials and interpretations of inter- pretations, or of derivative material, all engaging in interpretating the economy.

Some comments on the set of numbered quotations, by number: (1) The first sentence is tantamount to holding that the allocation of resources is governed by institutions, the institutions of the banking system. The second sentence belies the purported automaticity of the gold standard. Among the insights (to this reader) to be found are: (2) the implication that adoption and use of the gold standard was a matter of pragmatic considerations (say, rather than achieving "sound" money); (3, 5, 5a) preoccupations with price structure; (4) a prelude to Keynes' *General Theory*; (6) further insight into how institutions matter; (7) cumulative causation; (8) a tension between price stability, technological progress and economic instability, I hazard no guess as to whether any of these points were in Hardy's mind or would have made sense to him.

DISTRIBUTED MATERIALS FROM THE COURSE

1

PLANS OF MONETARY REFORM

I. Price Stabilization
  1. The Standard
      (Compare Hardy, Credit Policies of the Federal Reserve System, 202–219;
      Robertson, Money, Ch. 6)
    a. Wholesale Prices
      Keynes, Cassel, Fisher
    b. Consumption Goods and Services
      Keynes

    c. Prices of Factors of Production
    Hawtrey (Journal of Royal Statistical Society 1930, vol. 93, pp. 64–85 and discussion following)
    Edgeworth, Papers Relating to Political Economy, 1925, i, 428
    Haberler (reference below)
    Christianson – "Human Effort Monetary System"
    Bradford, Quarterly Journal of Economics, Vol. 43, pp. 668–671
    Leven, in Proceedings of American Statistical Association, March, 1928, 146–147

  2. Means of Effecting Stabilization – "Managed Currency"
    a. Bank Rate; Open Market Operations
    b. Currency Devaluation
    c. Public Works
    d. Unemployment Reserves

II. Stabilization of Employment and Production
  1. As a guide to central bank policy [Federal Reserve Board, Annual Report, 1923, Stewart and Strong testimony on Strong Bill
  2. The theory of deficiency of consumer purchasing power as a source of disequilibrium
    Marx; Hobson; The "New Deal";
    Foster and Catchings, Douglas [Major C. H. (not Paul)]

III. Stabilization of the Money Market
    B. M. Anderson, Chase Bulletin
    Hardy, "Credit Policies of the Federal Reserve System," Chap. 4.

IV. Neutral Money
  1. The Austrian position
    Haberler, (a) paper read at Harris Foundation Round Table, 1932; also (b) article in Schmoller's Jahrbuch, 1932. Vol. 55, pp. 993–1023.
    Hayek, article in Deutscher Volkswirt, Feb. 12, 1932, 642–645 [Prices and Production, Chap. IV]
  2. Money supply adjusted to volume of production, Bradford, reference above, 680–696
  3. The Snyder-Edie suggestion of a uniform growth of M and M_1 (Snyder, Review of Economics and Statistics 1928 vol 10, pp. 40–52 (?) Edie, The Banks and Prosperity, Chap. 4

  4. H. C. Simons' suggestion of <u>constant volume of bank deposits corrected for velocity</u>.

5. The suggestion of the Federal Reserve Committee on Bank Reserves for basing reserve requirements on velocity as well as volume of deposits.
   Hardy, Credit Policy, 318–327

V. Commodity Money
   1. Gold
   2. Bimetallism (Fisher, Purchasing Power of Money)
   3. Composite Standards

2

COLLECTION OF QUOTATIONS DISTRIBUTED BY HARDY FOR ECON 330

(1) The price and income structure of a modern economic community is in the first instance determined by the operation of the organized banking system . . . .. If the community is to remain upon the gold standard the task of the Central Bank amounts to controlling the effective volume of purchasing power in such a way that its aggregate amount does not exceed the amount dictated by the necessities of international equilibrium ["internal in the original; corrected by Ostrander in pencil]
   [T. E.] Gregory, The Gold Standard and Its Future, pp. 15–16.

(2) Great Britain has played a leading part in advocating "the rules of the gold standard" to countries in difficulties . . . . The country which did not "follow the rules" was Great Britain, and September 21, 1931, was the result.
   Benham, British Monetary Policy, p. 45.

(3) But the essential advantage of abandoning the gold standard is that the value of the currency can be adjusted to the point at which prices and costs are in equilibrium. Here is thee key to the unemployment problem.
   Hawtrey, The Gold Standard in Theory and Practice, p. 208.

(4) . . . we need a definite, dependable method of offsetting the deficiencies in consumer buying which at present are caused by savings, and which are never made up for many years at a time, and then only by chance. . . . Foster [and Catchings?]

(5) . . . the stability of the purchasing power of money involves the two conditions – that efficiency-earnings should be constant and that the cost of new investment should be equal to the volume of current savings . . . .
   Thus given the rate of new investment and the cost of production, the price-level of consumption-goods is solely determined by the disposition

of the public towards "saving." And given the volume of savings-deposits created by the banking system, the price-level of investment-goods (whether new or old) is solely determined by the disposition of the public towards "hoarding"[1] money.

(5a) ... a fall in the price of consumption-goods due to an excess of saving over investment does not in itself – if it is unaccompanied by any change in the bearishness or bullishness of the public or in the volume of savings-deposits, or if there are compensating changes in these two factors – require any opposite change in the price of new investment-goods . . .. (same, p. 145)

(6) Agreement among governments and central banks for a technical reform of the gold standard system, primarily with the view to: (a) introducing a greater degree of elasticity into its operation; (b) establishment of a system of adequate central banking collaboration, through the medium of the Bank for International Settlements, by the exchange of essential information and the coordination of national credit policies and money market conditions; and (c) creation of an effective international currency stabilization fund.

Paslovsky, The Necessity for a ,Stable International Monetary Standard, p. 54.

(7) ... over-indebtedness leads to deflation. ... And, vice versa, deflation caused by the debt reacts on the debt.

Fisher, The Debt-Deflation Theory of Great Depressions, Econometrica, Oct., 1933, p. 344.

(8) The stabilization of prices against the consequences of technological progress may involve creation of instability of productive activity.

Hardy, Credit Policies, p. 223.

3

F. TAYLOR OSTRANDER'S NOTES FROM C. O. HARDY'S COURSE IN MONEY AND BANKING, ECONOMICS 330, UNIVERSITY OF CHICAGO, 1933–1934

–Formerly a distinction between Money – the field of government, and Banking – the field of private enterprise.

  –Money had been made a government monopoly through the possibilities of profit through coining it.

 –Why has banking not been taken over? – Later. More complex (?) – shift of power from kings to bourgeois.

 –But, government begins to feel a responsibility towards banking, as the distributors of the main body of money (bank money).

–Distinction made since 1900 (Laughlin) – the financing of the government and the issuance of money should be rigidly separated.

–Hardy says:–financing of government and [blank]

–Banking is private as long as it is profitable, public when it is losing, i.e. the same private control of profits and socialization of losses that we see everywhere today.

–Problem of the Value of Money

  –Money defined by means of its functions.

    –Classical theory emphasized medium of exchange – brings up turnover.

      –But if exchange were always instantaneous, there would not be much need for money – it is not instantaneous.

    –Thus the function of money as a store of value.

      –Suspended purchasing power.

      –Where the real demand for money comes from.

    –The classical approach does not allow of any good connection between value theory and monetary theory.

    –Distinction between this use of money and hoarding is only one of degree. [In margin: "?"]

    –Aesthetic-emotional, engineering-measurement by definite units.

    –One function of money is to make possible cost accounting, alternative expenditure, etc.

      (F. T. O.? Is money necessary for these, or only money of account) [In margin: "?"]

    –Progress of engineering makes this more possible (?).

The Gold Standard

  a-Pure Gold Standard – no money except gold.

    –No management, no change in demand of arts [word uncertain; "articles"?].

    –Such a small proportion of new output each year.

    –Ordinary Gold Standard (plus credit)

  b-Gold currency (gold certificates), credit currency.

  c-Managed gold – broke down in post-war: nationalized currencies, internationalized reserves.

  [Diagrams: (1) Gold certificates atop gold reserves

    (2) Gold certificates, fixed proportion, atop gold

    (3) Variable currency atop gold

  d-Managed paper

  [References in margin: Gregory, Chap. I and II

    Hawtrey, Gold Standard, [in] practice; future]

International Aspects of Gold Standard
    –What would be an unmanipulated Gold Standard? There never has been one.
    –The Gold Standard provides a standardized export (gold) that will always move
    to balance an excess of imports.
    –Hardy says: It is the attempts to improve on the automatic system which are
    the fundamental causes of economic disequilibrium. [In margin: "?"]
    [In margin at top of next page: F. T. O. (What are the environmental, legal,
    manipulated, etc. factors underlying the "automatic" Gold Standard? – I.e. gold
    is manipulated so as to work automatically.)]

U.S. and England:
[Three boxes, numbered in reverse order. This is another diagram of boxes as
earlier.
Diagram 3. Deposits of commercial banks. Legal ratio.
        2. Deposits of [commercial] banks in central bank. [Notes atop gold
            reserves]
        1. Gold in central bank.
    Management and control comes in through action affecting 2.
        –Gold can come from within – no effect from gold mines, or from extra-
        national source.

Continental [Europe]:
    Loans of commercial banks
    [Diagram: Legal ratio
        Notes: Legal reserve
        Gold in central bank
        –Small legal reserve, but large actual reserve because loans will be withdrawn
        in full in notes.
        –Both these functions are inflationary while being built up. But not, once
        stable.
            –It is the expansion and contraction of this system that causes upsets.
        –1920–1923 – off Gold Standard – due to fiscal reasons.
        1931–1933 – off Gold Standard – due [blank]
        –Immediate effect of Liberty Loans was inflating just as paper money – but due
        to high rate of interest they went into the hands of permanent investors – [a]
        different end.
            –Bonds can not be pushed on from one person to another without making
            them a part of circulating currency.
            (F. T. O. –I.e. populace must have faith in enough stability of prices to be
            willing to hold bonds and accept interest.)

[Diagram of circular payments flow among farmers, merchants and traders, whose elements included money payments, national income, turnover, price level, and average balance.]

Issue of inflation vs. deflation is whether to do more business at a lower income or less business at a higher income.
  –Agricultural side has deflated.
  –Industrial side has inflated.
 –Rigidity of prices (trade unions, stabilization efforts, <u>lags</u>)
   –Creates unemployment on the deflationary swing.
   –Can not be conceived of, on any scale, on inflationary swing.
Gold Exchange Standard – reserves are paid interest, "having cake and eating it too."
        [Diagram with rate of interest on vertical axis and time on horizontal axis; downward sloping curve, marked "1928 = civilization, all rapid turnover;" upward sloping curve, market "1933 = barbarism, no future confidence."]
  –Buying commercial bills of other currencies, or treasury bills of other countries, or depositing in commercial or central banks in other countries:
    –"Sound" view is that central bank must not finance governments.
    [Two Ostrander questions:]
    –Was the whole impetus towards the Gold Exchange Standard wholly a matter of the desire to earn some interest on reserve funds? [In margin: F. T. O.]
    "How did the Gold Standard come into existence?
      –Certainly not to bring about those things the Gold Standard is claimed to do. Historical accidental growth;–growth of the "functions" of the Gold Standard – F. T. O.]
  –New York Federal Reserve Bank formed a market for the reserves of these Gold Exchange Standard countries.
  –Lack of confidence in future, encouraged a free market for foreign reserve funds to buy and sell in.
  –Potential disturbance in the existence of these foreign funds in New York and Paris (and London).
  –Gold Exchange Standard is no more than banking, but is just an added degree of pyramiding risk – and puts huge funds at the disposition of a very few people.
  –The lack of a central reserve for the world, with checks drawn on it for international payments, and then of cooperating policies of central banks – is all that sets off the post-war Gold Standard from a managed (international) system.

–How does a monetary authority arrange to keep the money in some relation to the national resources?
  –Discount rate – must react on the <u>credit structure</u> – charge interest on loans. Hardy: Pay interest on deposits – converts <u>money</u> into investments; a premium on not-spending.
  –<u>Change reserve ratios</u>. [In margin: Keynes]
  –Open market operations.
–<u>Great Britain</u> – Hawtrey – Gregory
  –<u>Stabilization</u> – not of real income, but of <u>prices</u>.
  –Big changes in prices over short periods are <u>never</u> the result of changes in the supply of money or the supply of goods – but of changes in the <u>demand</u> for money (or goods).
–The <u>prospect</u> of a <u>decline</u> in <u>value</u> of money does not of itself overcome the desirability of money as a <u>liquid</u> factor in unsettled conditions.
  –Liquidity attained by holding goods – expecting price rise – attained by holding money – expecting price fall.
    –Why is it that people are still speculating on a price fall? The issue is whether the strongest government in the world is strong enough to devaluate its own currency.
  –Governments can raise prices by issuing <u>greenbacks</u> or by issuing <u>bonds</u>.
    –[Greenbacks] may be held as an investment – hoarded – no change in prices.
    –Bonds may be held as investment – no change in prices.
    –I.e. both bonds or money may be spent, and may be held as investment – only difference between gold and bonds is one of degree.

Great Britain

–Hawtrey – English kept on a Gold Standard (too high) by a tight money policy – evidenced by falling price level.
–Benham – If prices fall due to tight banking policy – rigid prices don't fall nearly so fast as elastic ones (freight charges rigid, profits elastic).
  –But a fall in prices due to an increase in productivity does not have same effects – and never comes suddenly.
–Loss of gold in 1930–1931 was not allowed to influence prices – rate not raised enough.
–England went back to gold, gambling on the chance that price inflation in rest of world would obviate necessity of deflation and trade union struggle – or that England might increase its productivity faster than other countries, or that its productivity would fall more slowly than other countries.

–Alternatives: (1) deflate wage scale, money incomes – keep £ at 4.86; (2) or devaluate the £, keeping wage scales and incomes steady, (3) or raise tariffs- (temporary alleviation only).

–Maladjustments due to subsidiary price levels – affecting "structure of production."

$MV = pt + p_2t_2 + \ldots p_nt_n = \Sigma\, pt$ – transition to P. T. is hard

P = average price level; T = total of transactions – unhomogeneous units.

$M_hV_h = P_hT_h$ (buying horses)

$MV_a = P_aT_a$ = same thing, velocity of all of M not used for buying houses is 0.

$MV_c = P_cT_c$ Money turnover buying consumption goods.

$MV_s = P_sT_s$ Money turnover buying saving goods.

[In margin at top of next page: Fisher throws all emphasis on money as a medium of exchange.]

The Quantity Theory is a truism – if it does not work out – the fault lies with the manipulator's arithmetic and statistics.

–It is just as true for any isolated segment of prices and transactions as for the whole.

–For Fisher – V was fixed, any change in M forces a corresponding change in P.

–Keynes – $m = pk$

K = total purchasing power of all money.

P = prices, M = quantity of money

$\underline{K = M/P}$ Assume K to be always constant.

–Fisher emphasizes transactions.

Keynes emphasizes the value of money.

–Is superior – gives more rationality to the assumption of constancy.

–$\underline{V}$ is hard to measure. $\underline{M}$ is easier.

[Numerical example from blackboard, with conclusion:]

$\underline{T}$ being unchanged – the habits of the people with respect to the money they will hold being unchanged – the Keynes formula is convertible into the Fisher formula.

[Another numerical example from blackboard:]

Suppose a change in <u>productivity</u> . . .

–Community would not want to hold more money than before – i.e. would spend more often, i.e. V would rise. [Keynes]

–Community has not changed its habits re the proportion of income it will hold. [Marshall]

–Keynes' is a better formula for the beginnings of a rapid change in money (M).

–If community keeps same quantity of purchasing power as before change in T – you do not come out the same between Keynes and Fisher.

–If community keeps only proportion of income as before change in T – Marshall and Fisher are the same.

–Any surplus transactions – money against money, etc – do not affect income, but do affect M and V and T – divergence between two schools.

–Fisher assumes M/M^1 is a constant – on basis of pre-war, pre-Federal Reserve System experience.

[Diagram with four types of transactions: (a) income; (b) productive exp[enditure]; (c) capital transfer; and (d) gifts, thefts, intra-mural transfers.]

–Fisher intends to include a and b and c.

Keynes intends to include only a.

c – Transactions in money, don't figure as income.

–Fisher equation assumes that changes in c affect price level equally as changes in a or b.

–But, balances held to finance c are much smaller than balances held for others (a, b).

–Keynes has K_c, K_b, K_{ct}.

Professor Laughlin's Theory of Prices

–All forms of "money" merely represent a definite number of grains of gold. He throws all weight on money as the standard of value. The standard of value has value only in its commodity use (as beavers, oxen, etc.) – value obtained in regular channels of trade and by supply and demand for commodity use.

–Was not affected by existence of more forms of money than could be backed by gold. That merely proved that some people had sold gold or money short.

–What of irredeemable paper money?

–Redemption is held in future. Payment temporarily stopped. Value represents a speculation as to future possibility of payment in gold.

–In terms of Cambridge equation, K is affected by possibility of depreciation or appreciation if unspent balances. V will change.

–To what extent is a social institution (as money) a product of what people think it is.

–Obligation of State to pay in gold, is like any other obligation; may be deferred, but will be paid.

–Hardy has a preference for a commodity standard, but can not find a suitable commodity.

–Even such a commodity theory would not invalidate the Quantity Theory.

–Laughlin's doctrine is essentially that of the 19th century English "Banking School;" the Quantity Theory is that of the "Currency School."

–Laughlin says, income in quantity of money does not react at once on prices, but will lower the value of money, as its commodity value falls. K may change, so that the result on prices may not be the same as under the Quantity Theory. No Quantity Theory allows of redundant money, nor elasticity of money.

   –Banking Theory has "redundant" money absorbed by the Arts [?].

      –In "seasonal" period there is a good deal of variation of money, without variation in price.

      –But over long period there is a good deal of analogy between quantity and prices. Do not use Fisher's "verifications:" they are the worst things he does.

–Warren and Pearson – No short run collaboration of gold production with volume of industrial production. But a good deal of correlation in long run, especially in early days. But no correlation since the War.

   –Then they look for reasons to explain this lack of correlation – find many, of course. But they do not then apply these same reasons to the analysis of the earlier period to see if that correlation was too high.

–Hardy in favor of a commodity standard, but can not find a right commodity – wants one of steady output and demand, but one having utility in itself – not like gold and silver.

   –Warburton – ten commodities are money. 800–1000 price levels of other commodities – all money is representative. Reserves of these commodities set up. Government to stand ready to buy or sell fixed units of these commodities. If these ten make up a large part of the production of all goods in the country, this system will work as the Gold Standard was supposed to work.

   –"Objection" to Gold Standard is that so much of gold is money, there is not enough left to make a commodity in its own right. Under Warburton's scheme – the reserves of "money" will not be large enough to dominate the value of the commodities of which a part has been reserved.

   –Commodity Standard avoids all danger of inflation. Withdrawal of gold is for speculative purposes – withdrawal of commodities is for speculation, but also for consumption – because they are cheaper.

   –How get currency out except in terms of 100% backing.

      –Why then be on commodity standard? 100% backing of gold would be the same!

–Hardy suggests an <u>original</u> fiduciary issue – which shall not be increased, i.e. some <u>credit</u> but no credit risk. I.e. <u>elasticity</u> removed from <u>monetary</u> structure.

–Laughlin – Fiscal function and currency function must be kept separate. Assumes a <u>constant</u> currency, if fiscal function is separated, i.e. no credit.

–Changing the Gold Content of the Dollar.
  –This changes the number of dollars in hands of Treasury and Federal Reserve System reserve ratios changed.
    –This makes no difference when there are large reserves <u>anyway</u> – 80% gold backing – 50% cut of gold content.
  –Would a change of 50% in gold content change prices by that amount?
    –Increase in quantity of money may <u>reduce</u> V.
    –Hardy: It is not M that is important in controlling P, but <u>V</u>.
      –T reacts on M – say <u>commodity</u> theorist, if M will not change, V will change.
      –Certain transactions are more important than others, in influencing prices.
  –Starts from assumption that there is <u>some</u> level of prices and of output that will make the system fluid, even under present conditions.
    –I.e. put unemployed to work at such wages as their product will bring, in the present market.
    –But trade barriers will still stop flow of goods.
    –Flight from currency on side of dollar seller is a speculative purchase of money from side of foreign buyer – but both tend to reduce the velocity of money, but storing it abroad, rather than using it as purchasing power.
  –Commodity money is tied to something "independent."
    –It vs. managed money depends on one's confidence in the ability of managers.
    –Hardy does not believe in laissez-faire, but neither does he believe in monopoly. But State can not spend all its time <u>enforcing</u> competition.

–<u>Keynes</u>. Treatise on Money

Reviews:	Quarterly Journal of Economics, August 1931 – Williams
	Economica, August 1931, February 1932 – Hayek
	Art of Central Banking – Hawtrey
	Economic Journal, 1931 – Robertson
	American Economic Review, March 1931 – Hardy
	Journal of Political Economy, June 1931 – Hardy

–Whole Treatise is on bank deposits, i.e. is not a treatise on money – for it neglects money.

–Price level – includes all items that make up the cost of living – goods and services.

–Labor power of money – suggests, but not worked out.

–2nd equation is more important than 1st.

$$\Pi = \frac{E}{0} + \frac{I-S}{0}, \quad \Pi 0 = E + I - S, \; \Pi 0 = E + Q$$

Sale price = cost + profit (per unit)

Π = total price level

0 = total output

E = total money disbursements in production

– Arbitrary definition of profit: How can <u>more</u> or less <u>money</u> come back as earnings, than went out as expenses? [Double vertical line in margin alongside this point.]

    1–New creation of money (or disappearance of money).

    2–Hoarding, new or disgorging.

    3–Reduction or increase of reserve ratio.

    4–Speeding up or slowing up of expenditure, i.e. a change in cash balances, i.e. same as (2).

–Any existence of such disequilibrium means Q comes into existence, or I–S becomes a positive integer.

–Without Q, $\Pi 0 = E$.

–Keynes admits, at first, that Π may change because of a change in zero (productivity), but soon drops this possibility – assuming <u>every</u> change in Π to be a result of changes in I–S. [In margin: "Especially in Volume II.")

PT is a <u>turnover</u>, or <u>cash transactions</u> item.

Π zero is an <u>income flow</u>.

[Equations pertinent to the following omitted here.]

Total output = Output of consumption goods + output of capital goods. How does I' come to differ from I?

    –Cost of production of capital goods (I').

    –Price level (sales receipts) of capital goods (I).

<u>Price</u> of consumption goods is independent of price level of investment goods.

[Diagram indicating circular flow of goods and money, including E and Y.]

Amount not saved <u>must</u> be spent of consumption goods by definition, i.e. if S is equal to I′, amount spent on consumer goods must equal amount [word indecipherable] on consumer goods.

(p. 145 Investment goods include money.)

Price Level of Investment Goods (I)

– Keynes does not distinguish old from new capital goods.
– Hardy divides it. S is spent on <u>old capital goods</u>, but, the sellers of <u>old capital</u> then have the S to spend. If they spend it on C, all is in equilibrium again. If they spend it only partly on C (<u>new</u> capital goods) it is the same as if the first people had spent only part on C.
– K_3 is the relation of amounts of securities the people chose to hold to their total wealth.
– Price level of I is a function of the operation of the banking system – if security prices begin to fall, the banking system can create new savings deposits to offset the fall – keep I stable.
– Does Keynes aim at stabilization of (I–S)/0, or of E/0 too?
  – Same confusion on this in Treatise – especially in Volume II.
– Rate of interest regulates saving vs. investment.
  – If bank rate follows natural rate exactly, the value of investment equals amount of saving.
  Π is then determined by E/0.
    Efficiency earnings = [blank]
  – Did we have, in 1925–1929, an increase of I over S, an increase in E, <u>but,</u> also an increase in 0, to offset the others, so that price level did not change.
    – Keynes <u>really</u> means—central bank must offset changes in Π due to changes in I and S, but must not offset changes in E/0.
    – There was an inflation in 1925–1929, but we did not see it, as we watched only the price level.
  – Volume II adopts a Wholesale Commodity Standard – giving up all of Part II, Volume I.
    – What of a Labor Standard? – a <u>Human Effort Standard</u>.
  The Fundamental Equations and the Banking Policy: The bridge Keynes throws between them is the most important part of the work.
    – The banks are not in the equation.
    – Money is not in the equation. Page 144, Volume I, page 350, Volume II.

[Diagram of circular flow, as above, with arithmetic examples.]

Case I – Savings increase, propensity to hoard unchanged. Savings result in capital.

–Natural rate of interest falls.

–More I, less R – equilibrium again.

Case II – Has hoards of money – disposition to bearishness – Hoarding increases in rate.

–I' must fall, rate rises so as to offset tendency to bearishness.

–Price level falls – value of hoards rises – tendency to add to hoards ends.

[At top of next page: F. T. O. Thesis Subject: What is amount of <u>real</u> purchasing power held by people, <u>as</u> cash, and as deposits. – Analysis of K? How control it?]

–<u>Natural rate rises</u>. Bank rate should rise, to hasten the fall of prices, to end increase of hoarding.

–If central bank adds money to the system to offset the <u>new</u> hoards – Π, P, I, S, will all be stable.

  –<u>But</u>, the bank will have acted in the opposite direction to bringing its rate into alignment with the <u>natural</u> rate.

–In one case, the change in the <u>natural</u> rate is temporary, in the other permanent.

<u>Hoarding</u>	<u>Spending</u>
–In cash	–On consumer goods.
–In bank deposits	–On capital goods

  –If people decide to hoard in bank deposits, and cash hoards don't change, it may increase deposits of their account, or their bank's, but will not increase the <u>total</u> of bank deposits.

    –I.e. does not <u>save</u> from community point of view.

    –Other people must reduce their deposits.

    –Rate of turnover of deposits falls – only decline in <u>rate</u> of expenditures must be met by a decline in volume of bank deposits – or hoarding results.

–Hayek – Hoard is only one of a class of different degrees.

  –Long or short run, <u>liquid or tied-up</u>.

  –The hoard is the extreme liquidity – [word indecipherable] other extreme.

–Increasing inventories is the same as entrepreneur's loss.

Hardy says – whole concept of <u>natural rate</u> as discussed by all its proponents – assumes that there is only <u>one</u> rate of interest in society.

  –This, he says, would be true only in a totally <u>riskless</u> society.

  –But such a concept can not be compared to the <u>market rate</u> – which <u>must include</u> varying <u>risks</u>.

    –The average of all rates in the market has no significance.

    –This is a <u>line of preferences</u> – whose <u>slope</u> is the <u>important thing</u>.

–Aftalion and others include windfall profits in <u>income</u>.

[Diagram with unlabeled axes, with two horizontal lines, the lower one labeled "P. R." and the upper one, "E." Oscillating line drawn around upper line; with maximum distance between upper line and oscillating line indicated by lines.]

–Hardy, Robertson, Hayek, all assumed that change in I–S could come about only as a result of <u>monetary</u> changes.
　–Q can only be brought in by changes in monetary expansion (including velocity).
–Keynes says – amount of money and velocity remain the same.
　–Rate of savings changes, losses made, financed by reduction of cash balances (MV = the same as before – savers' balances increased), reduction of their own expenditure, borrow from people who save, sell securities to people who save.
–Decrease in S, profit to <u>consumer goods producers</u> – if <u>they</u> buy that part of capital formerly bought by savers, the capital goods producers do not make a loss – i.e. Q is positive, P and Π rise.
–I.e. +Q occurs as a result of changes in <u>rate</u> of saving, but with no change in quantity or velocity of money.
–There exists a huge pool of already created capital goods, <u>old</u> capital.
　–If this total, at a valuation, has that valuation lowered by the new increment, money is shifted from savings deposits to capital market, till equilibrium is restored.
–Keynes assumes hoards to be unchanged if the <u>demand schedule</u> for hoarding remains unchanged. (Hardy, Hayek, Robertson had assumed the <u>quantity</u> of hoards to be unchanged.)
　–Thus there <u>is</u> a change in velocity.
–Keynes assumes the rate of flow of consumption goods and of investment goods to be unchanged. (Cf. Harrod)
–Hardy's chart:
　[Diagram]
Introduction of new money by a government changes the propensity to hoard – i.e. shifts the schedule.
　–New stock of money, new propensity to hoard, or entrepreneurs getting a wrong number and not being able to sell securities to make up losses – all are the same in effect. [Line from final clause to brace alongside beginning of sentence.]
Extent to which bank-rate can control or affect the situation. – Bank <u>can</u> control the volume of savings deposits.

–I.e. really a <u>series</u> of propensities to hoard. [Diagram, unlabeled, with downward-sloping line alongside which is written: "Stocks, Bonds, Commercial Paper, Government, Hoards"]
–"Natural rate" is a complex affair.

The general British group approaches the cycle from the standpoint of a general price level.
–In general the standpoint of <u>monetary</u> theorists.
–But another group of monetary theorists rejects the <u>general</u> price level – uses the <u>price-structure</u> approach.
Wicksell, quoted by both sides.
–By Keynes, however, he is quoted in just the place where he is wrong. [Both "he" refer to Wicksell.]
von Mises: Theorie des Geldes – 1912, Causes of the Depression 1931
–Father of neo-Wicksell point of view.
–von Hayek, Machlup (Absorption of Credit in Stock Exchange), Haberler, Morgenstern.

Hayek starts from assumption that resources are <u>fully</u> employed. Natural rate of interest controls production at one end of the structure to the extent necessary to expand production at the other end.
–Interpretation of psychology of entrepreneur.
–Empirical proof – re facts.
–One [of] the two disproves of the logical chain of arguing from <u>his</u> assumptions. [Line from this statement to brace alongside the two preceding lines.]
–What of higher prices in boom the further away from the consumer you get? – The heart of the Austrian system; treated as only a <u>lag</u> by Keynes' system.
<u>Hayek</u> says we cannot talk about the price level, but must talk about a price <u>structure</u>.
–Can he then talk about an interest level, rather than an interest <u>structure</u> –
–New purchasing power brings increment of capital construction which can only be maintained with an increasing amount of purchasing power – a single increase of purchasing power must mean a change in the <u>rate</u> of output of purchasing power – constantly increasing total, due to constant necessity of increments of purchasing power to sustain the capital due to the first increment.

Proposals of Monetary Reform
–Price stabilization

–Stabilization of production and employment
–Monetary expansion at consumer's end
–Neutral money (keep monetary structure out of the picture)
–Labor standard
–Fisher – Over-indebtedness – Deflation (price level disturbances)
  –Debt liquidation leads to loss of confidence.
  –But only debt liquidation <u>plus</u> hoarding makes pressure on the price level.
    –And hoarding will produce the same result without debt liquidation.
  –Internal Debt vs. National Wealth
      1929   200,000,000   362,000,000,000
      1933   160,000,000   275,000,000,000
  –What do these figures mean?
  –The more debtors pay, the more they owe.
    –Solved by reflation of price level.
    –How reflate without new creation of indebtedness?

–Walter Stewart: Central banking control must be based on as <u>large</u> and <u>wide</u> a <u>base of observation</u> as possible – large amount of research.
  –<u>Rejects price level</u> as test, rejects <u>reserve level</u>.
  –Wouldn't worry about "profit" inflation, but about <u>income</u> inflation.
  –By 1922 – Stewart and [Federal] Reserve Board concluded that there was nothing to the discount rate without open market operations to support [it].
    –Thus the volume of open market operations has increased down to the present.
  –<u>We</u> were able to disregard reserve.
  –1923 – control of price level dropped – "accommodation of business" taken up.
  –Keynes breaks with the Anglo-Scottish-(U.S.) tradition that banks should be liquid and not invest in industries.
    –U.S. banks have always bought bonds very heavily, and real estate mortgages as much as possible.
    –Because, short-time commercial borrowing does not correspond [sic: respond] readily to changes in the rate of interest.
      –In the bond market, more possibility of control of investment by interest changes.
    –This is not so large a step in practice as it is in theory.
  –Federal Reserve System has never bought anything but government bonds (other central banks are not so strict).

–If Federal Reserve System buys only AAA bonds, it somewhat raises their price, making AA bonds more desirable to the marginal purchasers of AAA bonds. And so on down the line.

Choice of an index number for stabilization (following Haberler, Schmoller's Jahrbuch article, and Hawtrey).
  –Hardy surprised that so many – Bradford, Robertson, etc. have accepted a neutral money rather than stable money ideal.
  –Keynes wants services included.
    –Retail price index (consumption index).
    –Wholesale price index (working capital).
    –Index of valuation of productive resources (labor purchasing power).
    –General commodities bought in market
      –Including wages, rents, stock prices.
        –Snyder, Fisher.
        –Total income (Keynes' E) index.
        –Volume of employment.
    –Index numbers used for sake of comparing items of different nature or time period.
    –To study debtor-creditor relation.
    –To study stabilization of business cycles.

Haberler:

Index of Stabilization	Monetary		Non-Monetary		
	1 Inflation + m or + V	2 Deflation - m or - V	3 Growth of pop. No change of technology Growth of capital	4 Technological progress No increase in stages	5 Technological progress Increase in number of stages
Labor			Increased M/V Consumption steady E rises	M or V steady Consumption falls E steady	Increased M/V Consumption falls E steady
Total Income, "E"	Decreasing Money or Decreasing Velocity	Increasing Money or Increasing Velocity	Constant M/V Wages and Consumption fall	M/V Steady Consumption and wages fall	Increased M/V Consumption falls E steady
Consumption			Increased M/V Wages steady E rises	Increased M/V Wages rise E rises	Increased M/V Wages rise E rises

Wholesale prices go down or up more than consumption index in the cycle.

–Whether the new money comes in on the consumption side or not.

Warren <u>starts</u> with the statement – unproved – that farm products rise or fall more than other products – thus they should be specially protected!

Fisher says Rogers, Persons, Warren are three of best monetary economists in world! – three others in U.S. – six in England.

–Is debtor to pay <u>absolute amounts</u> or <u>relative amounts</u>?
  –First leads to use of commodity index.
  –Second leads to use of labor index.

Consumption goods index better in theory. Wholesale price index more practicable, labor index best from point of view of debtor-creditor.
  –Everyone who looks to the "price level" comes out with the wholesale price index.
–Böhm-Bawerkian analysis of production is not necessary to the acceptance of neutral money as an aim.
–Maintain consumer's demand in order to <u>justify</u> capital goods.
–Or maintain investment demand in order to <u>complete</u> the capital goods.
–If all were a matter of <u>quantity</u> of money there would be much point in a controlled inflation directed by a planning board.
–But too much of inflation is due to velocity, which is created on the side of the borrowers.
–Neutral money – not a price level or quantity of money is fixed, but the quantity of money will exert <u>no</u> influence on the otherwise (?) [F. T. O.?] existing state of demand and supply of goods and capital.
  –Opposed to Foster and Catchings – need of credit to consume.
–Depression isn't a time when there is less money, but a time when the increased money supply is not sufficient to offset the great decrease in <u>velocity</u>.
–Hayek disregards the problem of seasonal supply.
–Simons: –No incentive to hoard deposits as against current deposits (notes).
  –End of <u>discretion</u> by Federal Reseerve Board – managed money without definite rules is too free.
–Hardy: Velocity increase is of <u>much</u> more importance than quantity increase. (B. M. Anderson thinks, if quantity is taken care of, velocity takes care of itself.)
  –Is extremely reluctant to give up the Gold Standard – it has all the requirements of a money but one; it has little use in non-monetary ways.
–Warburg: warehouse receipts – a composite commodity of ten units.

–Substantial reserves, same uncovered amount.
–A precedent in Peel's Bank Act, 1844.
–Growing preference for these ten commodities as against all others.

–Foster and Catchings:
  –Doctrine comes out in relation to corporate profits.
  –Over-built industry due to reinvesting of corporate profits.
  –Money is used twice in succession to create goods, then only once to buy those goods.

Good = 100 units.

  1st year: Receipts 100, 90 distributed, 10 profit.
  2nd year: 10 units' worth new capital, thus a larger output. Goods = 110, but consumers have only 90 to buy with.
    –Why should price remain the same?
    –Really refers to a monopoly situation.
      –Never released the assumption of one corporation.
    –Corporations don't distribute their profits.
      –If savings are used to finance capital construction, still equilibrium; but, there are then more goods.
      –Keynes assumes that capital disbursements are made in the same period as goods are produced.
      –Profits are disbursed.
–Ford, Hoover, etc. – Recent Economic Changes (1929) – General Johnson. [Head of NRA (National Recovery Administration)]
  –Prosperity depends on payment of high wages.
  –Uneven distribution and lack of purchasing power.
    –Lauderdale, Sismondi, Say, Malthus, Marx.
      –Say – if production is geared to an unequal distribution you may have poverty, but not disequilibrium. [Double vertical line in margin alongside these lines.]
    –Hobson
    –So many capital goods, so much capacity to produce consumption goods, not enough consumptive power (purchasing power)
      –True if you reach saturation point.
    –Assumes prices steady, i.e. monopoly, true under this, or even bad competition.
  –Cycle in production of capital goods: too much production of them, falling return, depression.

4

OSTRANDER'S NOTES ON HARDY'S (1) REVIEW OF KEYNES'S *TREATISE ON MONEY* AND (2) "SAVINGS, INVESTMENT AND BUSINESS CYCLES"

4A

American Economic Review   C. O. Hardy   Review of Keynes' Treatise
   March, 1931

–Central theme of Treatise (not covering all of monetary aspects) is effect of changes in quantity of money on profits, productive activity, distribution of income, creation of capital.
–Equations – are mathematically sound, economically significant.
   –Constitute a realistic description of current economic behavior.
–Banks offering credit at a rate below natural rate, induce producers to use more funds than saving public is withholding from consumption by charging a higher rate than natural rate, discourage investment so that it falls below rate of saving.
–Assumption underlying this argument is that there is always some rate which would (if effective) induce an amount of investment just equal to the amount of saving which will take place at that rate, without any change in circulation.
This is Wicksell's theory. Keynes enlarges it, saying it would be true only in a barter economy. In a monetary economy, there are 3 variables. The willingness to save, the willingness to borrow to produce new capital, the relative attractiveness, as a store of value, of monetary funds and of other investments.
   –Savings made by purchase of new securities, or hoarding.
   –Investment made by borrowing from investors, or drawing on investors' hoards.
–Equilibrium requites I = S, also – demand for cash balances to be in equilibrium to [sic: with] demand for securities.
   –I.e. a rate structure.
–Keynes shifts meaning of "Natural Rate," – First, it means the rate which would equilibrate supply of savings with value of investment goods. Second, it means the rate which would induce entrepreneurs to borrow the whole amount that is being saved. (Market rate means the rate paid for that proportion of savings going to new investment. (Cf. II, 373)
–Monetary reform – objective – some inconsistency.
   –Vol. I – equilibrium of savings and investment, industrial stability involve conformity of prices to "efficiency earnings" (I, 166).
   –Vol. II – equilibrium of savings and investment appears to be assumed synonymous with stability of prices. (II, 220!)

–Vol. I – industrial stability and optimum output – ultimate objectives. (I, 17)

–Vol. II – stability of prices ultimate objective. (II, 222)

–Professor Mises: sole source of disturbance between market and natural rate is capacity of banks to expand effective currency in response to demand. Proposes all bank deposits to be covered by 100% gold reserves. Investment must equal saving (except hoarding).

–Hardy sides with Mises but advocates a fixed contingent of uncovered deposits (less drastic transition (?!)

   –No elasticity, no remedy for emergency situations because none could arise.

   –If Keynes' theory is correct, elasticity of the circulating medium is the primary source of cyclical instability.

      (–This is not true; it is not elasticity which causes cycle, but unregulated, or badly regulated, elasticity. FTO)

   4B

Savings, Investment and Business Cycles C. O. Hardy Journal of Political Economy, 1931

–Concept of relation of investment and saving, and prices and profits is realistic.

–Concept of "Natural" rate of interest is confusing.

   –Natural rate that which keeps saving = investment; price inflation and deflation caused by failure of market rate to keep up with natural rate.

   –But the natural rate can be obtained only by inference from the relation of saving and investment – inferred only from the phenomena it is supposed to explain.

      –Saving and investment can only be obtained by inference from the price level, or from statistics of credit and cash.

      –Thus any possible sequence of events supports the theory.

      –We are not [word indecipherable] in our trust or distrust of money rates as a cause of cyclical fluctuations.

–Seven historical cases – not inductive proof, but illustrations.

   2)- 1890–1896, high reserves in Bank of England gold doubled – Keynes admits open market purchases would not have stimulated investment; thus falls back on public works and government guarantees base on borrowing.

      –This is the only place where Keynes mentions this procedure, everywhere else it is a banking program, purely.

      –Keynes shows how central bank ($) policy minimizes the effects of changes in the supply of gold or the price level.

         –Hardy adds: Such changes in supply of gold work themselves out through changes in the relationship of investment and saving.

–Any new gold supply causes investment to be greater than saving.
–Criticism of Keynes' policy of monetary reform (banks stabilize prices by controlling the supply of credit).

NOTE

1. Using this term, for once, to mean their scale of preference for savings-deposits and other securities at different price-levels of the latter.
Keynes, <u>A Treatise on Money</u>, Vol. I, pp. 136, 144.

MATERIALS FROM CHESTER WHITNEY WRIGHT'S COURSES ON THE ECONOMIC HISTORY OF THE UNITED STATES, UNIVERSITY OF CHICAGO, 1933–1934

CHESTER WHITNEY WRIGHT: A SHORT BIOGRAPHY

Chester Whitney Wright (1879–1966) received his A.B. in 1901, A.M. in 1902 and Ph.D. in 1906, all from Harvard University. After teaching at Cornell University during 1906–1907, he taught at the University of Chicago from 1907 to 1944. Wright was the author of *Economic History of the United States* (1941, 1949); editor of *Economic Problems of War and Its Aftermath* (1942), to which he contributed a chapter on economic lessons from previous wars, and other chapters were authored by John U. Nef (war and the early industrial revolution) and by Frank H. Knight (the war and the crisis of individualism); and co-editor of *Materials for the Study of Elementary Economics* (1913). Wright's *Wool-Growing and the Tariff* received the David Ames Wells Prize for 1907–1908, and was volume 5 in the Harvard Economic Studies.

I am indebted to Holly Flynn for assistance in preparing Wright's biography and in tracking down incomplete references; to Marianne Johnson in preparing many tables and charts; and to F. Taylor Ostrander, as usual, for help in transcribing and proofreading.

Further University of Wisconsin Materials: Further Documents of F. Taylor Ostrander
Research in the History of Economic Thought and Methodology, Volume 23-C, 271–367
ISSN: 0743-4154/doi:10.1016/S0743-4154(05)23208-X

1

MATERIALS FROM CHESTER WHITNEY WRIGHT'S COURSE, ECONOMIC HISTORY OF THE UNITED STATES, ECONOMICS 220, UNIVERSITY OF CHICAGO, FALL 1933

Introductory Comments

Wright's introduction to the course was entitled in the notes, and most likely in the lecture, "Close relationship between economic and political history in U.S." It is important for several reasons – reasons that may not be obvious at first glance because the elements of the introduction are presented so tersely. First is the point articulated in the title itself – the close relationship ("interrelationships" would be better) between economic and political history – a point which runs counter to the non-interventionist ideology through which people have been induced to view the history of the economic role of government. Second, that "democratic government lends itself to influence by economic factors," helps both to specify something of the structure of interrelations between economy and polity and to explain the plutocratic nature of the system. Third, Wright establishes the importance of context, or environment, the particular large-scale forces within which individuals operate and which govern historical paths.

Among the contextual elements were: (1) advances in science and invention leading to abnormally rapid world economic development; (2) early independence from nationalism and foreign aggression due to geography – hence the largely passive advance of nationalism; (3) religious freedom and homogeneity – hence the subordinate influence of religion in political history; (4) the materialism of U.S. culture; (5) the combination of weak socioeconomic stratification (democracy and the absence of social, religious and bureaucratic castes) and that "opportunities for social prestige were from the beginning limited to ownership of wealth"; and (6) the influence of other countries' engaging in imperialism and colonialism. (By materialism is not meant Karl Marx's materialism in which the mode of production and the attendant social relations of production govern how people live and perceive their lives. By materialism is meant a preoccupation by individuals and families with economic well-being and the influence thereof on other social processes and phenomena. The two are not necessarily mutually inconsistent.)

Wright identifies, however briefly, some elements of the cultural materialism, specifying that most immigrants came for economic reasons; that the economic opportunity provided by a continent endowed with rich resources, was accommodated by world economic growth and moralized by a facilitating religion(s); and that economic success was promoted by status emulation taking the form of wealth, by successful economic development engendering further economic development, and by men of ability going into business. A materialist culture is one in which people are not only interested in – preoccupied with – making a living but one in which a group of people is preoccupied with organization *for* production and the organization *of* production, and associated financial manipulations, for the purpose of making money in a system of status emulation in which money matters most.

The fault lines of social development and history represent additional contextual or situational elements. One is that "Political and social order lagged behind economy." Economic growth itself tended to and was invoked to temper and limit political and social conflict and reform. Such conflict was also constrained by opportunities open, or believed to be open, sequentially in the West, by urbanization and by suburbanization.

All of the foregoing is somewhat summarized in the eleventh point, "Interaction between cultural and economic and political and social phenomena."

Wright began his introduction by saying that "In colonial times, relation of England to colonies was mainly economic." That is substantially true. What he does not say is anything about the struggle between two ways of life within the colonies, one preoccupied with religion, the other with trade, money and consumption. The latter won and that victory is why materialism took hold and strengthened and why Wright could say that religion had a subordinate influence on political history. Wright's twelfth point is recorded to have been that "History is record of man's struggle for freedom and self-expression." The point implicit in his introductory remarks is that in the U.S. that struggle for freedom and self-expression largely took culturally specific forms, namely economic freedom and pecuniary self-expression in a particular system of status emulation.

A few pages into the notes, Wright is recorded saying that the scarcity of labor, relative to the abundance of land, led to competition between the states for settlers. Proprietors had to make concessions in order to get tenants. As a result, the institutions of the country were considerably modified in the direction of "democracy, freedom, initiative." Thus did circumstantial conditions affect institutional structure and development – even if not permanently: the influences of labor scarcity, he noted, "lasted till well into 19th century."

Wright gave another perceptive interpretation, now of the origins of the American Revolution, one involving an incipient theory of public choice. As I read Ostrander's notes, Wright identified a change during 1773–1776 in the relative importance of political and economic issues, the former increasing and the latter decreasing in importance. The restrictions imposed by the Act of 1774 that led to the Boston Tea Party imposed negligible economic loss but adversely affected the political rights and liberties of a group at the center of public opinion – lawyers and printers – "who exercised an influence out of proportion to their numbers" – i.e. a matter of asymmetrical influence by a small-number group. Also, whereas (as we have already noted) relative freedom and homogeneity of religion paradoxically lowered the influence of religion on political history, surely an unintended and unforeseen consequence on the part of religious activists, immigrants who sought a different form of freedom, one centered on the individual, perhaps even in matters of religion (which made the Protestant Reformation attractive to many), gradually rose to the individualism of the Declaration of Independence. Here, therefore, we have a quasi-market involving: (a) changing marginal rates of substitution between religious, economic and political freedoms; (b) small vs. large number cases; and (c) asymmetrical influence by groups with intensively felt preferences.

A similar analysis is applied to the formation and adoption of the Constitution. The notes read, concerning the lengthy process of amendment:

–Due to <u>fear</u> of the masses – undemocratic.
–Whole movement leading to the Constitution was a <u>conservative reaction</u>; an effort to <u>protect</u> a <u>minority</u> group and interests
  –Made the majority as little important as possible and thus the Constitution made hard to change.

Here we find the problems of majority vs. minority and of a Constitution driven by the latter in protection of its interests.

One problem in constructing historical narrative of an explanatory kind is that of phrasing language. It is easy to introduce metaphysical and/or rationalizing terminology, because authors themselves have been acculturated in the national historical myths, or some of them. That Wright seems to have escaped this tendency is suggested by passage like the following down-to-earth formulation:

–Not a piece of political theorizing; but a document taking definite account of actual interests and conflicts – to meet the contemporary, not future, needs.
–Yet drawn up in sufficiently broad terms, that it <u>has</u> existed (however limpingly) to the present.

This does not mean that Wright's account is correct, only that his account appears to be of a particular type.

At one point the notes have Wright saying, "a <u>national</u> economy (self-sufficiency)." The development of a national economy does not necessarily and typically does not signify a self-sufficient economy. It may make better use of resources and be a more productive economy, and therefore be less dependent on foreign trade. But a national economy represents, especially in this case, a merger solution internalizing gains from trade; yet still require foreign trade for what cannot be produced domestically.

Wright is explicit and candid in taking up imperialism, by name, during the 19th century. Inasmuch as the same evidence has been cited in support of both the political and economic interpretations of imperialism, no conclusive way of choosing between them has been developed. (There is probably no need to choose. But not all scholars feel that imperialism is imperialism. Some sense that in some cases the driving force is national politics and in others, economic. In a recursive world, each engenders the other, as it were.) For his part, Wright's presentation, as recorded in Ostrander's notes, presents 19th-early 20th century imperialism as an economic phenomenon. Thus, some pages later we read,

–Use of the powers of States to wage economic warfare for private traders' gain.

And still further pages later, in a discussion of the peacetime advantages of a national merchant marine,

–In time of peace – "trade follows the flag" (sometimes).
  –Especially stimulating exports.
  –In reality, the flag follows trade – ships go where they will get cargo, that
    depends on other economic forces.
–thereby again adopting an economic interpretation.

Several of the foregoing points are illustrated by part of Wright's discussion of the results, by 1900, of the "end of free, public land, not least in importance his emphases on tendencies that have multiple causes and that may be counteracted and on increased interdependence as leading to the development of social consciousness:

–Economic imperialism – outflow of capital.
–Shift from exploitation of land to that of labor – end of bandit era.
–Conflict of capital and labor.
–Social Democracy of frontier of less importance.
–More interdependence, development of <u>social</u> consciousness.
–This list is one of <u>tendencies</u> – take time, may be counter-acted, are themselves
  the results of more than this <u>one</u> cause.
–1900 – end of one great epoch in our history, beginning of another.

Correlative to the foregoing is an identification and explanation of certain problems in terms not of their proximate causes but of their overriding or system causes. Thus we have not only multiple causes but degrees of proximity or the difference between systemic cause and the phenomena of life whose form they take. The railroads are not the important cause; the problems are due to modern industrialism; railroads are principally the vehicle of their delivery:

> –Railroads first brought the country face to face with the big problems of modern industrialism.
>> –Internal competition, coming from large fixed capitals.
> –First restriction on complete individualism – State laws, then Interstate Commerce Act 1887.
> –The problems of our post-frontier, industrial civilization, which are the main concern of present-day statesmen – first came into notice with the railroads in the 1880s.

One aspect of economic history is perhaps more apparent in Wright's course than in Nef's courses but is amply evident in both men's courses. It involves a parallel with macroeconomics. Macroeconomic forces are very important; the levels of saving, investment, liquidity preference, marginal efficiency of capital, tax revenues, government spending and the like. But they have no existence independent of microeconomic decision making in firms and households and smaller or larger iotas of incremental choices on all levels and departments of government. A dollar here, a dollar there, a vote trade here and there – they all add up. So too in economic history. Historical forces are very important; *inter alia*, they form the framework of individual and governmental decisions making. But they are what they are and have the influence they do because of incremental decisions at the micro level. Enough has been said by me above, and in connection in Ostrander's notes from Nef's courses, to preclude any reader from concluding that in the interpretive contest between the individual and historical forces I choose one to the total exclusion of the other.

Two-thirds of the way into Ostrander's notes from Wright's Economics 220 the reader will find what may well be – at least in the opinion of this editor – one of the most remarkable discussions found in any of Ostrander's notes from his year at Chicago. This is Wright's brilliant and accurate description of the process through which the institution of the corporation has been formed. What Wright taught at the University of Chicago at that time contrasts with what George Stigler and others taught there in the late 20th century, in part through criticism of the work of Adolph Berle and Gardiner C. Means. Wright's account emphasizes the competition between states seeking to both earn money from incorporation fees and earn reputation as pro-business. I state as positive propositions, first, that such origins of the institution are not unique to the corporation as such – they are found in the history of perhaps every basic economic institution; and, second, that being the case, it is difficult to take any position other than one combining cynicism, irony, and skepticism about all preaching on the sanctity of "the rule of law" (see Warren J. Samuels, "The Rule of Law and the Capture and Use of Government in a World of Inequality," in Samuels, *Economics, Governance and Law: Essays on Theory and Policy*, Cheltenham: Edward Elgar, 2002; and Warren J. Samuels and Arthur S. Miller, eds., Corporations and Society: Power and Responsibility. Westport: Greenwood Press, 1987). This applies to the modern Chicago School position that markets are ipso facto competitive and produce efficient (optimal) results, in part on the ground that every consideration that might interfere with such results are finessed by hypothesizing a relevant market: a market for promotion, a market for incorporation fees, a market for corporate control, and a market for control of government.

In the last fifth or so of Ostrander's notes, the alert reader will find numerous insights into Wright's thinking about government, from his description of changes in the economic role of government accompanying industrialization to its organization in the first World War.

Wright's concluding lecture presented an impressive list of "Objectives of [the] course." (A similar lecture was given early in Economics 320.) Some objectives are expectable – those, for example, having to do with training for citizenship, the culture expected of an educated person, and the substance of economic history. More subtle are those having to do with learning the concept of change, providing a background for other histories, and an aid to understanding ourselves and how we have been shaped. One set of items is:

–To see some significance in the facts of history.
    –Look out for operation of economic laws and principles.
    –Has legislation succeeded or failed?

In a Post Modernist period, to speak of the facts of history and their significance is to raise questions concerning the theory(ies) by which facts are fact and significant or not and how/in what way. As for the operation of economic law and principles, Wright seems not to have gone out of his way to specify them. And the success or failure of legislation raises questions concerning the criterion(ia) of success or failure, or of objective – actual or ostensible, and concerning the alternatives thereto that might have been followed. Wright also raised the prospect of "other histories," to which economic history was "background." His emphasis, explicit and implicit (in light of his lectures), on the interrelationships or interconnectedness between many factors and forces, is not unrelated to that prospect but also stands on its own. Finally, the notes record, within quotation marks, his humorous but pregnant concluding lesson (see page XXX).

Several lectures deal exclusively with topics of historiography and interpretation. These topics include: materialism; the economic interpretation of history and the problem of causation; the effect of religion, of nationalism, and of democracy on economic life; and technical details of historical method.

Throughout these lectures the reader of Ostrander's notes will find subtle and important insights provided by Wright. He suggests that the lack of a King, or of a ruling class of political, hereditary, family, religious, or military origin left the economic and material elements in life and government as the most important. He proposes that Brentano's approach to the relation of religion and economic life is more realistic than Weber's, suggesting that the rise of capitalism reacted on Protestantism and Catholicism. He suggests, perhaps ironically, that democracy in consumption habits allowed great standardization. Apropos of historical method, Wright cautions that the historian has "to get around group psychology and individual psychology," that the "first assumption is that every document is wrong until proven correct," and for "care in use of words (especially capitalism, democracy, etc.)" especially in light of the "tendency to read back into past history present day concepts." There is much more of scholarly interest.

At one point in the discussion of historical method – understood as the problem of evidence – the notes record Wright saying that the American economic historian "Must understand the economic order – the institutional background." Apropos of which the following points are apposite. First, understanding the economic order remains an objective of economists, including economic historians. One cannot presume either that it is already known or that the order is unchanging. That raises the question whether the same "economic order" underlies or otherwise applies to the sequence of economic systems in relevant economic history, say, Adam Smith's four stages. Second, the question arises as to the significance of the clause "the institutional background." Does Wright mean that the economic order as such resides in a set of institutions – if so, which ones? – or that the economic order is some generic abstract a-institutional conceptual system, or that institutions form actual systems, or something else? The Chicago School – whose doctrines it is not my intention to assign en masse to Wright – thinks of the economic order as a mixed abstract and institutionalized private enterprise system; Frank Knight's and Henry Simons's notions of social economic organization combine the conceptual market price mechanism and institutions.

Wright's lectures conclude with two mind-stretching presentations. The first is one of the most non-ideological treatments of laissez-faire in the United States to be found anywhere. The second consists of comparable discussions of the theory of progress, economic opportunity, democracy, and the adaptability of political to economic structure.

Ostrander' s Lecture Notes

Class notes
Econ. 220
Professor Chester Wright

Close relationship between economic and political history in U.S.
1. In colonial times, relation of England to colonies was mainly economic.
2. In 19th and 20th centuries, economic development was abnormally rapid throughout the world, due to advance in science and invention.
   –Political and social order lagged behind economic.
3. Democratic government lends itself to influence by economic factors.
4. Religious freedom, religious homogeneity, led to subordinate religious influence on political history.
5. Geographic influence: Nationalistic ideas and action for self-defense has been of less importance.
6. Materialism in the U.S.
   a. Most people came here for economic reasons.
   b. Age of greatest invention was age of greatest invention [Sic. Almost certainly "investment."] – increased possibility of earning.
   c. Economic opportunity in rich resources.
   d. Democratic society, no castes (relatively), no noble army, religious, or bureaucratic castes.
      –I.e. opportunities for social prestige were from the beginning limited to ownership of wealth.
   e. No social taboo on business activity; much of best ability has gone into business.
7. Exemplification of economic laws in U.S. economic history.
8. Pressure of the West – in last quarter of 19th century, urban movement took the place of the westward movement as dominant feature, 20th century – dominant problem was modern industrialism.
9. Rise of modern capitalistic industry.
10. Reaction of world conditions on the U.S.
    –Race for colonies, struggle for empire.
    –1815–1890 – political developments abroad did not affect us, Europe becoming industrialized, and a market for our goods.
    –In 20th century, we are competitive, not complementary.
11. Interaction between cultural and economic and political and social phenomena.

12. History is record of man's struggle for freedom and self-expression.

Economic history deals with the records of the process of getting a living.

[Three or four vertical lines in margin alongside this sentence, with "?" further out in margin and arrow pointing toward this sentence.]

   –A cooperative process between man and man, or between man and nature (and technology?).

–Nature of Economic History – the development of the methods of production and distribution, and how they functioned.

   –Progress = more full dependence on environment, not freedom from it.

The economic order of the American Indian.

–500,000 to 1,000,000 Indians in present confines of U.S., at discovery (now 350,000).

   –This was about as many as the country could support, with their technique.

–East of Mississippi River – fertile; corn main crop, wild game and crops.

   –Cultivation led to settlement, small villages.

      –50–100 inhabitants.

      –Palisades and wigwams.

–Semi-Arid region west of Mississippi River.

   –Bison chief food (dried flesh) – berries, roots, game.

   –Nomadic life (portable tepee).

–Columbia River area – little rain; depended on wild crops – nuts, seeds, fruits; shelter from reeds – about most backward.

–Plateau region – New Mexico, Arizona.

   –About most advanced.

   –Irrigated land to raise corn, melons, squash.

   –Settled life, in pueblos; used some copper.

   –Stone and wood, their chief materials; clothes of deer skin and grass fiber; –pottery.

   –Few agricultural tools.

   –Transportation: dog, dugouts (on streams), by humans.

   –Communication – oral only; little trade – mostly barter, some wampum.

–Unit of economy was clan; land held in common; private property limited to product and personal effects.

   –No division of labor between sexes.

   –Small wars constantly: struggle for food – blood feuds.

–Their resources inadequate to cope with whites.

   –Once a foothold was gained, they were lost, for they were an obstacle to white progress.

–Disposal of Indians: in Latin America; intermarriage, free association, attempt to Christianize them, large half-breed population.

–English did not fraternize with them or intermarry or try to convert – treated them as aliens, drove them out.

–Natives taught whites how to raise some crops, especially corn; considerable trade of furs.

Groups interested in colonization:

–<u>Nations</u>: economic contribution of colonies to national power and wealth.

–<u>Colonists</u>: religious motive fairly important: <u>economic</u> motive <u>most</u> important; political least.

–<u>Promoters</u>: economic motive dominant – some religious.

–<u>Company</u>, <u>Proprietary</u>.

<u>Population</u>: – Negroes, first brought in in 17th century (1619) – few came in in 17th century – but many in 18th century.

–1790 – population, 95% rural.

–18th Century: 30–35% growth per decade.

<u>Landholding</u>:

–In England land held in socage; could be willed or sold; but owed something to superior lord – land not owned outright.

–In colonies: Crown, or proprietor, or corporation (in Massachusetts) could extract a quitrent – not high, this a source of controversy.

–New England abolished primogeniture.

–In South, large holdings – <u>county</u> the form of government – or parish.

–In Middle States – small holdings – town government.

–In New England – town supreme.

<u>Scarcity of labor</u>, abundance of land.

–Competition between states for settlers; proprietors have to make concessions to get tenants.

–This led to democracy, freedom, initiative.

–Considerably modified the institutions of the country.

–And this influence lasted till well into 19th century.

<u>Manufacturing</u>

–Ownership: corporation did not exist till after Revolution – plants owned by individual – no fire insurance – much danger.

–Legislation: had little significant effect – artificial.

<u>Labor</u>

–<u>Very</u> scarce – great demand for it to use great resources.

–Productivity was high – small population – lack of skilled labor.

–Long hours – six full days work a week – little machinery – less <u>intensity</u> than now.

Education

 –State supported education – began in New England – a unique, not always too successful experiment.

 –In New England – religion a large factor in spreading education.

 –In Middle Colonies – less religious homogeneity – denominational and private schools.

 –South – scattered population – difficult to support school.

 –Most colonists had only a rudimentary education.

Wages – <u>rose</u> throughout 17th and 18th centuries.

 –<u>Scarcity of labor broke down apprentice system and blocked the introduction of guilds</u>.

Foreign trade – 1769 (only year of adequate figures)

 –New England – unfavorable balance with England and West Indies – favorable balance with Southern Europe – (<u>net</u> – slightly <u>unfavorable</u>).

 –Middle Colonies – unfavorable with England – with West Indies very favorable, with South Europe – net – slightly <u>favorable</u>).

 –South – trifle favorable with England, and West Indies. Very favorable with South Europe. Imports from Africa. Most trade with England. Net – slighttly favorable.

Smuggling

 –(1) Direct trade between colonies and continent.

 –(2) Direct return trade of certain good supposed to be shipped only <u>via</u> England.

 –(3) Trade of New England with foreign West Indies.

Expansion of market in South Europe encouraged trade with continent.

 –Great development of West Indian Trade in 18th century – thus the outcry over Molasses Act.

Shipping – the great <u>capitalistic</u> <u>field</u> of the time. [In margin, next to single vertical line: "?"]

 –Merchants often owned ships.

 –Lack of communication = risk; captain or supercargo given much responsibility; temporary dangers due to coincidence of several ships in one port; great risks of navigation – pirates.

 –Marine insurance by individuals, organized by brokers.

Colonies had duties – often against other colonies – largely for revenue, not protection.

 –Attempts to regulate slave trade were hindered by England.

 –Tonnage fees – England forbade discrimination in favor of colonial ships.

Currency – first used wampum and tobacco, then got specie from Spain, through West Indian Trade.

–Few English coins – due to prohibition of export.

–Paper money – inflation (Rhode Island and [blank] 1100% premium).

–Probably the cheap paper money, not the unfavorable balance of trade was the cause of scarcity of coin. [Double vertical line alongside in margin.]

–Development of bill of exchange usage – eliminated specie shipments.

Causes of Revolution:

a. <u>Depression</u>: <u>Callander</u> says it lasted ten years 1764–1774, <u>Wright</u> says it was probably at low point in 1764 or 1765, nearly over in 1771 and 1772, a little boom and reaction, 1773–1775.

–In Seven Year's War colonists sold to enemy and to British, a reaction from the rise of prices followed the end of the war.

b. <u>Specie scarce</u>: <u>Britain restricted use of paper money</u> – hit a large <u>number</u> of people.

c. Stamp Act hit lawyers, printers – who had vociferous influence.

Bubble Act of 1741 restricted land banks; restriction on New England paper money 1761; 1764 extended to other colonies. [Arrow in margin from "Specie scarce" to this line.]

–This hit the group which was most active in carrying on the revolution: <u>Merchants</u> turned Tory; but farmers, artisans, mechanics supplied main backing.

–Also British officials, and Anglican Church were Tory.

d. Quebec Act – prohibited settlement beyond the Alleghenies; hit colonies holding land there; fur traders and land speculators objected.

Index Numbers of Prices

Year	Index
1757	65
1758	70
1759	79
1760	79
1761	77
1762	87
1763	79
1764	74
1765	72

Index Numbers of Prices (*Continued*)

Year	Index
1766	73
1767	77
1768	74
1769	77
1770	77
1771	79
1772	89
1773	84
1774	76
1775	75

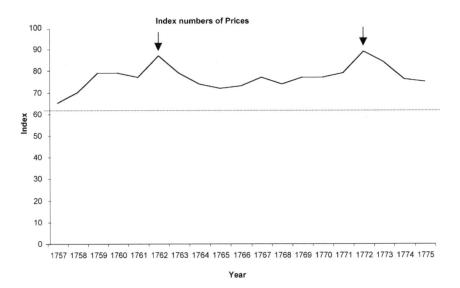

Economic events before Revolution:
(1) Up to 1764
(2) 1764 to 1776
   a. 1764–1773
   b. 1773–1776

(1) England felt she could not protect colonies without some benefit; yet without protection they would be seized.
  –Benefit would come from trade advantages.
  –But English people objected to bounties, monopoly given to colonists, etc.
  –Colonies complained of trade restrictions, prohibitions.
  –Probably the system benefited England more than colonies – but cost of defense was large.
  –Policy was one of regulation, not taxation.
(2)a- Colonies merely asked a return to prior system.
  –Effect of Seven Years War: – Removed France, thus loosened bonds of colonies and England. Put England in debt; colonies were expected to share some of burden.
  –Two mistakes: (a) regulations were thought to develop the Empire economically, (b) thought an insistence on the prerogatives of the King would strengthen the bonds of Empire.
  –Economic forces made the depression, but England was blamed.
  –Discontent with certain small groups having great power – especially in Middle and South – Quakers, one-fifth of population, dominated Assembly, sea coast in South dominated, land in New England.
  –Stamp Act of 1764 – others; led to first <u>non-importation</u> agreement.
  –1771–1772 – calm prevailed.
(2)b- Political issues rose to importance, economic issues sank into background.
  –Parliament grants East India Co. commission on tea – Boston Tea Party. Act of 1774 threatened chiefly the political rights and liberties.
  –British restrictions had hurt only slightly, economically, but their weight fell on groups able to agitate.
    –Were at the center of public opinion – exercised an influence out of proportion to their numbers.
  –Those who had migrated, interested in freedom – colonial. 17th century life fostered individualism – this little valued, <u>at first</u>.
  –<u>Half a million Indians</u> – living on a margin of subsistence – probably all that could be, accommodated by their methods.

Economics of Revolutionary War
  (1) Attempts to get goods and food (when and where needed).
  (2) Financing the War.
    –Scarcity of organized capital supply and loanable funds.
    –Hostility to taxation. Continental Congress <u>asked</u> States for money – borrowed $8,000,000 abroad – bought supplies there.
    –Congress borrowed $30,000,000, States $25,000,000.

–Congress put out $240,000,000 of paper money, States as much.

–States tried to force acceptance of Congress paper – said depreciation due to speculation, to effort of enemy to discredit currency.

–Attempts at price fixing, Congress, 1778, regional price fixing convention, prices to be 75% above pre-War level – next year advanced to 2000% above.

–1780 – Congress practically repudiated the currency – laid levy on States to be paid in this money – then destroyed it.

–Pay of army was usually worthless; paid in land grants to encourage them.

(3) Provisions for needs of civilian population

–Due to provincial economy, most of population was not very adversely affected; economic effects of war were localized to scene of operations.

–Fishermen wiped out; frontier not endangered, South was.

–Shipbuilding suffered – commerce hit hard at first as British controlled the sea; after 1778 a means found to evade the British, importation more possible; manufacturing stimulated, especially munitions.

–Most severe pressure was depreciation of money.

–1780 country looked prosperous – but a collapse and price fall after this.

–Total cost about $130,000,000 specie value – seven years.

Period of Confederation

–Problem of readjustment to peace time conditions, and a changed political situation.

–Individualism and provincialism had free play – nation almost went to pieces.

–Many democratizing effects of Revolution.

   –State constitutions more democratic; more power in assemblies, better apportionment of suffrage – disestablishment of Church – primo-geniture and quit-rents abolished.

–Movement of capital westward.

   –Shift in distribution of wealth.

      –Dispossession of Tories; effects of paper money.

–Creation of Public Domain – States gave up their Western lands – a nationalizing factor.

Economic Situation

–Deflation – falling prices, was worst bout 1786 – then very slow improvement.

–Agriculture – least hurt, especially where self-sufficient South had free outlet.

–Manufacturing established on large scale during was were hard hit.

–Commerce slow to recover, suffered from mercantilism of Europe – failure to get trade rights [there].

Economic Influences on Constitution
–A Convention to regulate commerce on Potomac was immediate cause of the Constitutional Convention.
–Commercial, propertied, conservative interests dominated.
  –A reaction from extremes of Revolution.
  –Five-sixths of them stood to gain from its adoption.
–Opposition – (small farmers, debtors) – poorly organized. Advocates extremely well organized – maneuvered.
–Provisions of Constitution reflecting these motives.
  –Directed towards remedying needs of confederation taking over debts of confederation.
  –Reinforce bankruptcy laws.
  –Congress only had control over money.
  –Taxation made legal.

Wright: Comparative study of the effects of industrialization, and of modern capitalistic, scientific, economic development, on various civilizations:
  a. Frontier civilizations – U.S., Canada, Australia, Brazil.
  b. Ancient civilizations (sudden impact): India, Japan, China, Russia.
  c. Ancient civilizations (slow transformation): Europe.

1789, Economic Interpretation of the Constitution
–Getting money to run government.
–Slavery.
–Coining of money.
–Control over Western lands.
  –Gave considerable influence and wealth to new government.
  –People interested in West looked to Federal government.
–Navy a protector of Congress, of trade.
–Date for elections set in November – after harvests, most convenient day to take off for voting – an agricultural [country].
–Congress meets the next March – due to bad transportation (at least 100 years necessary to get rid of this after it had become outworn).
–Regulations over States – corollaries of above – no import or export duties by States, no coinage, no taxes or limitation of tonnage.
–Federal government one of delegated powers – reflecting the time: provincialism, opposition to distant control, States' rights, etc.
–Balance and Check of Powers – slowness of amendment.
  –Due to fear of the masses – undemocratic.
    –Whole movement leading to the Constitution was a conservative reaction; an effort to protect a minority group and interests.

–Made the majority as little important as possible and then the Constitution made hard to change.
–Constitution a result of many compromises:
  –Senate = State – House = population; no prohibition of slave trade till [date blank];–majority necessary for navigation acts.
  –Methods of choosing Presidents.
"The Constitution was extorted by dire necessity from a reluctant nation," J. Q. Adams.
  –It was passed by nine, then thirteen States, only by political maneuvers.
–Constitution designed to meet a specific situation.
  –Not a piece of political theorizing; but a document taking definite account of actual interests and conflicts – to meet the contemporary, not future, needs.
  –Yet drawn up in sufficiently broad terms, that it <u>has</u> existed (however limpingly) to the present.

(1789–1815) <u>1775–1815 Period of Transition</u>
  –Abnormalities – wars.
  –From colonial economy to the beginnings of a national economy.
  –This studied: (1) by studying the Revolution; (2) the strange conditions of the Federation; (3) 1789–1815 – war. [Double vertical lines in left margin alongside these points.]
  –1789–1815 – the <u>immediately</u> most important factor was war and war reactions
    –Napoleonic Wars 1793–1815 – War of 1812.
    –Shipping and foreign trade most affected.

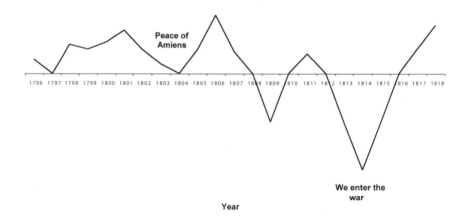

Shipping and Foreign Trade Most Affected

[*The units in the original graph are not specified. This chart was created using numbers generated to approximate a hand-drawn graph to show the wide fluctuations of shipping and foreign trade from 1796 to 1816.]

- –Tremendous profit from neutral trade – led us into war with England (complicated by political struggles at home).
- –Domestic exports became larger and more important in <u>relation</u> to foreign exports. (?)
- –A time of abnormally high prices – shipping prosperity.
- –Tendency from this to <u>prolong</u> the characteristic features of colonial economy – up to 1808 – Embargo, blockade.
- –After we enter war – shipping trade is ruined, manufacturing is <u>stimulated</u> (a line in which we had been backward) – a hastening of the new movement towards a <u>national</u> economy (self-sufficiency).

Acquisition of Louisiana

- –Importance of New Orleans as a port for Ohio, etc.
- –Napoleon gets Louisiana from Spain by secret treaty, 1801.
- –Free port ended – consternation in West.
- –[An] embassy sent to buy West Florida (west bank) [of Mississippi River].
- –By a peculiar chain of circumstances – <u>all</u> of Louisiana was thrown at their feet – never expected.
- –We got Louisiana by a <u>fortuitous</u> circumstance and didn't know what to do with it – had no concept of the future importance.
    - –1799 – Jefferson said, "1000 years to populate <u>to</u> Mississippi River.
- –Yet it was most significant event in our Western expansion.

*****

Assignments

First week
Bogart [1931]: Chapters I, II, III, pp. 123–126 – Chapter IV
Bogart and Thompson [1920]: pp. 1–22, 28–41
Callander [1909]: pp. 6–22

Second Week
Bogart, Chapter V, pp. 126–140, Chapters VII, VIII, IX, X
Callander, pp. 85–88, 122–141
B & T, Chapter IV

Third Week
Bogart, Chapter XI, pp. 248–258
B & T, pp. 175–200, Chapter VII, pp. 143–175

Callander, pp. 180–182
Schlesinger: New View Points in American History, Chapters 7, 8

Fourth Week
Bogart, pp. 418–426, Chapters 13, 15
Callander, Chapter 13, pp. 597–601, 345–348
B & T, Chapter VIII, pp. 376–404
Bulloch, Chapter II

Fifth Week
Bogart, Chapters 14, 20 // 18
Callander, pp. 337–41, 796–819 // 487–490
B & T, Chapter 17
Taussig – Tariff History, pp. 1–24, 46–67, 134, 135 (24–46)

Fifth Week
Assuming it true that slavery doesn't pay, how to you explain the continued expansion of the institution.

*****

1815–1860
   –(a) Western expansion more important than any other factor – accomplishing, in this epoch, the colonization from the Appalachians to the Missouri.
   –(b) The beginnings of capitalist enterprise is seen in this period – no revolution – slow growth, steady.
   –(c) European conditions ceased to influence U.S.
      –Marked decline in importance of foreign trade.
      –Development of national economy, from a provincial economy, dependent on foreign trade.
   –(d) 1790: Earliest movement to the West came from the South – South: Irish or German.
      –From Carolinas – through Cumberland Gap, into Kentucky (limestone area) and Western Pennsylvania.
      –Some expansion into Maine. Western New York little settled.
      –In the South more expansion inland from coast.
         –Indian problem: typical solution was a treaty by which Indians went West.
      1800 – Expansion into Western New York, and West Pennsylvania. Very considerable growth in Kentucky.
      1810 – Most of New York, and Pennsylvania settled. Westward emigrants going mainly through Pittsburgh – down Ohio.

–Spread of population all through Ohio and beginning in Indiana.

–Southern expansion into Tennessee; expansion of population about mouth of Mississippi.

1820 – After some check, due to War – a sudden new expansion – "Old America seems to be breaking up and moving West."

–Expansion along Lake Erie, Northern Ohio, Southern Indiana and Illinois.

–Spread up the Missouri – Spread out in Tennessee and Southern Mississippi.

–Filling up west of Carolinas.

1830 – Erie canal had been opened in 1825 – New England people now take this route to Buffalo, a sailing vessel then [thereafter].

–Spread about Detroit and South Eastern Michigan.

–Great expansion west of Georgia, filling in East of Mississippi. [Arrow from "Georgia" to "cotton," below line.]

–More expansion up Mississippi.

1840 – An epoch of great prosperity:

–For first time, Illinois (around Chicago) is settled – more of Michigan and Wisconsin. Much speculation in Western land.

1850 – Slower growth.

–Much expansion in South – West of Mississippi River.

–Westward into Iowa, filling up of Western Pennsylvania.

1860 – After another era of prosperity:

–Railroads built.

–Great growth of diversity everywhere.

–Most densely settled is coast from Massachusetts to Maryland.

–Southern New England, Central New York, Ohio, Pennsylvania, Chicago.

–Nothing of this density in the South.

1800 – only one-sixth of population west of Appalachian was North of Ohio River.

1830 – a marked shift.

1860 – population west of Alleghenies, North of Ohio River – was 50% greater than South of Ohio River.

Southern Illinois and Indiana – settlers came from South, before 1830.

Northern Illinois and Indiana – settlers came from North, after 1830.

–New England peoples had settled shores of Lake Erie and Lake Michigan – most of Illinois, Indiana, Northern Ohio, Southern Michigan – Central New York.

–New Englanders settled in groups – bring their typical institutions – town meeting, the Congregational Church – emphasis on education – free; small colleges.

–Foreigners: Mainly German – settled in river and lake towns, after 1850s.

Railroads – at first, wood covered with iron for rails – until '40s.

  –Dogs, horses, sails – no signaling.

  –Not till latter 1830s did locomotive come in mainly.

  –Were built with private capital.

   –Canals had been built with State aid.

    –Were long; were in thinly settled districts.

  –Early railroads were short; were usually built in thickly-settled areas, which had a good deal of capital for what was a very profitable venture.

  –Later on, railroads had to be longer and in less settled districts – need of aid.

   –State of Michigan began to build three railroads – Illinois had plans.

   –Then came the panic, and State aid was a discredited thing – collapse of State credit.

   –Thus private capital built them too, though states, towns, cities subscribed to capital.

    –Especially in South did states and cities aid, but also the B&A [Boston and Albany] aided by Massachusetts, Erie Railroad by New York State.

 –In '30s, railroads in New Jersey, Pennsyslvaniaa, Central New York, New England,Tidewater region: Charleston, Hamburg.

   –Boston had lost out on the possibility of Western trade by canal – thus got started early with railroads to tap that trade.

   –New York slow at first, had Erie Canal.

    [In margin: Chart. K, Coman [1912], [*Economic Beginnings of the Far West*], 235–238; B. Meyer and C. MacGill (1917) [*History of Transportation in the U.S. before 1860*]

 –in 1840s – New England quite well supplied by end of this period.

   –Erie Railroad in New York, Southern roads are extended, also Pennsylvnia roads.

   –One line across Ohio, and one across Michigan.

 –in 1850s – huge construction, of great significance.

   –Few additions in Northern New England, Erie Railroad extended.

   –Pennsylvania Railroad reaches Pittsburg (1852), New York City, New York to Albany (1851).

–Richmond to Chattanooga; New Orleans Northward connecting with Illinois Central, Mobile north – Rock Island reaches Mississippi River (1854).

–Most important was a mass of construction in the Northwest – Chicago gets rail connection with New York City.

–Standard gauge was not in general use throughout the country till 1880s – many short branch lines.

–Chief justification for a dividing point in American history at 1850 lies in this construction – the Railway Age.

–Railroad communication was good in settled regions, but had by no means reached the frontier – after the 1860s railroads became pioneers, passed frontier.

–Railroad land grants along Mississippi Valley – Illinois Central first, 1854.

–Beginnings of movement toward consolidation – Vanderbilt making New York Central – Pennsylvania Railroad created.

–1860 [in margin]

–More bond issues – dangerous.

–Superiority of railroad over canal pretty definitely established – heavy trade still used the railroads to get to best waterway.

–In South the roads all ran from seaports inland – to get upland cotton to the seaports.

– Few through lines.

–This acquired great significance in Civil War – South poorly equipped.

–After railroads the great volume of trade moved East and West – instead of South (on Mississippi River) and North (by ocean).

–Movement of bulky commodities was slow – railroads had not yet seen how they might cut rates and get traffic.

Development of Post Office:

1790 – one cent per year per capita spent on postal services.

1860 – 27 cents per year per capita spent on postal services.

1930 – $5.00 per year per capita spent on postal services.

[Double vertical lines alongside first two lines.]

–Machine-made paper – very cheap – enormous stimulus to printing and to newspapers.

–First penny paper (New York Sun 1830s); newspaper becomes popular.

–Agriculture predominates still; enormous increase of its area into one of richest agricultural areas in the world [the Great Plains].

–Shift from self-sufficiency, frontier agriculture to commercial farming for a distant market.

–Lumbering, fishing, fur trade became less important.

–West Indian trade had stopped growing.

  –Decline of output – declining fertility – <u>British</u> and <u>French</u> West Indies.

  –Expansion of Spanish West Indies (Cuba, Puerto Rico), keeping the trade from declining absolutely.

  –End of slavery in British and French islands.

  –Introduction of <u>beet sugar</u> into Europe by Napoleon completely altered the situation – and trade.

–We have probably <u>overestimated</u> the amount of Northwestern foodstuffs taken by the South.

–From 1844 on, with repeal of Corn Laws in England – the industrialization of Europe, growth of demand for food products, completely <u>revolutionized</u> the American good producing trade.

1860– Corn crop –	$500,000,000
Wheat crop –	$250,000,000
Hay crop –	(generally seasonal)
Cotton crop –	$166,000,000
Oats	68,000,000
Potatoes	58,000,000
Tobacco	48,000,000
Rice	7,000,000
Sugar	[no figure]

6th week [Assignments]:

B & T. Chapter X	pp. 524–545
Bogart, pp. 426–446	pp. 258–265, Chapters 16, 17
Callander, pp. 693–718	pp. 271–275, pp. 564–578

<u>Cotton and Slavery</u>

  –How could the world, especially England, afford to pay so much for a new crop?

  –Cotton did not represent entirely a <u>new</u> demand, but to a considerable extent was an <u>alternative supply</u>.

  –Egyptian, East Indian, Indian cotton supply declined.

  –Other fibers not used any more.

  –demand turned from wool and linen.

–10,000 families owned over 50 slaves a family. This tiny group was the <u>dominant</u> element in the South – controlled politics, but especially <u>they controlled public opinion</u> and <u>free expression</u>.

–We will never know whether slave labor was profitable or not – in the long-run sense (Cf. Phillips).

    –Except in certain sections it seems not profitable.

  –Why then did it expand?

    –Huge sunk-capital – like railroads – they would continue producing for a long time without "paying."

    –Non-economic: social prestige of owning slaves, fear of free negro, inertia.

    –Bad bookkeeping; monopoly position.

    –Overcapitalization – due to errors in optimism.

    –Short-sighted, not long-run calculation.

    –Extensive, exploitative methods of agricultural production.

      –Need for expansion Westward, and annexation.

–Effects: a backward region, no school system, few cities.

  –Most shipping, trade, banking, etc. was carried on by North Eastern and European capital.

    –A specialized system, dependent on outside world.

–South always on the defensive: dependent on a balance of power in Senate, the protection of minority rights.

–Denominational churches split over slavery.

1860 – Manufacturing

  –What explains the fairly rapid rise of manufactures shortly before this date, in spite of our remaining predominantly agricultural?

    –Big expansion of iron and steel. (1820 – produced one-third of our iron needs; 1850 – produced three-quarters of our iron needs.)

    –Huge expansion of cotton textile manufacturing (some woolen).

    –Lumber output; meat-packing; flour, boat and shoe industries; machinery.

  –New supply of cheap labor by immigration.

    –Overcoming older scarcity of labor (more labor used then).

  –Also new piling up of accumulation; overcoming older scarcity of capital (not so great).

  –Introduction of labor-saving devices [Alongside in margin: →]

    –Improving our comparative cost situation.

    –Many of our new industries were "domestic," did not enter into the international market.

  –Effect of tariffs ?

  –New use of abundant raw materials [Alongside in margin: →]

  –relative to Europe, our labor and capital costs were disadvantageous to us, perhaps still; but our resource cost was immensely cheaper.

  –Why did we not have an "Industrial Revolution"? – Wright.

   –I.e. (?) why did we not have the suffering and friction of the English "Industrial Revolution"?

   –England was much more advanced, more specialized (under <u>domestic</u> system(?)) than we were.

     –Introduction of factory methods brought trouble (domestic system = "<u>putting out</u>" in homes; (is this not from textiles, boat and shoe, only?)

     –We had no industrial system to revolutionize.

–Our population was increasing by leaps and bounds, but never pressing on subsistence; huge <u>expanding market</u>.

–Much of suffering of "Industrial Revolution" was really due, in England, to the Napoleonic Wars – which affected us in just the opposite way.

–Use of <u>family</u> domestic system reached its peak of expansion about 1830; after that larger industry expanded rapidly.

–I.e. in <u>sum</u>, we had no "Industrial Revolution" because we grew directly from agricultural to factory system.

–Even then, factory system grew slowly; factory system hard to define (?-no attempt!)

   –First in cotton manufacturing; then steam printing: '30s; ready-made clothing: '50s; shoe industry just after Civil War; packing industry – '30s and '40s; machinery and railroad supplies – all these [had] slow developments.

   –Real rapid growth comes after 1860.

–Tremendous influence of <u>transportation</u> improvements.

–Growth of <u>corporate organization</u> – with <u>larger</u> capitalization for industry.

   –Especially in cotton textile manufacturing.

   –Corporation <u>laws</u>; at first a new act for each corporation; then, after turn of [19th] century, <u>general</u> acts for certain lines, and after mid-century, <u>general acts</u> for <u>general incorporation</u> (few exceptions).

   –Slightly used before 1860 – was the beginning of an <u>important change</u>.

<u>Tariff</u>–

    1789–1816 – <u>Revenue</u> important.

    1816–1833 – <u>Protection</u>; high rates.

    1833–1860 – Protection (compromise of '33) falling rates – tariff of 1842, momentary advance.

  –If on goods not produced here, not likely to be produced, then presumption that it is for revenue.

  –If on goods produced at home – for protection.

  –If protective, brings in revenue also; but if protection <u>works</u> (?) revenue not yielded.

–If goods produced mainly at home – <u>most</u> of price rise due to tariff is burden on people, but does not reach government.

—If goods produced mainly abroad – most of price rise due to tariff goes to the government.

–War of 1812 – nearly ruined shipping and commercial trade.

—Imports cut off – a hot-house growth of new industries to meet abnormal war demands.

—At end of war – a flood of imports to the country.

—Thus the tariff agitation – successful.

—Large revenues from protective tariff.

—1828 – Tariff [of] Abominations

1827 – discussion of Missouri Compromise – tariffs also discussed – South began to turn.

—South had expected to develop manufactures, thus was favorable to tariffs at first.

—But they began to change – Europe was able to take all the cotton they grew – slavery and manufactures did not go together.

—Thus the South no longer supported high tariffs – which were not favorable to them.

—Fiscal situation – national debt paid off – a surplus.

—Infant industries – no longer infant – on their feet.

—But commerce died in New England – Manufacturing interests succeeded.

—Webster, 1828, goes over to high tariffs.

—Northwest in favor of tariffs – Home Market argument.

—But its wheat was too abundant – sent to England.

—Thus its enthusiasm for tariff decline.

—Other arguments for tariffs – only Infant Industry has any justification.

—List – we were passing from agricultural-commercial stage to agricultural-commercial-manufacturing stage – tariff needed to help.

—We had new industries already – and largely developed by hothouse methods of war-embargo-boycott and blockade.

—Then deflation; depression 1819; crisis in England, 1825.

—We were concerned, not with <u>starting new</u> industries; but with saving what we had – save them from the trial by fire they were undergoing.

—The tariff seems to have been justified.

—It helped, but that it changed the course of development much can not be held.

—Its influence must not be exaggerated or underestimated.

<u>Labor</u>–Immigration – huge natural increase.
   –<u>Large</u> proportion of labor supply was in working-years of age.
   –Small leisure class – long hours, few holidays.
   –Most laborers of high degree of skill and education.
   –Not too many women.

<u>Education</u>
   –Free, tax supported, general education begun in colonial times, spread <u>greatly</u>
    in 1820–1860 (academy for secondary education).
   –Result of change in political ideals.
   –Secularization, elementary and secondary education.
      –Growth of religious college education.
      –Growth of professional and woman's education.
   –Influence of education on labor supply – efficiency.
      –Keeping new labor supply off the market longer.
      –Education led the State governments into greater public expenditures.
        Persons gainfully employed:

	1820	1860
Agriculture	71.88	59.60
Manufacturings	12.15	18.35
Trade and transportation	2.50	7.44
Domestic and personal services	10.00	9.52
Professions	2.81	2.90
Mining	0.28	1.60
Lumber	0.17	0.26
Fishing	0.21	0.28
Total population	7,881,000	10,531,000

–Rise in money wages after 1820; a slight downward trend of price level until
  1845. – shorter hours.
–Labor Movement – beginning after panic of 1837.
   –1. 1821–1837, 2. 1837–1848, 3. 1848–1860 – beginning of modern labor
    movement.
      –Most successful among skilled trades.
         –Due to increasing competition, mobility.
         –Urge to standardize wages – less cause for cutting wages, for inflow of
          strange [foreign?] workers.
      –Concerned with large general reforms.
      –First enduring National Trade Unions begun in 1850s.

Merchant Marine	1789	201,000 tons
I-rapid growth	1810	1,424,000
II-reaction	1821	1,898,000
reaction continued	1829	1,280,000
III-slow growth	1840	2,180,000
slow growth	1850	3,535,000
IV-rapid growth	1861	5,049,000

–Equally divided between coastal, island, and overseas boats.
Percentage of Value of Foreign Trade Carried on American Ships

Years	%
1789–1793	52
1794–1810	89
1811–1814	73
1815–1819	78
1820–1830	90
1831–1846	82
1847–1858	72
1859–1861	66

7th week [Assignments]
 B and T, Chapter XV
 Dewey [Davis R.], Chapters 5, 6, 8 [11th ed., 1931]
 Bogart, Chapter 21
Exam, Thursday
 –<u>Our</u> percentage of total tonnage was not so great, i.e. we were carrying the
  more valuable cargoes.
 –Artificial stimulus as we <u>aped</u> the English mercantile legislation.
 –Impetus of neutral position in Napoleonic Wars.
 –Principle of reciprocity and freedom from restriction.
 –Foreign vessels excluded from <u>coastal</u> trade.
 –In 1840s a new design for American clipper ship – <u>speedy</u>.
  –Came at time of an increased demand for shipping.
 –Steamship – shift to iron boats – loss of our advantage over England in building
  wooden ships.
 –Regular transatlantic steam ship service did not begin until about 1840 – then
  for passengers, mail.

–Only replaced clipper ships for heavy cargo very slowly – say, 1890.

–Efficiently managed clipper ships gave U.S. a trade carrying advantage – training of crews, especially.

–Companies became more common, regular sailings – 1845 to 1860 we carried one-third of world's trade.

–But other countries caught up – speed less important for heavy cargoes; other countries could build steam freighters – skilled crew no longer an advantage.

Foreign Commerce

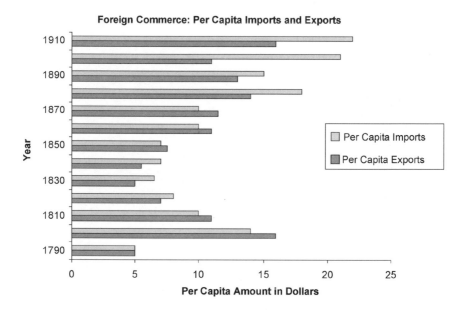

Foreign Commerce: Per Capita Imports and Exports

[Diagram is a reconstruction of original format.]

　–Slow advance to 1845, rapid to 1860.

　–Decline of West Indian trade, opening of China trade.

Balance of trade

　　1800–1850 – unfavorable balance of trade – imports of gold (and capital)

　　1850–1873 – unfavorable balance of trade – large outflow of gold

　　1873–1898 – favorable balance of trade – continued outflow of specie

　　1898–1915 – favorable balance of trade; smaller outflow

　　1915–1920 – 20 billion of exports; billions of specie inflow

1821–1849

Creditor balance (owed us)		Debtor balance (we owe)	
Shipping	450 million	Excess of imports	151 million
Net new capital	169 million	Interest on for. cap.*	224 million
Sale of ships	14 million	Immigrant Maint.	15 million
	633 million	Mexican War	25 million
		Tourists	95 million
			510 million
		Specie inflow	72 million
			572 [sic]

*and repayment.

Supply of bills on London   Demand for bills on London
–Exchange in New York should have been at gold import point.

1850–1860

Net new capital	188 million	Excess of imports	384 million
Shipping	243 million	Interest on for. cap.	203 million
	431 million	Tourists	165 million
Outflow of specie	420 million		752 million
	851 million		

Currency and Finance
  National Debt

1791	$75 m[illion]
1801	83 m
1812	45 m
1816	127 m
1835	0
1843	32 m
1846	15 m
1849	62 m
1857	28 m
1860	64 m

–Revenue: Tariff
    Internal revenue – repealed 1806
    War of 1812 – doubled tariffs – imports were small – finally put on excise taxes.
      –Mostly financed by borrowing – but government credit was not good – had
      to sell bonds below par.

Huge surplus piled up by higher duties of Act of 1816.

–Foreign trade fluctuates closely with prosperity-depression.

–Thus, getting our main source of revenue from tariffs – we were bound to have surpluses and deficits.

1835 – Whole national debt paid off – regarded as reworkable – greatly increased government credit, opened the way for large importation of capital from Europe.

1834–1836 – Receipts from sale of public lands became significant for first time – much speculation.

–Tariffs were typically 90% of total receipts; in 1810–1820, excises were a significant amount.

1836 – Surplus was paid out to States – in form of a loan – three installments paid – panic of 1837 brought a government deficit.

1843 – Government borrowing to make up deficit.

1846 – Surplus again.

1849 – Mexican War – government borrowed – good credit, sold bonds at par.

1857 – Debt reduced by surplus (public land revenue) but Panic of 1857 brings deficit, increased debt in 1860.

Problem of providing adequate circulating medium.

–Mint established 1792. – Gold and silver coinage [at ratio] 15 [silver]:1 [gold] (Market ratio $15\frac{1}{2}$:1)

–No gold presented. Silver arbitrage with West Indies – No more <u>dollars</u>.

Production:	1792–1847	Gold $24m[illion], Silver $.4m[illion]
	1848–1860	Gold 651m[illion], Silver.8m[illion]
Coinage: to	1833	Gold $12m to 1852 Silver 0.77m
	1834–1848	Gold $64m, 1853–1860 Silver 44m
	1848–1860	Gold $385m

Ratio:	Coinage	Market
1792	15 to 1	$15\frac{1}{2}$ to 1
1834	16 to 1	$15\frac{1}{2}$ to 1
1837	15.988 to 1	$15\frac{1}{2}$ to 1

(1934 off)

After 1834, little silver presented.

1853 Subsidiary coinage made token, by reducing ratio of silver value in coins to <u>14 to 1</u>.

–<u>Limited</u> the coinage of subsidiary silver (in amount).

1792–1860 – about $4million silver dollars coined.

–Practically speaking, we produced no silver [coins] till after the beginning of the Civil War.

–Previous to 1850 our supply of specie had been very small – after that we had plenty of gold.

–Actually, though not legally, we went onto a Gold Standard in 1834 (legally we were still bimetallic).

Panic of 1819-South least affected – cotton prices stay up.

–New England not so affected, inflation not having gone so far.

–Usual demands of a depression nature – stay laws, etc.

–Capital scarce; little knowledge of sound banking principles.

–Widespread feeling that presentation of notes for specie "wasn't done" by gentlemen.

–Around 1800, New England banks loaned out to operate.

1810–1820 – Middle States banks loaned out to operate.

1830–1840 – Ohio and South banks loaned out to operate.

–Place of note-issue, before Civil War, was all important.

–1850, circulation 50% greater than deposits.

–1855, total deposits exceeded note issues.

–1919, deposits 24 times as large as note issues.

–Bad assets – land

–Inadequate reserves – overexpansion of notes

–Suffolk system; facilities for redemption

–Safety Fund system; a form of deposit insurance, backed by all banks.

–Free Banking System, deposit of securities to back issue of notes.

Eighth Week [Assignments]

Dewey: [chapters] 12, 13

B&T: pp. 689–695, 783–792, 848–851, Chapter 19 (3& 4)

Bogart: pp. 600–607, Chapters 22, 23, 26

Enumerate the probable reactions upon the social, economic and political development of the U.S. of the disappearance of new free land and of opportunity to "go West."

–Louisiana Banking Law – reserve of one-third in specie, two-thirds short-time commercial paper – reserve against deposits (first time).

–Each bank could pay out only its own notes, had to send home the rest.

–State banks of Ohio, Indiana, Missouri, Virginia – all well run.

–Branch banking popular in South and West – died out after Civil War.

–Ever-increasing wisdom of banking laws in States – up to 1863.

–Yet, in 1860, the system had many defects:

–Decentralized, not liquid as a system, in stress.

–Lacked facilities for long-term loans.

–Growth of <u>savings banks</u> – trust companies – clearing houses. Stock exchange (1792, some such activity) – 1817 in New York City – after 1825 – New York City forges ahead of Philadelphia as financial center.

   –Foreign banks start branches.

   –Corporation securities.

–Development of insurance – maritime had existed in colonial period.

   –Fire and life – at first, small and local.

      –New York City, 1835 – large fire – wiped out [insurance] companies.

      –Raised need for larger organization.

      –Pressure by business interest to insure against fire.

      –Life insurance developed more slowly – no economic pressure.

–Accumulation of capital: (size of surplus, <u>savable fund</u>; <u>willingness to save</u>)

   –Many elements increasing per capita <u>productivity</u>.

   –Increased <u>facilities</u> for saving, increased <u>stimulus</u> to save.

   –Increased foreign investment in this country.

   –Growth of corporation organization to concentrate savings.

   –Evidence of a <u>periodic</u> depression.

      –Lengthening of production period.

      –Facilities for expanding credit grew – no control.

      –Increased specialization.

Causes of Civil War – were immediately economic.

   –North fought to save the Union, South, to preserve slavery.

   –Only one of a number of sectional conflicts and threats of secession – all economic at base.

	Population		Farm Land		Manufacturing		
	Free	Slave	Improved	Unimproved	No. of Estab's	Capital	Value of Product
Union	21.5m	0.4m	106m acres	100m acres	119,000	$913m	$1,730m
Confederacy	5.4m	3.5m	57m acres	143m acres	20,000	$95m	$155m

	Incorporated Banks				
	Capital	Deposits	Loans	Specie	Notes
Union	$317m	206m	547m	56m	147m
Confederacy	104m	47m	144m	27m	60m

Civil War Period – great prosperity (due to inflation and army demands) – in agriculture, manufacturing, transportation.
  –High tariff, 1862. Merchant Marine suffered severely. (300 ships captured, 1000 transferred to British flag)
  –Enduring results of wartime emergency measures – Banking, etc.
  –War ends with Union intact, and secession never again threatened because of economic differences – also economic bonds drawn tighter.

World background – 19th century
  1. Scientific advance – the century of material progress.
  2. Expansion of world commerce, world specialization of production, nearly free trade on large scale.
  3. Rise of modern forms of capitalistic production.
  4. Great rise of populations throughout world.
      1650–1750, 1 million increase
      1750–1850, 14 million increase
      1850–1920, 27 million increase
      [Are these figures correct? Even per year seems low.]
  5. Rapid growth of capital accumulation – and its spread to less developed areas – increased importance of capital in production.
  6. Increased mobility of labor and capital, economic freedom, laissez-faire, freeing of slaves and serfs.
  7. Growing spirit of nationalism, tendency to build up States (Italy, Austria-Hungary, Germany).
      –Increased national competition.
      –Ending in Neo-mercantilism.
  8. Spread of democracy – and more extreme political theories – many revolutions.

England
  (In 15th century Spain was most powerful nation.
      16th century, Holland becomes dominant commercially
      17th century, France becomes most powerful
      17th century, England wins her colonies away
      18th century, meteoric rise and fall of France
      19th century, England is the leading nation
      20th century, is for U.S.)
  –Textiles, iron and steel, railroads (less significant for England).
  –Until 1800, self-sufficiency, but not any longer, with growing population and export surplus.
  –Thus a complete shift in England's commercial position.

–Huskisson, Peel, Gladstone – free trade conquerors.

–Becomes leading financial nation.

–Self-sufficiency or specialization?

   –Chose specialization – dependent on outside world for food.

–Commercial supremacy, shipping and shipbuilding supremacy.

France

–Larger population than England's to begin with.

–Some changes in agriculture by Revolution.

–Frugality and much saving.

–High tariffs.

–Down to 1900, large use of labor in small plants – emphasis on artistic quality, not <u>mass</u> production.

–Greater freedom of trade down to 1880.

–Remained relatively self-sufficing.

–Railroad system rounded out by 1870.

–Rapid growth of commerce, 1800–1880.

–Burden of national debt and armament.

–In 1914, third nation.

Germany

–Thirty Years War – most devastating war in European history.

–1815–1838 small states, territorial organization, guilds still existed, internal barriers to trade.

–Zollverein [customs union] 1834 (2/3), 1852 (practically all).

–1850, exporting raw materials – foodstuffs – emigration constant (especially after failure of 1848 Revolution).

–Tariff shifts to protection, 1859. Turns away from agriculture. Capital grows, is exported.

–1915 – Germany is 2nd nation.

<u>Population</u>

[Rough diagram, showing population growth of the three countries: England starting below France (and Germany) but later exceeding France; Germany starting at about France's level and thereafter rising more rapidly.]

1912–1914	<u>Population</u>	National Income		Estimated Nat'l <u>Wealth</u>
		<u>Total</u>	Per capita	
U.S.	99m	$33.2b	$335	$187b
U.K.	45m	10.9b	243	86b

(Continued)

1912–1914	Population	National Income		Estimated Nat'l Wealth
		Total	Per capita	
Germany	66m	10.4b	146	76b
France	39m	7.3b	185	62b

	Value of mfg. in $B	Iron Prod. in Mill. of Tons	Coal Prod. in Mill. of Tons	Merch. Marine in Mill. of Tons	Exports in $B	Imports in $B	Per Cap. For. Trade in $	Rail Mile-Age	Foreign Invest in $B
U.S.	20	24	450	5.3	2.4	1.7	45	396	2
U.K.	9	10	276	18.7	2.5	3.7	151	37	18
Ger.	9	15	234	5.0	2.4	2.5	82	61	7
France	7	4	39	2.2	1.3	1.6	73	50	9

National Bureau of Economic Research.

Belgium, Holland, Italy, Austria-Hungary – slowly develop; after the 1890s, Russia comes on; Scandinavian countries advance on basis of their minerals. Canada began to develop slowly, but not rapidly till 20th century. South America very slow, Australia rapidly growing after gold discoveries; Asia opens trading ports. Imperialism during 19th century.

First period 1808–1875: cessation of active part played by governments in extending territories; political possession seemed to matter less; Manchester School claimed colonies were not worth their cost – some acquired however.

Second period 1875–1900: neo-Mercantilism; new spirit of nationalism (Germany) – England, U.S. and Germany develop rapidly in manufacturing. England reached her heights 1850–1875 – then increasingly imperialistic.

1- Seeking foreign investment, 2- Growing competition for raw materials, 3- Increasing competition for markets, 4- Increasing competition for foodstuffs.

–Less stress on gold than earlier Mercantilism – but stress on building up economic self-sufficiency.

–Struggle for possession of remaining territory led by France in Africa – England then Germany and Italy.

Growing capitalistic industry – by 1890 free, fertile land growing more scarce. 1890 last year of frontier.

Great urbanization:

City	Population in 1930
New York City	6,958,000
Chicago	3,373,000
Philadelphia	1,961,000
Detroit	1,564,000
Los Angeles	1,231,000
Cleveland	981,000
St. Louis	822,000
Baltimore	801,000
Boston	783,000

Increase in population per decade:

– to 1860	1/3 per decade
1860–1990	1/4 per decade
1890–1910	1/5 per decade
1910–1930	1/6 per decade

Density of population per square mile – 1929

U.S.	41
U.K.	484
Belgium	680
France	192
Germany	352
Italy	349
Japan	433

1930	
Rhode Island	644
New York	264
Illinois	135

Immigration (Charts: National Industrial Conference Board)

1921 – First law – severe – 3% of those nationals here in 1910 – i.e. 358,000 – instead of 1,000,000 pre-war.

–Result: restriction mostly on new immigration.

1924 – Quota reduced: 2% of nationals here in 1890 – i.e. 162,000 – but non-quota countries, Canada, Mexico, West Indies.

–Further reduction since then by official "interpretation."
Decline in immigration, and in birth rate (high standard of living at least partly due to <u>choice</u>.
    –Elimination of infant mortality and contagious diseases.
    –By 1970 – population of this country will be almost static, at about 150 million.

Ninth Week [Assignments]:
    Bogart, Chapters 24, pp. 698–709, 607–630, 674–698
    Taussig (IVth), pp. 361–371, 373–408
    B & T, pp. 813–847, 851–853, 644–655

<u>Disposition of the Public Domain to 1923</u>
    –Homestead Act 1862 – <u>giving</u> away the public domain – policy continued till 1900.
    <u>Conservation Movement</u> – pushed by Theodore Roosevelt especially.

Morrill Act of 1862, 30,000 acres for every State representative in Congress – to establish State colleges of agriculture and mechanical arts.
    –1866 – Mineral lands of great value (especially gold) discriminated from ordinary land.
    –1893 – Coal Lands Act – not more than ten miles from railroads – $20 an acre – over ten miles from railroad – $10 an acre – 160 acres.

Problem of arid land of West –
    –Valuable mineral resources, valuable timber resources.
    –Suited for grazing, lumbering, mining, dry farming.
    –Some new policy had to be made – though <u>too</u> frequently this land was treated as just farm land.
    –Tried a Timber Act (repealed soon 1891). 160 acres of homestead if farmed and 40 acres of timber planted.
    –Then tried selling at a lower price.
    –Finally, assessed land and sold it at that price.
        –Failed to consider that it is impossible to <u>grow</u> 40 acres of timber – profitably. Too long waiting and too large capital.
        –Land was usually transferred to timber corporations.
        –Desert Lands Act – sold it at $1.25 an acre.
            –Maximum available to single person 640 acres – but 2500 acres necessary to permit profitable operation by one farmer.
        –1894 – Preemption Act repealed.
        –Homestead Act amended (shorter residence).
        –Enlarged Homestead Act, 320 acres to one person in certain arid states.

–Grazing Homestead Act 1916.–Supply of free, fertile land was gone by 1890.

–In western half of country (middle of Dakotas west) – only:

–three large cultivatable centers – California valleys, Oregon valley, Eastern Washington (North Dakota) – other spots, along river valleys and in Colorado.

–less than $\frac{1}{4}$ fit for year-round grazing.

–even if every drop of rain water were utilized only 1/10 of this arid region could be irrigated.

–thus, there is no hope of much use of this – as land.

–National Parks and Forests – use up an appreciable part of West – also Indian Reservations.

–Public Lands Disposed of up to 1923:

Homestead	213m acres
Timber culture	11m acres
Desert Land	8m acres
Sales, cash & credit	220m acres (some duplication)
Timber and Stone	13m acres

–Grants:

–Railroad, canal, etc.	137m acres
Education	99m acres
Military bounty	68m acres
Swamps (to States)	64m acres
Miscellaneous	79m acres

–Reservations:

Forests and Parks	170m acres
Mineral and Power	48m acres
Indian	35m acres

–Unreserved – undisposed of –
unappropriated   186m acres

1–Main criticism – too much hurry in getting land out of public hands – was it desirable? –Or necessary?

2–Provisions of laws were never studied adequately; and needs never correctly met.

3–Lax and corrupt administration.

End of free, public land:
  Agriculture:
    –Intensification of farming
    –Increased product per laborer
    –Increased tenancy
    –Less pressure on Eastern agriculture

  Labor:
    –Less productive – increased conflict of capital and labor
    –Slower rise of wages
    –Restriction of immigration (emigration to Canada)
  –Growth of population? – birth rate.
  –Foreign trade – less imports of manufactured goods – shift of trade.
  –Tariff: protection for agriculture – some industry more anxious for free trade.
  –Economic imperialism – outflow of capital.
  –Shift from exploitation of land to that of labor – end of bandit era.
  –Conflict of capital and labor.
  –Social Democracy of frontier of less importance.
  –More interdependence, development of <u>social</u> consciousness.
  –This list is one of <u>tendencies</u> – take time, may be counter-acted, are themselves
    the results of more than this <u>one</u> cause.
  –1900 – end of one great epoch in our history, beginning of another.

Transportation – tremendous technological improvements from beginning to present – still going on: 1920–1930 – 25% increase in railroad efficiency.
  –What is the Industrial Revolution? – the <u>rate</u> of technological progress has
    immensely speeded up since the World War.
  –<u>Cheap steel</u> – Bessemer – rails, locomotives, bridges.
  –Standard gauge (in general use in 1880s).

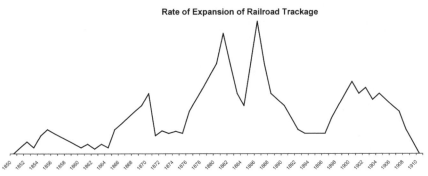

Rate of Expansion of Railroad Trackage

Year

*The units in the original graph are not specified. This chart was created using numbers generated to approximate a hand-drawn graph of railroad trackage from 1850 to 1910.

–Rapid construction in 1870s – great trunk lines – East and Mid-West.
　–Consolidation, competition, unfair methods, pooling, legislation.
　–Rapid fall in railroad [expansion] rates in late 1870s.
–By 1883, most of the big lines and important lines were finished – the railroads main spurt and stimulus to our life had spent its effects by 1883.
–Enormous land grants – as much as a quarter of some States – aid stopped after 1872.
　–But much did not go to the railroads, as they were not always finished on time.
–Feeling that there couldn't be too many railroads.
–Railroads first brought the country face to face with the big problems of modern industrialism.
　–Internal competition, coming from large fixed capitals.
　–First restriction on complete individualism – State laws, then Interstate
　　Commerce Act 1887.
–The problems of our post-frontier, industrial civilization, which are the main concern of present-day statesmen – first came into notice with the railroads in the 1880s.

–Effect of railroads – carriage of freight – huge saving of labor.

Decline of Waterways
　–After 1837 – no more canals built.
　–After 1860 – water traffic diminishes – many canals never did pay.
　　–Erie Canal – outstanding success at first – tolls abolished – even then traffic
　　declined – peak of traffic reached in 1882.
　　–Illinois and Michigan – also declined in 1880s.
　–Mississippi River also declined.
　–Waterway ports began to decline – Demand for improvements of canals.
　　–Barge Canal improved by New York (1916) – a disappointment.
　　–Ohio River improved – also a disappointment.
　　–Soo Canal of great importance – huge Eastbound traffic in ore – Westbound
　　in coal.
　　–Lakes-to-Gulf and St. Lawrence Waterway.
　　　–Always get support – local merchants, towns, cities, contractors – U.S.A.
　　　pays the bill.
　　　–What of economic aspects?
　　　–Will freight take to the water?

    –St. Lawrence has more to be said for it –
      –Traffic moves in that direction anyway.
      –A deeper channel and larger boats.
      –Connected with electric power creation.

Communication
    –<u>Cheap wood-pulp</u> paper invented shortly after Civil War.
      –Of great importance in rise of printing, e.g. the modern newspaper.
      –Advertising business.

Agriculture
    –Depression after Civil War – and in 1870s.
    –Better in 1880s – great suffering in 1890s (world prices fell).
    –Tremendous expansion after 1896 to 1920.
    –Then the worst depression of all.
   –Effect of urban development: truck gardening, dairying, fruit.
   –Beet sugar – 1930 nearly $1/4$ of U.S. consumption.
   –Export to Europe of foodstuffs – up till 1900 – then decline until World War –
    huge export expansion to war needs, depression after.

    1930–

	Value	Acreage
Corn	$1,378m	100m
Hay	1,135m	72m
Cotton	810m	45m
Wheat	517m	59m
Oats	453m	41m
Potatoes	326m	3m
Tobacco	216m	2m
Barley	129m	12m
Sugar	76m	1m
All crops	6,274m	

Growth of Farms
    –Improved land – steady growth.
    –Unimproved land – big growth 1900–1910 (grazing).
    –Number of farms rises – slower rate after 1900.
    –Size of average farm – decrease in '80s, slight decrease since.

Scientific farming advances – under direction and leadership of the government.
    –Farmer's small and numerous – unorganized.

–Farming more capitalistic, product-per-laborer has declined.
–Tractor, electricity.

Economic position of the farmer – his economic psychology.
  –Small scale producer – product goes into a <u>vast,highly competitive</u>, often <u>world market</u>.
  –Thus the control of the size of crop is very difficult – each farmer's crop is so small a part of the whole, he can see little effect of his action.
  –Seldom has reserve capital – is relatively <u>fixed as to</u> crop.
  –Is usually in debt – crop perishable.
  –Transportation takes large slice of sale-price.
  –The people with whom he deals are few and well organized.

<u>Corporation</u>: – in late years the corporation has gone into the field of wholesaling, and retailing.
  –It is only very recently that the corporation has come to dominate our economic organization.
  –The result of larger scale enterprise, and of changes in corporation laws (necessity of thorough study of evolution of corporation laws).
  –General Corporation Laws
  –1888 – <u>New Jersey</u> overhauls its laws, makes them more attractive (privileges, immunities, granted to officials) – made possible <u>holding</u> companies.
    –Simultaneous development of concerns with <u>large capital</u> – in later '80s – and especially after 1898.
    –New Jersey did a profitable business creating corporations.
    –So was followed by other States – hoping to make money.
      –Their laws – in the competition – became worse and worse, until certain of our States had the worst corporation laws in the world.
      –State utterly kowtowed to the corporate promoters.
    –At present [1933–1934] –
      –Ownership vested in stockholders – takers of risk.
      –Credit – advanced by bondholders.
      –Ownership quite divorced from control and entrepreneurship.
        –Directors can use their power at the expense of the owners and creditors – ability and temptation exists.
    –Corporation laws tended to protect the promotion, not owner.
      –Adequate safeguards not introduced.
      –Result: Modern corporation created in one of these States, is the greatest get-rich-quick devise ever created – for getting rich at the expense of other people.

–This problem is entirely <u>separate</u> from the Trust problem.

–The corporation problem is one of devising a type of organization adequate to large-scale enterprise, yet safeguarding the rights of <u>all</u> concerned.

–Necessitating federal incorporation – is it Constitutional?

　–Would improve our economy more than any other <u>single</u> factor.

<u>Tariffs</u> – Civil War introduces high protection.

–Would we have had high protection without the war?

–We had no preconceived notion that such was desirable.

–We needed large revenues and to offset currency depreciation.

–On return of peace – a surplus accumulated – some demand for reduction – and some duties were lowered – the revenue producing ones, more interested in them. Thus only the non-revenue duties were retained at their former high level.

–1870s –

　–Wool and woolgrowers tariff.

　–Copper tariff – passed over veto – few producers, high domestic price, low price abroad – rich ore, cheap production – exported copper – huge profits.

　–Steel rails.

–A lax period in public morals – <u>abuse</u> of the protective principle.

–Decline in Southern States' influence.

–Rise of protective feeling.

–1880s –

　–Surplus revenue – led to demand for lower tariffs.

　–Congress found easier solution: increase expenditures.

McKinley Tariff 1897 – higher duties than ever before – at a time when industry was further (and faster) advanced than ever before.

McKinley Tariff 1897–1909

　–Growing opposition by some groups of business men.

　　–Producers of goods for domestic market – who had higher costs.

　　–Producers of goods for export – high costs, retaliatory tariffs.

　–Farmers in Northwest thought they were getting the worst of the bargain. Tariffs on unimported agricultural goods. High cost of living.

　　–Rise in prices.

　　–Antipathy to trusts – which were considered the children of tariffs.

　　–Rise of opposition to special privilege, graft – muckraking.

　　–Conservation of natural resources – we were forbidding importation of raw materials, using up our own.

–Both parties stood for reduction in 1908.

–Payne-Aldrich Tariff 1909 – a failure.
  –Increase in many duties – special interest, graft.
  –Slight reduction of average level [of tariffs].
–Free trade with Philippines – great advantage to them.
–Tariff Board – gather facts – abolished 1912.
–Corporation Tax.

Tenth week [Assignment]:
  Bogart, Chapters 29, 28
  B & T, pp. 696–725, 729–737
  Dewey, Chapters 15, 17, 19
  Noyes, Chapter VIII (Panic of '93)
    –Democrats in 1913 – Underwood Tariff 1913.
      –Real steps toward reduction – less graft.
      –Income tax.
      –Subsidy for Merchant Marine, progressed.
      –Tariff Commission.
      –A shift in the incidence of taxation was involved.
        –Growing opposition to prevailing distribution of wealth.
    –Went through World War without any increased tariff.
      –Democrats in power; tariffs could not have been of much importance to
        total revenue needed.
        –New duties on sugar, dye-stuffs and chemicals.
    –1922 Fordney-McCumber Tariff – higher rates.
      –Return of Republicans.
      –Depression; depreciation of European currencies.
    –But we were now a creditor nation!
    –1930 Hawley-Smoot Tariff – higher rates.
    –The greater proportion of goods are imported on Free List.

[Two rough-drawn diagrams, with period 1860–1930 on horizontal axis. One
diagram illustrating free list as proportion of total: shows uneven but gradual
rise in proportion. Other diagram illustrates average rates on protected goods:
shows relatively short periods of rise, decline and rise, following by prolonged
steep decline and prolonged steep rise.]

–International bankers – a new group opposed to tariff.
–New groups favoring tariff.
  –Farmers are increasingly in a position to gain by tariff.

–Beet sugar interests.

–South is almost protectionist (Democratic party has not in past 50 years been sincerely free trade-ist.)

  –<u>New</u> industries in South.

  –West – is solidly protectionist – important in Senate.

–Use of the powers of States to wage economic warfare for private traders' gain.

  –Tendency towards self-sufficiency of National States.

    –Tariffs and a myriad of other restrictions.

–Effects of tariff have been grossly overestimated in U.S.

  –It has stimulated a few industries, but has not greatly altered our industrial growth.

  –It is a great burden, also.

<u>Labor</u> – factors affecting supply – population growth.

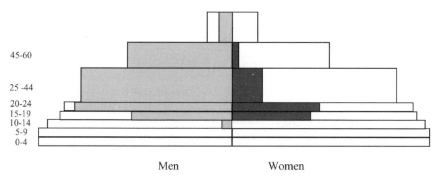

Men   Women

<u>Proportion</u> of total wage groups gainfully employed – by classes (age)

–Increased leisure time – but increased intensity <u>at</u> work.

–More time spent on education:

  –High school growth – 1880s (1840: 800; 1890: 2,000; 1920: 12,000)

    –General development of idea that a high school education is essential.

  –Kindergartens – vocational schools – adult education.

  –Growth of size of colleges.

–Population: 1890 –   50% of beginners got through 8th grade.

                            5% through high school.

                            1% through college.

1920 –   50% got through high school.

                            16% got through college

–After Civil and World Wars – wages fell, but not nearly so much as prices fell –
i.e. a substantial gain in real wages (based on hourly rates – and day's work has
shortened somewhat).

[Rough bar graph showing for 1860 large proportion in agriculture, small
proportion in manufacturing, and moderate proportion in trade and transportation.
For an unspecified later date, roughly the same proportions in each, i.e. fall in
agriculture and increase in the other two.]

1920 –	Employer's and self-employed	10.1m
	Home farm laborers	1.8m
	Wage earners (manual and clerical)	26.0m
	Salaried, professional	3.5 m
		41.5m

1870	1920	
7.1	17.2	Capital
26.6	42.4	Labor
58.2	35.0	General public
8.1	5.1	Non-classified

Industrialism's effect on labor
  –Decreased importance of skilled manual dexterity – opening up of most jobs
    to short period of learning how.
  –Speeding up of work – keep up with the machine.
  –Scientific management.
 –New prominence of Labor Problem.
  –Competition of laborer with laborer.
    –Increased mobility of movement in space, time, and job.
    –Geographical and international competition.
      –International Labor Office attempts at coordination.
 –Trade Unions – rapid growth 1900–1909, then plateau, again rapid growth
    1916–1920.
    –Increase in Transportation Unions, Building Unions, Metals and
      Machinery, Clothing.
    –Miscellaneous and mining remained steady.
  –1920, 20% of total employed in unions – 5 million – then drop to 3–4 million
    – up again in 1933.
  –Strength of unions concentrated in certain cities and trades.
  Competition between States in labor legislation – South especially is
  backward.

–Organized labor has been an aristocracy within the ranks of labor – not taking much interest in the unorganized, unskilled population of the laboring class.

–In struggle between labor and capital, the third mediating group (mostly agriculture, or "general public," has declined relative to the other two.

–There are endless conflicts in our industrial fabric. [Single vertical line in margin alongside entire discussion of conflict.]

    –Conflicts between elements of "capital," or between elements of "labor," between geographical interests, between farmers and workers, farmer and capitalist, farmer and railroad.

–There is not <u>one</u> class conflict – there are endless <u>group</u> conflicts.

1925	percentage distribution of realized income
Agriculture	11%
Mines	3
Manufacturing	21
Construction	4
Transportation and Public Utilities	8
Banks	1
Merchandising	15
Government	7
Unclassified	20
Miscellaneous	10

1925	Total <u>realized</u> income (includes income from <u>durable</u> consumer goods, and other non-pecuniary income).	
Wages	30.8b	38%
Salaries	15.0b	18
Pensions, Benefits	<u>1.1b</u>	<u>1</u>
Total employees	46.8b	57%
Rents, Royalties	10.6b	13%
Interest	3.9	5
Dividends	<u>4.1</u>	<u>5</u>
Total property	18.6b	23%
Entrepreneurial Profits withdrawn	<u>16.4b</u>	<u>20%</u>
	81.8b	100%

[In top margin of next page: Cf. Copeland's article in "Recent Economic Tendencies" [and] King – National Income and Its Distribution – 1930]

1926   Realized income

	0–5,000	5,000–25,000	25,000–50,000	50,000 & over
Income recipients	44,194,550	429,300	47,250	2,450
% recipients	98%	0.96%	0.106%	0.005%
Total income	$73,125m	$6,095m	$3,177m	$1,388m
% income	87%	7.275%	[not given]	1.656%

30 million families – about four to a family.

Wealth is more concentrated than income.
   Per capita (of total population) National Income –
      $700 in 1920
      $670–690 in 1922–1928
      $701 in 1929
The per capita income could not be greatly increased by equal distribution of wealth and income – its advantages lie in other spheres.
   –More can be accomplished by increasing the productive power of the country.

Estimated Expenditures of American (Realized) Income 1925
Food	$24,000,000,000
Clothing	$12,000,000,000
Rent and income on owned homes	8,100,000,000
House furnishings	4,751,000,000
Fuel and light	4,800,000,000
Health	3,600,000,000
Leisure	15,070,000,000
Savings	10,000,000,000

In Foreign Commerce – we are now (1933) back to the 1913 level of exports and imports – both imports and exports are less important for U.S. than for most European nations – 5–10% of our total annual production.
Imports – crude (tropical) foodstuffs – steady.
            –crude material for manufacturing – great rise after 1870s.
            –manufactured goods – decreases greatly after 1870s.
   Exports – crude foodstuffs – great rise in 1870s, fall off in 1900s.
            –crude material for manufacturing – great falling off in 1870s.

–manufactured goods – increase in 1880s.

–Cotton, machinery, automobiles.

–Europe declines in proportionate importance – Canada and Asia grow.

Imports – silk, coffee, rubber, sugar, paper.

–Europe declines as source, Asia and South America grow.

1850–1875 – Increasingly unfavorable balance of trade, outflow of specie (large).

1875–1900 – Favorable balance – outflow of specie.

1900–1915 – Huge favorable balance (one-half billion) – smaller outflow of specie.

1915–1921 – Staggering favorable balance (20 billion dollars)

1921–1929 – Smaller favorable balance – smaller inflow of gold.

1875 on – Lower transportation costs (rail and ocean), opening of the West – agriculture exported.

–Manufactured goods have comparative advantage.

–Tariff keeps out imports.

–Prices falling (in gold), due to depression of 1873.

–Steady rise of foreign investment made in U.S.

–Decrease of earnings of Merchant Marine.

–Growth of tourist expenditures, and immigrant remittances.

During and after War – we brought back two billions of our securities held abroad – loaned $18 billion – one billion of gold imported.

–This government took over task of loaning money to allied nations – by raising Liberty Loans – $11 billion.

–Came out of War a creditor nation.

–What of balance of trade? A paradox.

–We delayed solution by loaning more abroad.

Yearly Average of U.S. Balance of Payments 1922–1932

Creditor Balance		Debtor Balance	
Commodity balance favorable	$465m	American tourists	$492m
Balance of Interest on Foreign Investment.	$433m	Immigrant remittances	$283m
War Debt Receipts	$187m	Shipping & freight	$44m
Misc. & errors	$8m	Govt transactions	$52m
	-----	Foreign investments	$329m
	$1,273m		$1,200m
		Gold movement	$73m

Total Gold Holdings:
1914 2b
1918 3b

1924 4b
1933 5b
–Disorganization elsewhere, danger of inflation here.

Merchant Marine
  –Registered tonnage – engaged in foreign trade.
  –Enrolled and licensed tonnage – engaged in domestic trade.
  –Add to chart on balance of trade – on % of total foreign trade in American ships.
1920 – 43%   1930 – 34%
  –Add to American Merchant Marine – total tonnage

Foreign trade	Domestic trade
1922 – 10.7m tons gross	1922 – 7.7m tons gross
1932 – 5.0m tons gross	1932 – 10.7m tons gross

[Foregoing is an insert to chart not included in notes.]

–During Civil War we carried two-thirds of our foreign trade; after it, we carried one-third; this decreased until, by 1914, we carried only one-ninths of our foreign trade. 1920–1930, we carried one-third or more.
–Great changes and improvements in shipping and shipbuilding.
  –Shift from wood to iron vessels (disadvantageous to U.S.).
  –These brought about a rapid displacement of sailing [vessels] by steam vessels – up to 1893, over half of total world's tonnage was carried by sail – after that a rapid change.
  –England could build iron ships much cheaper than we, and our Register Laws forbade the register of foreign built ships.
  –Also our laws for a floating standard of living [aboard ship] were far higher than other countries – higher costs of operation.
–Foreign competition plays no part in our domestic shipping.
–Panama Canal Act – allowed ships not over five years old, if foreign built, to be registered in U.S.
  –Nothing happened at first.
  –We were, in fact, sending capital abroad to buy and operate ships on foreign register.
1914 – Ships over five years old could be bought and registered – German shipping wiped out. Allied shipping turning more and more to war purposes.
1915 – Seamans Act (LaFollett Act) to raise standard of living of seamen, and protect them by inspection, etc.
1916 – Shipping Board – to supervise building, to look over and veto rates, allowed to foster pooling agreements.

1917 – Outbreak of War – ships a <u>bottleneck</u> through which men and supplies had to flow – unparalleled expansion of American shipping – 162 [ship-building slip]ways, 1914; 1,000 ways, 1917 (August).

[Assignment due Monday, November <u>19</u>, 1933 Paper. Explain what seems to you to be the <u>chief reasons</u> why the government has not secured a wiser and more efficient <u>social</u> direction and control of the country's economic development. Why haven't we made greater progress?]

–But a majority were not finished in time for war – we could expand everything but time.
–After war – other countries expanded shipping.
   46m tons total world tonnage, 1914.
   60m tons total world tonnage, 1925 – U.S. second.
   70m tons total world tonnage, 1932.
–Higher surplus and overproduction of shipping.
–Jones Act: – muddled – sold ships to private firms, broke them up, etc.
–Total cost to government of ships about 3 billion.

11th week [Assignment]:
Lippincott, Isaac (Problems of Reconstruction), 3rd edition, 1933, chapter 7
Dewey, chapter 22
Noyes (War Period of American Finance), chapters 5, 8, 9
Bogart, chapter 30

–Jones-White Act – more favorable mail contracts.
–Advantages of a national merchant marine.
  –In case of war – auxiliary navy; transports.
  –In time of peace – "trade follows the flag" (sometimes).
    –Especially stimulating exports.
    –In reality, the flag follows trade – ships go where they will get cargo, that depends on other economic forces.
We are at a disadvantage in shipping.
  –High costs of shipbuilding (little chance for <u>our</u> industrial system).
  –High costs of operation – high standard of living on the seas – practically <u>requires</u> subsidies.
–Shipping industry has become "capitalistic" (?).
  –Huge ships, huge cargoes, huge construction costs – larger companies, larger capitalization.
  –Control of shipping has passed more and more into hands of great shipping combinations.

–Also, private ownership of shipping lines by United Fruit Co., Standard Oil, U.S. Steel.

–A ship is a large investment of <u>specialized</u> capital.

   –Extremes of prosperity and depression are thus characteristic of the industry.

      –Large building, then overproduction.

      –Cutthroat competition – combination.

   –Shipping "Conferences," "Pools," "Rings."

–Shipping Board allowed regulated pools.

Retail Sales Distribution 1929 (first time in census)

Food Group	$10.8b
General Stores	2.5b
General Merchandise	6.4b
Automotive	9.6b
Apparel	4.2b
Furniture & Household Gds	2.7b
Restaurants	2.1b
Lumber and Building	2.6b
Other Retail	7.7b
Second Hand	0.1b
	49.1b total sales

Retail Sales – Types of Operation

Single Store Independents	64.11% of total sales
2.3 Store [?] and Local Branch	8.84%
Local Chains	6.71%
Sectional Chains	4.46%
National Chains	8.06%
Others	7.82%

1.5 million <u>retail stores</u>

Wholesale Distribution

Total Number of Wholesalers	169,702
Total Sales	$169,291[m]

Free Silver Movement

–Production of silver – lowered market value.

–Interests of Western mine owners and mining States.

–<u>Commercial</u> Ratio [of silver to gold]

1870: 15.5 to 1	1900: 33.3 to 1
1875: 16.6 to 1	1915: 39.8 to 1

1880: 18.0 to 1	1919: 18.4 to 1
1890: 19.7 to 1	1928: 35.2 to 1
1894: 32.5 to 1	

–<u>Decline in output of gold</u> – but large demand for it – European nations going on gold standard – other silver stocks declined in value.

–1850–1860 – Huge gold production, stationary silver production.

    1860–1873 – Some falling off of gold production – rise in silver production.

    1873–1890 – More falling off of gold production – great rise in rate of silver production.

    1870 – Silver was undervalued by the mint – no dollars coined – silver sent abroad, never handed to mint.

    1873 – Market value of silver declined beyond mint value.

    –Demand for coinage of silver dollars.

    –Legislation forcing the purchase or coinage of silver.

–Demand for more money – falling prices 1880–1896.

    –Technological advance throughout world.

    –World goes on gold standard, just at time of decreasing gold production.

–After 1896 – gold production greatly increased – rise of world prices (new sources (cyanide process).

Average of annual gold production:

1801–1850	$15.7m
1851–1854	121.2m
1986–1900	177.7m
1901–1920	395.4m
1932 and 1933	500.0m

–Demand for free silver decreased.

Currency –

    Aldrich-Vreeland Act, 1908 – emergency currency based on other assets than government bonds.

State Banks – decreased after Civil War until by 1875, one-sixth of the national banks.

    –Moderate increase till 1886.

    –Then rapid expansion to 1920.

    –In resources, State banks rose after '86, more rapidtly after 1900 – didn't equal and pass national banks till 1916.

    Why? – Restriction of note issue (by tax) didn't end profitableness of state banks, due to the growth of importance of deposit-currency.

–Lax laws in States for State banks – though some improvement after 1887. Growth of Savings Banks – especially in North-East. Savings deposits in commercial banks elsewhere.
Growth of Trust Companies – after '90s.
  –"The department store of finance."
  –Demand for new agencies, new financial services.
  –Private Banks declined after Civil War.
National banks suffered in competition with State banks.
  –One of the objects of the Federal Reserve System was to remedy this, by extending the range of business of National banks.
Federal Reserve System – also aimed to give an elastic note issue.
  –Centralization of control – rate control.
–After 1920 an increase of State-Bank membership in system. 1922: one-third of Banks were National, which held two-thirds of resources.
Federal Land Banks, International Credit Banks.

With growth of corporate organization came the growth of stock exchanges, financial middlemen (investment bankers).
  Real Estate Bond Houses, Commercial Paper Houses.
  Installment buying, Investment Service.
  Blue Sky Laws regulating promotional activities.
  Building and Loan Association: first in 1831, a few after 1860 – moderate growth after 1880 – rapid growth after 1920 – 9 billions of assets.
  Life Insuranace – tremendous growth recently.
    1860, per capita insurance $5.50
    1932, per capita insurance $900
Industrial and Personal Insurance, former has more holders, latter has more value.
  –Extension of insurance into all realms of risk.
–Enormous growth of industrial stocks and public utilities.

  Final exam
    How have the American people proceeded in (carrying out and) satisfying their wants. [Single vertical line in margin alongside this sentence.]
      –Increase of national per capita income – especially over and above expenditure. Saveable income.
      –Increase of Wealth 1870–1920, $35 per capita per annum.
      –Each succeeding generation inherited a larger supply of accumulated capital (durable, technological).

Federal Finance: Interest-Bearing National Debt

June 30, 1860	$64m
1866	2,322m
1880	1,709m
1890	711m
1893	585m
1900	1,023m
1916	971m
1920	24,061m
1930	15,921m
1935	30,000m (estimated)

–Liquor and tobacco taxes were a permanent legacy of Civil War finance – were two-thirds as important as customs revenues in 1870–1895.

–Huge surpluses, even pork-barrel legislation could no stop them – national debt reduced.

–Spanish War was no financial burden – but navy and army were permanently greater expenses.

–Panama Canal financed out of revenue to two-thirds its cost.

–Corporation tax and Income tax become the chief source of government revenue after 1913.

–Customs duties drop in importance (to one-sixth of total, 1930).

State Debts – rapid rise after Civil War in South.

–Then decline and stable until 1890. Grew slowly until 1900 ($350,000,000).

–Then grew very rapidly – one and one-half billion, 1929.

Municipalities and Counties heavily in debt – larger in larger cities ($186 per capita of large cities, over one-half million, 1929.

State Taxation – approximately

$3 per capita, 1860.
$9 per capita, 1902
$57 per capita, 1931

–General property tax – the traditional.

–Income and inheritance – motor and gasoline – sales.

1913 – Local taxation most important.

1919 – Huge rise in national taxation, also in local.

1921–1929 – Fall in national taxation, rise in local, smaller rise in state.

Expansion of governmental activities.

–Little change in Constitution.

–Expansion of activities – <u>regulatory, positive</u>.

–<u>The State</u> an important factor contributing to our standard of living, <u>determining what it shall be</u>.

 –<u>Regulatory</u> expenses are much smaller for States, than <u>those expenditures which yield goods and services to the taxpayer</u>.

 –The <u>main</u> Federal expenditure is for past and future war.

–Decline of county government – <u>change of city government</u> – tendency toward home-rule, great increase in activities.

–One-seventh to one-eighth of national income goes to governments – redistribution of <u>real</u> income by taxation.

–"Old laissez-faire" lasts down to last quarter of 19th century.

 –Beginnings of revolt are seen in 1870s and later.

 –But main impetus of revolt came with [Theodore] Roosevelt and Wilson.

 –More impetus given by war.

 –Reaction after war – return to old cause under Roosevelt II.

The World War.

  –Economic problems of war in modern industrial society, and lessons for any planned economy.

 –War has become capitalistic – is an <u>industrial</u> affair predominantly.

 –We were strong in food, men, resources, finance.

 –Immediate needs were for <u>war</u> supplies, army, ships.

 –Conscription of men – why not of industry? – <u>possibilities</u> of it, legally – usually sufficient.

 –Getting goods and services – financing – taking care of civilian population. [Double vertical line in margin alongside this sentence.]

 –18 billion needed for first year (one-third of national income).

  –Decrease consumption, absorb savings, inflation.

  –How much to borrow, how much to tax. (Conscription given up.)

  –<u>Cost</u> of a war is inevitably the goods and services (destroyed) consumed by <u>war</u>, instead of civilian, purposes.

   –Must be <u>borne</u> by the war generation.

   –Later generations suffer only to the extent that a smaller supply of <u>accumulated</u> goods comes down to them.

  –But statesmen hoped to <u>shift</u> the cost of war to future generations.

   –Could really shift only <u>incidence</u> of burdens <u>within</u> the war generation.

  –Taxed to about one-third of war costs – income and excess profits taxes – internal revenue.

  –Excluding Allied loans – 43% of cost met by taxation.

Federal Finance:

Fiscal year	Ordinary Receipts	Ordinary Revenue	Surplus or Deficit
1916	$0.7b	$0.7b	+$0.04b
1917	1.1b	2.0b	−0.9b
1918	4.1b	13.7b	−9.6b
1919	4.6b	18.9b	−14.2b
1920	6.7b	6.1b	+0.5b

Liberty Bond	Issues	Issued
June 1917	1st	$2,000b
Nov. 1917	2nd	3,800b
May 1918	3rd	4,100b
Oct. 1918	4th	6,900b
May 1919	5th (Victory)	4,500b
	Total	19,000b

First year [April 1917-May 1918] – 4b taxes, 9b borrowed – excluding the loans to Allied governments, 50% was taxes.

–The main results of the 1912 Tax Act were felt in 1920 – $6^1/_2$ billion in taxation.

–Expenditures, 12 billion first year, 24 billion 2nd year.

–Total estimated direct and indirect cost to all nations of the World War was $330,000,000,000 – more than the total <u>wealth</u> of the U.S.

–Permanent change in revenue to Federal Government –

  –Main importance of income taxes.

  –Permanently higher level of expenditure.

  –Surplus from 1920–1930 – paid off 10 billions of debt – reduced taxes.

Government built up purchasing power by going into debt – based on public confidence – a legal limit in gold reserve.

1914 – Federal Reserve System – a base for expansion

  –Taking gold out of circulation – one billion.

  –Embargo on gold exports.

  –Lowering of reserve requirements.

  –<u>Everything</u> tending to <u>expand</u> credit.

Money in Circulation	Gold and Gold Certificates	Greenbacks Fed. Res. Notes	Total
June 30, 1914	$1.6b	$.3b	$3.4b
1917	2.4	0.8b	4.7b
1920	1.2	3.4	6.0

(*Continued*)

Money in Circulation	Gold and Gold Certificates	Greenbacks Fed. Res. Notes	Total
	1914	1917	1920
Total Bank Reserves	27b	37b	53b
Total Loans and Discounts	15b	20b	31b

–Inflation – kept credit easy and cheap – but increased cost of war – also increase cost through deflation later.

Wholesale Price Index

July 1914	100
Dec. 1915	98
Dec. 1916	147
Mar. 1917	161
Dec. 1917	183
Nov. 1918	206
Dec. 1919	238
May 1920	272
June 1921	148

–Price regulation during war – relaxed at end.

  –Great boom, then reaction.

–Cost of living didn't rise as quickly as prices.

  –Land doubled 1914–1920.

–Rise in prices – aggravated speculation, increased cost of war.

–Redistribution of income – farmers gained tremendously, some producers, labor – railroads, salaried, other producers lost.

–Estimated that 13 billions of cost of war (34b) came from increased productivity and production.

  –19b came from decreased consumption, mainly by creditor classes – and saving.

–Redistribution of wealth.

–People "wouldn't stand" higher taxes – meaning they were selfish, or ignorant (didn't know they couldn't shift the burden).

  –"Ignorance and selfishness are usually synonymous with 'political necessity.'" [Single vertical line in margin alongside preceding two sentences.]

–The war the greatest experiment in <u>social</u> <u>planning</u> in our history.
  –Price control, rationing, priorities.
  –Absolute inability to realize the needs and possibilities of war.
  –Chaos at first – then rapidly increasing expansion of centralizing agencies.
    –<u>Council of National Defense</u>
      State and Local Councils (184,000)
      Woman's Committee
      National Research Council
      Medical Board
      Engineering and Education
    –Food Administration (Hoover)
      Grain Corporation
      Sugar Board
    –Fuel Administration (Garfield)
    –Railroad Administration
    –Post Office Department – Telephone and Telegraph
    –Labor Administration
      War Labor Board
      War Policies Board
      Housing Corporation
    –Shipping Board
      Fleet Corporation
    –War Industries Board
      Sections:
        –Commodities
        –Priorities
        –Requirements
        –Resources and Conversion
        –Conservation
        –Price Fixing
    –War Trade Board
    –Treasury
      –Federal Reserve Board
      –Capital Issues Committee
      –War Finance Corporation
    –War Risk Insurance
    –Committee on Public Information (Propaganda)
    –Allied Councils:
      –Transport
      –Food

    –Munitions

    –Finance and Purchasing

Post-war years – and Depression.

  –Fundamentally a result of the <u>World War</u>.

    –Aggravated by disastrous Peace Treaty.

    –Immediate maladjustment in 1919 and 1920.

      –Tremendous expansion of credit after war.

      –Then precipitous drop in prices – yet few financial stringencies.

    –However, prices didn't fall as far as after Civil War – when the immediate drop did not complete the readjustment.

    –Prices, instead, stayed up on a level plan where they landed after immediate drop – until 1929, when they went down, till 1933.

    –Agriculture had depression all during '20s – culmination of two decades of <u>extraordinary</u> prosperity, ending in frantic prosperity of wartime.

    –[Arrow to "prosperity" just above.] European markets came back soon after war – with less purchasing power, and new competition by countries that had, like ourselves, become exporters during war.

    –During war a shortage of building – this rectified by tremendous building activity after 1924.

    –Remarkable technological advance.

    –Output grew – wages decreased slightly.

    –Prices controlled – thus <u>enormous profits</u>.

    –Increase in state and local debt.

    –Gold stock – $3b, $4b, finally 1931 – $5 billion – facilitated credit expansion and high prices.

    –Huge outflow of capital – stimulating exports – which kept up prices.

    –Enormous expansion of installment selling.

    –Capital flowing into real estate speculation – then stock market speculation.

   –All these elements kept up a falsely high, stable price level.

   –International conditions became increasingly influential on our economy.

    –Restrictions on gold flows, on credit flows, on trade flows – all increased existing maladjustments.

–Depression in U.S. inaugurated by stock market crash.

–Decrease of industrial production, and increase of unemployment were greater than at any other period of our history (relatively to population).

–Hoover measures – R. F. C. [Reconstruction Finance Corporation], Farm Board, keep up wages.

  –But credit panic in Europe; lower wages, hoarding, bank failures (10,000 in ten years) gloom.

–Closing of banks, 1933 – [after F. D.] Roosevelt inaugurated.

Two problems – Recovery – The New Deal:
1. Recovery – fundamentally a problem of price maladjustments – <u>within</u> the price structure, and between the price structure now and before.
   –Inflationist element – political power.
2. The New Deal
   –Redistribution of wealth.
   –Remedying those elements of capitalism that bring about crashes.
   –Aiding labor, the farmer.
   –Eliminating unfair and extreme competition, wasteful competition.
     –Sweatshops, child labor.
   –Financial system – banks, stock market.
   –Stabilize the value of money, check the overproduction.
   –Some control of the corporation.
   –Regulation of public utilities and new forms of transportation.
   –Protect the consumer.
     –Drugs and advertising.

–Bank crisis <u>had</u> to be met – but other remedies were matters of policy.
  –Especially the fundamental alternative of doing <u>something vs.</u> doing little or nothing.
  –"Do Something" Roosevelt.
    –Devaluation – to raise price level, aid exports.
    –Return to Gold Standard – for confidence – a psychological appeal.
    –Will devaluation work, in a country with so little foreign trade? – Should it be at 0.59¢?
    –What hardship will it work to some groups.
–Truly remarkable recovery since March 1933 – especially psychological – no longer going down.
–What of New Deal – why put them through at a time of recovery? – Get them through while Congress was obedient.
  –Some of them do not aid recovery.
  –N. R. A. [National Recovery Administration] – Get rid of child labor, low wages, bad conditions.
    –Spread employment – increase laborer's purchasing power.
    –Restrict unfair competition – especially in oil.
    [Brace enclosing preceding three lines, marked "Codes"]
  –Tremendous task – especially when attempted to be put over so suddenly.
  –Consumers' interest ignored.
  –Has probably held up recovery.

–Danger of monopolies of capital and of labor combining to <u>soak</u> the consumer.

–Banking Act – strengthen Federal Reserve System.

–Securities Act.

–Emergency Railroad Act – bolster revenues, remove duplication – plan a <u>nationwide</u> organization.

–Drug Act – Advertisement

–Unlikely that we will ever go back to extremes of individualism.

Objectives of course:

–Training for better citizenship

–Concept of past change, helping to an understanding of the present change.

–Some aid in making a living, conducting business in the light of a generalized past history.

–Purely cultural – as a part of the culture expected of any educated person.

–As a background for other histories.

–As aid to understanding ourselves – who are shaped by our past and present economic environment.

–To see some <u>significance</u> in the <u>facts</u> of history.

–Look out for operation of economic laws and principles.

–Has legislation succeeded or failed?

–Consider developments incident to the rise of Industrial Capitalism.

–Interrelationship between the U.S. and the rest of the world.

–Interrelationship between economic and non-economic aspects of our civilization.

–The problem of getting a living: the fundamental thing with which we have been dealing.

–The <u>way</u> the American people have gone about the business of satisfying their wants.

–Cooperation of Man and Nature – of Man and Man.

–Improving of institutional setup.

–Necessity of getting a concept of the standard of living of the past:

–An <u>advance</u> unparalleled in human history.

–<u>Due</u> to <u>unusual</u> progress of invention.

–And to <u>unusual</u> circumstances of a virgin land.

–Plus social and political possibilities of a <u>new</u> country.

–Problems left unsolved, often – and new ones rapidly arising.

–Main one: How to live?

"You may be through with Economic History – but it is not through with you!"

2

MATERIALS FROM CHESTER WHITNEY WRIGHT'S COURSE, ECONOMIC HISTORY OF THE UNITED STATES, ECONOMICS 320, UNIVERSITY OF CHICAGO, SPRING 1934

Introductory Comments

Wright begins the course by saying, in effect, that economic history is the history of economic development, particularly its effect on the business of making a living. He distinguishes that view from the economic interpretation of history and from the economic aspects of political history, i.e. the effect of economic development on political history.

Unlike the concluding lecture in 220, Wright now specifies economic laws. Wright presents economic laws as a matter of conditions and influence rather than in a deterministic manner. The laws he identifies (as having been operative) are not homogeneous in nature but are many and wide ranging.

Economic laws seem to have been influencing our economic life – instances:

> Comparative costs; modified quantity theory of money, Gresham's law, optimum theory of population, marginal productivity, diminishing returns, decreasing costs and resulting monopoly, diminishing utility, supply and demand, balance of payments, division of labor and size of market.

He then takes up the relation of legislation to economic principles. As already indicated, the success or failure of legislation raises questions concerning the criterion(ia) of success or failure, or of objective – actual or ostensible, and concerning the alternatives thereto that might have been followed. Notwithstanding these and other issues, Wright provides a list of legislation that he deemed to have failed because they ran "contrary to economic principles." The reasons he presents for the failures are few and simple:

> American legislation typically ignores the economics of the problem – through idealism, ignorance, <u>haste</u>.
> –Seldom has our legislation ever been based on a thorough-going economic analysis.

– as if economics was a set of doctrines immediately applicable to policy in such a manner that they yielded one and only one solution to a problem. Surely Wright was aware of the complaint – voiced by economists and non-economists alike – that economics did not yield such solutions.

Class notes
Econ. 320
Professor Chester Wright

Bibliography

[Editor's note: This list is in longhand, presumably dictated by Wright.
Corrected titles are given, plus added information in square brackets.]

Journals

Supplement to Economic Journal
Journal of Economic and Business History – Best for U.S. – now defunct
Economic History Review
Revue d'Histoire economique et social (begun 1908) – Best for France
Annals d'Histoire economique et social (begun 1929)
Zeitschrift für sozial- und wirtschaftsgeschichte [1893–1900] (continuation of
Zeitschrift für Nationalökonomie [?: 1929–])

Encyclopedias

Encyclopedia of the Social Sciences
Palgrave's Dictionary of Political Economy – out of date (revised edition 1925)
Conrad's Handwortsbuch für Staatswissenschaft (4th edition 1929)

Maps

Phillips – (1901) "Library of Congress list of Maps of U.S." [Philip Lee Phillips,
A List of Maps of America in the Library of Congress, 1901]
Library of Congress – "List of Geographical Atlases"
Paullin – Atlas of the Historical Geography of the U.S., 1932 [Charles Oscar
Paullin]

Bibliographies

Channing, Hart and Turner – "Guide to the Study and Reading of American
History" [Edward Channing, Albert Bushnell Hart, and Frederick Jackson
Turner; 1912]
Hasse – Index of Economic Material in Documents of the States of the United
States [Adelaide Rosalia Hasse; numerous individual states, varying years]
Statistical Abstract of the U.S. (begins 1878)
Commerce year book (U.S. Department of Commerce)
Census – (especially 1880 with historical material)
Hockett – Introduction to Research in American History [Homer Carey Hockett;
1931]

Coulter – Guide to Historical Bibliographies [Edith Margaret Coulter; 1927]
Allison, Fay, and Shearer – A Guide to Historical Literature [William Henry Allison, Sidney Bradshaw Fay, Augustus Hunt Shearer and Henry Robinson Shipman, eds.; 1931]
Sabin – Dictionary of Books relating to America begun 1870–1891 – finished through S. – Best thing – and unique. [Joseph Sabin]
Library of Congress Cards
Union Catalogue
Evans, American Bibliography, 1629–1820, 8 volumes, in process, listed chronologically. [Charles Evans; 14 volumes, 1903–1959]
Bradford – Bibliographical Manual of American History, 5 volumes, 1917 – useful for documents of states, cities, towns (Cf. Index, vol. 5)

Biography
Encyclopedia of American Biography – Appleton
Dictionary of American Biography

Textbooks
Bogart – Economic History of the American People – most satisfactory from point of view of economists. [Ernest Ludlow Bogart; 1931]
An Economic History of the United States – elementary. [Ernest Ludlow Bogart; 1929]
Lippincott – Economic Development of the United States – looks interpretative, factual, dry. [Isaac Lippincott; 2nd edition, 1927; 3rd edition 1933]
Jennings – A History of Economic Progress in the United States – tremendous amount of facts. [Walter Wilson Jennings; 1926]
*Kirkland – A History of American Economic Life (1932) – readable, excellent companion volume to an economics text – many novel problems. [Edward Chase Kirkland]
*Faulkner – American Economic History – a historian, who succeeds fairly well in meeting needs of economist. [Harold Underwood Faulkner; 1928?]
*Carman – Social and Economic History of the United States (volumes 1 and 2, down to 1875-). [Harry James Carman; 1930–1934]
Bolles – Industrial History of the United States, 1879. [Albert S. Bolles]

Political Histories
American Nation Series – 30 volumes, index volume – Hart, editor (good bibliographical chapters – pretended to cover economic history – didn't succeed. [Albert Bushnell Hart, editor; 28 volumes, 1904–1918]
Social and Economic Forces in American History – an extract of those chapters dealing with economics. [1913]

History of American Life – 12 volumes – Schlesinger and Fox, editors – the new history – broadened – civilization. [Mark C. Carnes, general editor; Arthur M. Schlesinger, consulting editor]

The Rise of American Civilization – Beards [Charles A. Beard and Mary Beard; 1930]

McMaster, J. B. – History of the People of United States, 1789–1860, 8 volumes – first use of newspapers – mass of material wretchedly organized. [John Bach McMaster, A History of the People of the United States during Lincoln's Administration, 1 volume, 1927]

Channing, editor – A History of the United States – 6 volumes, through Civil War – scholarly, remarkable. [Edward Channing, 1905-]

Rhodes – History of the United States from the Compromise of 1850 [8 volumes, 1910–]

Chronicles of America – Yale University Press – 50 volumes – popular, but written by scholars, brief.

Pageant of America – Yale University Press, 15 volumes – all pictures, maps, transcripts.

Colonial Period

Chitwood – A History of Colonial America, 1931. [Oliver Perry Chitwood]

Journeyman – Epoch Series on Colonial Period

Greene, E. – The Foundations of American Nationality [Evarts Boutell Greene; 1922]

Jefferson and Madison

Henry Adams – History of the United States of America during the administrations of Jefferson and Madison [9 volumes, 1921 edition]

Beard – Economic Origins of Jeffersonian Democracy [Charles A. Beard; 1915]

Revolution and After

Nevins – The American States During and After the Revolution, 1775–1789 [Allan Nevins; 1924]

1860 and After

Hacker – [Louis M. Hacker and Benjamin B. Kendrick, The United States since 1865; 1932]

Readings

Bogart and Thompson [Ernest Ludlow Bogart and Charles Manfred Thompson, The Industrial State, 1870–1893; 1920]

Flugel and Faulkner – begins with 1780. [Felix Flügel and Harold U. Faulkner, Readings in the Economic and Social History of the United States, 1929]

Callender – ends with 1860. [Guy Stevens Callender, Selections from the Economic History of the United States, 1765–1860; 1909]

Miscellaneous
   Simons – Social Forces in American History (Marxian). [Algie Martin Simons; 1925]
   Semple – American History and its Geographical Conditions [Ellen Churchill Semple; 1903]

Economic History
   Colonial Period
      Weeden – Economic and Social History of New England, 2 volumes – poor [William Babcock Weeden; 1890]
      Bruce – Economic History of Virginia in the 17th Century, 2 volumes. [Philip Alexander Bruce; 1895]
      Osgood – The American Colonies in the 17th Century, 3 volumes [Herbert Levi Osgood, The American Colonies in the Seventeenth Century 1904–1097, 1930]
      Osgood – [Herbert Levi Osgood, The American Colonies in the Eighteenth Century, 1 volume, 1924]
      C. M. Andrews – The Colonial Period [of American History; 4 volumes, 1934–]
      Adams, J. T. – The History of New England, 3 volumes [James Truslow Adams; 1921, 1923, 1926]
   Colonization
      Bolton and Marshall – The Colonization of North America, 1492–1783 [Herbert Eugene Bolton and Thomas Maitland Marshall; 1920]
      Beer – Origins of Colonial Policy – 1500–1660 [George Louis Beer, The Origins of the British Colonial System, 1578–1660, 1908]
            The Old Colonial System, 1660–1754 [1913]
            British Colonial Policy – 1754–1765 [1907]
         [Arrow from Beer to under J. T. Adams, 3 lines above.]
      Cambridge History of the British Empire, volume 1 – best book on British imperial background.
      Donnan – Documents Illustrative of the History of the Slave Trade to America – 3 volumes. [Elizabeth Donnan; 4 volumes, 1930–1935]
      Bond – The Quit-rent System in the American Colonies. [1919]
   West Indies
      Pitman – The Development of the British West Indies, 1700–1763 [Frank Wesley Pitman, 1917]

Ragatz – The Fall of the Planter Class in the British Colonies, 1763–1833 [Lowell J. Ragatz, 1928]

Ragatz – A Guide for the Study of British Caribbean History, 1763–1834 [Lowell J. Ragatz, 1932]

May – Histoire économique de la Martinique [Louis Philippe May; 1930]

Satineau – Histoire de la Guadaloupe sous l'ancien régime, 1635–1789 [Maurice Satineau, 1928]

Revolution

C. M. Andrews – The Colonial Background of the American Revolution [Charles M. Andrews; 1924]

Schlesinger – The Colonial Merchants and the American Revolution, 1763–1776 [Arthur M. Schlesinger, 1918]

Van Tyne – Causes of the War of Independence [presumably, The American Revolution, 1776–1783; 1905; Claude Halstead Van Tyne]

Egerton – The Causes and Character of the American Revolution [Hugh E. Egerton; 1923]

Jameson – The American Revolution Considered as a Social Movement [John Franklin Jameson; 1926]

Sumner – Financier and the Finances of the American Revolution [William Graham Sumner; 1892]

Nevins – The American States During and After the Revolution, 1775–1789 [Allan Nevins; 1924]

Constitution

Beard – An Economic Interpretation of the Constitution of the United States [Charles A. Beard; 1913]

Farrand – The Framing of the Constitution of the United States [Max Farrand; 1913]

1789–1860

Pitkin – A Statistical View of the Commerce of the United States of America (1833 edition) [Timothy Pitkin; 1835]

Niles Register, 1811–1849 (indispensable)

Hunt's – Merchants Magazine 1839–1870 [Edward Hatton, The Merchant's Magazine, or Trades-man's Treasury]

DuBois – Review 1846–1870 (in South) [James Dunwoody Brownson DeBow,et al, Debow's Review: Agricultural, Commercial, Industrial Progress and Resources, 1846–1880]

[James Dunwoody Brownson DeBow, The Industrial Resources, etc., of the Southern and Western States . . ., 1853]

Bankers [word indecipherable] 1846–1870 [?]

Civil War

Fite – Social and Industrial Conditions in the North during the Civil War [Emerson David Fite; 1930]

Schwab – The Confederate States of America, 1861–1865; A Financial and Industrial History of the South During the Civil War [John Christopher Schwab; 1901]

Reconstruction Era and After

Commercial and Financial Chronicle, 1865 on

The United States Industrial Commission, 1900, 19 volumes, volume 19 – a summary

Durand – American Industry and Commerce, 1930 [Edward Dana Durand]

Later

Clark – Industrial Activity during the World War [?]

Crowell and Wilson – The Giant Hand: Our Mobilization and Control of Industry and Natural Resources, 1917–1918 [In series, "How America Went to War"] [Benedict Crowell and Robert F. Wilson; 1921]

Willoughby – Government Organization in War Time and After. Carnegie Foundation Series. [William Frank Willoughby; 1919]

Recent Economic Changes in the United States, 1929. [Recent Social Changes in the United States since the War . . .; edited by William F. Ogburn; 1929]

Hunt – Audit of the U.S. [Presumably, An Audit of America: A Summary of Recent Economic Changes in the United States; 1930; Edward Eyre Hunt]

Recent Social Trends in the United States, 1933

Economic History by Topics

(1) Immigration and Population Growth

1900 – A Century of Population Growth – Summary by Census

William Paul Dillingham, corporate author – Reports of the Immigration Commission – United States Immigration Commission – summarized in two volumes [1907–1910; 1911]

Stephenson – A History of American Immigration, 1820–1924 [George M. Stephenson; 1926]

Jenks and Lauck – The Immigration Problem [Jeremiah W. Jenks and W. Jett Lauck; 1917]

Abbott – Historical Aspects of the Immigration Problem, 1926 [Edith Abbott]

(2) Westward Movement

Turner and Merk – List of References on the History of the West [Frederick Jackson Turner and Frederick Merk; revised edition, 1922]

Turner – The Frontier in American History [Frederick Jackson Turner; 1920]

Paxson – History of the American Frontier, 1763–1893 [Frederic L. Paxson; 1924]

    Paxson – The Last American Frontier (popular) Frederic L. Paxson, 1910]

Coman – Economic Beginnings of the Far West [Katharine Coman; 1912, two volumes]

Riegel – America Moves West, 1930 [Robert Edgar Riegel]

Webb, W. P. – The Great Plains, 1931 [Walter Prescott Webb]

Thwaites, Reuben Gold – Early Western Travels (32 volumes – good index) [1904–1907]

Tuckerman – America and Her Commentators, 1864 [Henry T. Tuckerman]

Nevins – American Social History as Recorded by British Travellers [Allan Nevins, ed.; 1923] (extracts from travels)

(3) Transportation and Communication

Meyer, Balthasar H., and Caroline E. MacGill, History of Transportation in the United States before 1860, 1917 (a definitive work)

Ringwalt – Development of Transportation Systems in the United States, 1888 (technique emphasized)

Cleveland and Power – Railroad Promotion and Capitalization in the United States [Frederick A. Cleveland and Fred W. Powell, 1909] (early railroads)

Hulbert, Archer Butler – Historic Highways of America, 16 vols.,1902–1905 (good topical study)

Dunbar – A History of Travel in America, 4 vols., 1915 [Seymour Dunbar] (Illustrated, popular)

Riegel, Robert Edgar – The Story of the Western Railroads from 1852 through the Reign of the Giants, 1926

The American Transportation Problem, 1933 [Harold G. Moulton]

Moulton and Hardy [Probably, Harold G. Moulton, The American Transportation Problem, 1933]

Kelly – United States Postal Policy, 1931 [Clyde Kelly]

(4) Agriculture

Bradley – Title Index to Publications of the United States Department of Agriculture, 1901–1925, Journal of Agricultural History, 1929 [Mary A. Bradley, compiler]

Bailey – Cyclopedia of American Agriculture [L. H. Bailey, editor; 1907–1909]

Schmidt – Topical Studies and References on the Economic History of American Agriculture, [Louis Bernard Schmidt; 1919]

Schmidt, Louis Bernard; and Earle Dudley Ross, eds. – Readings in the Economic History of American Agriculture, 1925

Bidwell and Falconer – History of Agriculture in the Northern United States, 1620–1860 [1925]

Gray, Lewis Cecil – History of Agriculture in the Southern United States to 1860 [1933]

United States Department of Agriculture – Year Books – since 1860, especially 1921–1926

Colonial:

Carrier – The Beginnings of Agriculture in America [Lyman Carrier; 1923]

Anonymous – American Husbandry, 1775, 2 volumes

Movements:

Buck – The Granger Movement [Solon J. Buck; 1913]

Hicks – The Populist Revolt [John D. Hicks; 1931]

Wiest – Agricultural Organization in the United States [Edward Wiest; 1923]

Lands:

Hibbard – A History of the Public Land Policies [Benjamin H. Hibbard; 1924]

Treat – The National Land System, 1785–1820 [Payson J. Treat; 1910]

Donaldson – The Public Domain, 1884 [Thomas C. Donaldson]

Sakolski – The Great American Land Bubble [Aaron M. Sakolski; 1932]

Mines, etc.:

[James Elliott Defebaugh, History of the Lumber Industry of America, 1906]

Ise – The United States Oil Policy [John Ise; 1926]

Rickard – A History of American Mining [Thomas A. Rickard; 1932]

(5) Manufacturing

Clark – History of Manufactures in the United States (3 volumes – definitive) [Victor S. Clark; 1929]

Bishop – A History of American Manufactures from 1608 to 1860 – 3 volumes, 1864 [J. Leander; 2 volumes, 1861–1864]

Cole – The American Wool Manufacture, 1926, 2 volumes – best case study [Arthur Harrison Cole]

[Frank A.] Southard – American Industry in Europe, 1931

(6) Labor

Commons – History of Labour in the United States (best – on organized labor) [John R. Commons et al, 4 vols., 1918–1935]

– A Documentary History of American Industrial Society, (society, labor, slavery) [John R. Commons et al, 1910–1911, 11 volumes]

Jernegan – Laboring and Dependent Classes in Colonial America, 1607–1783 [Marcus Wilson Jernegan; 1931]

Ware – The Industrial Worker, 1840–1860 [Norman J. Ware; 1924]
   – The Labor Movement in the United States, 1860–1895 [Norman J. Ware; 1929]

Phillips – American Negro Slavery [Ulrich Bonnell Phillips; 1918]

United States Bureau of Labor Statistics – Bulletin 495 – History of Wages in the United States from Colonial Times to 1933 [1934]

(7) Trade and Commerce

Johnson, et al – History of Domestic and Foreign Commerce of the United States, 2 volumes (best) [Emory R. Johnson et al; 2 volumes; 1915]

Day – History of Commerce of the United States (good) [Clive Day, A History of Commerce, 1922]

Frederick – The Development of American Commerce, 1932 [John H. Frederick]

(8) Finance

Taussig – The Tariff History of the United States [Frank W. Taussig; 8th edition, 1931]; Some Aspects of the Tariff Question [Frank W. Taussig, 3rd enlarged edition, 1931]

Stanwood – American Tariff Controversies in the Nineteenth Century [Edward Stanwood, 2 volumes, 1903]

Williams – Economic Foreign Policy of the United States, 1929 [Benjamin Harrison Williams]

Dewey – Financial History of the United States (good bibliography) [Davis R. Dewey, 11th edition, 1931]

Sumner – History of Banking in the United States (to 1860 – rich detail) William Graham Sumner et al, A History of Banking in All the Leading Nations, vol. 1, The United States, by William Graham Sumner, 1896

Review of Economic Statistics – Harvard

Warren and Pearson – Prices [George F. Warren and Frank A. Pearson; 1933]

Thorp – Business Annals [Willard L. Thorp, 1926]

Miller – Banking Theories in the United States before 1860 [Harry E. Miller; 1927]

Bolles – The Financial History of the United States from 1861 to 1885, 3 volumes [Albert S. Bolles; 1 volume; 1886]

Persons – Forecasting Business Cycles, 1931 [Warren M. Persons]

Beckhart – The New York Money Market, 4 volumes (good history) [Benjamin H. Beckhart et al.; 1931–1932]

Miscellaneous

Merriam – A History of American Political Theories [Charles E. Merriam; 1910]

– American Political Ideas [1920]

Hillquit – History of Socialism in the United States [Morris Hillquit; 1910]

W. I. King – National Income and its Distribution [Willford Isbell King, The Wealth and Income of the People of the United States, 1915; The National Income and its Purchasing power, 1930]

– Income in the United States, Its Amount and Distribution, 1920 [Willford I. King et al.; 2 volumes; 1921–1922]

Federal Trade Commission – Report on National Wealth and Income, 1927

Institute for Public Service – Monographs

[Lloyd Milton Short] – The Development of National Administrative Organization in the United States [1923]

*Kaempffert – A Popular History of American Invention [Waldemar Kaempffert; 1924]

Sweet – The Story of Religions in America, 1930 [William Warren Sweet]

Rowe – The History of Religion in the United States [Henry K. Rowe; 1924]

Johnson – American Economic Thought in the Seventeenth Century, 1932

Seligman – Essays in Economics, Chapter IV [Edwin R. A. Seligman; 1925]

Cambridge History of American Literature, 4 volumes, [William P. Trent, et alia, editors] 1933, Chapter on American Economics

*Lynd – Middletown: A Study in Contemporary American Culture [Robert S. Lynd;1929]

*Williamson – The American Hotel, 1930 [Jefferson Williamson]

*Parrington – Main Currents in American Thought, 3 volumes [Vernon Parrington; 1930]

[Francis R.] Packard – The History of Medicine in the United States, 1901]

Talmadge – The Story of Architecture in America [Thomas E. Talmadge; 1927]

Manchester – Four Centuries of Sports in America, 1490–1890 [Herbert Manchester; 1931]

*Earle – Two Centuries of Costume in America, MDCXX-MDCCCXX [Alice Morse Earle; 2 volumes; 1903]

McClennan, E. – Historic Dress in America, 1607–1800 [McClennan, Elisabeth; 1904] [Historic Dress in America, 1800–1870; 1910]

Howard – Public Health Administration and the Natural History of Disease in Baltimore, Maryland, 1797–1920 [William Travis Howard; 1924]

Taussig and Joslyn – American Business Leaders, 1932 [Frank William Taussig and Carl S. Joslyn]

Munford, L. – The Golden Day: A Study in American Experience and Culture [Lewis Mumford; 1926]

Beer, T. – The Mauve Decade. [Thomas Beer; 1926]

Siegfried, A. – America Comes of Age, A French Analysis [André Siegfried; 1927]

Ostrander' s Lecture Notes on Economics 320

Detailed study of small area vs. general study of whole history with aim of making it significant from the point of view of "economic history" with social and cultural fringes.

First paper, due April 11th: "What are the main factors or developments making possible a higher standard of living for the American people in 1900 than existed in 1793?"

–Economic history is primarily concerned (just as economics is concerned!) primarily with the business of making a living.

–I.e. with the evolution of the economic order towards a more efficient and more complete satisfying of their wants.

–Understanding this process gives human significance of the mass of historical facts.

Second paper, due April 18th: "What ought to be the objectives and the specific content of the study of economic history?"

Reading:

Clapham, "The Study of Economic History''

Unwin, "Studies," pp. 3–36

Economic History Review, Vol. I, Gras, Ashley (articles)

Encyclopedia of the Social Sciences, Vol. V, Economics, "The Historical School," "The Institutionalist School"

American Historical Review, March 1932 – Homan – The Institutionalists

Bury, Selected Essays, pp. 3–59

Encyclopedia Britannica – "History" – (Shotwell)

[Richard H. Tawney, "The Study of Economic History," Economica, vol. 13, February 1933, pp. 1–21];

[John Bates Clark, "The Future of Economic History," Quarterly Journal of Economics, Quarterly Journal of Economics, vol. 13, October 1898, pp. 1–14]

[William J. Ashley, "The Study of Economic History," Quarterly Journal of Economics, vol. 7, January 1893, pp. 115–136]

Seligman – "The Economic Interpretation of History"
Sée – "The Economic Interpretation of History"
Bober – "Karl Marx's Interpretation of History," Part 5, pp. 265–346.
Matthews – "Spiritual Interpretation of History," Chapters 1, 2, 3

What effect has scarcity of labor and scarcity of capital had on the economic development of U.S. – relative to the European situation.

Historians treat economic development from point of view of its effect on political history – this is hardly "economic history – it is economic aspects of political history.

Economists treat economic development from point of view of:
    a- Their effects on the business of making a living – functional point of view.
    b- [incomplete]

Historian is in the stronger position than economist to discuss the economic interpretation of history – but this is not economic history.

Scarcity of Labor – its effects.
    –Introduction of slavery.
    –Indentured servants.
    –Laws and customs holding workers in industry – failed.
    –Breakdown of apprentice system and of efforts to establish guild system.
    –Kept wages high – standard of living high.
    –Prevented organization of an organized labor movement.
    –Large immigration – mixture of nationalities.
    –Great mobility of labor – less stratification.
    –Spirit of Independence – great influence on Democracy and political freedom.
        –Competition between colonies and states to attract workers leading to greater religious freedom (Pennsylvania) and political freedom (Virginia).
        –In 20th century immigrants given franchise by Western states before they became citizens of U.S.
    –Delayed introduction of manufacturing
    –Conservation of labor in agriculture – extensive "[words indecipherable]]"
    –Promoted invention of labor saving machinery.
    –Made the development of manufacturing more rapid, when it did come.
    [Brace in margin encompassing preceding three items.]
1– Economic laws which have been operating to influence and shape the economic development of the U.S. – instances.
2– Legislation that has proved unwise or futile because it ran contrary to working out of economic principles – instances.

3- Reasons for contention that economic forces and conditions are <u>particularly</u> important to an understanding of the political history of the U.S.?

What turned New England from colonial economy to an industrial one?
  –Less scarcity of labor and capital.
  –Availability of a large market – in West, particularly important with new machine technique.
 –Characteristics of American industry to this day were set by the early scarcity of labor.
 –Influences in development of a merchant marine.
 –Affecting character and direction of our farming, trade.
  –It becomes chiefly complementary to Europe, manufacturing [goods] imported, now materials exported.
  –As labor becomes abundant – we export manufacturing to non-European countries, import raw materials from non-European countries.
 –Social reactions – greater democracy, less class stratification and struggle.

Rising standard of living:
  –What determines the productivity of a country at any time?
    –Factors entering this – quantity, quality.
    –Changes in these factors.
    –All institutions in so far as they affect economic life.

–<u>Total Wealth</u> –	1790	$\frac{1}{2}$ billion
	1900	89 billion
	1920	320 billion
<u>Per capita Wealth</u> –	1790	$40
	1850	300
	1900	1165
	1922	2900
<u>National Income</u> –	1860	4.4 billion
[date missing]		14.0
	1928	89.0
		(52 m in 1913)
<u>Per capita National Income</u> –	1860	$140
	1913	368
	1928	452 (1913 $)

(Such figures only suggestive.)

Factors of Production – Natural Resources
 –Territory – additions to it.

–Louisiana Purchase – tripled area of country – not resources.

–Quantity of national resources was being depleted – lumber, fur-bearing animals, coal, oil, iron ore.

–Capital – cumulative effect of increase of capital.

   –<u>Saveable fund</u> being increased by all developments increasing per-capita income.

      –What of "desire to save"?

        –Education – institutions making saving more attractive.

        –Institutions protecting property rights.

        –Absence of <u>serious</u> burden of destructive expenditures – war – armaments.

        –Absolute amount of saveable fund was rising – proportion going to expenditure probably was constant – i.e. rising absolute quantity of expenditure.

–Improvement in quantity of goods and services.

–Improvement in quality of goods and services – largely due to technique and invention.

Labor – growth of population – small leisure class.

   –Long hours, few holidays, long working period.

   –<u>Spirit of work</u> – no social taboo on labor.

   –Few crafts or skilled hand trades.

   –High level of intelligence among workers.

Business management

      –High level of entrepreneurial ability – taking best ability in country.

      –A product of lack of taboo on work – and of <u>great opportunity</u>.

      –Unrivaled chances to make money.

      –Enterprising, active, ambitious, willing to take risks which usually didn't turn out to be risks.

      –General policy of laissez-faire.

      Development of corporate form of organization – scientific management.

Developments

   –Improvements in transportation.

   –Retail vending, institutions.

   –Financial institutions.

   –Development of banking – stock exchange.

   –Risk taking institutions.

   –Increasing mobility of labor and capital.

Political Institutions

   –Development of government activities.

Economic development of the rest of the world.
  –Supplying us with capital, raw materials, markets.
Banking as a better means of organization and exchange.

Term papers
  –Standard of living in 1770, or 1860
    –A subject left out of most economic history textbooks.
    –But study of economics and economic history is primarily directed towards
    the progressive changes in the standard of living.
    –Difficulty of understanding what the standard of living was, in a former age.
    –The concrete elements of former standards of living – both goods
    and services:
      –Housing and furnishings.
      –Food and clothing.
      –Leisure time-amusement.
      –Government services and goods (1770 and 1860).
    –Enjoyed by the masses.

Economic history – can be a series of mental gymnastics – or it can bear out the
one fundamental objective of improving human welfare and having significance
for human value.
Economic laws seem to have been influencing our economic life – instances:
  –Comparative costs; modified quantity theory of money. Gresham's law,
  optimum theory of population, marginal productivity, diminishing returns,
  decreasing costs and resulting monopoly, diminishing utility, supply and
  demand, balance of payments, division of labor and size of market.

[In margin at top of page: (Shift of a civilization from Old to New World – with
slight vested interests interested in perpetuating old institutions.)]

Legislation failing because running contrary to economic principles.
  –Anti-trust legislation (lack of skill).
  –Colonial attempts to promote silk culture in Carolinas.
    –Efforts to fix wages – to force men to follow crafts.
  –Public land policy applied without change to arid and grazing land.
  –Missouri Compromise – failure – slave vs. free labor as one system.
  –Attempts to bolster up our merchant marine.
  –Molasses Act.
  –Attempts to fix interest rate.
  –Civil War law against speculation (and in Revolution).

American legislation typically ignores the economics of the problem – through idealism, ignorance, haste.

–Seldom has our legislation ever been based on a thorough-going economic analysis.

Cheney – Law and History, American Historical Review, 1929.
Encyclopedia of the Social Sciences, vol 10, pp. 216–220 – Historical Materialism.

Paper [Assignment], Wednesday, April 25
"Explain the so-called Materialism of the American people." Question it.
–Economic activities of getting a living consuming an undue proportion of time – as contrasted with European civilizations at same time.
-a- Earlier stage of economic development.
-b- Masses of all countries – always are materialistic – our civilization pointed its culture to these – no upper class, not important enough to have a "representative" culture.

Objectives of Economic History
–Stigler [This must have been a statement by George Stigler, a fellow student in the course.] – History not a science – no systematic generalizations, no laws of historical development – multiple connections.
–Is essential – to what? – to almost every field of human activity. –Is a tool (objectively, impartially) scientific.
–As a social phenomenon is a discipline or tool to be adapted to each application.
–As economic history:
a/ Isolates a fairly definite set of data – uses a technical equipment – specialization.
b/ Complement and corrective to economic theory (with statistics). Institutionalism.
–Content:
(I) Institutional background.
(1) Political activities.
a- Regulator of economic activity
Social philosophy – interests.
b- State enterprises.
c- Fiscal.
d- Relation of society to consumption
e- Distribution of wealth.
(2) Legal backgrounds
(3) Social factors

    (4) Physical background (resources, geography)

    (5) Place in world economy (and place of economic activity in man's
    life [philosophy.

  (II) Economic organization

    (1) Resources (population, land, minerals, etc.)

    (2) Organization:

       a- Form of enterprise

         –Legal nature of business unit.

         –Size (technical economic) of unit

       b- Economic institutions

         –Banking, transportation

         –Credit, marketing

         –Labor

    (3) The individual

    –Economic life

    –Classes – basis

Cournot – in history, chance is a factor.

  –Sought long time forces, influences – generalizations.

  –I.e. a philosophy of history – in a limited sense.

Wright – a key to, or underlying thread of, history.

    –As Unwin – man's efforts to obtain greater freedom.

      –At least dominant groups at any time strive for something.

      –Progress can be watched, or we can fail to see it – different from
      determination to trace progress.

   –First generalization – is specialization, division of labor.

   –Second generalization – increased cooperation between man and man.

  –Man's efforts to obtain greater freedom in so far as that was concerned with
  material resources and welfare.

    –Western civilization seems to have chosen (?) the way of a maximum
    dependence on material aspects of the full life.

      –Without care for contemplation – standard of living raised in the same
      way as rent – by material goods.

–Economic History – training for citizenship or understanding of present economic
order – how it has evolved, problems raised.

    –A question of rise of efficiency.

    –The way a people has set out to solve its problem of making a living. (?)

    –Way the individual has solved his problem of getting a living.

    –Cultural purpose.

–Understanding one's self – as a product of economic environment.
–Understanding of economic backgrounds – for economic theorists.
  –Background of theory – and its assumptions.
  –Theory suggests the facts to be looked for.
  –Through history one can best understand the present evolution of society.
  –The similarities of the evolution: and the dissimilarities due to different environments.
    –Institutionalism – to some extent every economist studies institutions – and possibly should do it more than he has.
      –But this no excuse for remolding the study of economics – at least not until the "institutionalists" have put forth something positive and constructive.
Content – by Wright.
  –The way man has gone about the business of getting a living.
  –Natural resources.
  –Population.
  –Cultural heritage.
  –Institutions – Economic organizations.
  –Processes of econ[omy] – conditions determining: (a) the total; and (b) the distribution of, the national income.
  –Agriculture, transportation, manufacturing, building, personal services – production.
  –Inventions, science, quality of production.
    –How far go into the technological side of machinery? (Tool-making machines)
    –General and scientific development is probably more important! – as technological side of agriculture.
  –Content of economic history is different for the economic historian and for the course given to students.
  –Exchange-transportation, marketing.
  –Distribution of product to resources.
    –Orthodox division.
    –Actual divisions – comprising the whole complex of economic conflicts.
    –Economic struggle in history is a struggle for income.
      –Social desirableness of distribution.
  –Non-economic institutions.
  –Introduction of world conditions and events.
    Guess that there has not been any great percentage change in the distribution of income to classes or groups since the colonial period.

–Why so large a predominance of economic aspects in U.S. political history?

–What reason is there for the evident attention paid to the economic sides of U.S. history and politics:

–Historians have stressed this side of history – the enthusiasts of economic approach in history are largely, and were first, here.

–Religious freedom and religious unity took that aspect away from a large place in our history – sects fought themselves, but no one tried to dominate.

–Lack of a King, or of a ruling class of political, hereditary, family, religious, military origin left the economic and material elements in life and government – as the most important.

–Opening up of a new continent – economic aspects of life predominate – settlers looked to advancing their standard of living.

–Our political life was lived entirely after the change in economic life due to industrialism – whole world tending towards economic predominance in politics.

–Lack of any necessity of interest in political or diplomatic maneuvers – no political rivals – plenty of resources.

–We had already gained by our Constitutions (state and national) most of what other countries fought for on political lines.

–Most racial issues solved by amalgamation and the "melting pot." (But did racial diversity stop growth of a national culture?)

–Due to rapid development – a family had to continue its work, or fall behind.

Paper [Assignment], May 2: Enumerate the ways in which the common man could advance himself economically have been increased, or decreased, since 1800.

–I.e. what is chance to get ahead?

–Not to weigh the balance – but enumerate the positive and negative influences.

Hadley – Economic Problems of Democracy.

Adams – Ideals in American History

Materialism – by Wright

Non-materialism

I. Stressing cultural [activities]

(a) Simple life – minimum of material goods. Asceticism.

(b) Rich – requiring many material goods.

II. Stressing non-cultural activities
   (a) Idleness.
   (b) Sensuous pleasure (requiring wealth).
–All four found lacking by foreign travelers – but stress put on untutored approach to arts.
–Activities so exclusivity devoted to business.
–I.b-lacking most.
–Cultural arts lacked most.
–But <u>other</u> ideals not lacking – humanitarian, social equality, democracy, liberty.
–Critics came from upper classes – but <u>they criticized upper class activities</u> – for lacking in pursuits of a well endowed leisure.
  –Such was the <u>product of a social environment</u>.
    –In Europe – Christian hangover of asceticism.
      –Chances to enjoy fruits of material wealth not many.
      –Wars – Protestant Ethic.
    –Commerce – Far East – New World.
      –Opportunities for accumulating wealth by <u>business</u> methods grew (as separate from plunder, exploitation).
      –In spite of faith – upper classes sought material goods.
    –Old World <u>caste</u> attitude towards business – breaking down slowly.
      –Overemphasizing the proportion of leisure time spent in cultural pursuits.
      –Their culture required many material goods – though they did not enter the <u>business</u> of getting them.
    –In America:
    –Selective process in immigration-
      –Adventure, political and religious.
      –But mainly lower class artisans with economic motive first – improve their position.
    –Abnormally augmented population – from lower classes.
      –Never have more than one-half of adults of country been of native parentage.
    –<u>Freedom</u> of initiative and economic opportunity.
    –Cheap, valuable resources – virgin land.
    –Democratic spirit – spirit of enterprise.
      –Weakening of aristocracy – absence of castes.
    –Every attraction into business.
    –No wars or destruction of property.
    –Lack of stability. [sic]

–Great preponderance of <u>rural</u> element (arts thrive in urban concentration (?).

–<u>No</u> caste in country – isolation.

–Excessive resort to business.

–Lack of resort to leisure time pursuits of cultural interest.

–American materialism was a result of environment.

    –Was "American" only because this new country gave full play to such features. [Single vertical line in margin alongside preceding two sentences; another such line alongside next sentence:]

[Assignment:]"Explain the factors responsible for the <u>rise</u> and decline of the so-called laissez-faire, in the U.S."

    Cf. Keynes, End of Laissez-Faire

    Hoover, H., American Individualism

    Materialism was not inherently American, it was the 19th century – which a series of circumstances brought about first in this country. It is evidenced in older countries – since the end of the Middle Ages – but held back.

–Economic interpretation of history has tended to be <u>applied</u> to political history as already written – problem of causation in history?!

    –Individual action – where are influences to stop, before they reach the primeval slime.

        –<u>Immediate</u> causes; secondary, tertiary, etc.

        –Which is more complex, near or very distant causes?

            –Economic interests in immediate cause – supposed motivation, <u>actual</u> not.

            –Other factors entering into more remote cause.

    –Is there such a thing as <u>cause</u>, in the singular – in social sciences.

–<u>Any</u> number of <u>phases</u> of the interpreting of <u>history</u> – the record of man <u>in</u> his environment – physical and human environment.

    –We <u>usually</u> consider man as the more active factor.

        –Consider him in all his activities.

    –The economist merely chooses <u>those</u> of his activities which are economic.

–Economic interpretation of history is just as important as the economic activities of man – no more. F. T. O.

    –Useful to stress the economic for certain purposes.

    –Justified by the facts of our lives which are so much spent in getting a living.

[Assignments] Wednesday, May 9: Enumerate the various ways in which religious, nationalistic and democratic ideals have reacted on American economic history.

Recent Social Trends, Introduction, 9, 10, 17, 18; Chapters 1, 2, 5, 16, 25, 26, 29
Ogburn, Social Change, pp. 43–89, 146–169, 200–280

[Assignments] Wednesday, May 16: Economic group efforts to affect the distribution of wealth and income, 1789–1860 – describe the variety of economic groups struggling to increase their income and wealth.
Economic history is a record of changes in the national income, and how it is distributed.

Effect of religion on economic life of U.S.
  –Freedom of worship – brought immigrants.
  –The Protestant Ethics; its effects.
    –Wright proposes Brentano's approach to this as more realistic than Weber's
      –Rise of capitalism reacted on Protestantism and Catholicism.
      "Der Wirtschaftender Mensch in der Geschichte" – [Lujo] Brentano
  –Ideal of service – an offshoot of Christianity – into business and advertising.
  –Connection of Protestantism with democracy, of lack of religious authoritarianism.
  –Religion was the main mover for education.
    –In colleges for ministers.
    –In Protestant belief in education.
    –Though this became political, in 19th century.
  –Religion and laissez-faire-individualism.
  –Temperance movement as a result of religion – its effect on economics.
  –Denominational rivalry and its effect.
  –Religion and the missionary and the frontier.
  –Lack of State (Church-State) control of universities, hospitals, etc. – usual to Catholic Church.
  –Development of Newfoundland fisheries – and religion.
  –Absence of religious feast days.
  –Conflict of Catholics and Protestants for the Western territory.
  –In Colonial days – theocracy.
    –[name indecipherable], Roanoke, Jamestown – did not have the persistence and perseverance of Plymouth and Boston settlers – due to their religious faith.
  –Attitude of Protestants and Catholics toward the Indians – contrasted.
  –Attitude of Protestants towards Sunday.
  –Relation of birth control to religion and to economics.

Present day relation of religion to economic history – lack of former basic rivalry between sects.
  –Leads to a stressing of the fundamental aspects of Protestant-Christianity.
    –[Catholic] Church takes a wider view of, and interest in, economic affairs.
      –Gaining influence?
      –Giving effect to "practical Christianity."
        –Spirit of humanitarianism.

Effects of nationalism on the economic history.
  –Tariff
  –Revolution
  –<u>Subsidies</u> (agricultural) (Beet sugar)
    –<u>Transportation</u>
      –Every phase has received subsidies
      –Merchant marine – always nationalistic
      –Telegraph and railroad to Pacific in '60s was nationalistic.
      –<u>Panama Canal</u>
  –Banking – especially with First National Bank – restriction of coinage to government
  –Federalist movement
  –Civil War
  –Purchase of Louisiana
  –War of 1812
  –Monroe Doctrine
  –Everything that furthered sectional specialization [word indecipherable]
  –Policy of isolation
  –Conservation
  –Open door policy in China
  –Dollar Diplomacy – Economic Imperialism
  –Spanish American War
  –Policy of hastening growth, in early years

Effects of democracy on economic history
  –Franchise
  –Control of monied interests
  –Free banking principle
  –Trust busting
  –Democracy in consumption habits – allowing great standardization
  –Spoils system
  –Rise of socialism
  –Opposition to militarism – minimum of war expenditure

[word indecipherable]

In universities – 75 years ago – history was the history of all mankind

–Then lopping off – economic history, social history, history of science, of literature, political history.

–Nothing left.

–Then, for last 30 years, a trend towards giving l' histoire integral – a synthesis of life, past and present – Cultural history – i.e. much overlapping.

–Specialization versjs view of the whole.

–Historian doesn't object to the separate study or teaching of subjects. But claims the right to the synthesizing of them – for all the overlapping.

–Cf. History and Historiography in Encyclopedia of Social Sciences

Beer and Febvre – Nevins.

–Charles V. Langlois and Charles Seignobos: Introduction to the Study of History [1912]

J. M. Vincent: Historical research

Allen Johnson: Historical method

Historical Method

To discover truth,

To eliminate all sources of error.

–Recreate the picture of the past.

–Has to get around group psychology and individual psychology.

–On part of author of material.

–On part of writer of history.

–Subjective (wrong) vs. objective (good) history.

–Keep the personality of the writer out of the history.

–German Historical School.

–Began here with Johns Hopkins survivors – influenced by Germany.

–But we know that it is impossible to keep a personality out of history written by human beings.

–Tendency is towards a subjective history of interpretation – not just personal bias, but interpretation based on the facts – if possible!

–Problem of laws

–God in history.

–External environmental influences.

–Cheney – American Historical Association, 1926)

–Laws of history

–Physical analogies.

–How predict in nature and humanity?

–Problem of determinism – progress!

Evaluation of Material
  –External and internal criticism of documents.
    –First assumption is that every document is wrong until proven correct.
    –External:
      –Is the document authentic,accurate?
        –To what extent?
        –Forged? Plagiary.
        –Did a traveler speak what he'd seen? Or heard? – for no overt reasons?
        –Genuine or tampered with?
      –Any doubt about authorship?
      –Is assigned date correct?
      –Is it honest, genuine? Or written to deceive?
      –Language – does it belong to the correct period?
      –Contradictions?
    –Internal:
      –Is what the authentic author really said true?
      –Personal background of author – race; religion; patriotism and
        nationalism; leaving out unpatriotic details; class; occupation.
      –Favorable or unfavorable to subject.

  –Historical analysis.
    –Find out and know all the details about material before beginning to write.
      –Causal relations.
      –Environment, character of people.
      –Distance from markets; transportation, etc.
    –Historians stay away from choosing hypotheses beforehand – (but how
      else proceed? F. T. O.)
    –Other events at same time, out of the whole complex of history.
    –Necessity of being able to throw away notes.
    –Care in use of words (especially capitalism, democracy, etc.)
      –Tendency to read back into past history present day concepts.
    –Correct cultivation of historical imagination.
      –Vital for recreation of picture.
      –Dangerous.

Hackett, pp. 56–103 – Introduction to Research in American History
Palgrave's Dictionary, revised edition, Vol. 1, Appendix, American School of
political economy, pp. 804–811
Seligman – Essays in Economics, Chapter IV
      And Seignobos.

Historical Note Taking
- a- Complete and perfect quotation – accuracy.
- b- Running abstract – outline language and <u>order</u>.
- c- Abstract in your own words – dangerous.
- d- "Shorthand" notes – valueless.
- > Keep opinions and comments very separate (Cf. Earle Daw – book on note taking).

Historical Synthesis – putting the thing together.
- a- Chronological – difficulty of subject, dispersion.
- b- Topical method – chronological sequence <u>within</u>.
  ("The thin gloom of meantimes.")

<u>Fitting language to the evidence</u> – very important

<u>Interpretation</u>:
- –Every age has an intellectual atmosphere (James Truslow Adams).
- –The historian interprets his data in terms of his own intellectual environment.
- –What the historian believes about life and thinking is the framework of his interpretation.
  (Cf. Tawney – each generation must write its history over again for its own uses.)
- –Periods of optimism, and of pessimism.
- –Few historians are able to get rid of <u>taboos</u> – mainly for reasons of social position, pressure by friends, etc., etc.
  - –As religion, patriotism, race.
  - –Economic History Association has recently said that history must be written in a way that creates <u>no</u> hard feelings.

<u>Footnotes</u>
- –An important statement of fact – <u>unless it is generally known</u>, must be substantiated by references and evidence.
- –Mistakes of rising references – statements on insufficient evidence, or mistaken generalization, or generalization contrary to the evidence.
  - –Or lack of correct chronology, using as evidence, a reference from later or earlier period – time error.
  - –Some mistakes <u>re</u> area, classes, etc.
  - –Vague and indefinite language.
  - –Relying on the testimony of <u>one</u> witness.
  - –Stretching too far the argument from analogy.

        –Omission of evidence contrary to statement.
        –Plagiarism – solved by giving references.
            –Not citing where the evidence came from.
            –Or using evidence without reading it.
        –Too great reliance on secondary authorities.

Wright – What is "historical method"?
    –It is not anything, in a strict sense, as a method peculiar to history.
    –History has no distinct method separate from induction, deduction, etc. – it can
        not experiment.
    –What is called historical method – is the problem of evidence – the same as in
        law. [Two vertical lines in margin alongside this statement.]
    –The "historical" method is used in every phase of applied economic study.
    –The material which the American economic historian deals with is different
        from that used by the historian of other ages.
        –American economic historian needs some knowledge of statistical method.
            –But adds the background of the data.
        –And some knowledge of accounting.
        –Some (! [F. T. O.]) knowledge of economic theory.
        –Must understand the economic order – the institutional background.
    –In the case of political history, chance is a much greater factor than in economic
        history.
        –The single individual is much less of a factor.
        –The mass[es], large groups, predominate.
        –A single motive predominates – profit.
            –Making explanation and interpretation relatively easier.
        –Intelligent action – correctly reasoned.
        –Rational action – reasoned, but inaccurately, insufficiently, reasoned.
            –Emotional action.
            –Economic theory must study rational, and/or intelligent action.
            –Economic history can study emotional action – as description.
                –and usually studies mass action (Cf. Cournot – who held that such study
                    was usually better than individualized study).
        –Is there the same motive for putting out falsity of interpretation – or the same
            chance – in economics, as in political history?
–Wright thinks not so much in economic history. (!? [F. T. O.])

Gras, N. S. B. –"Concept of a Metropolitan Economy," *American Historical
Review*, July 1922.
                –Introduction to Economic History, pp. 186–187, pp. 281–329.

–Journal of Economic and Business History, May 1930 – *"Stages in Economic History."*

Laissez Faire – in U.S.

a – Non-interference of government in business – historical origin. (Where draw the line?)

b – Ability of business man to do what he wants – same theory with approach of 19th century.

–Maintenance of competition.

–? Confusion, requires government interference, and end of <u>freedom</u> of doing what one wants.

–Freedom to do what one wants usually ends in a lack of competition.

–Freedom of individual initiative.

–What explains the prevalence of this idea in the U.S. up till recently?

a –Urge to <u>get away</u> from the elaborate system of regulations of Europe.

–Which were not suited to the <u>new</u> commercial and industrial situation of the world and brought suffering.

b –We were an agricultural country – with widespread private ownership of land.

<u>c</u> –A virgin country was being exploited.

–Freedom of economic opportunity.

–Opportunity to make a self-sufficient living, to get one's own land.

d –Slow development of factory system.

e –Size of country, diversity of economic conditions.

f –Limited powers of federal government.

–What of actions of State governments?

–Cf. Frankfurter's study of early legislation in [the] East [of the United States] – small total, but largely regulatory or giving bounties.

g –Spirit of liberty – dislike of <u>any</u> regulation.

–Impossible to determine the degree of laissez-faire accurately – nearest approach is to go to the statutes – of all governmental bodies – national, state, local.

Colonial period:

–Hangover from England – wage laws, guilds – both [word undecipherable] and abandoned.

–Agriculture – stimulus (mulberry trees, silk worms).

–Industry – bounties (local aid grants).

– mercantile regulations.

–Communication and transportation – post office.

Early National Period
  –Constitution – is it a laissez-faire document?
    –A transfer from states to federal government of some (problems and)
    powers.
      –Is this laissez-faire?
      –Is it a move towards less governmental interference in business?
    –Since 1789 – by interpretation and development – it has become more
    of a bulwark of private property and private initiative.
  –Manufacturing – tariff, regulatory.
  –Labor – decrease in efforts at regulation.
  –Consumption – end of blue laws, less price fixing.
c.1860s:
  –Transportation – canal building, road building.
  –Labor – beginning of legislation.
  –Consumption – education by state, poor laws, libraries.
–Any less, or more, interference of state than in colonies?
Since 1860:
  –Labor legislation.
  –Anti-trust legislation.
  –Public utility regulation and control.
  –Regulation of banking, insurance, stock market.
  –Consumption changes.
–No doubt of State control, positive or regulatory.
–Was the 19th a century peculiarly laissez-faire?
–Interdependence grows – social effects of any action grows.
–Effect of depressions.
–Legislation is behind the times.

Summary of Theory of Progress and its Development (Summary of Bury) [J.
B. Bury, *The Idea of Progress: An Inquiry into its Origin and Growth*. London:
Macmillan, 1928]
  –Idea of progress is relatively recent.
  –Controversy over ancients vs. moderns evoked the first idea of progress.
    –1620 in Italy – flourished in France, [Charles] Perrault, moderns have more
    knowledge.
    –[George] Hakewill – protested idea of degeneration.
    –1660 Royal Society, 1666 Royal Academy.
    –[Bernard Le Bovier de] Fontenelle – the first to stress idea of continuing
    progress into an infinite future – advance of knowledge.
    –[René] Descartes – stability of laws of nature, reason (deism, rationalism).

–French thinkers stress social life – progress idea enlarged to include general progress of human race.

–Abbé Saint Pierre third quarter, 18th century – suggested civilization was only in its infancy.

–French of last part of 18th century were optimistic.

–[Adam] Smith supported idea of progress.

–Socialism.

–Germany – necessary progress.

Economic Opportunity

–Preparatory to making a living.

  –Less physical handicaps, less deformity, etc., better health, better medical care.

  –Paternal legislation.

  –Free education.

  –Rising standards of living of common people – better family life, more advantages.

–Making a living.

  –Access to labor – easy.

  –Access to business – easy, mobility.

    –Some restrictions in professions.

    –Less in recent years in those fields of industry where large scale industry prevails.

  –Cf. Taussig and Joslyn, *American Business Leaders*, 1932.

  –Access to upper position out of farming is cut down.

  –Look at large fortunes today – how many go back even one generation? Two.

    –Where have they been earned?

Democracy and Economic Progress.

–Its effect on production, distribution and consumption.

–On conservation.

  –What of future invention? Will it make conservation useless?

  –Democracy does not tend to conservation.

–On capital – made it easily and widely obtainable.

–On labor – respect for work, much mobility within laboring class, between groups.

–On entrepreneurship – respect for business – starvation of ability in other lines.

Distribution – democracy tends towards more welfare of common people.

  –But development of the power of money – especially where large fortunes exist and are readily made.

–Slowness and lag in remedying evils of economic organization.
  –Class and sectional interests.
  –Spoils systems – lack of ability in public office – failure to pay enough.
  –Tendency to refuse to grant power except to legislative bodies.
 –Handicaps to democracy's effective functioning.
  –Rapid development.
  –Framework of government – division of powers.
  –Lack of able people in public service.
  –Problems of future will increase burdens – need of more and more regulation.
  –Lack of social direction – in past and in present.
  –Lack of foresight.
  –Careless formulation of legislation.
  –Sublime faith in a law – no realistic approach to facts and factors.

Lack of ready adaptation of our political structure to our economic structure.
 –Due to rapidity of economic change facilitated by individualism.
 –Stiff framework of government and little opportunity for change.
 –Growing interdependence of economic life.
 –Growing area of economic life – to a national continental scope.
 –Growing development of industrial capitalism – forms.
 –Rise of large cities – metropolitan area – its problems.
   –Relation to the State and Federal governments.
   –More power needed – separate states.
 –Lack of inventiveness in the adoption of culture.
   –Lack of interest in other than personal, private affairs.
     –Slow changes in social mores.
 –Strong power of vested interests – 15th Amendment.
 –Constitution – minimum powers to solve conditions of that time were granted
   to Federal government.
 –International relations.

[Final] Examination Questions

–Enumerate the chief developments in the rest of the world which reacted on the
  economic history of the U.S. 1800–1914.

–Into what periods would you divide the economic history of the U.S. since 1607?
  Characterize those periods.

–What factors seem most important in determining the growth of American cities?
  – i.e. one as against another.

–What have been the chief differences in underlying factors shaping the economic development of the U.S. and some European country since 1750.

[Additional references:]

Middletown, Chapters 4, 8 and 29.
Recent Economic Changes, IX-XXV, 1–12, 841–910